THE PRINCIPLE OF AUTHORITY

THE
PRINCIPLE OF AUTHORITY
IN RELATION TO CERTAINTY, SANCTITY AND SOCIETY

AN ESSAY IN THE PHILOSOPHY
OF EXPERIMENTAL RELIGION

LECTURES BY

P. T. FORSYTH, M.A., D.D.
PRINCIPAL OF HACKNEY COLLEGE, HAMPSTEAD

"Abeunt in mores"
"The knowledge of the holy is understanding"—Prov. ix. 10.

Eugene, Oregon

Wipf and Stock Publishers
199 W 8th Ave, Suite 3
Eugene, OR 97401

The Principle of Authority In Relation to Certainty, Sanctity and Society
An Essay In the Philosophy Of Experimental Religion
By Forsyth, P.T.
ISBN: 1-57910-019-8

This book is dedicated to
Mike Munk
Friend, brother, servant

PREFACE

BY way of preface I have only to say briefly how very much I am indebted to others in the effort to find my way into the interior of the subject of my interest.

Besides the authorities referred to in the text, my largest creditors among many are these—and in parts I have followed them closely, but, I hope, judiciously, both in what I take and what I leave.

IHMELS: *Die christliche Wahrheitsgewissheit*, 2 Ed., 1908.
PFENNIGSDORF: *Der religiöse Wille*, 1910.
SCHAEDER: *Theozentrische Theologie*, 1909.

CONTENTS

PROLOGUE 1

A.—*CERTAINTY*

I
EXPERIENCE AND FAITH 19

II
CERTAINTY AS FAITH 38

III
AUTHORITY, CERTAINTY, AND SANCTITY . 54

IV
THE SOURCE OF CERTAINTY 82

V
BELIEF AS A WILL TO RECEIVE AND OBEY . 101

VI
PAST FACT AND PRESENT POWER . . . 125

VII
THE GROUND OF RELIGION—THE HISTORIC FACT AND THE PREACHED WORD . . 137

B.—*SANCTITY*

VIII
THE OBJECT OF RELIGION 163

IX
THE VOUCHER OF RELIGION 187

X
THE FOOTING OF RELIGION—THE REAL AS THE REDEMPTIVE—THE FINAL AUTHORITY OF THE HOLY 199

XI
AUTHORITY, HISTORY, AND DESTINY . . 223

CONTENTS

C.—SOCIETY

XII
THEOLOGY AND CHURCH 237

XIII
PLEBISCITE AND GOSPEL AS AUTHORITY . 253

XIV
LIBERTY AND ITS LIMITS IN THE CHURCH . 280

XV
AUTHORITY AND INDIVIDUALISM . . . 297

XVI
AUTHORITY, FREE PERSONALITY, AND FREE THOUGHT 319

XVII
AUTHORITY AND HUMANITY 345

XVIII

AUTHORITY IN CHURCH AND BIBLE . . 361

XIX

THE THEOLOGY OF CERTAINTY—ELECTION . 382

XX

THEOCENTRIC RELIGION 409

EPILOGUE 443

PROLOGUE

A FEW years ago we were all deeply exercised about a great constitutional question—the Veto of the Lords. And every now and then such questions arise in one form or another which is but a variant of the perennial issue. A constitutional question is so great because it raises in a political form what appears also in other forms as the final question of life. For the constitutional question is the question of authority, which, in its religious form, is the first and last issue of life. It is indeed a question of Lordship. As soon as the problem of authority really lifts its head, all others fall to the rear.

The question of the spiritual authority is very closely bound up with that of the public authority. Our views about the Church must affect our views about the Throne. It is not always accidental, and not artificial, and not merely perverse, when certain modes of religious authority are found conjoined with certain modes of political. There are views of the Church which make it not only tactical in men to espouse one party, but impossible (in the spiritual logic which rules great movements) to do otherwise. There is something more in it than corporate self-seeking, party blindness, class interests, or social push. Our idea of authority lies so near the heart of life that it colours our whole circulation. Men and societies are totally different according as their ruling idea is to serve an authority or to escape it, or according to the authority they do serve.

PROLOGUE

No one, I think, can view with any insight the ferment among the workmen without realising that we are getting well out into the stream of a social revolution; nor can we take the true dimensions of youthful indiscipline, or of the movements among the women, without perceiving that we are even getting into the rapids and are in some danger of a spiritual catastrophe. The woman movement seems often to be least gauged by those who promote it most. It goes to the very foundations of all that has hitherto been known as society, and even of the spiritual order. In most of its advocates it acts as little more than a nature-force, but in its essence it is a spiritual principle—whether for evil or good. That is a question, however, which I do not venture to discuss here. I only note the fact for what it seems to me to be—the index of an unexampled social and spiritual revolution, compared with which even the questions about Church or State that occupy our senates or enrage our parties are small. Parliaments, after all, with whatever tumult or friction, can but register in enactments the great moral and spiritual action which other powers and guides have been preparing far behind the order for the day.

In this unprecedented social revolution, so indicative of a spiritual, the question that naturally becomes imperative is the question of an authority. For Society it becomes a greater question than ever before, because in all previous forms it has been conceived in terms, and staked upon issues, comparatively external. It has been more or less imperial. It has concerned forms of governments, or the areas on which governments should be based, seat of force or the range of franchise. But it now becomes a question of any government at all, of any control, in our moral temper. Is duty dead, and the moral ideal reduced to this, "I must live my own life and be true to myself"? Is obedience a pure curse, and escape from it a pure boon? Does the soul come to itself by a career or a master? Is all submission but slavery? Is liberty man's chief end, or has it its condition in a prior and creative control? Is the principle of authority the salvation of society or the bane of the race?

The conviction in these pages is that the principle of authority is ultimately the whole religious question, that an authority of any practical kind draws its meaning and its right only from the soul's relation to its God, that this is so not only for religion strictly so called, nor for a Church, but for public life, social life, and the whole history and career of Humanity. Society cannot be founded on sympathy alone, but upon right. No amount of fraternity will preserve it; but fraternity itself rests on due and true authority, brotherhood on fatherhood. The doctrine of the divine right of kings was wrong only in the form of the kingship. Society does mean sovereignty, even if it be the sovereignty of the people (however the people may be defined). And sovereignty draws its right to claim obedience only from the Sovereignty of God, conceived concretely, as He reveals His will in history that it should be conceived. All the authority essential in an ordered society or state has its right in proportion to its proximity to, or charter from, the last authority of all. And that is an authority to be appreciated and ordered only by the soul. The religious authority at last settles all things. All questions run up into moral questions; and all moral questions centre in the religious, in man's attitude to the supreme ethic, which is the action of the Holy One. We must all start with something given, something imposed. We create neither truth nor right. Is the Giver a blind power inferior in dignity to our rational will ? Or is it the Holy One bestowing, from the least gift to the greatest, His own holiness, and establishing His own righteousness, in a love whose true response is not merely our reciprocity but our obedience ?

There is no social future without authority. Yet we have come to a pitch when liberty threatens to go to pieces, of its own momentum like a racing fly-wheel where they have shot the engineer. And there is no authority without a religion—none for Humanity without the religion of Humanity. And the religion of Humanity is not a mood of the widest fraternity, nor a cult in which mankind worships itself. It means a God, and a God not of benevolence but of holiness, who treats the unholy with the right, the judgment, and the grace which are after all our commanding ideals, and which are making the New Humanity in Jesus Christ. The one practical authority for human society is the God who in Christ comes in such judging and redeeming action that we are no more our own at all. If we will be as thorough as the soul or its God, that is the only authority which at bottom sanctions a social order even about drains, justifies a fellow-creature's commital to jail for twenty-four hours, mulcts him of a shilling, or which at its height provides him with a throne and a loyalty that make public order a spiritual hierarchy, liberty a sacred passion, patriotism noble, sacrifice divine, and obedience a pride.

What do we mean when we speak of the Holy so often and so centrally as we here shall ?

It is of course a religious idea—*the* religious idea ; in what region of our nature shall we seek the nature of religion ?

For long it was sought in the region of theory—of the rational consciousness. What was asked about a religion was " Is it true ? " That is to say, " How far does it fall in with those rational principles which make our *a priori* axioms and standards of scientific or philosophic truth ? " And there are many who treat the question in this way still.

But the modern movement broke away from this quest for theoretic truth as the prime thing in religion. The day of orthodoxy went by, and with it the night of Rationalism. With Kant came a new order of things. The ethical took the place that had been held by the intellectual. The notion of reality replaced that of truth. Religion placed us not in line with the rationality in the world but in rapport with the reality of it. And the ethical was the real.

As Kant handled the principle it was much hampered by the circumstances of his day, but his route was right. It is true that religion belongs neither to the rational, the æsthetic, nor the ethical side of the soul exclusively. It draws on the whole soul's being and energy. But the Christian religion at least involves if not the solitude at least the primacy of the ethical. If Reality is to reach us it must be thus. And what Christianity means by the holy is best expressed in ethical terms as the absolute moral Reality. We too are holy according to our relation to that power, or rather according to His relation to us.

Now it is distinctive of the moral consciousness that it is not, like the philosophic, single, simple, and harmonious, but double, divided, and even rent. It is not monistic but dualistic. A solution of the world which is determined to be theoretic above all must end in Monism, which is the death of religion; but if it be moral, if it be religious, it must begin with the experienced and certain fact of the divided conscience,[1] a standing state of collision war, and sin. It begins with a state of the consciousness anterior to its branches as theoretic, æsthetic, or ethical, a state underlying all these. It must begin with that fundamental antinomy of the conscience which emerges in the conflict of " must " and " ought," of instinct and obligation, of natural law and moral norm. To realise the deep distinction between law and norm, between our psychology and our conscience, between the make up of our natural constitution and the state of our moral will, between our substance and our sanctions, to realise this is essential to a right start in the matter. And it leads us on to the farther recognition not only that the distinction rises to collision but that the war between the law of instinct and the norm of duty is a civil war; it is waged within the unity of the person. The defiance of the moral norm seems to be as much bound up with our nature as obedience is. And this creates a problem quite insoluble for any philosophy as yet.

But apart from the success of philosophy in the matter of such a theodicy, our practical experience convinces us of the " ought " of the moral norm. The ideal is that that should rule. In God such an ideal is reached always, and in Him alone. Unless life is to be detached from reality and thrown into hopeless schism both with itself and the universe, Absolute Being must be identical with the absolute moral norm. God wills good because He is good, He is good because He wills good. That is the holiness of God, the identification of the moral norm and the ultimate reality of the world. The holy is the ideal good, fair, and true, translated in our religious consciousness to a transcendant personal reality, not proved but known, experienced immediately and honoured at sight as the one thing in the world valuable in itself and making a world. It is a con-

---

[1] *Cf.* Windelband, "Praeludien. Das heilige," p. 419, 1907. (There is a later edition.)

ception justifiable to no philosophy, as I say. For it seems to involve (what is a moral impossibility condemning any theory) that all reality, even that of evil,[1] should be a part of the absolute moral normality. It seems to require that the norm of all reality should cover what is contrary to a moral norm, that absolute reality, ruled by the moral norm, should yet have the morally abnormal among its appearances or products.

When we are dealing with the holy, therefore, we are in a region which thought cannot handle nor even reach. We cannot go there, it must come here. We are beyond both experience and thought, and we are dependent on revelation for any conviction of the reality of that ideal which moral experience demands but cannot ensure. Life is ruined if our greatest moral ideals are not fixed in the greatest reality; yet we have no means in our own power of any conviction of such fixity. The holy is both urgent and inaccessible. It is imperative, yet unapproachable. The situation is only soluble by a miracle.

That is the miracle of Revelation, of Grace. The unapproachable approaches, enters, tarries, lives, dies, conquers among us and in us, knows us into our only knowledge of itself, subdues all things to its sanctity, and establishes its good and blessed self in us and on us all. The norms, the " oughts," become for us the motives that instinctive laws and " musts " used to be. We are ruled by the imperative and not the clamant, and we are united by love where we used but to meet in passion, and in passion slay.

But the effect on us of the moral ideal is not simply admiration; it is confusion; it is accusation; it is judgment. We do not only desire it, we dread it.

[1] Which can never be treated as a mere unreality and negation without ruining both the place of conscience and the agelong passion for redemption.

Its very grandeur fills us with a sense of weakness, nay, of blame, shame, and despair. We are not only weak but helpless. And it is chiefly by our fault, crime, and sin. So we do not simply worship afar, we repent in the dust.

But what does that mean ? It means that the Revelation of the Holy can only come through Redemption by the Holy ; that to us, ruined by sinful act, the only truth that represents Him is an act ; that the absolute reality of the active and mighty world in its actual case is expressible only in an Eternal Deed ; that the holy nature of God comes home by no prophetic exposition, even through Apostle or Saviour, but only by the priestly act in which the saving person consummates ; that it cannot be taught us, it must be created in us by that act ; that the Cross is the creative revelation of the holy, and the holy is what is above all else revealed in the Cross, going out as love and going down as grace ; that the Holy Spirit's point of departure in history is the Cross; and that while our justification has its source in God's self-justification of His holiness there, our sanctification has the same source as both.

I shall often have to return to these points to expound and expand.

The prime service to our vast problem must be rendered by the Church ; even if in doing it it should have to be changed out of all recognition by its past leaders, so long as it maintained the continuity which is not in its structure but in its trust, not in its machinery but its message, the continuity of its Gospel. The Church in its many forms has rendered vast service to human freedom, ever since the day when it converted the huge machine of the Roman Empire, or the later day when it provided the conditions that called into being the nations of Europe, or the day,

PROLOGUE 9

still later, when, within these nations, it raised the head of successive *couches sociales*. One need not forget the disservice to the same cause by particular ages, churches, or churchmen, in order to say that. One need but remember the work of the mediæval church for nationality, or Calvinism as the true creator of modern democracy. And the Church has done this even more by the kind of authority it has provided than by direct exhortations to men to rise. Men do not rise because they are bidden, but because they are inspired. And the grand inspiration for human freedom is human redemption.

To-day, as ever, the Church has to control, lead, and secure human freedom. And to-day, as ever, not by idolising freedom, but by its old method of authority, by providing an authority whose very nature creates freedom—the authority, that is, not of the Church itself but of its Gospel and Saviour. There are Churches in which the note of liberty has been detached from the note of authority, and the liberty has begun to degenerate and the Church to decay. On the other hand there are Churches where the note of authority has been severed from the note of liberty, and where the degeneration and decay of authority are no less sure. The only Church adequate to the demand made by new liberty for divine authority is that in which the supreme authority is such as being the liberating power, the authority which has not liberty as a corollary but as its nature. And that is the Church of the Gospel of God's constant and immediate presence in action as Redeemer—as moral Redeemer from sin, as holy Redeemer from guilt. There is no hope for society in the long run but in such a Church ; and there is no hope of such a church but in such a gospel. Why does a religion which is but liberal, rational, and humane, tend always to run down into interests but trivial and secular ? Because it has not the secret of the moral soul, the lift of the guilty soul free in the Holy God. The control of the great and long social revolution must, more than ever before, lie in such a radical, spiritual revolution, which God makes and not man. The society which is the first charge upon the interest of Christian people, therefore, is the society created by that Gospel which makes them Christian. It is the Church. But in the Church this is now widely and practically denied. A free State gradually settles in, like the camel of the oriental fable, upon possession of a free Church. And we are in danger of an Erastian habit of mind and interest as fatal as any established by law (Chap. IV.).

Logic is rooted in Ethic, for the truth we see depends on the men we are. Ethic is rooted in theology for we are made men by the gift and grace of God. And theology is rooted in living faith—which is the Supreme Gift of God *in* man, because it is the response evoked by His supreme revelation and gift of Himself *to* man as Father, Saviour, and King.

Of course these considerations are of no more use in election mêlées than the Fourth Gospel on 'change; but, if they be always scouted or even challenged, it means that our Christianity is ill-prepared, for lack of insight, to handle the issue that settles all. It is not a welcome truth to-day, but true it is, that one of the very first conditions of dealing with a great question is the power to see how great it is. And if we shelve the problem of authority, if we lose ourselves in all manner of clamant and proximate issues, and evade the the issues which make any of them worth while, it disqualifies us so far for being more than politicians. It is only the power of handling ultimate issues that gives religion any claim to guide Humanity, or any voice of real weight in the greatest public affairs. But we are too lightly deflected into the loud issues of the

PROLOGUE

hour; and we are too foreign to the powers that ride over all such matters, and break them small as the dust of the balance, and fuse them up as a very little thing.

If it is not so, why is there such a meagre literature in our own tongue on this supreme matter of authority? Why is so much of it but on the middle register? And why are so many of us prepared with no solution of the question of authority except a rejection of the idea; which is a course as crass, mindless, and unspiritual in its nature as many of the forms of authority we resent? Why has the idea of the authority of the Church, for instance, almost wholly vanished from sections of the Church? Or why has it sunk to the rude political arbitrament of a living majority, when the real spiritual majority are the dead? Why all this in a Church which is one and continuous on each side of a veil so transparent, so pervious, from the other side? And why is it thus in a society like the Church, which has always been a spiritual power just in virtue of that which is bound to make it a minority on earth? Has the offence of the Cross then ceased at last? I read the other day, in a book by a Nonconformist, that "the loss of the essential belief in the Ecclesia—as it has been held in all ages since the time of the Apostles—is perhaps the great religious peril of the modern world." To see that is to qualify for discussing the subject.

For the same purpose we ought not to feel bewildered when it is asked what is the religious *a priori* in the soul; what in the soul rules the soul; how any such *a priori* in the psychology of history can come to have, in the case of Christ, an absolute value for Humanity at every conceivable stage; in what sense an authority can become more objective by becoming less external; what is the difference, so vital in these days, between a rational and a moral authority?

The great question is not really as to the seat of authority, but as to its nature. The one question is psychological, and can wait, the other is theological, and cannot. What constitutes the absolute claim? Does "the experience of my finite soul that it is possessed with God" give me a God infinite and absolute for the whole *human* soul's *eternal* destiny? God in Christ was not God in a soul, but God in a person greater than all Humanity. Even Rome admits that in the last resort the *seat* of authority is in the soul. All turns on what makes authority authoritative there, on what legitimates it. Is it enough to say that the organ of authority is "the soul in communion with God"? That does not touch the question what it is in God that makes Him authoritative for the soul. The idea is too empirical, and too little ethical, as if the mere contact and impression were enough. But the effect of Christ was not mere impression; it was reconstruction; it was the new covenant with God, and the new creation of man. A tremendous impression does not necessarily give a legitimate authority. A true authority is an authority for action on the scale of all life; its assertion, therefore, must be in an act of the living God which has the *right* to control all possible action of man, to control history viewed as one colossal act. The question is not, therefore, How has God appeared? but, What has God done? God did not come to be seen but obeyed. The Christian answer is in the Cross of Christ. The nerve of Christianity is expressed in such a great and sweeping word as "Ye are not your own; ye are bought with a price." It means Christ's absolute property in us by a new creation. The sinlessness of Jesus, His ideal perfection, is not enough. It is too negative for authority. It really means the active holiness of Jesus, not merely as keeping Himself unspotted from the world, cherishing a pure experi-

PROLOGUE

ence, or going about doing good, but gathered to a universal, victorious, and creative head in the Cross. The whole range of right and demand opened by the holiness of God and its judgment must be surveyed. It is there that we have the absolute and its authority. It is there that the crucial issue of the Cross lies. It is in this nature and action of the Cross that the solution lies of the question of authority for Christianity, for history, for ever. It lies in the absolute holy right of the new Creator of Humanity. It does not lie in the consciousness of Christ, construed psychologically and acting æsthetically or by impression, but rather in His personality as effectuated in an act which changed the whole of human relation and destiny. That is to say, the work of Christ's person must be taken into prime account, His power not only to know and show His perfection, but to perfect His perfection in the new history of a sinful race. He had power not only to present His death-crowned life *before* us, but to present it *to* us as offered for us to God, and so to make it the life of His Church and of the new race. This was done only by His death. Jesus becomes for us historically both Christ and Lord (*i.e.* absolute authority) only through His death and resurrection (Romans i. 4). Authority does not lie in Christ as the Superlative of the conscience, but in Christ as the Redeemer of the conscience and its new life. The kingship of Jesus can only be established in the Cross, His universal and absolute kingship. It is not the authority of excellence, but of grace. He is not simply the soul supremely, sinlessly, in communion with God, the perfect saint, the saintly superman ; He is God reconciling. The authority of Christ is not simply the pressure upon us of the divine obligation which He so perfectly embodies, but the action in us of the New Life founded for Humanity in His death taken as the crisis of His life and person. "The sinlessness of Christ," says one, "means His lordship of the human race in all the things of faith." I am afraid the meaning of this is not clear, till from sinlessness we rise to a holiness which was more than a supreme and unbroken communion with God; it became an act identical with that holy and Eternal act of God which secures His will always, and which sustains the universe, even to its Redemption.

The question of our authority is the question of our religion. It is a religious question first and last. We have no absolute authority over us except in our faith; and, without it, all relative authority becomes more and more relative, and less and less authoritative. There is no final answer to the question of any authority but the answer contained in our personal faith. And the first business of our religion is to provide us with an authority—an authority which shall be at once as intimate to active life as Mysticism is to the life contemplative, and more objective than the most Roman Church.

For life is as its religion. And religion can never now be less than Christian faith. And faith is in its nature an obedience; it is not primarily a sympathy. It is sympathetic obedience, truly, but obedience always. Eternal Life is absolute obedience, an attitude to One Who has a right over us high above all His response to us, One to be trusted and obeyed even amid any dereliction by Him and refusal of His response. He is our God, not because He loved and pitied, but because in His love and pity He redeemed us. God is for us and our release only that we may be for Him and His service. He is for us, to help, save and bless, only that we may be for Him, to worship Him in the communion of the Spirit and serve Him in the majesty of His purpose for ever. First we glorify Him, then we enjoy Him for ever.

PROLOGUE

The whole nature of authority is changed as soon as it ceases to be statutory and becomes thus personal and religious. It is no longer then what it is to most people—*a limit*; it becomes *a source of power*. It is not, in the first instance, regulative and depressive; it is expansive, it is creative. Like personality, it is not a delimiting circle, but an exuberant source. It makes the soul to be more than in its egoism it could ever be. It means increase, augmentation (*auctoritas*). By the true obedience we *are* more. It is the great culture, the great enrichment. Our great authority is what gives us most power to go forward; it is not what ties us up most to a formal past. It is of Grace and not of law. It cannot be a doctrine, nor a book, nor an institution; it must, for a person, be a person. And a person who is not an æsthetic ideal of perfection, but an active source of life, a person who is gathered up and consummated in a creative, redemptive act. There is no revolt when the authority is realised as the Lord and Giver of Life; for it is the passion for life and its largeness that is at the root of rebellion.

These are the lines on which the following lectures purpose to move, with due attention to some contemporary forms of the problem, and no wilful neglect of the vistas that open on all hands as we rise in that high air.

A.—CERTAINTY

I

EXPERIENCE AND FAITH

THERE is only one thing greater than Liberty, and that is Authority. And there is one thing we have widely sacrificed to Freedom, and that is Certainty. No sacred freedom is freedom to be unsure about its source and right.

The intellectual, and especially the moral, situation of the age raises with evergrowing force what I have called the central question of religion, and therefore of everything,—the question as to *authority*. True religion is the solution of life; but in a variety of forms we are faced by religion as life's difficulty. And what makes the religious difficulty is some challenge that rises in us, or round us, to a fact, truth, or power, which has come down as authoritative—with the authority of, say, the Bible or the Church. Let us take, for instance, the matter of the soul's salvation by Christ's atonement. That is in the foreground both of Bible and Church. Both have declared it throughout to be central to Christianity as the core of the apostolic doctrine. But much of the religion round us—not only the world, but much of the religion round us—challenges all apostolic doctrine as such, or even treats it as obsolete; and many people in consequence are thrust into great moral and intellectual difficulty.

What, then, is the exit from such difficulty ? What is its proper treatment ? Is it enough to put the foot down, and say with prompt heroism that the Book is final, or the Church ? Is it enough to show that the belief is morally rational ? Neither line is satisfactory. If we are asking the soul's question, and not merely raising problems in religion, it is only a religious experience of the whole man that gives us our outlet, only a remorseless moral realism, only the personal experience by the guilty conscience of a holy doom and grace. In the absence of that realism and that experience we do not know to what we can appeal. But to one who has really gone through this life-experience the fact of such a salvation is the truest thing we can know ; it is more of a fact even than the soul it saves. To him it is at the least *as* true as his own soul and his own sin. He knows that salvation, that Redeemer, as he knows his own life—nay, more intimately ; he stakes his eternal all on such knowledge. That is to say, such truth becomes its own authority. God takes our conviction in hand when others can do nothing with us. And then our difficulties (especially our intellectual difficulties), if they do not disappear, are yet submerged. They can wait, but our salvation cannot. They are thrown down to a secondary place, and do not give grave or fatal trouble. We do not ignore them, but we can wait. We have the answer, if not the solution. Everything must be true in the perspective of its necessity for that gospel. Life—the soul's life—is not arrested by central doubt. We do not then live upon truth in any form of it which is vulnerable to intellectual challenge, nor upon an ethic which depends on moral evolution. We do not live on its traditional statement or dogma, but on its inner distinctive power—not vaguely its power, but the moral power interior and peculiar to it, its genius, and its Word verified in experience.

For Christianity is not a matter of mere spirituality, but of the Holy Spirit. And it is not a belief in truth, in truth's great power in general, and its destiny to prevail. But it is belief in truth of a

EXPERIENCE AND FAITH

special and practical kind; yet even then not in its trueness but in its power—as life-truth, in its central and creative reality for our person, and not in its congruity with other truth. In that respect its form may be irrational, and its power thereby is none the less, or even more. The truth is suspended, floated, in the personal effect. Christ did not come to teach us truth, but to make us true. He did not come to teach us to tell the truth, which can be damning enough, but to tell it in love. And that again means worlds more than a precept for Christian manner, that we tell it kindly, considerately, urbanely; it means (like being " in the Spirit ") that we speak, with whatever urbanity, less or more, from within the special order of holy love and grace which belongs to Christ's redemption, so that we tell men the truth in a love of them for His sake. And we can only believe in redemption to practical purpose by believing in the Redeemer—by a personal relation of committal for ever to that Person and His act of capture. A redeeming Christ thus becomes His own authority with us; and that not because He is passed by our natural and general standards of truth or worth. We can have no standard for our absolute Judge and Saviour. We know Him with at least as much certainty as we know any fact or law, cosmic or psychic; by another order of knowledge perhaps, but with far more intimacy, and with much more practical effect on life. And what is knowledge but truth that corresponds in kind to objective reality, especially the reality of life and experience? It need not be truth which locks into an objective scheme; but truth that responds in kind to an objective and personal act.

What, then, does this involve in regard to authority? First, that the last authority is religious and not theological (in the current sense of that word), that it is an authority for the person for the soul, and not for the mind and its truth; and that the soul cannot live on an external authority as one merely traditional and liable to intellectual challenge. Of course, empirically, educationally, we do depend on external authority in the first part of our discipline. The order of time is not the order of reality. As children and youths (of whatever age) we must. It is a necessary stage of our growth. It is a mark of our minority. We depend on statements about religion made by other people who are in some historic position of religious authority over us—parents, teachers, churches, or apostles. That is to say, our most direct contact at that stage is not with the object of religion, but with people produced by that object. The authority for our faith is not yet the object of that faith; it is certain people who themselves have come to own, serve, and worship that object.

So it follows, secondly, that when by these stages we come to religious maturity *our only authority must be faith's object itself in some direct self-revelation of it.* Our authority is what takes the initiative with our faith. Only so is the authority really religious, only as creative. *Our only final religious authority is the creative object of our religion, to whom we owe ourselves.* Every statement about God is challengeable till God states Himself, in His own way, by His own Son, His own Spirit, His own Word, His own Church, to our soul, which He remakes in the process. And the challenge, coming at the right place (alas, for the heartlessness of those who force it!), is God's ordinance, to drive us onward and inward upon the soul's centre and King there. The present criticism of Church and Bible is, on the whole, providential. "He saith of Cyrus, he is My shepherd, My anointed, whose right hand He hath holden." It is meant to disengage crude religion from all temporary and pædagogic authority, however valuable, and to force us for

EXPERIENCE AND FAITH 23

our moral manhood upon the only authority truly religious, truly speaking the tongue, and meeting the need, of the adult soul.

In the last resort, therefore, the only religious authority must be some action of God's creative self-revelation, and not simply an outside witness to it. For instance, as to Christ's resurrection, if we had signed, sealed, and indubitable testimony from one of the soldiers at the tomb who saw Him emerge, it would have a certain value, of course; but it would not be a religious authority. It would not be equal in that respect to Peter's or Paul's, though they did not see Him rise. It would be more *historisch* and scientific but less *geschichtlich* and sacramental than theirs. It would not prove that the Saviour rose in the triumphant power of his finished work over the world of nature as well as of man. It would only prove reanimation; so that He might, perhaps, get over His first failure as Saviour and try again. It would be no part of God's self-revelation through apostolic souls whom the risen and indwelling Christ taught with regenerative and final power. The soldier would be but a bystander of an event, not an agent of revelation, nor a subject of it. Men are an authority to us, to our conscience, not as they may be able to stand cross-examination by historical and critical research, but as they are made by the power of the God, the Christ, Who reveals Himself in His regeneration of their souls. The Apostles are authorities for Christ only in so far as Christ made them so, not as infallable chroniclers but as elect souls. And even these men fade into the rear when they have done their work; and they may crumble and dissolve, like the sacramental bread—so long as they have brought us to direct communion with God, with Christ, as His own voucher, and stirred the evidence of His Spirit's action and power in our soul's new life. The best documents are human sacraments. Holy men are the best argument of the Gospel, short of the Gospel itself, short, *i.e.* of Christ's real presence with us in the Holy Ghost as our active Saviour. And when men have done their proper work, when they have introduced us personally to God and left us together, it is not fatal if we find flaws in their logic, character, or faith. There is so much spiritual truth as that in the Roman principle that defect in the priest does not destroy the effect of his sacrament. Defects in Church, Bible, or apostle, defects in the logic of creed, or inconstancies of conduct in Christian people, need not destroy the real religious witness they bear on the whole, their sacramental mediation of the Gospel to us. Secure in the God to Whom they led us, we turn at our ease and leisure to examine their flaws with a quiet and kindly mind, knowing that they do not cost us our soul's life. " A thousand difficulties do not make one doubt."

When we trust an apostle, for instance, it is not his foregone infallibility we trust—of which we have no evidence but his own, whose infallibility is yet the thing to be proved. Nor is it the penetration of his perceptive power, his genius, his skill as a gifted observer, a heart's analyst, a searching seer or spiritual psychologist. Nor is it his veracity, nor his competency as a reporter of dictated truth. But we trust his truth as an integral expression of his personal experience and reality in a select historic position, his truth as an organ of the Spirit, according to the vocation of his person, lay or apostolic. Even the words and teachings of Christ are most precious to us, not as the insight of a spiritual sage whose moral vision was detachable from His personality (as genius so often is); but they are valuable as the transcript of His own experience, as facets of His own soul.

EXPERIENCE AND FAITH 25

They are all indirect autobiography. We do not trust them as the flashes of an unequal genius (like Bacon), nor as the conclusions of an exceptional but detachable intelligence, but as coined from His whole personality and issued from its divine experience. For instance, when at the sight of the poor widow and her mite, He called up His disciples and startled them with words so revolutionary to all their upbringing under their religious authorities as that she was worth more to God than these consequential leaders and givers— what was behind it? Was this the remark of a born teacher of moral revaluation, with a quick eye for an effective text, and a happy knack of finding object lessons for certain principles he had reached? Would that not be to reduce Jesus to the level of an expert preacher always on the alert for subjects or texts? Was it not said rather because He was so deeply moved that He could not be silent—because He was stirred to the centre by that in the woman which held so much of His own Spirit of life; because of the free-masonry of the Cross signalling from her heart to His, His own soul finding itself in her; because they had the same standard of spiritual value; then because He must seek in His disciples some to whom He could overflow (since it would have spoiled all to overflow to her); because He must draw them into the circle of His moved confidence. He was not instructing His postulants, lecturing them with a view to the sound principles of their future ministry; He was giving vent among them to the emotion which the incident stirred in a heart that always answered swiftly to His Father's grace in men.

But as soon as we move from external inspiration or authority to take our last stand upon a direct inward experience we are faced with a series of difficulties. We have to expect questions like these.

How do you reach in your experience the real objective which is so essential to the idea of authority? Or (as it is not so much a case of reaching it as of being found by it) where does it find you? How is it related to your previous experience? What is the religious *a priori*? How do you know that you are not the victim of a self-delusion? Moreover, how do you go on and venture to assign universal value to this personal experience of yours? How can you come to believe, about a God Who moves and masters *you*, things which are beyond any possible experience of yours as yet, such as the certainty of His effectual salvation at last of the whole world? And if we had this belief universally, how should we know that it was not a case of racial self-illusion? How are you, how is Humanity, to be secured in the objective reality behind even a universal experience? If all mankind confessed an experience of God, must it follow that a real God was behind it and produced it? Might God not be a mere postulate of ours, not to say a wish, to explain the experience and its range—a postulate, rather than its true cause? And might the rival postulate of a subliminal Humanity not have a good deal to say for itself? How do you pass from experience to faith? The experience is actual enough; what in it is real?

These questions could easily be multiplied. And, academic as some of them may seem to a too practical faith, they are real concerns and irritants to many to-day, when faith is not robust, and when it is easily disturbed by questions which its more vigorous health would shake off. If they could not be answered practical faith would in due course decay.

Some of the queries are not so hard to deal with. The suggestion of self-delusion we can escape from in more ways than one I shall return to it at a later stage (Chap. X.). But I may anticipate a little here.

EXPERIENCE AND FAITH

We can note the frequency and pertinacity of the experience in our own case. It becomes not only recurrent but continuous, and masterful. It controls us in everything that we regard as life's reality, so that if reality be anywhere it must be here. It turns to our habit and quality of moral life. We do not simply repeat certain novel experiences at intervals, but the new experience is what we can only call a new life. We experience not a novelty, but a regeneration. We do not live to ourselves and our experiences, but to Christ. We feel, moreover, not merely that we change, but that we *are* changed, and changed in one decisive way. We live no more to ourselves, but we are sent to a great spiritual servitude for life; which develops a freedom only to be described as a new creation, and not merely a new experience. And if we know anything about our own soul at all we know that this new life does not rise out of our own interior, or spring from our own resources. We are not the cause of our new life, we know. We are not the creators of our own new career and destiny. We did not, and could not, forgive our own past, which was not sinned against own own soul merely or chiefly. The conscience, so swift to accuse, is powerless to forgive. Nor could we infuse new life into ourselves. Neither could we insure our new life to be eternal. Our new life of faith is a miraculous creation, attached to our " old man " indeed, but not growing out of it; the old man can provide the commissure but not the current; the spiritual man is suspended, so to say, by the natural man, but it is not the natural man prolonged and transfigured. Rather it is a new man created in Christ Jesus.

Again, we pass outside our own experience, its repetition, its continuity, and its external reference. We find the like experience repeated and continuous in a vast multitude of other people. We have a whole historic Church, the greatest product of history, resting on its confession. Our own experience arose in the bosom of that community. And there are thousands and thousands, there have been millions and millions, with the same tale. And they collectively refer it, under its own compulsion, to the same fontal historic source, as well as the same creative spiritual power. And it has stood for ages the test of all their difficulties and challenges, which are substantially those which we moderns feel in ourselves. There has been enough testing, in all the modes of moral experiment, to cancel individual variations, and eliminate the mere visionary and individual element from the living, historic, case. No consensus of truth has ever been established by such an extraordinary *variety* of testimony from all ages, lands, and stations of men, simple and critical, men of all gifts and of none. It is useless to remind us how an error like the Ptolemaic astronomy [1] held the whole world for the greater part of its history. That was but a view, a theory, accepted by a *fides implicita* from the experts, and having nothing to do with personal experience or conviction or life-committal. Besides, the Ptolemaic system was upset by new facts; and it will hardly be said that comparative religion, for instance, provides us with a new firmament of facts calculated to destroy the reality of the Christian experience, however they may modify some views of Christian theology about its uniqueness. Other faiths, like Islam or Buddhism, will indeed provide us with cases of a mysticism subjectively and individually as deep and sure of itself as anything in Christianity. But how rare they are, how individual, how poorly ethical and social, how little the possession of masses of believers, how incapable of forming a Church, such as we have in Christianity—people who would never by temperament have risen to that mystic

[1] Ihmels.

EXPERIENCE AND FAITH

relation to Christ which is now their daily experience, and to a Life deeper and truer than their own lived through them, to the blessing of all they meet. And this is a unity of witness which is not destroyed by all the ecclesiastical divisions of Christendom.

But the chief guarantee of the value of an experience is not given by its actual universality, by its popularity, but by its content. Was it really God that touched me, or did I fancy it ? Was it Christ I met, or did I live in a dream ? I certainly did expect Him ; did I therefore project Him ? My Christian certainty begins with being a self-certainty ; I had the experience, most surely ; does it end there ? Was it all but a mode of me ? That experience is the strength of Christian faith ; it is also its weakness ? Does it reduce everything to a mere subjectivity ? I begin by being sure of myself as affected by God ; is that certainty the mere envelope of a delusion ; is it mere imagination if I end by being surer still of God as affecting myself ? Does experience act in a normal, reliable way of spiritual logic when it leaves me surer of the content than of the experience itself ? Or is that a pathological eccentricity, a morbid aberration, an egoistic extravagance masquerading as its opposite ? Is it an imagination, desperately hypostatised by people who feel they must, at any price, be sure of something not themselves ? Is it an illusion canonised ? Is it a psychological fiction, which became steadied into a hypothesis, and then rooted with a dogma ? Have I really had that in experience which carries me beyond experience, and turns it to faith, in the specific and crucial sense of the word ? I have the experience of being saved ; do I pass lawfully to the greater certainty that it is really Christ Who has saved me, and not an idea of Christ into which my subliminal consciousness, my deep, far spiritual destiny, has emerged and crystallised? And, going further, I have the certain experience of being saved by Christ; how should I extend that to the certainty that He will save, that He has redeemed, the whole world? I cannot experience the salvation of the world, though I can experience my own; how am I to believe it? How translate experience here also into faith? Merely because the information was once given to a divine penman, who correctly reported it?

We are here pushed within the experience to its content. And the first thing we have to say is that the content is the only thing that gives the experience religious value, or any value other than psychological. It is the content that turns psychology into theology, thought into revelation, and experience to faith. We do not believe things *because* of an experience, but we do *in* an experience. They are true not *by* the experience, but *for* it. The content transcends in reality the experience whose language it speaks, and whose psychology it follows. Faith is a religious experience, but religious experience is not faith.

And the thing which guarantees the reality of the content in experience is this, that in so treating it, in treating it as real, we acquire our souls for life. At bottom, indeed, it is a miracle. There is no denying it. It is a miracle of the Gospel Word when it strikes on the soul that turns experience to faith. When we analyse faith to the bottom we are brought up there, as I hope to show later. It is a creation. It is not of ourselves—it is the gift and creation of God. It is the Gospel that creates the power to believe the Gospel. Revelation would be impossible, it would be mere exhibition, it would not get home, were it not also, in the same act, Redemption and Regeneration. That no lesson is really taught till it is learned is a valuable principle of the new

EXPERIENCE AND FAITH

pedagogy. It is no more possible for the natural man to believe what God has done in Christ than to do it. It is, to any psychological science, always a mystery how we decern the Lord in our experience. Here we are placed beyond the mercy of Pragmatism and its somewhat utilitarian regards. Before it "works" we know and are sure of its power to work. And it is only by this foregone certainty that it does work. But when we have secured this proviso there are pragmatist considerations which are of immense value. Faith does "work." Yet it is not mere experience that works, that brings us to ourselves, but the experience both of an active God, an approaching, revealing, recreating God, on one side, and of the act of surrender on our side which replies. It is this twofold, this reciprocal act, which completes our personality, and really gives us to ourselves. And can anything be surer to a personality than that which realises it?

Of course, if we start with the advantage of the Theistic idea, and the belief that God created us for Himself, it is clear that every experience which makes us more for Him must be one which also makes us more for ourselves; and it must be one which comes home at last to every conscience He made. If man was made for God, with God's image for a destiny, then he makes himself only as he practically gives himself and all his experiences to God. Only so does he rise to true free personality like his Maker's, and is perfect as God is perfect. But surely also, even when we do not start there, if we do not start with our creation for God's image, yet if the faith that our experience is God's visitation fill, fortify, and settle for life our whole moral personality, we have the surest escape from the idea that that objective in our experience is imaginary. Much may be illusionary, and illusion may play a great part in our education, as we shall see. But at a point it must stop unless we are to dissolve everything. The philosophy of the "as if" has a limit in something final. A belief which does the last thing for personality must have behind it an objective something not less real and valid than personality and action themselves are in life. If we then treat the impression of objective reality as an illusion, it is at the cost of life's reality and of personal value sooner or later (Chap. IX.).

And especially so as we grow sensible of moral defect and sin. To treat God's rescue there as an illusion is to go deeper and deeper into self-servitude. To treat God's redemption in Christ as a valuable fiction hardened into dogma is to fasten on ourselves the bondage it was meant to destroy. It is to enslave ourselves as deeply as we were redeemed. If God be not our supreme deliverer He is our chief burden. To deny the reality of God in the saving experience is thus but an extreme case of that self-contradiction, that schism with ourselves, which is the nature of uncertainty, of unfaith, and of sin. The secret and unity of true personality is real faith in something, some authority, some creative and personal authority, that comes from without, lifts us out of our warring selves, and gives us a unity of reconciliation. We do not achieve ourselves; our soul is *given* us as a prey. Self-salvation is a self-contradiction, and means dispeace. To refuse the reality of God in experience is to divide the soul against itself. A man then sets himself against the genius of his own personality, and starves himself of its chief food. In a word, unless the object of our soul's experience is real and personal, religion vanishes and the soul with it. For religion is trust. And without a real object trust is meaningless; else it means but self-trust, or trust in one-half of self against the other, with the interminable civil war which that implies.

EXPERIENCE AND FAITH 33

And when we point the question in the farther way I have said, and ask why, because I experience that Christ saves me, I believe He can and will save the world, we are specially thrown back for our faith on the *content*, the object, of our experience, its creative fact. Could we doubt the larger faith we should be doubting no mere statement, no mere intellectual truth, but the eternal and invincible nature of Christ's person, as it stands in history and works in our own new creation. We were created again by one who knew and who said that He did it as a part of His work for a world. And there is the further fact that He consummated a long national history with a universal mission and destiny in it. By such doubt we should be challenging both the faith He created in His apostles and His own belief about Himself. And if He was wrong there He could not save me; and so my own experience of His salvation is reduced to a delusion. The greater, the more humane, the soul feels itself to be the more it demands a universal Saviour. It is thus at first the content of the experience that extends it from a mere experience to a living and reliant faith. And it is then the content of the faith that, when we have committed ourselves to Him *for ever*, compels and enables us to commit to Him also *the world*. *My* Eternal is *the* Eternal. When we are justified by Christ it means that He makes ours the whole justice of God, which is the great objective reality of universal things. When we sinned it was not against a God who was our private patron and tutelary deity, but against the righteousness, the one moral order of all the world. Offending in one point we offended in all. Anything that Christ did with God for us was done with the whole holy God of the whole sinful world. And any salvation of us must be the salvation of all that God's holiness covers and claims, *i.e.* of the whole universe. I am saved only in a world

c

salvation. The great matter therefore is not *that* I feel, but *what* I feel. If I believe in Christ it is not because I *feel* Him, but because I feel *Him*. And the experience of Him in my conscience, perfecting me, perfects me in the region where human unity lies —in the conscience. It is the perfecting of the world by a moral redemption.

When we fall back for authority and certainty on experience, and especially on a personality there given, on an authority not simply for our acts, nor for our thoughts, but for our souls, we escape from one mischievous fallacy as to faith. It is a state or act of the soul, it is not a piece of its property. We have too long been brought up in the belief that our certainty of faith concerns a *deposit of truths*, committed to us, and detachable from our personality and its history. It is a parcel made up and put in our charge. This has been especially noxious when applied to the Church as custodian of a creed which has ceased to be the living expression of its corporate life. Or faith is by some regarded as a rest-and-be-thankful spot, which we attain at last, occupy, and even fortify. We can stand, or even repose, upon this something with security; and we can devise it to those that come after us. It is a closed whole with a scientific frontier. Possessing it we can enjoy the peace of knowing that all conflict is over in connexion with its delimitation and acquisition by ourselves, all except the duty of preserving it as our spiritual inheritance against others. It is a piece of spiritual estate. Of course we recognise that battle is a part of our life, and healthy for the soul; but it is only battle to keep marauders off our religious goods, to defend the Ark and its contents. We have a touchy and turbulent creed rather than a militant faith. It is not battle in the spiritual way of reappropriating the property and developing it, of preserv-

EXPERIENCE AND FAITH

ing amid growing knowledge our own certainty of what is committed to us, and of keeping it always fresh in the new lights, and supreme among the new forces round us. We think of the conflict as an effort to keep invaders off faith's domain, rather than to keep our own instructed personality always in command at faith's centre. We bank our capital of belief, so to say, instead of investing it. We lodge it in an old strong room, instead of putting it into the moral commerce and conquest of the age. We may even bury it in a napkin.

But to hoard this manna is to have it go bad on our hands. We must always be reacquiring our faith in the Gospel if we are to retain it. We must always keep verifying our personal reference to the Cross. We cannot settle down on it. True, we must not always be plucking up salvation by the root to see if it is firm ; but we must (at least the Church must) keep verifying it, testing it and our faith in it. We must keep adjusting our compass, by asking always, and showing, if it is still equal to the new moral situation, and still lord of the new problems of life. Faith can only exist as an inner warfare. That is why the easy Christian public hates apologetics, and calls them mere polemics. But we can only keep our faith by constant reconquest. Our certainty must move on with our enlarging personality and our waxing world. As a life it is a constant decision of our soul, a constant functioning of our life-decision in new conditions ; it is not a mere relapse upon a decision we made years ago. To possess our souls we must always be mastering our souls. We receive our legacy under conditions of active tenancy and yearly improvements. The sure Christ of our frolic youth would not be a sufficient certainty for our tragic old age.

In the region of faith and personality this must always be so. Our material goods, the results of our civilisation, we can lock up and pass on. We consolidate and transmit them. We transmit our improvements. But our spiritual goods we must daily regain, daily adjust, and daily fecundate. The certainty of yesterday will not do for to-day. It must be recertified to-day. Always we must go back to adjust our compass at the inexhaustible Cross. We must return to our living authority for our obedience and reassurance. What we are so sure of is a positive Word, with features changeless and always recognisable for what it is; but it is also a living and waxing Word, as living for to-day as for yesterday and for ever, which the more it changes is the more the same. It is a Word, and not a scheme. It is a personal power, and not an intellectual palladium which we snatch up, throw on our shoulders, and carry out of the fire. And therefore it is that moral progress is so slow—because we cannot make a *thing* of it, and transmit it, as we do material gain. Each man has to verify for himself, and to acquire his legacy. He may accept gravitation, but he has to acquire sanctification, and win his soul.

And through the whole history of the Church this has been the case with vital faith. It has had to fight its way in every age. It is true the *form* of the assaults on it to-day differs from their form in ages past. But the root of the antagonism is the same. The genius of it is the same—the principle of the world against the Word, and of man's self-salvation, his self-justification, against the grace of God. The intellectual difficulties of our own age are only a special case of those that have always confronted faith. If we really mastered the second century we should be in substantial command of the twentieth. Indeed, the real solution of any age is what solves all ages. The way to overcome our difficulties is substantially that which has done it always. It is not better apologetic, but more positive, more creative, religion. The only religion with hope

EXPERIENCE AND FAITH

in it is a religion which is not set, above all things, on peace, composure, bland mysticism, or quietist piety; but it is bound up with an inner warfare, in which the Cross extends its territory in the conscience by victory upon victory, and by ever fresh command of thought and life. Constant certainty is only to be had at the price of constant surrender of our inertia. Faith is no mere charter for comfort. It has no *rentiers*. And the experience of salvation's ripening power is the only real way to continued certainty of its truth. Apologetic is not so valuable to convert the world as to confirm the Church which does convert, to give faith a foundation in the world's reality, and to unify its knowledge of the Son of God. The same Apostle of the first Epistle to the Corinthians, who insisted in the second chapter that faith did not come by the arguments of men, but by the power of the Spirit, goes on in the fifteenth chapter to confirm the Church's wavering faith in the resurrection of Christ by many infallible proofs.

II

CERTAINTY AS FAITH

There are many people prepared to speak readily of Christian preaching, Christian personality, Christian work, Christian influence, or the Christian Church, for one who can or will speak freely of Christian certainty. Sympathy has taken the place of certainty. Many can say they love, or they labour, for one who can say " I am sure." Amid all our energy there is a deep aversion to asking what we really believe, where we really are with a creed which makes any love divine, or anything worth doing at last. Which is as if a man of business refused to face the stock-taking, and never balanced his books. Yet for a Church what it surely believes is of prior moment to what it does. For all it does is done for what it holds as its real creed.

And even when interest is roused in what we think we hold, it is more difficult than ever to compel attention to the way we hold it, or the grounds for doing so. We do not interrogate our pietisms. We do not make our current religious phraseology stand and deliver an intimate ultimate meaning. We have impression without insight. The Cross does not break open to us. Eternity is not set in our heart; and therefore our religion cracks in life's fires and snaps in life's stress. We are not on rock. For current inquiries cannot now be answered by a wholesale reference to a Church or a Book. They carry the modern man deep into his moral interior; and to most men the inner man is a ghost, or at least a haunted room ; few care to explore that region till they are forced. It has to haunt them, they do not court it. And being forced work it is apt to be work ill done. The true faith and fear of God is arrested and benumbed first by inertia, then by ignorance, and then by a fear that if we really explored the deep reality beneath our shining sympathies we should find a cavern, an abyss, no God, or none that could carry life, none that could make life an enthusiasm, no God so sure as trouble, doubt, or death, none of Whom we can be more sure than we are of ourselves. Naturally and initially, of course, there is nothing of which a man is so sure as he is of himself. For, practically, we begin life in the nursery by asserting ourselves at the cost of all else, and claiming the gas, till our limit is burned into us. And, psychologically, we begin by trusting our self-consciousness and its report. Naturally, initially, that is so and must be so ; but fundamentally it is not so. The mature work of grace certainly leaves us otherwise. By a long process, out of our egoism is distilled a spirit of surrendered faith. We renounce self—not necessarily in the sense of mortifying self, but in the sense of committing ourselves to an absolute Lord and Master. We come to be both more sure and more concerned about Another than ourselves, more about His sanctity than our salvation. Within the self consciousness itself, using its language but not its voice, arises another power, whose right it is to reign. It takes possession of us and our certainty. And what we become more sure of than anything else is that God has done what makes Him surer of us than we are either of ourselves or of Him. Our chief certainty is God's certainty of us in Christ. And our religious knowledge is not to know God but to know that we are known of Him. That is religion ; the rest is but science, more or less loose. All other knowledge of God is but some form of science, less organised or more.

The question of religious certainty is, in its form at least, quite different to-day from anything it used to be when either Church or Bible made a court of final appeal. For it is not simply a question of what is true, but of what helps. Or rather, perhaps, truth is not a matter of systems but of values. It is not a matter of congruity (which is its scientific sense), but of reality (which is its moral sense, and the sense it has especially in the New Testament). That is to say, the soul has no disinterested knowledge. It is not truth as cold fact that concerns us, but truth as living experience; and as experience which *promotes* the soul, involves its destiny, and does not simply *exercise* it. It is no religious truth that is meant when it is said:

> " It comforteth my soul to know
> That, though I perish, truth is so."

That is plausible poetry, but it is amateur philosophy, and to speak of comfort is here an abuse of words. It could comfort no soul to know of the existence of a truth with which he had absolutely nothing to do. A certain strength of a Stoic kind, a certain " mantling spirit of reserve," might be given by such conviction, but nothing that deserves the name of comfort, nothing really and positively religious, and nothing that promotes the soul's proper life. It would lead to hardening rather than consolidation. Reality is no reality for religion until it supply something more than a world or a power that outlives the soul, or overrides it. It must supply a footing; more than a footing (Chap. X.). When we use that image of a footing we think of a man on a rock, of a foothold that we can exchange for another without serious change in ourselves. But in religion it is not a question of our foot but of our root. We do not stand on something solid like a rock, but we grow in something vital like a soil. We are rooted and grounded

CERTAINTY AS FAITH

in Him, in a personality congenial to our own. The reality in religion is not something to stand on, but something to live from. It does not simply hold, it helps and feeds. The connexion between us and it is organic, and not merely local. We are not merely inserted into our foundation. It is more than ground that will not give way; it is a source that will not fail or dry. We draw life from it, and it is a medium in which we live. It does not simply uphold us—it carries us, feeds us, slakes us. It is not only true for us, but mighty with us. It supports us as food does, and not simply as a floor does. It is better, of course, to be on rock than sand, but to be in soil is better still. We are rooted, and not only grounded, on our God. And, though it is true, as we shall see later (Chap. XX.), that God does not exist simply to establish and prosper man, it is also true that we cannot reach what we exist for in His revealed purpose except by His help, service, and nurture of us, as a faithful Creator who has not taken His creating hand from us. The truth in religion is not simply true nor simply helpful, but creative. It not only stays us but quickens, nor only quickens, but redeems. It is organic to our soul's life, however miraculous to our natural experience. It is not only truth, but salvation. It is not the truth of a fixed world, but of a mobile yet changeless will, and a moving but purposed history; the truth not only of what things are but of what they have power and commandment to be, not only of order but of destiny. The vital sciences, and especially history, have altered the whole complexion given to truth by the mechanical sciences. They have turned the divine reality from being the world's first cause to be its living ground, and from its ground to be both its Saviour and its Goal. And especially He is the Saviour of the world of Humanity, the moral world, the moral soul. We have to do with a God who is for man, but chiefly to enable man to be for God. Whether we take the Reconciliation idea which ruled the philosophy of Hegel, or the Redemption idea of Von Hartmann, modern thought has to do with the process and destiny of a world that lives, and moves, and grows, and not with the structure or substance of a world of still life. Therefore the goal of the world is of more moment than the ground of it. Or it would be more accurate to say the goal and the ground are one. Or, in language still more technical, we identify Finality and Causality. To put it still otherwise, philosophy, becoming more teleological, grows more theological. It becomes engrossed with will and purpose, and especially with the idea of redemption. It is dominated by the interest of salvation, as it contemplates a realm of ends, as its thought becomes more subordinate to action, as its facts become more moral, its law less mechanical, its anomalies more intolerable, its sympathies more social, and its habit more teleological. It is thus concerned about the nature of God the Saviour even more than God the Creator, about a creative redemption more even than a creative evolution. It regards the attributes of God less, and the purpose of God more. It is God's purpose more than His nature that it finds first in Revelation.

When we speak of certainty, what do we really mean by it ? For the thing we are sure of will settle the nature of our certainty who are sure, and the thing we are most sure of will determine the nature of ourselves The nature of certainty about the last things is not to be found by any amount of psychology, but by the nature of the revelation which emerges in the psychology—the sure word of prophecy. Psychology is a mere science of observation or experiment ; and science can never give us reality, nor certainty about it.

CERTAINTY AS FAITH

By the question, of course, we mean at the outset a religious certainty? We do not mean the mere objective consciousness of science, nor the empirical experiences of common sense. We do not mean a conviction of God's existence, nor a certainty of His power. There is a fixed belief about these things on the part of beings who only tremble at their remembrance, and whom we do not credit with any such religion as we desire to share. With the creed and church of the demons we seek no communion. Our Christian certainty, objective as it is, is much more subjective and intimate than that. It is not a thinker's conviction of God, but a sinner's communion with God, and, farther still, his direct communion with a holy God. It is not a mere conviction of God, nor even a temperamental impressibility by God, a spiritual susceptibility; for that may be good, bad, or indifferent. God is not sure to us just because He meets our needs or tastes. What makes Him most God is something whose deep need in us we do not know till His gift awake it. It is not that we are naturally sensitive to a divine presence of a mystic sort, nor that we respond to impressions of a devout kind, nor feel that God must be the ideal goodness of the world. It is not a matter of mere spirituality; we must prove the spirits whether they are of God. Nor is it even that we answer spiritual goodness with goodness of ours. God's is a special kind of goodness, which we must answer accordingly. It does not spread over us like a sky, it comes to us. And we must become partakers of the particular order of goodness in which He comes to us, by which alone in the moral nature of things the Holy can come home to the guilty. We do not echo God, nor corroborate Him, we obey His self-revelation. We do not thrill to an awful and mystic presence, we answer a moral person, act, and message, universal yet individualised to ourselves. We do not simply have contact with a supernatural person, we enter communion with His advances of Holy Love. And our certainty is, by the Holy Spirit, a most incredible thing—it is a function of the certainty which God always has of Himself. It is a certainty of experience truly, but it is more than experience ; it is faith ; it is a reflection of His own self-certainty. It is His own self-certainty immanent in us by faith. He never doubts Himself, and He lives in us. The things of God are only known by the Spirit of God, whether in Him or in us. We rise to newness of life by the very self-same power which raised Christ from the dead. So that if God be holy grace, the sure faith is the faith that answers grace in its own holy kind, and reflects the holy conditions of its revelation in the Cross.

I spoke just now of God's goodness as a special form of goodness. It is not the self-contained goodness of the upright, but the outgoing goodness of love ; and of love that goes out under the conditions of holiness, that reaches us only so, and determines our certainty as a personal response of that kind. The source and authority of Christian certainty, of all moral and final certainty, is the revealing, atoning, redeeming cross. It is a hard saying if we weigh words.

We can never be sure of the goodness of God except in connexion with the justice of God. The one fixed and certain thing in all the world, its bedrock, must be sought in the moral world. We believe in the substantial and final justice of the universe. How shall we be triumphantly sure of that ? The mere intuition of conscience will not give that certainty, in the face of the challenge raised by history, and its anomalies, by life and its shocks. Yet also conscience has no meaning apart from the morality which is the nature of things. To part with that conviction is

CERTAINTY AS FAITH 45

moral chaos. The mighty power we call God is a just power, *the* just power, the justice of the universe. The worst challenge that man raises of God is caused by things that make us doubt or deny His justice, not by the existence of suffering but its bad distribution. The deep certainty of God is one that rests upon His righteousness. We are not ashamed of the Gospel chiefly because therein the righteousness of God is revealed. We can continue to believe in forgiveness only if we realise that righteousness was secured in the manner of it, that it is not immoral, but that universal mercy is absolute right. Yet the question of God's general justice is not the issue on which religion rests—at least, it is not the issue on which Christianity rests. The question becomes more poignant, less remote, than that. Certainty is not an impersonal matter, like gravitation; it is a personal, like salvation. How is it between that justice and me? How do I stand with that justice? That is the central question of religion and its certainty.

It is not a general justice, which goes its way irrelevant or indifferent to me, " God's in His heaven, All's right with the world." But a justice which is the sure and fixed thing in the world is *my judge*. What crushes my conscience is not a taunt from another individual, however great, but an indictment from the moral universe. I did not break a bylaw, nor transgress a regulation; I collided with the moral unity of things, with the absolute holiness of God. *I* have to do with Him, and He with me. All the holiness of God bears down on my soul. Not His power, His influence, but His holiness. I am not a sensitive atom affected by Him, but a moral monad judged by Him. The question of personal religion therefore (the prime question, if not the first), the matter of most urgent certainty, is, How do I stand before my Judge? The Eternal Justice of the world, absolute and holy,—is it for me or against me as I stand ? As I stand—that is, in my actual moral case. It is not an abstract question of the room there might be in a universal power for a particular soul, or even of His goodwill to it as the patron of its weakness. And the issue becomes more pointed still. God's justice, of course, must be for me if I am for it. It must aid those who seek it and serve it. It must be for those who live for it. He pitieth them that fear Him. Yes, but what of those who fear Him not ? That allegiance which elicits His pity does not describe me, a sinner, a malignant, perhaps, me with the rent and warring, yet indivisible, personality, me who have been against His righteousness as well as for it, and who know not on which side my total soul may be held at last to stand. I have disliked that holiness, ignored it, withstood it, defied it. I have not been small only, or weak, but hostile. Is it still for me, or, is it against me for my sin, my serving of two masters, my better service of the bad, my mockery of the good ? That is the question Christianity answers. It is the world-question. It is the religious question. It is the question on which all other certainty rests. And it is not a question for my intelligence. It is not a question *about* religion, but a question *of* religion, raised by religion ; it is religion as question. It is not a question of thought about the soul ; it is the soul's question about itself before the Holy Soul. Nay, when we come to close quarters, I am not concerned about my soul ; it is my soul that is concerned ; and about another—my victim, perhaps. Ultimately it is concerned about God, about His holiness and my damage to it. That is the central pang of repentance. And that is the question Christianity comes to answer with a certainty, fundamental not to itself alone but to the whole moral world. That is the nature of Christian certainty ; the last root of all certainty ; which is therefore soul-certainty and not

CERTAINTY AS FAITH

rational certainty ; a certainty which is the state of a soul, and not a truth held by it ; and the state of a soul in a moral universe, with a Holy God.

The answer is from God ; and it is the gift of Himself, engaged in the act of securing His holy sovereignty in things, making His holiness good for the world, and especially in me. And to such a personal answer our only due rejoinder is personal also. It is self-donative. Our certainty is practical. Our religion is absolute self-committal. It is the gift of ourselves, the gift of our eternal selves eternally, our holy, and therefore whole, surrender to holiness and to communion with the Holy. And even that self-surrender is created by Him. The just and holy One is not against me but actively for me with all He is and all that He can for ever. That is the revelation. His authority certifies the conscience. His justice is all mine. His Holy One is mine. I have not His mere sympathy and help; I have with me all His holy justice, His Eternal Son and Other Self. " His justice is mine." It is a tremendous thing to reach, realise, and stand upon. "*I am thy salvation.*" All the righteousness, that is, all the reality of things, all the Eternal Holiness is mine. Joined to Christ by faith's committal I am loved in the love that the Father for ever spends on His Eternal Holy Son. It is a tremendous certainty. It plants us in the eternal centre of the world. And the whole soul goes to eternity on it—in the fellowship of the self-certainty of Him Who cannot be shaken, but remains for ever and ever. It is a tremendous certainty, an overwhelming certainty, an energy of faith which grows more foreign and unintelligible to the too busy churches. It is only to be revealed by a redemption, by a regeneration even of the spiritual and by conversion of the good. It is incredible until we are redeemed into the power of believing it, and it is credible only by the new creature; so that the belief of it is nothing less than a miraculous new life.

That is the Christian certainty — not simply certainty about Christianity, but certainty in Christ, about the divine reality, stability, and destiny of a shaken moral universe. And how does it come? How is it made mine? Not simply, How do I reach it?—rather, if it is a function of God's self-certainty, How does it reach me? How are we made sure? The sureness is a part of the gifted, the donated, salvation. The certainty here is being saved, it is not preliminary to it. *Faith is salvation*; it is not a condition of it, but the life of it, the function of it. It is not certainty about salvation; it is salvation acting as certainty. It is not my belief about justification; it is justification at work in my belief. Faith is not a means of certainty, it *is* certainty—though not of myself and my salvation, but of Christ. How, then, does it come? In Christ? Yes; but that alone is too historic, too external, it may be, too æsthetic, too impressionist. It is not near enough, not intimate enough, not specific enough, not close enough to my conscience nor to the world's moral case. It comes not simply by Christ the historic figure, but by Christ as the Justifier; not merely by Christ the historic fact, but by Christ the divine act. It is not by Jesus as the great transparency of God's love and pity, but by Christ as the agent of God's self-reparatory holiness, and by Christ the Spirit reaching me. That is the meaning of Justification, which must never be detached from Sanctification. Nothing can justify but holiness. No amount of suffering or dying ever can, but only holy obedience. By means best known to God, the Giver, we are united to such a holy Christ and set for ever inside the justice of God, which is no more over us, and no more confronts us,

CERTAINTY AS FAITH 49

but is within us, and we within it. There is no more condemnation nor guilt. In a holy living Christ we are integrated into the holy eternal self-satisfaction of the whole world's God. It is the act or process in which an accusing God is in His grace greater than our accusing hearts, and knows not only a more damning indictment against us than our conscience draws, but, still more, knows all the costly and cosmic things He ever did to take us inside His holiness in Christ.

The relevant experience here is that of the evangelical conscience, and not of the natural in any degree of purity. We are quite sure, when we do come to the ultimate doubt and question of the soul's conscience, only in Christ the Justifier at the central point of history, conscience, and being; only in union with Christ our Righteousness, in Whom God's own justice becomes our true acceptability, our infinite security, our experienced new life in a renewed race. God's holiness in Christ is the one security the world has of His love and its changelessness. To take that justification, that new life (and not any theory of it), is our faith. And the culture of that positive faith is the culture of the final certainty which makes sure everything else. God's holiness is the reality of all things, and it is mine. The Holy God is mine (or rather, I am His) as absolutely as He is holy. That, I say, is tremendous, glorious, and incredibly sure. And it is only possible if Christ, His Holy One and man's Holy One, is mine, if I have in Christ the eternal holiness of God handling me and my sin in a new creation; if in Christ I am uncondemned because in Him I am all that I am not.

If that absurdity be not yet the experience of all Christians, it is none the less the faith of the classic elect, who are the first fruits of all, on whom the Church lives, and who inhabit its holiest place. The great

D

Church is a host of concentric circles deepening inward, and that is the innermost of all.

You believe in Christ. You are sure. Sure of what? Sure, æsthetically, of His wisdom, depth, dignity, beauty, majesty, sinlessness, love, and pity? It is well. But what do they mean for you? What is their bearing on you and your destiny? What have you to do with them? In what sense are they yours? For contemplation, admiration, love only? Only for your infection by them? Your imitation? You, driven to your last hold, penned in your last corner, making your last stand, before the last bar and the holy judge of all the earth doing endless right—what do these things in Christ mean for you? All that He is, and you are not and never can be, all that you might have been and lost the chance of ever being—what is it for you now? Does He give it you all back? Is He the very justice of God; and in Him do you stand inside that justice? For that is being justified—being taken to stand and live inside the holy justice of God, and to work with it instead of standing and collapsing before it. What religion needs most is certainty of this kind. What all certainty needs is this religion at its root. With the interest in justification there has ebbed religious character, sureness, stability, and reality — much as the demand for realism has increased, and the feeling of sympathy. It is a demand that can never be met except by the loving, unsparing moral realism of the New Testament, its sense of the sinfulness of sin rather than of the number of sins, its certainty of the apostolic Salvation, of being, by God's act in Christ, in right and eternal relation to the holy love and justice of all the world, which sanctity we have injured, and which, had it been left to us, would have collapsed. (For to offend on one point is to offend on all, since it is against one absolutely holy person.) Outside that

CERTAINTY AS FAITH

justice we cannot stand. And Christ's task was to cast it over us, to take us inside it; where, having done all, yet we stand—having done so many things we dare not name, yet we stand. That is our justification. That is our sanctification. They are one. They mean establishing once and for ever the sanctity of God in the universe, and putting us inside it; so that one day it shall be sanctified in us as we are already justified in it; and we pray without ceasing, Hallowed be Thy name in its eternal sanctification in Christ. That is the kind of certainty central to the soul, and therefore to the world. It is the soul-certainty of God's justification of us, His final forgiveness of us in Christ, *i.e.* His restitution of a moral universe, and His assumption of us into its holiness.

We must frame theories of that Justification, based on our moral nature, and God's, and the action of their laws. But every theory of Justification has its test here—in its power to produce this life-certainty, to promote it, or explain it. The great certainty thus concerns the conscience and the will. And the settlement of it is in this moral, this holy region of sin and guilt. Our central certainty concerns the treatment of these, their treatment not by us with our levity, but by the holy and injured Party, from whom the initiative must come. It is the certainty of reconciliation, and its experience of communion. It turns upon God's initiative of grace and reconciliation. And Christian faith is faith in the Justifier, the Reconciler, the Sanctifier, and not merely in God the Father. It is the soul intimately certain as to the world's saving, redeeming, forgiving, regenerating God in Christ. We may be patient of ourselves and our lower stages in our progress to that, but it is that to which they progress; and that is the Church's Word trusted to its teachers—if the New Testament is not the mere relic of an out-grown fictionary phase of faith. Our certainty of faith is not an impression of Christ, but a life-experience in Christ. It is our regeneration by and in Him. It is neither a conviction, nor a mood, nor a manner of life, but a life indeed. Essential Christian certainty is thus not a rational but a miraculous thing. We are not convinced of it but converted to it. They have much to say for themselves who say that the central Christianity is Regeneration. And the Soul, Humanity, has but one Authority—its New Creator.

It is central to what I say in these pages that the meaning of faith should be taken in all the earnest of the soul and its situation, moral and historic. To that situation a definition of faith as but loyalty is inadequate. Loyalty is a defective account of faith, even to faith taken as the soul's relation to Christ, and not merely to a cause. For loyalty means the relation to a king of one who is yet, in relation to that king, a freeman, possessed of a conscience whose shrine even the king must not invade. But we are the absolute property of such a king as is here contemplated in Christ; and there is nothing in us hid from His light, His sight, or His right. It is absolute self-committal, it is not only loyalty that is involved here. We are not our own in any part of us as against Him.

But especially is loyalty an inadequate version of Christian faith when it is turned but on a universal cause or mission instead of an eternal and absolute person. Faith has recently been defined[1] as devotion to a Cause, which is described as " some conceived, yet also real, spiritual unity, which links many individual lives in one, and which is therefore essentially superhuman, in exactly the sense in which we found the realities of the world of the reason to be super-

[1] In Dr Royce's fine book, "The Sources of Religious Insight." T. & T. Clark, 1912.

human" (p. 199). Be loyal, says this lofty moralist, to some such Cause, "superhuman in the scope, the wealth, the unity and the reasonableness of its purposes and of its accomplishments." "So be loyal, that is, so seek, so accept, so serve your cause, that thereby the loyalty of all your brethren throughout all the world, through your example, through your influence, through your own love of loyalty wherever you find it, as well as through the sort of loyalty you exemplify in your deeds, shall be aided, furthered, increased so far as in you lies."

It is very great and high. But it is the note of the school rather than the Church. Emerson would have so expounded the cultivated stoicism of New England had he lived to-day—the religious ethic of a young nation's invincible optimism, and of its self-confidence somewhat untried as yet in the inmost moral fires. Who can deny that Christian faith has often lost this note of loyalty, and the chivalry that goes with it. But all the same this is something less than New Testament faith, something too modern, ·to be just to the Gospel, and too abstract to make an authority for human nature. "Your true cause is the spiritual unity of all human beings." That is not Christian till we find the source and guarantee of such unity in Christ: "You are safe," quotes our author, "only when you can stand everything that can happen to you." It might be Marcus Aurelius. But that is not the Christian salvation, though it should be a fruit of it. "I can endure the loss of all things that I may win Christ." "I can do all things through Christ who strengtheneth me." "If any man be in Christ, there is—not a grand heroism but—a new creation." Our first charge is Christ; His Cause is a first charge only on Him. The whole of us and our resources are quite unequal to it. But He is equal to it and more.

III

AUTHORITY, CERTAINTY, AND SANCTITY

The question of authority is, I have said, at another angle, the question of certainty. Under the last certainty, as over the supreme worship, there must be an authority. The truth may be a shock to some stalwart ideas, and some prickly rights of private judgment, but certainty is really obedience. Without that note it is but a mode of self-assertion, in which we are more sure of ourselves than of each other or of anything. If we strove to avoid self-assertion, and if we erased from society all authority, by the way of reducing the greatest relation of the soul from an obedience and a duty to a sympathy and a *fraternity*, there would still be in the end no certainty. It would dissolve into the doubt of vagrants, who would but call to each other in the night. And therewith would dwindle and die any real power to give fraternity its own effect. Nor is certainty something we arrive at out of the mêlée of a common *freedom* ; it is something given us to start with for the sake of freedom ; it is a factor necessary for the achievement of freedom. And the one condition of true and permanent *equality* is the equal obligation of all to the one gift and grace of God, which is at once the supreme authority and the central certainty of the soul—at least as Christ read the soul and its destiny. " To every man this penny."

The seat of authority, I have also said, is one

AUTHORITY, CERTAINTY, & SANCTITY 55

thing, the source and sanction of it is another. The seat of it, of course, is subjective to us. Real authority is a thing that must be experienced, but it is not the experience, which is but a mode of ourselves. And so with the certitude which is authority's correlate. We cannot say of anything " it is certain " without saying " I am certain " (though we cannot always say " it is certain " with the same force as we can say " I am "). Certitude is not, indeed, the absence of difficulty or contradiction *in our views* ; but it is a state in which we cannot think otherwise without getting into contradiction *with ourselves*, and destroying our subjective harmony, and ultimately our personal unity. Yet all the time it is certitude *about something* in which we find ourselves in a bracing way ; it is not certitude of ourselves as certain. If we speak of the sanction of our certitude, that is not subjective. It is experienced, indeed, but it emerges in experience ; it is not evolved from experience. It is implanted, it is not produced. We have an experienced *faith* in an engrafted *word*. Faith is a mode of our experience, but the Word we trust at its core is not ; it is *to* our experience. Nothing, truly, can be final authority which is not experienced, but the experience is not the authority. Our experience becomes authoritative for other experiences, according as it links us and them with a reality which is authoritative for itself. Certainty is an experience and not merely an impression, it is an assurance of something. We know not that we feel somehow, but that we feel something. It connotes not only our certitude as its subjective side, but an objective worth. Certitude is valuable according to the certainty, the certain thing, it carries at its heart—which is in it but not of it. It is not religion that is really valuable, but God. As a mere experience, as a subjective state, as mere certitude, it has no great value except to the possessor as being a mode of himself; or it has an æsthetic one for the artist who represents it, or the psychologist who studies it. It can even be an obsession to its subject. It has force enough for ourselves, for we can be very obstinate about what is really quite uncertain or false; but it has not value in itself in a region like religion or ethics, where we worship, sacrifice, and obey a not-ourselves. It may rally a man without rectifying or justifying him.

The prime value of an objective and absolute reality is not even the power I have named of harmonising the subject in his states. It is not that it pacifies, or even exalts us, makes us feel a quiet or a dignity. Things may do that for a time which we afterwards find to be unreal—things in the nature of opiates, and with their sequelæ. This is the bane of much popular religion, and the source of its wide collapse. People are hypnotised rather than converted. They are acted on by suggestion rather than authority, which lowers their personality rather than rallies it, and moves them by man's will rather than God's. Some treat as the great certainty that which merely enables them to study to be quiet, to court comfort, and pass a peaceable life cultivating their garden; they have no test beyond the calming power. Truth is then a quietive, not a motive, faith a sedative and not a tonic; so that a crisis becomes a break-up, and age is but a slough of petty egoisms and draggled regrets. But the great obedience we render not for the sake of peace, not for its by-products and reactions on us, but for its own sake; not because we court calm, but because we worship right, royalty, and sanctity. In like manner the sharpest sting of our repentance is neither the fear of punishment nor the loss of self-respect, but it is the sense of wounding, unhallowing, and to our power destroying the Holiness eternal. The precious thing

AUTHORITY, CERTAINTY, & SANCTITY

about the objective reality of which we are so certain is its right to reign, and its power through obedience to create personality. It is not its Catholic power as a quietive, but its Evangelical as a motive; its power to make us not only study to be quiet, but to do our soul's business; power which makes us strive toward making rather than to repose on aught found made; power to make us meet our God, face our actual moral position, acquire moral personality, and unite our soul in the fear of His name. The test of its value is its moral majesty and its moral teleology.

Thus religion, which is based on an authoritative certainty, is less enjoyment than inspiration, less comfort than strength. The crucial hour on the cross had no comfort; but it had eternal strength and redeeming power. Religion is not æsthetic, but ethical and practical. It deals first with our conscience. It realises in it a divine vocation, and an upward calling. We acquire moral standing, on the scale of the divine and redeeming purpose for the race. The things most valuable, most sure, and most commanding are the things that most contribute to that. It is not what just makes us feel good. Christian religion is not a sense of spiritual well-being or soul-repletion; nor is it the rapture of intuition; but it is the satisfaction that radiates from the holy authority alone, goes with its obedience and at last gives us ourselves therein. It is the sense of fulfilling rather than the sense of being filled. His will is our peace. We are not so much adjusted to ourselves and trimmed to the spiritual symmetry of the Christian gentleman, but we are reconciled to Another, Who emerges in our experience, and Who does so not to magnify, beautify, or dignify that experience, but to constrain and dispose it for His purpose of love. God's chief end is not to glorify man, but man's is to glorify God. The object of our certainty compels us by its revealed nature to think of it in a particular way; we do not so think of it only to escape the *malaise* of self-contradiction.

The real ground of our certitude, therefore, is the nature of the thing of which we are sure, rather than the nature of the experience in which we are sure. (Chap. VIII.) It is what we are sure of that enables us to say why we are sure of it. The object of certainty is a creative power which obliges us to say of our faith, when we would account for it, that it is not of ourselves, it is God's gift and His product in us. The object gives by its intrinsic and creative quality the ground of the certainty. It does not verify itself to our reason, except as it evokes our will's preference and decision. (Chap. IX.) It has its own secret, and its own order of authority. We are sure of a coming eclipse for very different reasons from those that make us sure that a debt will be paid. We are equally sure of each, but upon grounds which differ according to the nature of the event. We are sure of our philosophic theology, our theosophy, in a way different from our saving certainty of Christ and its positive theology. The authority is different. If Christian truth were a plexus of doctrine, our certainty would rest on one kind of authority (which would probably be a finally authoritative Church). But Christian truth is not that; it is not propositional or statutory; it is not a gift, a revelation, of formal law, but of spiritual reality, divine life, personal grace. It is not theological but religious, in so far as the distinction exists. The faith of it is in an experienced state and carriage of the soul. It is not first concerned with belief but with a soul believing, and a soul which in its belief knows itself not to have attained but to be re-created. It means communion with the God self-given to us in Jesus Christ. And all the several truths connected with it, however scientifically

AUTHORITY, CERTAINTY, & SANCTITY

organised, must be owned and rated according as they contribute to that end for the soul, as they serve and expound that kind of faith.

Therefore, for such Christianity, for the truth which is a personal response and not a mental assent, which involves a choice rather than a creed, the authority cannot be lower or less direct than the choosing, saving God Himself in action. He alone by His action creates that choice and guarantees that communion. The object of our faith, as it is its creator, so also is its authority. Our final authority is our new Creator. The authority cannot, therefore, be either a Church or a Book—both of which are historically the products of such communion with God. They did not exist till it did, and therefore could not be the cause or the authority of its existence. The only final authority for Christian faith is its Creator—God Himself acting on us in the Christian way of a new creation, *i.e.* God asserting His holy Self in Christ's historic and regenerative work, and in its perpetual energy in the soul. It is God emerging in history by a superhistoric and timeless act which also emerges and functions in each soul, the same yesterday, to-day, and for ever. (Chap. VII.) It will not do simply to say, generally and mystically, the Authority is God. The mysticism here must be the historic mysticism of positive and redeeming revelation. The authority of the source lies not in its mere power of pressure (far less its mere presence), but in its positive nature, its action, and its effect. It is not dynamic but qualitative in its effect. It is God with a special nature shown by express action, God the All-holy rather than the Almighty, God in a special mode of action freely chosen by Himself, and necessary to His moral freedom—God giving Himself, indeed, but giving Himself freely, historically, and positively, in a particular way determined materially by His holy nature and only formally by the human crisis. It is God so acting that the principle of the action is not to be grounded in our subjective religious state, nor tested by our first and warmest impressions, but it is grounded in Himself and His work as the objective fact which created that state. God's grace is not certain just because it satisfies our need, but because it has pleased Him to reveal it in a historic, authoritative fact which creates the chief need it fills. As a matter of fact our religious soul has been made by the Christian history, and especially by the first century of it. The features of our faith do not form its ground. Its features are created, subjective, and experienced, but its ground is creative, objective, and historic. The principle of salvation is not to be found in our faith or our need, but in the revelation which created the faith and deepened the need—in Christ and Him crucified. It is a certainty which, however mystic it be, is always mediated by the historic apostolic Christ.

How that is possible, how ancient history can become a conscious presence, or, conversely, why the Christ present in our consciousness should be absolutely identified with the historic Jesus—is discussed elsewhere. (Chap. VII.) I only say here that, were it otherwise, then the Christian certainty would be no more than theistic, mystic, or subjective—like much Unitarianism —a rationalist monotheism invested with Christian sympathies and ethics. Or its tribunal might be the Christian consciousness; whose mentality at a given stage of growth might be taken as the authority, standard, and measure of Christian truth. The truth would then be an unfolding or analysis, or discovery of subjective religion from time to time, and not a statement of the real historic revelation that created and develops it. And it would always contain an element of illusion, which succeeding stages must escape. We

AUTHORITY, CERTAINTY, & SANCTITY 61

cannot measure the wealth of our revelation from God in Christ by our best ideas, nor from our " Christian spirit," however Christian. We do not wait till we are perfectly in tune with God in a Christian spirit before we realise the final truth as it is in Jesus. But this we should have to do, were the Christian consciousness our objective, our finality, and authority. Christian truth lies fontal in the historic and immortal source of the authority, not in its subjective seat; in the objective, creative sanction of the authority, not in its subjective sphere or effect; which is a mere register of truth, and not its treasury, far less its judge. We do not wait to believe in Christ till we see if He " works "; else how could men believe at the very first, before they could say if He was to work or not, and while His victories in history were yet unwon?

We can be quite sure of our communion with God and its eternal security only as we are sure of the realities that create, saturate, and sustain it, only in Christ, only as we are sure of the Son of God in us. These realities emerge in the region of experience, and unfold in its warmth. They talk its language, and have their scope in its occasions. But it is not their matter. We are surer of Christ and His salvation than of our faith; but it is certitude of a Christ Who can be understood only by faith, *i.e.* by personal contact with Him. We have not two certitudes about these supreme matters, produced by authority *and* experience, but one, produced by authority *in* experience; not a certitude produced by authority and then corroborated by experience, but one produced by an authority active only in experience, and especially the corporate experience of a Church. Christ is the food we live on, not the voice we echo. We appropriate Him, else we do not fully appreciate Him. We are more sure of the Cross which destroys our sin than of the sin to be destroyed; and it is a Cross that really makes us cease to be sinful, and not only cease to feel condemned.

But the weakness of current religion is its infection by modern subjectivity to an extent which makes it too careless of its objective content, its historic base, or its searching ethical quality. We evade the theology of the moral soul. We ask only for temperamental or impressive religion too regardless of belief ; or we heal the wrongs subjective to man, too careless of the more deep and dreadful wrong from man to God. Religion has become psychological at the cost of being theological, and it is therefore much more sympathetic than sure. The Incarnation, for instance, where the name is kept at all, is treated from the subjective and æsthetic point of view, as a symbol of the glorification of Humanity, and a guarantee of the development of man's spiritual nature. It is occasionally conceded that the Church doctrine has something to be said for it, as a rude envelope of ideal truth. The concession wears an air of historic impartiality and philosophic liberality. But that God was in Christ reconciling and redeeming rather than developing man, that the Incarnation drew its first necessity from the free movements and requirements of God's own holy nature more than our human need, that its root is the ethical necessity of the holy rather than the æsthetic prospect of a splendid Humanity—such considerations are "theological." The real meaning of which is that they do not cater to the egoism of Humanity, to its prompt and elemental affections, and to its self-centred, self-satisfied pre-occupation with its own needs, possibilities, and glories. They do not gratify the Thrasonic religion which is engrossed and aggressive with the glory of this excellent creature man, and oblivious of the duty and love due in penitent worship to a holy God.

AUTHORITY, CERTAINTY, & SANCTITY 63

Much of the religious writing of the period which is most attractive to minds on the threshold of culture is the work of subjectivists, who are more interested in impression than in reality, in the sweet than the holy, in mystic piety than moral faith, in literature than in Scripture, in the heart and its affection than in conscience and its justification, who are more at home with religion than with God, and more sentimentally interested in the dead dog for its white teeth than with the wound to the living God in the loss of a creature's faith.

> " Our interest's on the dangerous side of things.
> The honest thief, the tender murderer,
> The superstitious atheist, demirep
> That loves, and saves her soul in new French books.
> We watch while these in equilibrium keep
> The giddy line midway."

The track that I here pursue of course starts from a unique emphasis upon the Cross of Christ as the ultimate act of universal moral reality, and the final seat of authority in history; and this whether we regard it as an act condensed at a focal point of time, or the same act "functioning" by the Spirit in the Church's detailed experience. The Cross is here viewed not as a martyrdom mainly passive, or a sacrifice chiefly æsthetic and exemplary for us; nor is it regarded as an act detached from Christ's life; but it is seen as the consummatory act which points the whole of His person, and is the spearhead by which the inner life of that person effectively enters all time. Nay, one is carried beyond the idea even of an act to another idea which must not be rejected simply because it has become encrusted, for a business people, with commercial associations. It was a great *transaction*. Or we can use the old word of a "covenant," if only we secure the idea of a reciprocity without a bargain. For we have here more than an exhibiting act of God, more than a didactic, more than a prophetic; we have an act, creative, decisive, and reciprocal. We have an act which involves both sides alike, and which settles their whole future, and indeed eternal, relation. We have a central, fontal, constitutive act of God, creating faith by its very nature as a corresponding reaction to it in man, just as the first creation made human freedom with all its energies, reacting even on the Creator. Faith is no less crucial than the Grace it answers; and equally with Grace it is the supreme energy of a person. If there is any authority over the natural man, it must be that of its Creator; and, if the New Humanity has any authority above it, that authority must be found in the act of *its* creation, which act is the Cross of Christ. If the authority is Grace the certainty of it is faith in Grace.

Authority, we keep finding, is only a religious idea. In science it does not exist, and in politics it is but relative. In any ultimate sense it concerns but the soul. There only is it absolute; everywhere else it is but relative. And it rules through the soul, by the response of the moral personality. It is a personal relation and a moral, the relation of two wills and consciences. It is the authority of an absolute, holy Person. And in religion nothing is authoritative except in so far as it shares the authority of God Himself, and holds of the holy. The degree of its authority is that of its true sanctity. But the holy is the absolute conscience. So this divine authority is exerted upon a conscience. But on a conscience which, as soon as it realises the holy, realises itself in the same act as sinful and lost. "Depart from me, for I am a sinful man." It is therefore, farther, the authority of a Saviour (for nothing damns like what saves). It is the authority of a Saviour Who effects a new creature, with the absolute right

AUTHORITY, CERTAINTY, & SANCTITY 65

over it that creation always must give. It is the new-creative action of the perfectly holy conscience of God on the helplessly guilty [1] conscience of man. It is life from the dead.

Hence it is a miracle. Who shall explain the secret of the influence of one person on another ? It is as mysterious, and as real, as love always is. Authority is in the nature of miracle, as appears every time a man quells a mob. And the more absolute, so much the more miraculous, the more creative. It creates its own obedience, rather than extorts or even elicits it. Its Gospel creates its own belief. We know not how. Our faith, like our freedom, is a creation of God—yet so that we are responsible for both. The authority of God, and especially of God the Saviour, is more miraculous than explicable. His Gospel is more of "foolishness" the more Gospel it is. When Paul describes his own experience of the *bouleversement* it made of everything that had been engrained in his rational religion, he can only say that it pleased God to reveal His Son in him. He never speaks of the success of the Gospel as lying in its appeal to his better self, or its consummation of his prior self, or its transfiguration of his natural self, or its corroboration of his rational self. There is nothing miraculous when I explain. When I explain something, I command it ; and it is natural to seek to command. But to obey is not natural—the less natural the more I have disobeyed—and to make me obey is miraculous. There is no miracle like that which changes the whole direction and complexion of a will. The supreme authority, in so far as it is effective for my obedience, is the supreme miracle, which remakes me and my will, rather than the supreme reason which extends me and my domain.

All of which issues in this—that authority at the

[1] I do not say "totally corrupt."

last has no meaning except as it is understood by the evangelical experience of regeneration in some form, which is the soul's re-creation, surrender, and obedience once and for all in a new creation and direct communion with the God of the moral universe. Nothing else quells for good the defiance by human egoism even of its Creator, or subdues our heady liberty to humble and hearty worship. And nothing else gives us our cosmic place. Nothing else establishes us for ever on the impregnable rock of the saving purpose of God in a world. The last certainty is only ours as a personal experience of an Eternal Salvation. And so it is there also that we realise our absolute Authority, Whose we are, and not our own at all, being brought with an infinite price.

It is current to say that the seat of revelation and of its authority is the soul or the conscience; which in a sense is true. But it is not in the individual soul. Its sphere is there, we have seen, but not its source, not its throne. But also not its range. Nowhere in the New Testament do we find that the supreme and authoritative truth about Christ and His work is constructed out of the individual experience, little as it would mean without it. It comes to that experience from a public, social, national fact and history, with a claim and a truth independent of a soul's experience. Such experience is the medium but not the canon of religious truth. Nothing final and universal can be assured from the narrow resources of the individual experience. True, revelation can only speak the individual's *language*, but it utters much more than an individual *word*. The great truth is given and promised to a Church. The Apostle to Society is a Society. A final and universal authority must speak with a larger utterance even than that of Humanity. It must speak from Eternity. It must speak to the

AUTHORITY, CERTAINTY, & SANCTITY 67

soul eternal things with the weight and intimacy of history. And, lest it become the appanage of inductive and scientific historians in search of general laws or principles, it must speak at a point which is central to history. Yet not simply in a man's experience. It must proceed from a soul, but one which is much more than individual. Its word must, indeed, be more than commensurate with the whole human soul, else it were not authoritative for man. It must speak in a God-man, Who is not amenable to the judgment of the whole of Humanity, but is Himself its Judge. *Securus judicat orbem terrarum.* Without that, *orbis* spells mere Positivism. It is useless, it is trifling even, to say that the source of revelation and authority is Humanity ; that it is through the voice of collective Humanity that God speaks, and in its achievements that He acts ; that man is the revelation, and his amendment the only atonement. Where are we to find the final voice or the crucial act of a Humanity so rent with division of every kind, on every issue, as actual Humanity is ? Besides, the authority of a personal and eternal God cannot be expressed by any *grande être* of impersonal Humanity whose career is as yet incomplete. It must be heard, answered, and made incarnate in a person who *is* the New Humanity in principle, and who is for each individual the authority of God as Humanity's new Creator.

This brings us back to say that the authority must be pointed not in a truth simply but in a deed—not in an impressive idea pervading all Time, but in a crucial deed uttering all Eternity. The supreme Revelation is the final Redemption. And the supreme Authority is the agent of an Eternal Salvation. It is an authority founded on a revolution it created, on a revolution which is not merely an acute evolution, not merely a stage of progress precipitated and condensed (as the multiplication of the loaves has been explained to be but the hastening and compression of the natural processes which lead the seed through harvest to the oven). It is a revolution which turns our face the other way, and steadfastly sets us to the Jerusalem we had left.

It is saying the same thing when we answer the question, What is the Christian fact? (Chap. VII.) by declaring that it is not a mere historic event but a historic word. That is, it is an event which is a divine act uttering and effecting the divine will. And as divine it is an act interpreted by itself, an act inseparable from its own account of itself through men it raised up for the purpose. We can have no faith in a mere fact, but only in a personal power working and reaching us through the fact. When we ask if a historic fact can become a present experience, so that the history do not starve the experience, nor the experience ignore the history, the first step to an answer is to become quite clear that the fact is not a mere occurrence but a salvation. What we need is not merely a fact that can become sacramental, and sacramental for individual edification, but one that is creative for a Church's faith and life—the act of God's Gospel.

In all social authority we must have a head and centre of it. We must have a positive law and a positive ruler. Truly these act in a diffused spirit and *milieu* of law-abiding; but without a positive centre the social spirit itself is soon lost. It "dies of diversion," and evaporates to futility in a mere haze of fraternity. Now the counterpart of the social authority, with its activity and positivity, is found for religion in the central and frontal place of the historic Saviour and His crucial transaction, for the race and with it, in the Redemption of the Cross. He is a King who does not succeed to His Kingdom

AUTHORITY, CERTAINTY, & SANCTITY 69

but conquers and creates it. What we need, and here have, is not the authority of a grand spiritual personality, æsthetically viewed, or impressively and magnetically felt, but One who is ethically, spiritually, experienced by us as regenerative, and reciprocally met in a relation which is more than contact, and more even than intercourse. It is a standing communion, a life communion (and not a mere rapt colloquy), created by Him who says, " I am thine, and thou art Mine," in a wedlock equally real whether the day pass in glow or grey.

Impressive preaching is not the ideal Christian type, which is regenerative. (Chap. XIX.) A deep impression is not yet a new creation; and to create an impression is not to new create a soul, nor to set up an authority for all life. This is one reason why out of much impressive preaching to which audiences crowd we have not so much in the way of personal conversion or Church power. Churches are made by conversion, rather than by mere impression. It is not easy to say how much impressive preaching yields in the way of deepened communion with God as a habit of life. Yet nothing less than such communion, on the basis of forgiveness, is the object of Christianity. Christianity is nothing less than habitual communion with a God of holy love on the basis of a historic revelation and redemption.

Theism leaves room for commerce with God, but it has more room than power for it. And it takes much more than Theism, it takes something more mediatorial, to establish and maintain the direct Christian communion with God. The source of that, in man's actual, moral, sinful case, is an act which sets up the new relation by a new creation, by an actual, historic, and absolute impropriation of the forfeit soul, by its redemption into the communion of the creative grace; so that the saved soul says, " I am Thy loving slave, and I am not worthy to be called Thy son " : and the Saviour God, " Thou art My son, this day have I begotten thee."

The final authority for all life, we have seen, must be a religious authority. The absolute Lord of Life must be found in life as religious, in personal communion with a personal God; and we can be surer of God than either of the world or of man. But religion to our modern soul has two features. As ethical it must be essentially an act, and not a sentiment only; and as psychological it must be an experience. And to these subjective features of religion must correspond its object. That must be a person putting Himself into an act for an experience. Our relation, as living persons, to an influence or an idea is not religious. The final authority must therefore be such a communing person as I say. It can be neither a statement, nor a symbol, nor a society like the Church. For a Humanity with a history it must be the Christ of the historic and redeeming Cross.

The difficulty so many feel about an authority is due, *first*, to the tough and venerable fallacy that religion is assent to certain truths—for which we should have no final authority except an infalliable book or an infallible see. ' Who shall tell me surely what to believe about Christ ? ' None can. No Church can. No book can ; no saint, no theologian. None can but Christ Himself in actual presence—it may be without a word that I could report, or a theme I could frame —by overwhelming my soul with its greatness and its evil, its judgment and its salvation, in His invincible word of death, resurrection, and glory. One recalls Sir Walter Raleigh's fine saying, " A mighty teacher is Death. He reveals the secret of the whole world without saying a word."

And, *second*, the difficulty is due to the ancient shyness and inertia which makes it as hard to enter personal and religious dealings with the personal Saviour as it is easy to swallow an imposing creed.

We must, however, come to this personal and experient communion of a supreme personal act on the scale of the race. The Cross is not only a finished act or transaction, but a perpetual, like creation itself. But here the objection is obvious. ' Can I, can every man everywhere, enter experienced communion with a person or an act in the remote ages of Time ? I can be acted on mightily by a great far prophet ; can I actually, directly, and reciprocally deal with Him ? Can the Jesus of yesterday be every one's most present Christ to-day and for ever ? ' This is the real issue in the question about the final and absolute authority. The great question thus put I deal with more fully on another page. (Chap. VI.) I will only say here that to handle it we must get rid of the notion of saving truths in the sense of truths that save ; that is mere Orthodoxy, whether they be few or many.[1] While we may pursue them as truths about salvation, or insist on them as statements of it, we must be rooted in the fact, faith, and feeling of a saving person and His work. That is, we must start with the principle that all stateable truth about that person flows out of experienced personal relations with Him ; it does not create these. Truths about Christ are really sure to the Church only as they arise out of its experience of Christ. It is not truth that saves but reality ; and reality comes home but to experience ; it has to be stated only in being conveyed. Truths about salvation rise out of experience of salvation. The idea of a chronic communion between Christ and the soul is only certain by the experience of that com-

[1] See *Hibbert Journal*, Jan. 1913.

munion. Our construction of the great person and act, its theology, arises out of such faith in it. We must love him ere to us He shall seem worthy of our love. Our experient faith is our living fellowship of Christ's person and act as the closest, surest, dearest certainty of our new, deep, eternal life. And the act of our redemption, especially, is as intimate to Christian experience, and therefore as present and as constitutive of it, as the person of the Redeemer. For the act is the person in power, the person is the act in reserve. The whole Eternal Redeemer was gathered in the act. And, if that historic presence is for Christian faith a perpetual presence, much more must His act be an *eternal act*, like the act of creation which always makes the world; and it must interpenetrate every act of faith, to create and to command. We shall be sure of an actual, final authority in proportion as we have had the experience of being absolutely mastered by the moral act of redemption which made Christ King of human history. What recreates the conscience masters the cosmos in so far as the cosmos has a moral foundation. Our authority, therefore, is not simply Jesus, nor simply Christ, but Jesus Christ, our Redeemer, our Conqueror, who in one act breaks us and makes us for ever. We are here far beyond discipleship and its amiable quest. We are found and bought. We are more than His disciples. We are His property and His confessors. The great fact is not His person, not even His inner life; for (as Johannes Weiss points out in criticism of Herrmann) its impressiveness is too dependent on a temperamental susceptibility varying in individual cases. But the great fact is His person in that objective office and function of redemption. Our conversion may be sudden or slow, but its type and idea is given in the swift, sharp, decisive and permanent

AUTHORITY, CERTAINTY, & SANCTITY 73

cases of it represented by St Paul's. These give its nature, however unconscious of that nature the subject may be. It is a breach with the natural man and his egoist world. The truths truest to us and most sure are those most inseparable from that experience of radical change. And the reason why many doubt such truths is that they have lost the experience or never had it. Some have missed it through preoccupation with other interests; some, having had it, have lost it, either through such pre-occupation, or even through engrossment with religious interests excessive and mechanical. So that they can think, and even preach, of the divine service of worship as being chiefly a preparation for the real service, which is philanthropic. And some may even come to look back on the blissful hours they once enjoyed with the kindly smile that we bestow upon dear illusions faded now. Or, worst fate of all, they may turn on them a bitter and hostile eye as mischievous delusions that wasted the time and tribute of the soul.

The question of the final authority is really another way of handling the moral question, which is the question of life, and the solution of all questions below it.

And the solution of the moral question is the religious solution, because the religious question is moral at its heart, and means the question of the race's guilty conscience and its peace with honour to a holy God. There are forms of religion which do not mean this, which are ideal, mystic, humanitarian, æsthetic, pathetic, and egoist, which know practically no greater Deity than Humanity, and whose voice, even about Humanity, speaks in this wise: 'This is my enlarged self in whom I am well-pleased.' But, if religion and ethic are ever to be reconciled, it must be by their union and consummation in the supreme moral (and even metaphysical) idea of *holiness*. That must be the ruling idea of the ruling religion; and the securing of that holiness its supreme task.[1] It must treat as the chief end of man the life-worship and confession of a God self-revealed as absolute and holy Love. Such worship is the one consummating attitude of a righteous Humanity; for sublimated righteousness is the very nature of God. *Bonitas est substantia Dei*, says Augustine. "The Holy Lord shows His holiness in righteousness," says Isaiah (v. 6). If such righteous holiness be the nature of the last reality, and therefore of the last worship, it gives us the last standard of man's worth. It is his last judgment. By this measure his righteousness and his reality throughout must stand or fall. Such goodness is his reality. His reality is to be righteous thus. His supreme concern and disquiet is his dislocation from such holiness. His joy and crown is to be attuned to it. The fulness of the whole earth, of all Humanity, is no procession of evolutionary cycles shining in endless day, but it is the glory of the thrice holy God from whose absoluteness all evolution proceeds. Our final religion is not the proud and happy sense of a splendid well-being, which has the ethical note and takes decent account of God; but it is this absolute and perpetual and humble worship. Our salvation is the restoration of holiness. The central concern of religion is God's holy restoration of personal holiness to the guilty conscience of the race. All else is added to that. That is evangelical religion, pure religion and undefiled. It is the religion of grace, else it would only judge us to condemn us; and of the atoning Cross of Christ, else the grace were severed

[1] May I refer to my book on "The Work of Christ" (Hodder & Stoughton) for the rationale of this?

AUTHORITY, CERTAINTY, & SANCTITY

from judgment and less than holy. That is the only religion charged with the solution of the moral question, which is the real problem of the race.

Religion is our relation to the absolute as holy. Without such an absolute there is no faith, no obedience, because no authority. If it be not holy it is not a moral absolute; and if it do not save it does not love. Mankind finds and confesses its one authority in a Holy God as a Saviour—in the Holy God, not viewed in a moral æsthetic as merely pure, but ethically, lovingly, and practically viewed, as saving and sanctifying, as absolutely mastering the world's one moral crux, its unholy sin. Before such a God the modern autonomy of the individual is broken into moral concern. His self-sufficiency passes beyond the classical submission with its subdued despair. It passes beyond mediæval resignation with its chastened calm. And it passes beyond modern fortitude with its mild regret. It rises to be lost in God's will of grace as our peace, and to the personal obedience of faith with its godly joy. And by this obedience of faith, of course, is not meant the obedience that grows out of faith but, here as always, the obedience that is faith—faith being the greatest act a will can do, as its absolute self-assignment to the grace of the Holiest and His holy love. This Word is the authority of the world, the experienced, proud, sated, and distracted world.

In all this, of course, it is not meant that in every soul the form of faith should reproduce the history, say, of Luther or Augustine, with their tragic, and even violent, experience of the world collision of grace and guilt. That were to standardise faith too much for its good. All that is meant is that this, rather than merely being in love with Christ, should be recognised as giving the classic and normative idea of faith. It is the idea which should dominate the message of the Church; but which, being the message of a Church, and not the expression of individuals, should give shelter to many forms, or rather stages, whose present experience has not yet come to that maturity and fulness.

It is not easy to secure due attention to such a line of thought at the present moment, when the interest of Christian reality has given place so largely to that of Christian sympathy, and certainty is less a concern than beneficent activity (which may even be an anodyne for its loss, or a phase of unrest). A variety of reasons account for that difficulty. For one thing the most active and passionate assertions of the evangelical principle have unfortunately fallen into the hands of an order of mind and belief which represents a meagre and metallic orthodoxy too secluded from the best social and intellectual influences of the world; and Low Church in all the Churches is a Church in a corner. A century ago orthodoxy and its valuable philanthropies not only renounced the dictation of the Illumination, but its company. It broke with it. And in this country it was driven as Nonconformity from the offices and universities of the state to take its own seminarist way and sectarian creed, which its piety fixed deep in the mass of the people. And though, during the nineteenth century, great efforts were made, and fruitfully made, both here and abroad, to pick up the connexion, and regain for positive belief an ideal tone, they were too late to recover the rank and file of the Protestant public, or overtake the sterility of the popular theology, and escape its jungle of desiccated phrases. Orthodoxy lost the public note, and the ethical, in a sectarian pietism. On the other hand the Illumination suffered, in what might be called an antithetic, though com-

AUTHORITY, CERTAINTY, & SANCTITY 77

plementary, sympathy, as one eye does in the disease of the other. If Orthodoxy lost atmosphere, the Illumination lost footing. If the one lost idealism, the other lost reality—even in its pursuit of realism. It lost moral reality. If the one could not mount the sky, the other could not search the soul. If the one ceased to convince the mind, the other failed to convict the conscience. If the one was unable to charm and attract, the other was unable to repent and atone. If the one lost the eye for the old life's beauty, the other lost the power to produce the new life at all.

And to-day the rational and the æsthetic worlds have but an external idea of ethic; which hardly passes beyond conduct or character, individual and social, and which has no power to regenerate those ultimate sources of action where the great issues of character and conduct are determined. In an age like the present, when culture has become more varied and general than ever before, and when elaborate civilisation has combined with great wealth to set men free to follow easy ideals, interests, and hobbies at the cost of hard righteousness, the sources and guides of action are not the highest (though they are not the lowest). The greatest issues of the soul are rarely handled in our current Literature, which, with its sterile passion of moral mutiny, contains no spiritual guidance, and little or no spiritual insight. Meantime the range of action has grown with the growing world, and the results of a step which used to affect but a country or a continent now vibrate or crash across the globe. And yet the wider the action the higher the motive must be.

As action grows more wide and even universal, so much the higher must its sources and motives be, if it is to be guided to human safety and final gain. What we find, therefore, is that, in our civilisation, the height of our source and the weight of our control do not fit the breadth and variety of our energies. And that is where we may well feel concern. The widest and humanest ends, being moral and spiritual, cannot continue to be pursued upon rational and æsthetic principles alone. Action has become social, and culture is not social but individual or cliquish. True social action must have a moral inspiration, more even than a sympathetic. It is in the moral region that the real unity of society lies. The only true universal is the conscience. And control of a horizon so wide as we see must proceed from something less individual and less self-centred than either the atomic conscience or the culture of sets, something which reaches the heights and depths of the racial conscience, inspires its heroisms, and above all heals its helpless wound.

Since the break-up of the spiritual unity of Europe, at the close of the Middle Ages, the factors of that disruption have never yet found a true synthesis. These factors were two in chief. The first was Humanism in its two aspects, the early aesthetic in the Renaissance and the late scientific in the Illumination. And the second was the moral Evangelicalism of the Reformation. The ideal of the former was natural autonomy, of the second, spiritual obedience—only to the Gospel instead of the Church. Up to the present things have come no farther than to a choice between these two rather than their co-operation. And they run on lines so far apart that it is still possible for even scholars on either side to treat the other as if it did not exist. For instance the fascinating movement known as Modernism, which engages the very *élite* of the Roman Church, is drawn almost entirely to the rationalist, the illuminationist, the Socinian side of Protestantism, which in all matters of criticism and thought has influenced it very greatly. But it seems

AUTHORITY, CERTAINTY, & SANCTITY 79

not only uninfluenced by the great evangelical theologians or discussions, old or new, it seems quite ignorant of them—almost as ignorant of them as its enemy, Curialism, is of rationalism. And in so far as it knows them, it dislikes them. This is the more remarkable, as so much of the Modernist interest is ethical and human, while it is upon the profound ethic of Humanity in its conscience that the evangelical theology is so thorough, and the rationalist theology so thin. There is nowhere such searching acquaintance with the psychology of sin as in the great Reformers, or in that modern " Pascal of the North," Sören Kierkegaard. Some of the most able and genial writing of the Modernist School goes back with a clear somersault over the Reformation to the mediæval idea of mystic love, as if the evangelical idea of faith were but a negligible aberration, justification a juridical fiction, and the Protestant movement the black sheep of the Christian family which it was charity to wrap in silence.

It cannot be on the lines of any rationalist modernism that the great and necessary synthesis must take place. Nor can it be on the lines of a traditional orthodoxy, or a popular pietism. Both sides are starving for lack of the synthesis, and their ignorance of each other is part accident, part affectation, part crime. Here, as on all the great human questions, the solution must not only be a moral one, but more profoundly and searchingly moral than either the ethicisms or the orthodoxies that have failed. It must be the solution of the supreme moral problem, the relation of the conscience to the holy, especially in terms of the modern challenge. It is in that world, high over the rationalism of either orthodoxy or heresy, that the synthesis must probably be sought. And then everything depends on the terms in which the problem is posed. It is not the problem of individualist or of social ethics. It is no mere problem of the private conscience and its subjective peace, or the fraternal conscience and its mutual harmony. It is the question of the great solidary human conscience and its objective, its ultimate relation, its ground of confidence, its final authority, the question of man's judge and man's guilt. It is the world question at the last, for it is the question of the world's God. It is the evangelical question, the central question of the whole Church, as real for Rome as for us (though answered so very differently), the question of the soul's obedience to a holy grace, according as grace may be construed. It is the question of moral manhood in relation to God, of God in His moral nature as holy, of God not clothed with the imperial authority of an Almighty Creator, but with the gracious authority of a moral Redeemer. It is the question of a God more mighty by His love that blesses than by His power that creates, and more effectual by the grace which forgives than by the love that charms; more of our Lord by His new creation of us from our sin than by His first creation of us from the dust.

To keep central the moral problem of authority for society we must, with stern moral realism, keep central the problem of guilt, so dominant to the great seers—whether to the Aeschylean poet, or the Christian apostle, or the Reformer of faith, or the modern dramatist. And the question of the final authority then becomes the question of a Redeemer. It is the question between God in Christ as that Redeemer and Humanity as its own Redeemer. But it is a matter of redemption, either from grief or guilt, as the pessimist thinkers like Von Hartmann so clearly see. To ignore that is to move the previous question and leave the meeting. And, if we are to trust the true experts, the expert here is the soul that has

AUTHORITY, CERTAINTY, & SANCTITY

tasted of God's grace, passed by its means from death to life, and knows thereby the eternal and immutable morality in the facts of a historic and personal salvation. If such a soul is not the chief expert he is the great dupe. The social product of that salvation, the great Church, can have but one article central to theology, ethics, civics and all else. It is the absolute loving authority of Holy Grace in the perfect atonement it makes for guilty society in Jesus Christ and Him crucified.

The Church has now in many sections well learned, and in some overlearned, the lesson of love, in one kind at least; so that its note becomes that of muliebrity rather than virility. It wooes where it should rouse and rule. It soothes, and even coaxes, where it should judge and mould. A Mother Church hides a Sovereign Father. And its influence is minished on men and affairs. It becomes the butt of thin satirists in the name of a moral realism which gets no farther than honest human nature and its satisfaction with itself. They think it their call (though often it is no more than their bent) to scourge its hypocrisies on stage or page, and strip its falsities away to get down to honest manhood. They will stand no moral nonsense, and in the name of sincerity they will recall us to the religion of the child of nature and naïveté, where a man sets forth his beloved Soul in which he is well pleased. But what is any such moral realism compared with the seeking, piercing, unsparing judgment, the confounding, dissolving, redeeming judgment of a holy God in the Gospel of *His* love, with its power (and certainly its right) to shatter the self-righteousness of the very satirist into a speechless penitence for himself and his kind! And this is the note that the Church most needs to strike at this hour of moral mock-heroics, poseur prophets, and critics who spare nothing but their own souls.

IV

THE SOURCE OF CERTAINTY

THERE is one danger which we incur in carrying out the modern transfer of faith's foundation from dogmatic inspiration to current experience. We run the risk of putting theology at the mercy of psychology. And this is no imaginary peril. In many quarters it has become an actual surrender. And the result has been not only to put belief at the mercy of the laws of thought but to develop an alarming subjectivity, and even debasement, in religion, its preoccupation with inner processes, problems, and sympathies, and its loss of contact with the reality behind these, or the authority over them. For psychology, like all science, can but co-ordinate experience or process; it is but descriptive; we must turn elsewhere, to a theory of knowledge, to a metaphysic, or to a faith of the will and conscience, for our grasp of reality, or its grasp of us.

It is unfortunate enough when in such a transfer the content of faith is handed over to the experience of the individual, and the tradition of experienced ages in the history of a church becomes of no account before the subjectivity of the spiritual amateur and his impressions. This is a special risk where the skilful preacher takes the idolised place in democracy which the theologian had in the seventeenth century, and his mixed crowds, royalist or rebel, claim to possess the arbitrament of belief. But even if we escape from the individual, even when we go beyond the experience of

THE SOURCE OF CERTAINTY 83

the hierophant, the crowd, and the age, even when we extend the area of the experience to the whole history of the devout Church, we do not evade the danger of a religion which is merely or mainly subjective in its tests and tone. Not that we need ignore the claim, which religious psychology now sets up, to be the final forum of Christian truth, and to move the venue to that court *ex foro Dei*. No harm but good is done if we mean by the claim only that the *court* is changed, or the language changed from external dicta to experience. The change of a court, or the change of the language used in a court, matters less. What does matter is the change of the judge, of the law, and of the authority they represent. What matters is the change from external authority to none. For the autonomy and finality of mere experience is an end to all authority. A real authority, we have seen, is indeed *within* experience, but it is not the authority *of* experience, it is an authority *for* experience, it is an authority experienced. All certainty is necessarily subjective so far as concerns the area where it emerges and the terms in which it comes home. The court is subjective, but the bench is not. Reality must, of course, be real for me. It must speak the language of my consciousness. But it makes much difference whether it have its *source* in my consciousness as well as its *sphere*—whether for instance the authority of reality is merely the total volume and weight of monistic substance (prolonged into an atom in me, and urging me so), or whether it be the moral action on me of another will. We may apprehend the movements of the reality only in the guise of subjective experience, and we may perceive that its immediate form is always that of psychological act or process, and not of voices in the air. But it is another thing to say that there is no more reality behind than that which is subliminal to the process, that the momentum is only the weight of the submerged part of the process, the unexplained residuum, *ejusdem generis et molis*, of the conscious experience, something which the progress of psychology may hope in due time by its own methods to explore and explain. Were psychology much farther advanced than it is for long likely to be, we should yet not have reached by it the objective reality which is the first condition of true religion. And we should not have acquired a standard whereby to test reality. For, I repeat, psychology after all is but a science; and science cannot go beyond method. It has no machinery with which to reach or test reality, and therefore it has no jurisdiction in the ultimates of religion. When it is a question of the reality of an object and its value, we are treating it in another dimension from that of science; for science but co-ordinates our impressions, and cannot gauge their ultimate weight or worth. The Judge of all the earth is not an object of knowledge, but of obedience and worship. He is to be met neither with an intuition nor an assent, but with a decision, a resolve. (Chap. VIII.)

Still the problem is not solved by the hasty heroics which warn criticism off the grounds, whether it be psychological criticism or historic. We are long past the day when faith could secure its own by erecting notices to trespassers and threatening penalties. The only warning in place is one against tramps or trippers—if we may use such metaphors for those discursive minds who, without competent knowledge, demand precedence for vagrant intuitions or smatterings on matters of so much venerable delicacy and moral difficulty. The real problem is one of adjustment. It is to adjust the belief in an objective, and especially an historical, authority with the rights of sound criticism, the results of

THE SOURCE OF CERTAINTY 85

tradition, and the facts of the spiritual man. We have to recognise that criticism has destroyed the ideas current in the Reformation age about the Bible and the creeds ; it has destroyed the unpsychological views of that period as to their external authority. We have further to recognise that a later Protestantism was often too much concerned with the delineation of the religious objective in a school theology, and too little with its action in the spiritual psychology of a living faith. Whatever the new view of authority may be, it must allow duly for critical and psychological principles, and give them their place without owning their sway. And our task is to preserve the reality of a religious authority while we change its locale, or its speech, or its procedure. We are crossing a heavy stream and we must not change our horse—though we may not land at the same spot where the old ford did. Authority remains as the ruler of religion in the stream of time. But religion is passing from the old bank of the Bible's verbal inspiration to the new bank of a historic experience. It is readjusting the old Protestant ideas of the relation of Scripture and tradition. It is passing from an *ipse dixit* of the Bible or the schools to the Church's long and classic experience of the distinctive source of our salvation—the experience of the new Creator in a saved and enlightened conscience. All the reformed confessions, however various and however antiquated on many points, are at one upon that. That is their Christianity. And, when that is surrendered, the holy Church is simply merged in the excellent world. It is made to be but the admirable world on its religious side.

Now, this is Erastianism in heavenly places. (Chap. XIV.) It is the subtlest Erastianism of all, and one that easily besets the freest churches, and it may tie them with bonds more stifling than those of the State which they seek to break. Christianity is what it is in the spiritual region by its *peculium* and not by its *continuum*, by confronting other creeds and not prolonging them, by the distinctive thing in it and not by what it shares supremely with other beliefs. It is not under the control of natural religion, of general spiritual truths enacted in some parliament of religions. Such rationalism is the worst Erastianism. Christianity is not the dominant partner in the world's religion, the *doyen* of equal faiths. And the distinctive, classic, permanent thing in its experience is not God's guidance but His unique, final, and continuous act of new creation on the moral soul of the race, in a historic redemption by Christ; which is not mere emancipation, and not mere enlargement, nor refinement; nor is it in Christ a compressed evolution; but it is such a forgiveness and regeneration into communion with Himself as revolutionises to the very bottom the moral world. In this new life and grace its believers, however few, are so searched and so sure that it does not need artificial protection against criticism. It is really impervious to it. Criticism, whose tide submerges orthodox Canute and his prohibitions from the sand, breaks in vain upon this rock certainty, or only detaches loose fragments that were ready to fall. It breaks in vain upon it, just as all the strictures or changes of marriage cannot quench love or arrest the race. This experience, this certainty, belongs to the prime massive realities of permanent Humanity and eternal life. It is all over with Christianity when forgiveness falls to the rear of the natural or pious affections. And it is recognised by careful and reasonable criticism that this is so. Such criticism only proposes to detach with its valuable acid the human alloy, and clarify to us what is the pure and direct action of God. It thus leaves us face to face with an authority which is *the only final authority known to religion, namely, the authority which is*, not an echo nor a vicar, but *a part of God's own*. In history

THE SOURCE OF CERTAINTY

it leaves clearer than ever for the Church the Godhead of the Saviour by its detachment from an obsolete metaphysic. And in experience it disengages, for our deepened certainty, the invasion of us by that Saviour, His emergence upon us, and His mighty *creative* hand upon us as Saviour. It may dissolve much of the historic elements without destroying the sacramental effect. All the criticism of the Church's career, whether it be historical or moral criticism, cannot cut the red thread of its evangelical continuity in experience and message. More and more we learn to wonder at what surgery can remove to save life and to enhance it.

And when we have secured the autonomy of this saved certainty under the living and preached tradition of the Church, a reasonable and sympathetic criticism will also regard its innate and specific quality. It will give it its own. Like all true science it will respect the nature of the particular fact, and the modes of treatment appropriate to it. It will treat the fact by the fact's own laws, and not by those of the world in general; just as it will connect, but not explain, consciousness with the laws of inorganic nature. The history of redemption is a history within history, superhistoric, distinct but not detached—as surely so as psychic history has its own process within physical history and as moral freedom exists within psychic law. It has other laws and ideals than general history. It is indeed articulated into the history of society by an immense complex of fibres and commissures. The points of attachment are almost incessant. And it is far from insensible to the currents of influence which act upon it from the world of affairs. But it has never been quite lost in the world, it has never wholly succumbed to the secular infection. It has always circulated with more or less vigour through all its veins, nerves, and fibres, its own autonomous life.

The Reformation was much more than a reform, it was the re-establishment of Christianity. It never claimed nor proposed to destroy the Church; it continued the true Church by a resurrection; it prolonged it on a new foundation which was the re-discovery of the old, a new commandment which was from the beginning. It set it on a new subjective foundation at least; for the objective foundation was Christ and His salvation, after as before. The Reformers, rather than contemplate such a destruction of the Church and the Church idea as some of their Christian posterity have reached, would a thousand times rather have remained where they were. It was for the sake of the Church that they moved as they did; it was as a Church they moved; only they knew that the existence and work of the Church demanded a new temple on the old rock.

They started, as we must start, with the idea of a new moral creation as the base of the personal Christian life. We, too, if we are to bring psychology to the closest contact with theology, must see that it is the moral psychology of sin, faith, and regeneration. But did the old Church not start from such a creative point, in the notion of baptismal regeneration? That is truly so. Both started, as the Church always must do, if it remain a Church, from a real regeneration. They differed when they came to define the nature of its reality. For the Reformers it had to be in the region of personal experience and not of subliminal magic. It was theological, and not theurgic. The evangelical regeneration was an experienced regeneration and not an institutional effect. It was inseparable from some form of real conversion. It was upon a felt certainty that the soul stood, and not merely on a lodged security. The saving certainty was in the region of experience, of radical moral realism. That was the fertile psychological element in the new departure.

THE SOURCE OF CERTAINTY 89

Yet it was not a mere certainty of experience sure of itself, but of faith sure of its Saviour. It was not a mere mode of consciousness. What faith was certain of, what it trusted, was not the experience, but something rising in the experience. The religion was neither pietist, nor romantic, but evangelical. It was a faith, and not a mere subjectivity. It did not simply occupy and even fill men's interest; it committed them for life. The soul was not simply impressed; it was assigned. Its constant word was "Into Thy hands I commend my spirit; Thou hast redeemed me, O Lord God of Grace." Mere experience, mere consciousness is too mobile. It comes and goes too much for eternal purposes. It is too temperamental, too æsthetic, and too little ethical. A saving certainty must be within the experience of our moral world, in that region where we find ourselves confronted with an object that we can neither deny nor face. It is there that the conscience, which is the most real thing in us, finds its congenial objective to be the most real thing in existence. Where we find the Judge of all the Earth, we find the reality of all the world; while in His salvation we have all aspiration, all idealism, consummate. And the life we find in His absolution is the real eternal life. It is not so much peace we crave, not comfort. That may be but an experience. What we crave is strength, power, confidence, a stand-by (Παράκλητος) — One Who is our peace. To grasp that is faith; and by that we live, and not by our experience as such. We live not by experience, but by something experienced, not by knowing but by being known. (Chap. IX.) It is not on the experience we lay our soul but on its content, on the God in that car. But we do place the accent on the subjectivity if we think of faith only as one variety of human experience instead of the whole man self-bestowed in a certain way, self-assigned to a God Self-given. It is a subjectivity if we think of it but as a sense of spiritual *bien être*, of release and expansion of soul ; even if we think of it as a deep sense of the power and desirability of goodness ; yes, even if we think of it but as the sense of having and enjoying God, if we regard it as a sensibility, more or less constitutional perhaps, to the moving, genial, and expansive aspect of God, coming to us through Christ. A strong faith is engrossed with the reality of God's crucial and creative action, whether on history or on us, more than with our sense of it, or our perception of the way it takes.

Certainty, I have said, must always be subjective in one sense—in the sense that it is for the subject that it is certain. But we must go farther than " I am certain." That gets us nothing forward. My neighbour, who is wrong, is as certain as I who am right. The anarchy of the hour arises from the multitude of units who are all equally certain of various values. For any fruitful purpose we must go beyond " I am certain " ; we must reach, " It is certain." My certainty, the certainty *of* me, turns into a certainty *for* me. My sureness contains something which should insure yours. Otherwise we cannot pass beyond the region of mere mystic impression and unstable opinion. That is the morass and abyss of all certainty merely subjective. It sinks to mere mood or opinion. And we land among a mass of squabbling amateurs, each shouting that he has as good a right to his opinion as the next man. Which is really not challenged, as his opinion may be wanted by none. What such people miss in their egoistic heat and hurry of private judgment is this, that certainty means certainty *of something*, which we do not arrive at but which arrives at us. If I am certain, it does not really mean that I am certain of being certain. In religion, at least, I

THE SOURCE OF CERTAINTY 91

am certain of something beyond my certainty and creating it. And it is this something that is the chief concern of all who have outgrown the stage where liberty is brandished more than harnessed, and claimed more than used. Of what am I certain? How far does it unify me (" Unite my heart to fear Thy name ")? And how far does it agree with that of which my neighbours are certain?

The more we fix our attention on the object of our certitude, the more we humbly realise that it is a something *given*. Its source is not in us. It is of grace. The men of discovery, of inspiration, tell the same tale. Truth finds them, not they it. All that is in us is a welcome, a response, a correspondence to it— not indeed a passivity but a receptivity. And, when that has been realised, the only farther step to be taken for the purposes of religion is this, ' Does it give itself? Is the revelation a self-revelation? Does the supreme Object of all human knowledge *give Himself* to be known? Does the Core of all experience give Himself to be felt? ' That is the dispensation of the Eternal Son. And then with one step more we ask, ' Does He so give Himself to our knowledge or experience that our certainty of Him becomes a part or a function of His own certainty about Himself? ' That is the certainty and the mission of the Holy Ghost.

But a question recurs which I have dealt with in one way already. (Chap. I.) How do we jump off mere individual certainty? How can we venture to claim for any certainty of ours universal validity? Is it impertinence to be missionary? What distinguishes the true missionary from the crank, the meddler, and the bore?

I said that all experience in us is a congenial response to a something given to the soul from *without it*. But does that not tie us up in a subjectivity which ends in individualism? Does it not mean that we can never step out of our circle of self with the gift, step out of our private faith to preach a certainty given for all? Does it not mean that God deals with each soul by private bargain, and on special terms? Not so. We feel more or less clearly that what is true for one in this region ought to be, in proportion to its truth, true for all. It need be neither absurd nor overweening to claim for our individual experience universal validity. The fact that there is a datum in our experience delivers us from the charge of egotism in pressing it We may mistake a fancy for a datum, but we press it in the belief that it is a datum and not a fancy. It is that subconscious belief that is our justification in urging our view. It means the conviction that not we only but everyone else acted on in the same way by the same fact ought to come to the same recognition of it. If I am quite sure of anything positive, my certainty carries latent in it the conviction that everyone with exactly the same relation to the real fact must come to think of it in the same way. It does not matter a farthing whether they agree with us or not as yet. There might be a very general denial of our mode of certainty of it. But we are bound to believe, by the very nature of certainty, that every intelligence which is in our contact with the same fact must share our certainty. If we came to think that with exactly the same relation to the same fact there could be a variety of opinions about it, then all certainty would collapse. That is to say, wherever we have certainty, we have the implicit conviction of its universality if it had its rights and conditions. The more sure we are of any truth, the more universal we feel it must be. So little is certainty, because it is subjective, also individual. It is subjective in its manner, but it is universal in its note, range, and destiny, if it had its due. So that

THE SOURCE OF CERTAINTY 93

real certainty is by its nature universal and missionary. It preaches, striving to bring the hearers into its own relation to the fact. It claims the world. What is surest for me belongs with equal certainty not to me only but to all men. It is not my certitude I offer them; it is my reality, my God. And the converse lesson is that to increase missionary effect the objective certainty must be increased more than the subjective ardour; which in the long run only objective certainty can sustain. Missions live on evangelical faith, and droop under sentimental, pietist, or humanist religion like that of to-day.

There is a valuable distinction which should be observed in connection with the psychological treatment of faith and its certainty. The process of conviction (the *ordo salutis*) does not follow the order of reality. The foundation of belief is a different thing from the reason why we became believers, and it is realised much later through our faith. The ground of salvation is not always the same as the motive that decided us. Nor was the first movement the deepest through which our personal history has passed. The future belongs to the Christianity of the mature, not of the young. The true foundation is revealed in the veteran certainty of those who *have already become* Christians before realising it; it is not discerned by the natural man and then used as his reason for becoming Christian. He became a Christian by a miracle. So far Baptismal Regeneration is right. It was not by an inference, by a conclusion, by a verdict. It was not a verdict but a decision, an obedience. It is not an inevitable inference seized in an hour of vision from universal truths already admitted. Apologetic on such a base is valuable, but it does not make Christians. The real foundation lies in another dimension, to which our Christian faith gradually opens our eyes and tunes our sense. It is discerned by the regenerate man, after more or less experience, as the real ground which was acting but partially to his growing consciousness, among all the sacramental influences and pychological stages which made the deepening process of his knowledge of it. We are changed not by the logic of facts but by their sacramental power, not on a base of historic evidence but by response to a historic act. The conscious motive is not the efficient cause, though the cause is working in it. Why I now believe is a different question from how I came to believe. Probably I could not have believed then on the grounds on which I must believe now. We shed much and alter much ere we arrive. And we acquire with labour and sorrow that which yet was with us at the first, without which indeed we could not begin. The threshold by which we enter is not the ground on which we rest. It is true that Christ is both door and ground. For the very first Christians it was so. He was way, truth, and life. But this came home by degrees. It was by Christ the prophet, passing upward to Christ the Messiah, that the Apostles arrived at the heavenly Christ, as the active personality and the eternal ground, through all stages, both of their faith and their salvation. Through Him it was that they had come to live in Him. He made Himself their resurrection and their life. It was under His own guidance as teacher, both on earth and from heaven, that they came to believe the heavenliest things about Him as Saviour. It was Jesus the prophet that extorted their belief in Jesus the Messiah ; and it was the fate of Jesus the Messiah that drove them to believe in Jesus, the eternal and atoning Son, whose Sonship underlay all His Messiahship. He who first taught them to pray a prayer which had no allusion to Him, and yet was uniquely bound up with Him, went on, as He put forth all that was in Him, to teach them also to

THE SOURCE OF CERTAINTY 95

pass deep within and pray to Him. Those who began with Him were led on to found and end in Him, the Alpha and Omega, the same yesterday, to-day, and for ever. It was revealed to them that the author of their faith was also its finisher, and the Son of Man one with the Eternal Son of God.

We come to see that Christ is for us both door and ground. We learn to identify the Way, the Truth, and the Life. And we have to be patient with those to-day who are but in the early stage of that process—so long as they do not claim to be the higher stage, and insist that the whole Church, in so far as it has passed beyond them, is the victim of speculative, not to say morbid, delusions, which it is the mission of their crude religion to destroy. With a temperamental religiosity, a youthful experience, and a mind theologically virgin it is not hard to present a case for a simple religion resting on a piety purely " religio-ethical and humanitarian," a mere practical mysticism. It is not hard to appeal to those " ethical ideas that are the essential element in the spiritual experience of the modern world." It is plausible to point to the teaching of Jesus, and that personal impression of His being a supreme prophet which He made on the first disciples, and to deplore the insertion by Paul of the leaven of the Pharisee and to the Gnostic poison, and his seduction even of John. It seems to save much spiritual trouble to rest there in port, and shun the seas of thought and experience on which the Church immediately embarked, to its alleged confusion and misfortune. Let us stay, they say, by Mark's Gospel, or its rudiments, and James's Epistle, and we may write off Paul as a spiritual splendour, but also as a speculative excrescence and a blind alley for the true purpose of Christ.

It seems very reasonable to remind us (as Johannes Weiss does) that the first Church contained all three tendencies and forms of Christianity with an equal right. It comprehended the reverence for Jesus the prophet, the allegiance to Jesus the Messiah, and the worship of Jesus Christ, the eternal and only Son of God. It held the Jesus of the public, the Jesus of the Twelve, the Christ of Paul and John ; though this last (it is said) rose out of an extreme and elaborate preoccupation with the Cross, which seemed so fatal to a Messiah, and necessitated stories of resurrection and theories of atonement to explain it away. Or it seems the enlightened view, proper to the modern and careful regard for history, to see in the first Church two distinct types—those who followed Christ and those who worshipped Christ, those who lived like Him, and those who lived in Him. And people who to-day belong to the imitation school remind themselves that they are so near the sound realism of simple truth that they may with ease be compassionate and tolerant of the more extravagant type who worship Christ as God—unless that type claim monoply. Both sides are reminded by the genial Christian with the bland ethical spirituality that, as they lived together in the New Testament, they should live and teach together in the same Church, with equal right, mutual respect, and common charity, in the twentieth century.

To pleas of that kind we must oppose the principle with which this section set out. The foundation, the reality, of a belief is different from the motives or stages that introduced us to it. The message, teaching, and foundation of the Church is not to be reduced to the measure of its catechumens The faith of the Church is the faith of its mature, as at the first it was the faith of its Apostles. Our authority is not the Church of the first century, but the Apostles who were its authority. The Church does not rest on its inchoate stages (which would poise it on its apex) but on

THE SOURCE OF CERTAINTY 97

its eternal foundation—a Christ Who, in His apostolic Self-revelation, is the same deep Redeemer always. Individuals may linger long in the early stages of the Church's attainment. But while members are to be sympathetically handled who are but moving to the centre, what is chiefly required of a ministry is the preaching of the foundation from the centre. The rights of the Church flow from its foundation not from its inception, from its Gospel not from its infancy, from its Word and not from its history; or, if from any history, surely from the substance of the apostolic inspiration, and not from the embryonic conditions of the society, or the stage of its clarifying ferment. Those who argue the equal right and place in the Church to-day of views where Christ is but a prophet and views where He is God the Redeemer, strangely forget what they are at other times too forward to urge—the evolutionary nature of faith within the New Testament period. They forget that Christ the prophet gathered about Him only disciples and not a Church; that, when it is a question of a Church, its foundation was the risen heavenly, incarnate, redeeming Christ in His Pentecostal Spirit; that the evolution from the prophet to the Christ was the process of the New Testament Revelation and not a perversion of it (unless the New Testament is a record of spiritual decay). And it was over (in the Apostles at least) before the Church was founded. What founded the Church was not the life and teaching of Christ, but the preaching of the theology of His death and resurrection. It is one thing to be patient with a faith which is *in statu pupillari*, and is growing to larger things; and it is another to tolerate such a state in the ministry of an apostolic Church when it offers itself as the true and final faith, with but little patience and some insult for the Church's Creed. It is one thing for an inchoate community like the

G

first Church to contain a variety of crude notions slowly settling down to the mature self-consciousness which gives it a distinct existence, footing, and message ; and it is another thing to recognise the same right in such crudities and their publication when faith has come to itself and seized the crowning and final revelation that was once arriving through them. In the light of finality all the right of the crude stage is relative to its early time or minor place.

The process, the stages, the conscious motives in reaching a belief, therefore, are one thing, and the *real* foundation of the belief is another ; and it is not always formally obtruded at the beginning. It may arrive at a later time, corresponding to the age when we reach our majority, or become adults And, when it has been reached, the Church cannot consent to do all the work over again for each age, repudiate the attained finality, start afresh as if it had not so much as heard of the Holy Spirit, and give equal rank in its teaching to the apostolic heralds and the tentative seekers. The whole course of the first period was to bring to light the true foundation out of the actual motives and stages, to secure the theology implicit in the inspired psychology of faith, to clarify inspiration into revelation, to complete the Word as the meaning of the fact. We now have, and long have had, that finality in substance. The kingdom is in substance come. To return to conceive of Christianity but as the finest Judaism is reactionary. It is to belittle and ignore history. It is to turn one's back on the decisive things that have arrived—on the Cross, the Resurrection, the coming of the Holy Ghost, and the Holy Catholic Church. It is to identify or to equalise the foundations of belief with the motives that acted consciously on young believers.

Our Lord said propædeutically to the ingenuous scribe that the greatest commandment was to love

THE SOURCE OF CERTAINTY 99

God above all, and our neighbour as ourselves. And truly, if Christian faith were a matter of commandment or precept, and Christ were but its promulgator, there we might have an end. But with Christ standing there, and all that we now know to have been in Him, we are much beyond that. When the scribe agreed, he was only told that he was not far from the kingdom. *He was not in it,* as those in Christ are. Nor was the Baptist. It is only when we set about repenting or loving with all our heart, soul, strength and mind that we discover our impotence to do either, and therefore realise the prime necessity of what most sharply differentiates the best Theism from evangelical faith. We can neither repent nor love with our might till we have come to terms with that holiness in God which assumed in the Cross its own complete satisfaction and power. The fine Theism of the precept was not the constituent principle of the Kingdom, nor was it the foundation of belief, though it was a great stage on the way to it. This scribe was in the morning twilight with his face to the light, and he was so handled; but if *we* stopped at this stage we should be in the evening twilight. We should be parting with the light. We should be turning our back both on the decisive thing Christ did at His life's end and consummation, and on His final interpretation of it given to apostles within the period of New Testament evolution. How fruitless are these efforts at repristination masked as simplicity! How reactionary repristination always is! How laboured the simplicity, and how ineffectual! And how such efforts persist under dogmatic (or rather anti-dogmatic) prejudices, even among capable historians. As the historian is seldom a revolutionary, he is apt to miss the experience of the evangelical revolution. It is not possible to give to a section of the Christians of the first years after Christ's death, to the Church as distinct from the apostles, an equal right for the present time with those of the thirteenth century, or with the Reformers. That were mere traditionalism. If we are to go back to the simplest thing, Judaism is much simpler than Christianity. It is not possible to cut out of the organic history of New Testament revelation those crowning stages of it in the apostolic interpretation that give their just place and meaning to all below. We cannot as a Church reproduce to-day, and offer to the world, the inchoate Christianity of the Judaist disciples. They had a historic right where they were as catechumens, as disciples; but they became apostles; and it does not follow that their rudimentary stages have the same right on this side of the Pentecostal watershed of revelation as on that. Those who teach at that level only have not the same right within a Church in being that they had in a Church in the making. They refuse light which did not then shine. The adolescent intelligence has in no community the rights of the mature. Any rights it has are rights to tutelage and education. It has rights in a Church which must feed its lambs. Only not the right to be recognised among the lambs' teachers, or the Church's guides.

V

BELIEF AS A WILL TO RECEIVE AND OBEY

How should we deal with the psychological plea that the morphology of knowledge, the laws of thought, the limits of the mind, forbid to us the revealing authority of a divine personality, or any credit to His miraculous action?

Here (leaving for a moment the point of difference between our thought reaching God, and God's will reaching us) it should first be observed that the vital question and practical is not, What *can* we know? but, What *do* we know? If our real knowledge of God, of Christ, of salvation be challenged on the ground that a true theory of knowledge makes such knowledge impossible, this may be no more than a philosophic pedantry. Neither philosophy nor psychology is there in order to determine what we *may* know, but to find and set out the conditions of what we *do* know. We know first, and then investigate the conditions of knowing. *Solvitur ambulando.* We cannot wait for knowledge till we have a satisfactory epistemology to license it. Are we to exercise no function till we are sure of the science of it? How can we reach the theory of a function until we have had it at work? How shall we ever reach the theory if we suspend the real function, or treat it as a mere gymnastic? Is research in physics to cease till we settle a theory of sense-perception, and discover exactly how the behaviour of matter stirs our forms of consciousness in dealing with it? Is our science not pursued so fruitfully on the basis of what is as yet a mystery no less than a reality ? So, also, because it is a great mystery how soul can act on soul, and A's unseen personality behind his body affect or capture B's, are we to challenge the action upon us of an unseen present or an unseen past, and even its mastery of us ? The sense of God, the communion with Him, the union with Christ cannot be made to wait on a psychology of religion. Have we no practical business with the Infinite because thinkers may tell us that the nature of our faculties forbids knowledge of it ? No theory of knowledge can destroy the fact of knowledge, no conception of our mental impotence condemn us to agnosticism. Surely the experienced reality of revelation is the material on which a philosophy of revelation or of religion must begin to work.

Moreover, God is an object of certainty quite different from those we deal with in any theory of our knowledge of things. The ordinary theory of knowledge discusses our relation to an object we approach ; but, when it is a question of religion, or indeed of any personal relation, our knowledge relates not to an object but to a subject who takes the initiative, not to what we reach but to what reaches us, not to something we know but to some one who knows us. (Chapter IX.) It is knowledge not of a known thing but of the knowing God. It is not a case of our limited mind reaching God, but of an infinite God reaching us soul to soul.

Our theory of knowledge must be adjusted accordingly. We must avoid the fallacy of taking the conditions of one order or one stage of knowledge, say the psychology of scientific knowledge, and making them universal and normative for all the rest, say the moral knowledge of a living person. A science of the mind's deportment will not yield the secret of the will's act. The knowledge of a person who knows us back and acts on us is very different

A WILL TO RECEIVE AND OBEY 103

from that of a mere object of our knowledge. And the difference is still greater when it is a case of His knowledge of us being the source of all our knowledge of Him ; of our finding Him being but our reaction to His finding us. Revelation has other laws than discovery though it does not ignore them ; it may break in as the spark when all the tinder of heuristic method is laid, and we are eagerly looking in another direction. The autonomous knowledge of grace is not to be limited by the canons of nature, nor by the process of an idea.

It is sometimes said that theology is a deductive science, as the explication of an idea ; but this a statement which will hardly hold for theology of the more modern kind, which rests on experienced religion, and strives to be religious always in the way of realising a fact, and not explicating a dialectic. If it were based on a great and pregnant idea, it might be so described—as a warm dialectic. A philosophy drawn out in a genetic way from a first principle which was the germ of a whole system might be called deductive ; and a theology might likewise be so described, in proportion as it shared the nature of a philosophy. And its chapters would then have to be bound together by a logical sequence which aimed at an order and beauty of its own, and came at the end to a rest it did not possess at the beginning.

But that is theosophy ; it is not the true nature of theology. Our theological capital is not ideas we arrive at but experience we go through ; it does not rest in conclusions but in perceptions of a spiritual kind, perceptions of a spiritual fact, pervading and emerging from the experience of life and history. The theologian is not a syllogist but an experient, an observer. He gives an account of faith, and especially of his own, as a creation by a historic fact and not the dialectic of a fertile idea. In him the intelligence of faith reports itself in an orderly way. His new life states itself with more or less fulness as it realises more and more of the effect of the creating fact, and as the fact acting on his person is a person. He has to do with movements and processes of the soul which exist alongside each other, and complement and qualify each other, and do not arise in a logical sequence. The order of treatment is not a process of proof so much as a piece of orderly testimony. It is less dialectic than didactic. If one part is discussed before another, it does not mean that the one produces the other. It is less deductive than descriptive. The order is not a law of logic but the suggestion of a travelled experience as to contiguous provinces. It rests on an anthropology of the supernatural man. There is no suggestion that faith in Christ grows by any ideal concinnity out of the premises provided in the natural man.

We should also meet the psychological difficulty I stated by asking what is meant by the laws of thought which limit will and its contacts. Do they mean anything else than the normal formation, or the habit of behaviour, in a thinking personality, where the thought is the servant or organ of the spontaneity, initiative, and freedom, bound up in the very idea of personality? Yet are we not continually tempted to treat these laws by way of abstraction, to hypostatise them, to invest them with a detached existence, an *a priori* value, even a despotic autonomy, and then to force them on the personality as if it were another existence to which they were led up? But, if they are what has been described—the thinking personality's organic and normal mode of action, then it is surely impossible to say that this habit of action forbids either our access to the personality within us,

A WILL TO RECEIVE AND OBEY 105

or its own departure from habit on due occasion. If it so forbade, the constitution or "nature" of the personality would submerge its freedom in mere process, and therefore destroy the personality. No abstraction can prescribe or dominate life. No process exhausts personality. We may not say how a divine person should act, we can only observe how He does. It is history that rules thought, not thought history.

The laws of thought are no more than the observed biology of our personal spontaneity, or the physiology of our productivity, and the life of it is beyond them. They are the texture of our personal activity, the normal type of its working, but they are not the dynamic. And, as I say, they are not a mere mental form which is applied *ab extra* to personality, as if that were some other quantity, with a collateral and inferior existence, up to which they were brought. Such forms would be quite empty. They would be mere abstractions. There never did exist a thought separable from the subject thinker, the object thought, and the experience that unites them. There is no form of thought in consciousness which did not arise from the activity of living men in the world. And the passion for truth is at bottom a passion for no abstract system, no symmetrical figure, and no closed scheme, but for an intellectual unity reflecting the indissoluble unity of the student's moral and active person, serving it, and doing it justice. The laws of thought, therefore, pursue a unity which is not theirs but the thinker's, which is not so much a seamless robe brought from the mind's wardrobe and put on the restless soul, but rather is the skin, the mould, the fashion of the soul's own unity, the unity of a moral person, a unity capable of a fresh spontaneity and new departures without inner schism, especially in the region of action.

A theology, therefore, which is organised on a

system of thought closed and self-contained can never be a due expression of that action, that revelation of a personal God, which creates religion ; and certainly it cannot be its measure. A theology is scientific not according as it is syllogistic, as it is in logical continuity with a philosophic preamble, nor even according as it harmonises with a " preconformation " of man to Christ ; nor, as it satisfies human need (which is only truly felt through revelation) ; but according as it does justice to its creative fact, and serves as the expression, or exposition, of that revelation. The ground of real knowledge is perception, it is experience, it is our reaction to fact, it is not ideas ; and it is experience not of our need but of something that rouses it, and then does more than fill it. Theology therefore does not appeal to a prior and surer philosophy ; but a philosophy comes later, and it must take due account of the facts, and especially of the revelationary and experienced fact which theology expounds. The concrete precedes the abstract ; history, philosophy ; life, thought ; religion, theology. Our Ego is not the final measure of the world ; it receives its content from nature, and history, and especially from revelationary history, which has done most to enhance and consecrate personality. How perverse it is for the philosopher to accuse the theologian of abstraction or of playing with abstractions, when he reports the effect and the significance of his creative facts.

A familiar form in which the dictation of the laws of thought is applied to quench the possibility of knowledge may be found in *the distinction*, so common since Lessing, and so attractive to the rationalist level, *between necessary truths of the reason and accidental truths of history*. (Chapter VI.) It is a distinction made in order to found the contention that the latter

A WILL TO RECEIVE AND OBEY

can never guarantee the former; they are not *in pari materia*. The fallacy which underlies the contention is the fallacy of abstraction. There is really no such thing as a truth of reason abstracted and detached from a truth of history, prior to it and independent of it. All our truth has come to us from history. The mind has its content from history. We do not know the one by one means and the other by another. There are not two parallel movements, one of which puts the ideas into our minds, while the other gives us concrete facts for the ideas to organise—as if the one provided us with the faculty of pure reason, the other with the faculty of experience, and the problem of any theory of knowledge were to describe the relation of the two, of form to matter, and thought to impression. That is a conception now too Hellenic and antiquated.

The fact is, as I say, we have no forms of knowledge which are not produced by particular contacts and experiences in ourselves or the race. In the great act we call life we have various forms of experience, but they are all of a kind in this—that they are all on the one hand conditioned by laws we do not create; and, on the other hand, so far as they are productive, they all produce notions which are not empty but charged with the prior history. We may speak disparagingly of accidental truths of history, but they are all we have. They make our whole mental property. Our ideas come in that shape, by that route. They pass through these forms of nature and history, and they subsist in them. There is no such thing as faith or knowledge apart from the believing or knowing men (as there are no decrees of God with an existence detached from a God willing them). Every idea grows out of some perception which we handle, which reaches us as a *donum* through man or nature, which we appropriate and integrate into our

Ego, and transmit. There is no such thing as thought apart from thinkers, or ideas apart from souls. The idea is a result of our thinking, not its origin; it is a product of our thinking power in fertile contact with facts; it is not something that makes it work, or maintains work's energy. Of course the categories are valuable. We need not distrust them, and relapse on mere Empiricism. Only let us not turn reception and production, the fact and the thought, against each other. Reception is the basis of production, and it demands it. We *must* frame ideas out of impressions, and by a real art of thought, not a casual artifice. We must produce them, and in no fantastic or groundless way. Only we have nothing, no knowledge, no foregone truth, alongside experience and before it, to which we must submit it. Our ideas do not found, they are founded. They are the blossom, not the seed. And, when we speak of unity or causality, for instance, we mean not a ready-made category into which facts must be squeezed, but something that is quickened in us by contact with facts, something we exercise in every act of life where we grasp or realise our personality at all.

This personality, it has been said, the idealists constantly tend to bully and tyrannise. If you do not have their ideas for ultimates, you have no science. But we must experience the facts for ourselves; and so, by real contact, by experience of life and contact with history, we find our own foundation, and escape their dogmatism.[1] For the objectionable dogmatism is not an immense and imperative certainty; every great faith must have such certainty; it belongs to the fact which creates the faith. It is the dogmatism of fact, and finally of God. But dogmatism is objectionable when we take thoughts or ideas and impose these as such certainties, with a claim to be autono-

---

[1] Schlatter, "Briefe über Dogma."

A WILL TO RECEIVE AND OBEY 109

mous, to override or ignore the laws that emerge from real experience, and to declare a life-experience to be an illusion. A good example of a high kind of this method has been found in Anselm's ontological argument for God, which deduces the certainty of Him, not from living contact with His behaviour, His historic and revealed reality, but solely from the necessary content of the idea of God in us. Certainty can be founded on no idea, but only on the soul's relevant experience of its facts—in this case on God's historic Self-revelation as we take it home. It is the understanding of some fact that we realise. It is emitted, exhaled, inspired, from a fact; it is not deduced from an idea. Any conclusion we draw is certain only as we know that the premiss is given us in the very fact and act of concrete life. Our general ideas have not their law, necessity, and authority in themselves, however imposing they are, but in the concrete history from which they are drawn. Such notions as Reason, Philosophy, State, Religion, easily become tyrannical hypostases when we give them an authority and a reality detached from the intercourse of living people who act, think, or believe together in a concrete life.

The truth is we can neglect neither the experience nor the thought. If we ignore the experience which shapes us, the seeing and hearing, the historic *provenance* of the idea, then we claim that thought is a creation of ours and invested with life we give it, instead of being given us and determined. And, if we ignore the mind's action, in judgment, which integrates our perceptions with our Ego, all we do is to accumulate matter which remains outside of *us*; and all our knowledge is but learned and loaded ignorance. The given is not really given, because it is not really received.

Our thought and its laws, truth, our knowledge,

though appropriated by our will, is not the creation of it. It is something we find to our hand, something given, something created. It is laid on us, not laid down by us. It is a law and a gift of our Creator. He gives our knowledge, and shows our truth as gold embedded in the ore of experience; and, as He gives by will, by will we take. A rationalism which has a closed system, sufficient for itself and receptive not at all, which makes its word out of its own resources, as the evolution of the idea, is godless. There is no thinker then behind the greatest thought. The greater the idea the less room there is for any one whose idea it is. And, at the other end, the same is the case with a mere empiricism, where a procession of experiences or sensations passes before our Ego leaving us unmoved, appropriating nothing, asserting nothing, losing character in mere science. That is godless and nothing less, with the kind of atheism that dazes smart society in an incessant shower of sparks.

We create neither truth nor God. And, if we repudiate the creative reality of God, we destroy the idea of truth. An atheistic science has prepared its own demise as science. For we pursue truth, because we believe it attainable. And we attain it only by receiving it, only because we believe in a power that gives it, and put us there to find it. If thought create its own world, there can be no objective perception either of ourselves or anything else. Thought but broods. But, if we inhabit a world which is thinkable, if we have thought which is in real relation to a world of thought, we have the idea of a Giver, of God, of an Authority Who is not simply our own superlative.

God is not thought raised to infinity. The authority for thought is not more thought. It is not identity with an idea that makes religion for a living soul; not that we are part of a great thought process which is held to make reality. But religion is communion

A WILL TO RECEIVE AND OBEY

with God, the relation of a living person with a living person. Our thought and its laws reflect His thought. It is not a matter simply of affinity and intellectual love but of difference and of intellectual fear, rising from the limitation of our thought and not its absoluteness. We have no absolute knowledge. We have but a knowledge that we are absolutely known, and therefore a complete trust. We do not deify, we do not idolise Humanity as the ideal become personal in multitude. We, and all being, are thought, are known, are loved, by an infinite Lover of Souls. A theory of knowledge must start with the prime knowledge, the knowledge that we are thus known.[1] Our knowledge of ourselves rests on God's knowledge of us. We are most certain of our thought when we know that God is thinking us and through us. " Das Wahre ist das Bewährende," Baader says. The root certainty is not, " I think " ; it is, " I am thought " ; not, " I know," but, " I am known." If we know that, we need not fret at the limitations of our ignorance. It has been well said that there is a great truth in the taunt that the idea of God is but an asylum for our ignorance. It is encompassed by the all-ruling thought of God. Such faith saves our necessary ignorance from being a burden and a curse.

Our thought will prosper, and our science, as we realise that it is not the first thing but the second. It does not till then realise its own place and right. To see God and hear Him is prior to all thought about Him or His world. The perception of faith is the condition of any science of God ; religion founds all theology. The world we are in is not ours but God's. We therefore revere its reality, and own a wisdom wiser and greater than ours. We do not create truth, but receive it. We do not command it, but obey it. Wisdom is over the thinker who loves it and seeks

[1] I expand this in chap. viii.

it. And the infinite wisdom is the holy Lord, King, and God.

Certainty, therefore, is at bottom no matter of intellect alone, nor of thought; it cannot be there without an act of will, an act of appropriation by the personality. A process of thought apart from an act of will would bring us to no conclusion, to nothing that could be called certainty. It would be but a mental panorama, a cinematogram played to a house of one. What is exhibited before us by thought must go through another process and must become our property; and we cannot affirm it till it do. When we say it is true, and we are sure of it, that is what we mean. And our certainty shows as faith when we weave it into practical life. If the will challenge it, it is doubtful; if the will do not control it, it is mere fancy; if our will absorb it it is faith. So that logic involves ethic; and truth which we are in any earnest about can never be parted from personality. Thought is a work, an art, a duty, and not a mere process nor a mere spectacle. We are *under obligation* to seek and think the truth; we may not merely play with it, we may not loll in the stalls as it passes before us. It is a task, it is not a treat. And we do not legislate for truth; we have to see that the law of thought has its way with us. Our chief act of will is practically recognition of a gift. It is obedience to a grace, even in science.

This is the exit from Intellectualism into Voluntarism. But here too we need to be careful. Voluntarism means only the primacy of the will, not its monopoly. A will, acting without the reason, on other than intelligent principles, is not a will but a mere instinct or impulse. The will is never free to create truth; it is dependent on its donation. The

A WILL TO RECEIVE AND OBEY

thing willed is no product of ours. It is a given: what is ours is our appropriation of it, our self-committal to it, our identification with it, our self-expenditure on it. Even in life's conduct our true originality does not lie in creating the course or form of duty, but in following it, in putting our personality into it. The line of duty (though not its sanction) rises from the law of reason, or the tradition of history; and it may be independent of our will, whose ground and content it yet becomes. It presses on us and solicits. It becomes ours by a decision, swift or slow; and choice is but appropriation and self-devotion. The will is not the cause of truth but its recognition, its service. Even in God Himself, His will is a perfect and eternal appropriation of His nature. It is eternal, for there never was a time when a divine nature began to impose itself on the divine will; it is perfect, because there is no part of that will that does not move by that nature. The causative process in our will is not so monopolist as to extend to the invention of truth (for which we have a short name) but only to its treatment. The intellect may be the instrument of the will, but it is not its creature. For the full process of thought we must be active as well as receptive, but not creative at the upper end, any more than merely passive at the lower. Truth is a matter of observation, or the co-ordination of observations by acts of judgment; and the place of the will is to see that the observation is pure, and purely directed on the truth, so as to make the pursuit of truth a moral act and discipline.[1] No earnest science is in its real nature more theoretical than a judicial inquiry or a parliamentary commission. We think of God, we entertain the idea of God, as we think anything else that is reasonable. But what everything turns on for the truth of the notion is the discovery of a right

[1] Schlatter, "Das Christliche Dogma," I. § D.

and a claim in it. It thinks us, it does not merely think itself in us. We are its humble creatures and not merely its proud organs. Everything turns therefore on the decision with which our will owns the claim set up upon us by that idea in its exigent truth and reality. What matters is the force with which we appropriate and obey the fact as a revelation, a gift. It is not a product of ours, any more than we are a passing product of it. The formation of the idea and its claim are not due to our will, but the recognition of it is. The method and goal are given us; our will but unites us to them in the various forms of veracity.

Such veracity, of course, means much more than truth-telling. But it also means much more than intellectual consistency. Here again the intellectualists are apt to bully. There is a subtle but common kind of Pharisaism which begins by dogmatising with an *a priori* idea or movement of ideas, draws out certain inevitable consequences, and then accuses of unveracity, of carelessness for truth, or slovenliness of mind, those who cannot accept the conclusion. This is arrogance. It is arrogant to monopolise the love and service of truth for those who will take but our reasoned way out of contradiction. It often betrays no more than a philosopher in a hurry, a precipitate system-building, which proposes to organise the world on the basis of one observation.[1] That sequacity is not veracity; which means treating the pursuit of truth as a great and long moral act, resting on a dogmatic gift and a disciplined personality. It means, first, the *finding* of truth by great moral pains taken in the matter of observation. If means, second, the *unifying* of the observations we make, by the selective and co-ordinating act of judgment, working from a tendency or an instinct which demands that truth shall reflect the unity of the moral personality. And, third, it

---
[1] Schlatter.

A WILL TO RECEIVE AND OBEY

means the *fortifying* and establishment of truth in the relations of life, the conduct of men, and the course of God's revealed end with history. But the power to see that end truly in the creative fact which contains it is greater than the power to reason correctly, one that makes more draft upon what we are, one that implies much more self-discipline for the observer's personality. It is also more valuable for truth itself, where the great thing is our pregnant facts, our data, our premises, our revelation. The ethic of intellect depends much more on the quality of its personality than on any code of its procedure. It is obedience to heavenly vision rather than observance of correct precept.

The process of thinking then involves an act of will (that is of obedience); otherwise the unity of our personality is destroyed, and a fatal gulf fixed in its midst. The receptivity which is the foundation of consciousness is not a mere passivity. It cannot be detached from the activity which is of the very being of personality, the act of life. A " wise passiveness " is a deliberate one; one we determine to exercise. It is only possible because of the vitalism of all existence, because life itself is a uniting *act*—both our own personal life and the life of society. Our perceptions, and therefore our thoughts, are made what they are for us by our place in nature and history. And that place, that set of relations, means our part as actors in the active context of things. It is action that makes thought possible. He, who will do, shall know. Ideas are the product of experience and of conduct. History is the factory of ideas. Even when we pass beyond mere perception and the part the will plays there, when we come to forming a judgment on our various perceptions, what have we to work with but the mental capital with which history has provided us, the condensed action of the past, including our own past? What acts freely in our judgment is the condensed history of the past, either our own or that of the race. We cannot break loose from our chain of antecedents, nor break the spiritual entail. We can never reach an objectivity of judgment which entirely severs our continuity, our identity, with ourselves and our kind. We who judge are the agents (though not the mere products) of our past experience and action. The formation of thought is the creaming of a history. There are thoughts that we cannot reach, there are some that we cannot understand, till we have lived them out. We are not ready for them. They cannot be inserted at any part of our career we please. That would be mere dogmatism, mere intellectualism—just as, at the other end, we might have mere practicism, which is all action and no thought. Dismiss action, hypnotise the will, and you discard the only conditions which separate thought from dreaming and brooding. Dismiss thought, and you reduce action to mere activity; and for want of coherent intelligence it sinks in driving sand.

Certainty, we have seen, is no matter of the intellect alone. It involves a prime act of will. But do not let us forget that it is an intelligent will. There is no small temptation offered us, in any system which works with the primacy of the will, to drive a wedge between that and the intellect, and to proclaim an agnosticism on the side of thought only to be redressed by the moral witness of conscience. As if our personality, acting as mind, were atheistic, and theistic only as conscience: as if one hemisphere were always dark and one always light in the Lord. As if thought by its laws and categories were not a given thing with a witness of the Giver. Many have so learned Kant.

A WILL TO RECEIVE AND OBEY 117

But a schism of this kind cannot be permanent, however strategic at a juncture, or useful as a device in disentangling a process. It carries a challenge to that unity of the personality which means so much for the foundation both of thought and of religion. We may admit that the laws of knowledge or thought will not give us an object of religion to engage our whole personality—we may admit that, without denying them all value in that direction. When we have found our soul's God on other than intellectual lines, it is quite possible for us to return to our mental process, to the logic of thought, and find in its donative quality features which corroborate the will's faith, and share in the convergence of all our powers on the God whose gift they are.

There are three great monopolies to-day which rival and threaten the true monopoly of Christianity, and threaten it from within. They have been said to be the æsthetic, the philosophic, and the theological constructions of religion. They are literature, speculation, and orthodoxy.

The æsthetic is the peril to religion from the monopoly of the feelings. Abroad its medium is art, in this country it is literature, with its debauch of sentiment in the feebler types, and of passion in the stronger. The besetting sin of literature in the region of religion is unreality, pose. Expression runs away from experience. Even sermons grow literary and to an extent unreal. Instead of faith speaking, we have the words and thoughts that faith might be imagined or expected to speak. Expression outruns realisation; facility, profundity; grace, truth; and charm, matter. Impression is mistaken for regeneration, and to move men is prized as highly as to change them. Emotion, which is so valuable for literature, becomes of prime value for life, and tends to become its law.

Ethic becomes erotic, or the delightful engrosses the respect due to the real and true. Culture is defined as mere susceptibility. Temperament takes the place of character, sympathy of insight. The writing of an adulterer with a touch as light as his morals may be more popular than that of a deep prophet like Carlyle, because he had household jars.

The philosophic peril approaches religion from the side of the intellect. It is its apotheosis and monopoly. Christianity becomes a religion of ideas instead of facts. It is cut adrift from its history, and cherished as a system of religious ideas, which are either evolved from thought or, permeating life, are elicited from it by an induction, instead of given in a central revelation. We are not saved by Christ, but by the principle of redemption or sacrifice pervading life, and inviting us to place ourselves in line. We are practically self-redeemed, by giving course to the humane principles that pervade the soul, or the spiritual processes that work up out of the depths of life. But even if the redemptive idea be kept it is emptied. The sanity of ethical process replaces the tragedy of spiritual crisis, and reality is organised in a moral philosophy rather than revealed in a moral Saviour. Attention is fixed on the grand resources of human nature instead of the impotence of the human will. And for this dehistoricised religion a place is claimed in the Church of equal right with the faith whose sole object is Christ and His Cross.

The peril of orthodoxy is also intellectualist, though now it has come to be debased intellect. It is an old intellectualism fallen into poverty. It was the intellectualising of Scripture, as speculation is the intellectualising of the soul. It is often conjoined with a facile piety, and (to be fair) with a devoted and valuable philanthropy. It has a tenacious hold of the Church's rank and file, who find belief

A WILL TO RECEIVE AND OBEY 119

easier than faith, both to cultivate in themselves and to apply to others. It asks first not if a Church has the gospel but if it has the pattern standardised, say, in the Victorian age. It hates the intellectualism of the critics with a family hatred. It is devoid of moral insight into the better genius of its own creed, and has no literature which could nurture its inquiring youth in the world-principles of its world-appetite. Its passion tends to the note of ascendancy and militarism with a peculiar mixture of hardness and timidity.

Each of these spiritual perils is a peril only through being misplaced, through a head of department being placed in imperial control. Each has an indispensable element to contribute to a true faith. Where should we be without emotion in our religion, without thought, without Scripture? We should have neither heart, mind, nor gospel. But where are we through their struggle for illicit monopoly? In serious danger of losing Christianity altogether. Because their common result is the submersion of the ethical element, of the centrality of the conscience, and the authority of the holy. Even the ethical element claims but the hegemony, the primacy—the control of the rest, and not their expulsion. The conscience is a passionate conscience, which makes the world's salvation its tragedy. Let that be granted to æsthetic. It is an intelligent and veracious conscience, a conscience for the whole scheme of life, with a system of the world latent in it. Salvation is the plan of the whole creation, with which it groans toward the manifestation of a universal and holy reality. Let that be owned to philosophy. And it is a conscience in such a case, so made and marred in history, that it can only be divinely handled by a historic treatment, a historic gospel. Let that be conceded to those who find the Bible to be everything. Everything to the point here *is* in the Bible, in the gospel (which we have only in the Bible), of a guilty conscience redeemed by the Holy. Christianity does insist on the supremacy of the ethical as the condition of revelation and the avenue of the real. But it is conscience, as the core of all life, as the axis of all thought, as the element of all final weal. It is not a conscience in a corner but a conscience saved only by an act of which saves the world. The whole man is redeemed to a vast fulness of life; but it is by the world-redemption of his conscience. It is by the obedience of man's constitution to his will, and to his obedient will; by the obedience of human nature to a divine will which speaks in the conscience the authoritative word and exerts from the conscience the final control.

May I recapitulate as I close this lecture? We start from the very nature of truth. It is given us. We do not make it, we have to yield to it. The laws of our thought, the conditions of our knowledge are not framed by us. Here we are not free, not creative. So far from being free, thought is beset before and behind by necessity laid upon it. Our mind is not a mere vitality, moving featureless like the wind; it has a formation, a destiny, which emerges in all evolution, but is not created by it. It rules evolution as its latent goal and deep burthen. Our mental constitution we find to our hand with a living *nisus* at every stage. There is no hope of anything if we do not obey it. We do not prove it, we perceive it; and its observance is the condition of our proving anything. Our mentality descends on us both from heaven and from history. It comes with an authority from without and from above. Ideas are not ultimates. Thought does not create its own foundations or necessities. It does not make the laws of thought. It sees them, owns them, and thus alone is fertile thought. It does not prove them

A WILL TO RECEIVE AND OBEY

but starts with them as conditions of proof. We are often told we cannot prove God. But God is not the only reality we cannot prove. The notion of space, of colour, of other personalities, nay the fundamental act of our own self-consciousness—all these (it has been often pointed out) are beyond our control. They are laid on us, they are donated—by what kind of power we have other and surer means of knowing. But they are given, that is the point. They came from a thought before man's thought. Our root certainty is not "I think" but "I am thought." We cannot tell just how they arise in us, as we cannot watch our own birth. Neither memory nor observation is the source of our belief in them. An unconscious passivity precedes all our consciousness, and consciousness is but a growing appropriation of what was given us before consciousness arose. All we know is the experiences in which they come to light, which compel us to think them, as we are compelled by parallel experiences to the idea of God. Our proof of Him is little more than setting forth in an orderly or impressive way the situation or experiences in which He is borne home on us. It is not a case of syllogism but of observation and experience. In our religious teaching we are really but coming in aid of those processes, which lie outside our own causal power, and are rather causal to it; just as we can only teach mathematics by falling into line with the pupil's notion of space or sense better than he can. All the great religious teachers take God for granted, and go on. All our knowledge arises upon us concretely out of certain actual relations in which reality approaches us. And so our certainty of God can only be based on the approach and action of the power which alone can set up the real relation between God and man. And that is God Himself. God thought before we did, and He moved first.

The point is that the foundation of the intellectual life is itself given, revealed, and authoritative, though the full significance of the revelation appears in another quarter of our being. But the principle is not fatally different in each sphere. It is not as if the intellect (in its nature as distinct from its use) were incurably sceptical or self-sufficient, while the will witnessed to a will over us. In both regions we are dependent on what descends on us with a claim, on the authoritative.

Not indeed as if with the merely given we had the certainty of God, as if He were but stamped on us. For that would leave us too passive for faith. It would be too mechanical for religion. Our spontaneity is more involved than that. We have to contribute a judgment on the data in order to reach certainty. The mere notion of God, though it arises on our intelligence, like other objects of thought, does not make us religious. It involves our personality, and must even engage it. It must be affirmed or denied by us, appropriated or rejected, taken down from the region of notions that pass before us, and incorporated with our practical life. Sight turns faith as soon as it is made active in practical life. "Faith," says Baader, "is the act in which we allow influence over us. It is the owning of *value* to a thought—value for life." The thought of God must be adjusted continually, whether in life or theology, to command the new situations or the new knowledge that continually arises. But, as we grow more and more religious, we return to find the very notion of Him more and more of a given thing, a descending, commanding, authoritative thing. The more we know of His love the more we know it as that of a Master and not a mate. That is to say we begin with God and His donation in thinking about God. If we acquired that habit of philosophic mind, we

A WILL TO RECEIVE AND OBEY

should boggle less when we came to deal with the historic origins of Christian faith. God gives reason, else reason could not give God. "Any knowledge of God which begins without God is a challenge of God." It contests His relation to our knowledge and to the possibility of it. We really know him only through Him as the Giver of knowledge. We think Him because we are His thought. Herein is thought, not that we think God, but that He thought us.

Any other conception of the matter is rationalistic, as if faith were the result of the noetic process, or God a result of thought, instead of its ground; as if we had something more certain or real than He is on which we could base the certainty or reality of Him.

But, it may be urged, with a parting shot, if our mental formation and rational categories are given us for a start, and are no product of ours, does that not the more oblige us, in reverence, to submit to our reason all the other data that reach us with God's name and claim, say, in history, in the Christian revelation? And so do we not come to a religious rationalism, to rationalism as God's will? But reason could not assure us of the God that gives it its first title. Nor can it secure us in any final and rational purpose of the world, which is the real matter. There is a farther and more explicit revelation which takes command of the first. Our rational faculties are not all of us. They run up into our whole moral personality. The gift of God is more impressive and authoritative on our moral side. The conscience, which began its witness by owning the moral obligations of thought, comes to itself and its authority only as God saves it by His final light. That is what is meant by the primacy of the will for life or faith. It is the gift and will of God that we should find this final authority in the moral region of experience, of personal contact with Him, of communion with the holy, will in will. The only point it is desired to make here is that the authoritative note is not a monopoly of our moral judgment, but is at the base of our intellectual processes also. It is articulate in conscience, but it is also active in thought. And our constitution is not in this respect cleft, nor the morphology of one personality rent, by a civil war in its being, however it may be with the uses to which our will puts it.

VI

PAST FACT AND PRESENT POWER

How can any fact of the past ever be an object of personal experience, or final authority, or absolute certainty ? How can the historic Jesus be a part of my present life—not simply an interest, but a part of it, to say nothing of the ruling part ? How can He live and reign in me, and I in Him ? I can study Christ and admire Him, how can I live Him ? I can study Socrates ; is the result of my dwelling in Christ no more than the result of my immersion in Socrates ?

This is, of course, a different question from one with which it may be confused ; how a present experience can guarantee a historic fact, or make it more at most than a postulate to account for it (which is short of a presence that creates it). And yet the two questions are at bottom the same, and differ but as converse modes.

The famous saying of Lessing still holds its ground in many uncritical quarters : " The accidental truths of history can never become proof for the necessary truths of reason." Of course much turns on its interpretation. It is wrong if it is taken at its face value, or swallowed whole. It reflects the eighteenth century and the rationalist way.

If we try to get at its real meaning, or what it strove in that eighteenth-century fashion to say, we may usefully begin by distinguishing between history in the great sense and history in the small, between history as a tissue of great ideas and powers and history as a mass of empirical events, between history as divined and history as proved. There is *Geschichte* and *Historie*.[1] *Historie* is history as it may be settled by the methods of historical science, where our results, like those of all science, are but relative, and either highly or poorly probable. *Geschichte* on the other hand is a larger thing, out of which *Historie* has to sift, but which may embody and convey ideas greater than the critical residum retains power to express. It is tradition, which may be sacramental even if its elements crumble before science. But not only so. Tradition is also creative. It is not a mere matter of the past, but it reaches organically down to the present. It not inly influences us, it makes us.

And where we feel the past to transcend the *sacramental* and to be *creative* for us it cannot crumble. A creative effect cannot proceed from a friable cause. The author of our new creation cannot be dissolved by critical science, though the source of a sacramental impression may. The man who was the sacrament of our regeneration may fall into soul-collapse without entailing mine; but the Saviour who was the Creator of it cannot, without involving me in the *débâcle*. A picture that drew me near God for days may be burned, and I suffer no loss beyond what can be covered by regret; but if the gospel story were pulverised my soul would make part of the spray.

We are far removed from the facts of *Historie*, it may be, and we can hold them at arm's length and peer at them with a disinterested knowledge; but we are woven into the tissue of *Geschichte*. It has made us. We cannot be disinterested here. Ἐκ γὰρ τοῦ γένος ἐσμεν. It works out into the present, into

[1] *Cf.* Wobbermin, "Geschichte und Historie in der Religionswissenschaft," 1911.

PAST FACT AND PRESENT POWER 127

us. It is the evolving organism of mankind taken as a moral and spiritual unity. If Nature made us, this history made us still more, far more inwardly. *Geschichte* regards the individual fact or person as to its place in this living whole. It has to do with the actual course of civilisation in the gross more than with the net results of science applied to that course.

Having distinguished thus we may interpret Lessing's phrase to mean that detailed facts of *Historie* will not prove the eternal truths of *Geschichte*. We answer, they may not prove, but as a matter of experience they convey. Defective documents may be great sacraments. Lessing's own phrase is wrong too. Truths are not accidental. What is true excludes accidents. If we speak of the accidental we do not mean truths, historic or otherwise.

Again, all truths are historic in the sense of *geschichtlich*. They emerge into history, and, in proportion to their truth, play an organic part in the whole. Hence we cannot speak of necessary truths of the reason in contrast with truths of *Geschichte*. All truths are necessary in their place. There are no truths of the reason in Lessing's sense, in the sense that the reason can discover and prove such truths purely from its own resources apart from historic experience. But if we mean that all truths are truths of reason in the sense that they are founded in a supreme Reason which guides history—that takes a religious faith for granted.

These great spiritual truths, then, belong to history. They reach us so. And they affect us mightily, both to shape and to enhance us. But they are not at the mercy of the historical science which deals with single events. In a word, such events do not prove the truths; they convey them. They are not proofs, but sacraments or sources. The death of Christ does not prove anything. It conveys the Grace of God, and it is the source of a new life. It is not evidence but action, the outcrop of an eternal act.

We must fit the method to the nature of the fact, and not the fact to the method. It is easy to say that historic Christianity cannot be the absolute religion because no single point of history can be absolute. But it sounds too much like an *a priori* judgment to which the historic fact must be squeezed down by deflation. It is trimming a fact to a method instead of framing the method on fact. The historic Christ *has* founded an absolute faith.

And therefore in order to answer the question we must become clear about the nature of the fact concerned. Are we not begging the whole question when we call it a purely historic fact that is the object of our present Christian experience? It has already been said that the final Christian fact is not simply a phenomenon, nor even a person—it is a person culminating in His eternal act, and both coordinated in an interpretation, through Apostles, by the same Holy Spirit whose was the divine power of the act. " Jesus Christ, who in the power of the Eternal Spirit offered Himself unto God." As a matter of historic fact, the Divine person of Christ, as construed by the apostolic Word or preaching of Christ, did become the Christian foundation, the object of the Church's faith, and its source. Or, if we speak of the historic Jesus as the fact, we may say that, in all our sources of information, the fact is never there without the luminous *aura* of inspiration about it, and a certain interpretation. It is only in an inspired interpretation of it that we have any cognisance of it, so far as history goes. Apart from this, in epistle or gospel, it is inaccessible to us. And this *aura* is not a mere envelope put about an inert fact, but a radiance emitted from the fact, and as integral to it as the

PAST FACT AND PRESENT POWER 129

ray to the sun. The manifestation and its self-interpretation, gospel and epistle, make the one great fact, as Father and Son are one in the Spirit, or as man and wife are one spiritual personality. It is this perennial, intrinsic vitality that makes the great fact more than historic, that makes it a present thing to us. It is more than *historisch*, it is *geschichtlich*. It lives in its Church. Christian certainty, our present possession of Christ, is inseparable from some form of the active tradition and experience of the long and living Church. The great fact is the historic phenomenon, Jesus, *plus* its " meta-historic " Word, the fact active only in its Word, acting therefrom always as living, life-giving Spirit. And this apostolic interpretation, this sacrament of Christ in the Word of Him, claims to be the Word for Humanity as a whole, and not for a certain early stage of it. It is contemporary with every age. It is not only *in* history at a point but *for* history throughout Only that which solves all ages can be the radical solution of any age.

By being thus integral with its Word, in an economy of the Spirit, this fact of Christ is differentiated from all other history. No other tradition is like this tradition of the Church, which carries the initial fact, active in it and creative, wherever it comes, and does not simply echo it, or testify to it. The fact is the Lord the Spirit, the consummate and perennial achievement of an Eternal Person, the Eternal Act of spiritual Reality made historic. It is a timeless act, detailed to the individual not from the remote past alone but also from the deep present, not simply from a historic Lord but from the Lord the Spirit (2 Cor. iv.-fin.). It was the act of a timeless person and present, and therefore an eternal act, co-eval for ever with every age and soul. Here is the action of the Holy Spirit, an action different from the general spiritual presence of the Creator in His universe, inseparably bound up with the historic act of Jesus Christ, and differentiating that act from every other that has taken place in history, as the pointed outcrop of the Moral Act which is the soul and sustenance of things. Apart from the Holy Ghost, with His individualising and time-destroying action, there is no means of making the past present in the Christian sense. Only the Lord the Spirit, by the Word of the Gospel, makes the person of Christ so near as to be the ever-present revelation and ever-creative redemption by God. The revelation which came to mankind in Christ, *i.e.* the real, intimate, and ageless act of God, comes to each man as Christ comes to him in the Holy Ghost. The historic fact of revelation that we are taught becomes the Word of revelation that we hear. Such is the Christian experience.

It is not to be denied that in this there is something without parallel or analogy, something inexplicable and dogmatic, essentially different from our contact with every other piece of history. The relation is not evidential, nor is it merely continuous. It is sacramental. Nay more, it is a creative relation, acting in a creative evolution. There is an element of miracle in it, and therefore of freedom.[1] The Spirit, acting in the historic fact and series, *creates* the power to believe. We are not coerced by data. We do not bestow assent, we are captured for it. We do not credit the fact, we are "apprehended of it." The fact, being spiritual in its nature and not merely in its effects, creates its own belief; and it does so in the face of such obstacles in us as no mere historic fact has to contend with. By the apostolic *word* of Revelation, the Spirit brings the historic *fact* of revelation, the person and act of Christ, so near that it becomes the revelation of God equally present to every age—as we must believe God Himself

---

[1] It is odd that in an age almost drunk with freedom there should be such an aversion to miracle.

PAST FACT AND PRESENT POWER 131

to be on any theory of His reality and immanence. The Spirit stands, like the great angel, with one foot on the old fact and one on our new soul. And fact and soul are united in His consciousness, which we share.[1] We become certain of the revelation itself only by this experience under the apostolic Word of revelation, and not by going round it or behind that Word, in the way of some critical construction which destroys it. The Word which historically arrives *at* the Christian is spiritually a Word *to* him; and that not by a formal and collateral authority (like miracles or an episcopal succession) vouching it to be of God, but by its own creative content and nature, its intrinsic, miraculous, regenerative action in us. At Pentecost the Apostles' word was owned as God's Word, not by external vouchers and credentials, but by its nature and effect. It was not by the mere power, as of an irresistible gust. That might be interpreted as a violent subliminal upheaval, closing in explosion a long process of irrationality fermenting in our unintelligible, and therefore non-moral, depths. But like all the action of the Holy Ghost in the New Testament, it was bound up with the person of Christ and His felt, moral, and redemptive meaning. And it made its way and pricked their hearts by this content, through the greatest obstruction and doubt in the soul. This obstacle was not an old, cold, indurated crust of habit or indifference which was volcanically burst, but an earnest obsession by active, hot, and hostile convictions, interests, and prejudices. It was the same with the conversion of St Paul. It was the meeting of two fires. Pharisaism was as earnest and passionate as Christianity.

Every other historical fact than the Gospel finds the human mind with such a disposition for truth that

---

[1] I have said elsewhere that our certainty in this kind is really a function of the divine self-certainty.

it has merely to present itself with sufficient evidence or attraction. It appeals to the instinct for natural certainty or excellence. But with the Christian certainty it is otherwise. The element of natural certainty or proof in it is very subordinate. Its rational appeal is always inadequate, and its desirability is not at once apparent. Nay, it has a power all its own of rousing antagonism and even hate. Its certainty comes with a blow to human nature and human reason, or with an unwelcome demand for submission, or at least preferential treatment. It has no *foundation* in either nature or reason, but only contact, only points of attachment for appeal. It is more despotic than constitutional, so far as rational law is concerned. How is the natural man to verify a gospel which takes the confidence out of human nature and its instincts, and destroys the egoism which is its first certainty? How can the foolishness of such a Gospel commend itself to man's native wisdom? And is the Gospel not such? I am not speaking of religion. Religion is natural to man, faith is not, Christianity is not. The Gospel revelation means self-condemnation and no confidence in the flesh, in human nature. It upsets the ordinary bench of appeal. Its protectorate begins by dissolving parliament. How then is it to be effectual by its *nature*, and not as a mere superior force, by quality and not mere dynamic? To this question there is a proximate answer to which I refer elsewhere. But there is no ultimate answer but a miracle. The response to the Gospel is an act of will, an act of preference and committal as unto the higher, with all the miracle of moral mastery, of moral freedom in it. (Chap. IX.) Paul could only say, " It pleased God to reveal His Son in me " amid the *débâcle* of everything that was certain before, or that made the test of certainty. The Gospel must *create* the power to believe it.

PAST FACT AND PRESENT POWER 133

Revelation here is so radical that in the same act it must be Regeneration. The calling voice of a holy God to us sinners is such a judging, crushing voice that it becomes effectual only as a new-creating word.

> " The prayers I make shall then be prayers indeed
> If Thou the Spirit give by which I pray." [1]

The deeper the revelation *of* the love, the deeper is the holiness revealed *in* that love ; and we are delivered from the wrath of God, *i.e.* His holy judging demand, only by the gracious act of His holy atoning love. The Gospel creates far more sense of sin than it finds in the natural conscience and its accusals ; which conscience is always trying to put itself right, but deepening its despair in every effort, and so blinding its spiritual eye to the very Gospel it is scared into seeking. The Word of the Gospel comes not only to blind but to slay, and in the same act to re-create, to create a confidence in self-despair. At its hand we die to live. The same word which deepens the doom saves us from it, and rouses our utter self-condemnation—to be certain that there is now no more condemnation in Jesus Christ.

Clearly if such psychology of sin and salvation be sound, if it be not a case of popular insanity and epidemic delusion, there is more in the Gospel than the divine impressiveness of Christ's character or even the ideal message in His person. That historic and eloquent phenomenon is, as a mere impressive fact, not the whole fact. It is made a Gospel by that person's creative act and effect as the very act of God, and not as a witness to it or message about it. For a Gospel to man through his conscience the ideal Christ must be pointed, not to say moralised, in a specific but universal work—His adjustment of

[1] See the whole of Michelangelo's Sonnet in Wordsworth's version.

love and holiness from the side of God, and His new creation of us on the side of man. No mere impression from Christ will make Him more than a great historic figure for us, or make His moral greatness more than æsthetic. It may influence us deeply from the past, but it will not make the past fact the present life. That can only be if the past fact is of such a miraculous nature that it judges and saves and re-creates us individually, if it is with us in saving action as the life of our life, and not simply as an exemplary memory, an impressive heroism, or a winning spectacle. It can only be if it quell our every effort at self-justification or self-condemnation with one perfect, loving, and final justification by all the damning power of a holy God now turned to our eternal life. There is no full forgiveness except by the eternal damnation of sin in the same act — an eternal damnation of sin which sears it out of the sinner, and has for its obverse our eternal life and holiness.

So that the certificate of the Gospel to us is really its own unique and unimpaired work with us. It lies in a personal experience of it. And those who are devoid of the experience are *ultra vires* when they challenge the reality of its object or the nature of its process, to others so deep and sure. It is quite true that the psychology of vision tells us that we do not see the object but its image on the retina. But it is the experience of vision, and our direct touch of reality by it, that makes that very science of it possible. And it is possible, moreover, and the philosophers can only work, in a society where the reality of the objects thus seen is a condition of practical affairs. So the certification of the Gospel and the theology of it rest on an experience of it whose final psychology must always be beyond us, and on an experience of it in a corporate society.

Faith is a creation. It is not of man or man's will,

PAST FACT AND PRESENT POWER 135

nor is its secret within man's scientific knowledge. The certainty in the religious life is bound up with the autonomy of that life, its uniqueness and its independence of other knowledge. Our natural modes of rational certainty are but points of attachment, or under-agents for the certainty of faith ; they are not germs of it, and they are not tests of it. And it is the autonomous verdict of the will in this new-created experience that the grace of the Cross is there only by the judgment in the Cross—whatever offence this may give to the sympathies, charities, or generosities of a natural religion, to our belief in human nature. The new creation so changes me that it removes the weight of my sympathy and concern from that excellent creature man to the side of God's holiness, to consider first the creature's wrong to it and its requirements. I am no more a special pleader on man's side to mitigate the justice of God's plea, and to urge considerations that may have a certain weight in an individual case—his early disadvantages, his excuses, his remnant of right. I do not then voice my friend's theological scruples, and his too, too tender conscience, as he questions the possible justice of any divine judgment that falls on another than the culprit. What if the object of my chief concern were man's prior infliction on the Holy One ? Before I boggle at vicarious judgment on men, have I secured my standard of all justice by securing the holiness of God in the face of what was so gratuitously inflicted on it by man's sin ?

The point to note is that the effect on the soul is not due to the power or Spirit of God corroborating Christ like a second revelation. Nor is the action of the Spirit that of opening the heart, by a new and collateral act, for the fact of Christ, and so letting the inner nature of the fact exert its due posthumous and psychological influence on us. But it is the action of the whole Gospel fact itself, of the Lord the Spirit. The Spirit acts from the fact and not simply with it.[1] It is the power of Christ's saving act functioning in the saving Word, that in the same moment both breaks a way in and plants in a life. Least of all can we refer the Gospel to have its claim tried before some native God-consciousness or ideal on man's side ; as if there were some sure and supreme natural knowledge of God prior and permissive to the Self-revelation of God. A lower revelation may prepare for the higher, and provide a psychology for it, but it cannot measure, and therefore cannot test it nor vouch for it. There is no final and innate revelation of God in human nature, nothing so much deeper and surer than the Gospel that it can lend it a licence —there are only points of attachment or modes of action, an economy for a revelation when it comes.

So then the experience which makes Christianity real and its knowledge sure is inseparable from the historic, apostolic, and creative Word of its ultimate fact. It is inseparable from the Gospel, towards which such experience must always behave as its product and not as its superior, to which experience must also go back as to its source, and whose nature is its norm. Faith has its object only in that Word, and it arises through that Word certified as God's Word by no collateral authority, but by the miracle of its native effect.

Our ultimate authority, then, which justifies every other authority in its degree and measure, is the Creator of the New Humanity as such. It is the Power Who, in His loving will in Christ, bought up the claims upon us of the moral universe and of His own holy nature ; whose grace, therefore, became our one creditor, so that faith became our one debt, to be paid with our soul and person alone.

[1] See the first two chapters of my "Faith, Freedom, and the Future." Hodder & Stoughton. 1912.

VII

THE GROUND OF RELIGION—THE HISTORIC FACT AND THE PREACHED WORD

WHAT is the objective Gospel for which supreme authority is claimed in human affairs? It is a question already proposed, but it calls for more incisive answer than I have yet offered. What is the fundamental fact of Christianity as final for the soul? What is the unit great with all the Christian power and the world's future? What is it from the past that is presented to our present experience to make it Christian?

The offhand answer of the modern Christian who wishes to be more religious than theological, and who would be positive, and generous withal, is that the fact is Christ. But that is really no answer. What do we mean by that? Do we mean the historic Jesus (or what is left of Him in the crucible of criticism), apart from the Apostles' faith in Him, or do we mean the whole New Testament Christ, as interpreted by that faith? Must the Christ who makes our Gospel be the Christ pre-existent to his earthly life and post-existent, risen from the dead, and royal now in Heaven and in the soul? Or, again, is it the inner life of Jesus or His atoning death? At least it is no relevant answer to say the fact is the historic Christ, when we understand the question. It cannot be meant that the supreme and final Christian fact is a figure historic in just the same sense as Socrates was; a figure whose historicity it is enough to prove, in the same way as that of Socrates, by strictly historical evidence; and who occupies, therefore, a fixed place in the procession of personalities that fill the first century. More must be meant than that Christianity turns on recognising the historic reality and ideal influence of a person who urged certain truths about God, and man, and His own relation to both; irrespective of the question whether these ideas were dreams of His, or realities eternal and component of His person. For Christianity the personality of Christ is much more than a historic quantity. Then, what more? What is " meta-historic " in it? To say that Christ is our grand fact means little till we can answer that question, till He is more than a formal fact, and becomes to us a material fact and a spiritual, whose value lies wholly in its nature, quality, and interpretation. The valuable thing is not the fact nor its integration in the historic series, but its super-historic meaning and content. It is not Christ but His Christology. It is not the appearance of a tremendous prophet, but the identity of His message with His person and work, and of both with God's final reality for the world.

The great and rending issues of the hour are not outside the Church, but within it. And perhaps the greatest of these is not that (which passion fans) between the Christian public and the Christian priest, but that (which sentiment smothers) between an Apostolic Gospel and either a spiritual instinct or the Theism of a refined Judaism. Is our Christian foundation the Christ of the Epistles and Apostles—*i.e.* Christ as He revealed Himself to them for the equipment of the Church—or is it a prophetic Jesus, taken apart from the apostles' faith in Him, a spiritual splendour distilled critically out of the Synoptics? It is even denied by some that there ever was such a thing as an

THE GROUND OF RELIGION 139

apostolic Gospel. It is urged that the leaders of the first Church were at sixes and sevens as soon as they passed beyond the mere memory, or the parousial hope, of that glorious sage who so dominated their reverence.

If this be true, and in proportion as it is felt to be true, the Church must subside like the Venetian Campanile—only never to rise again. It just becomes the religious side of the world, and sinks into a piece of culture, like art, which only symbolises man's best ideas instead of effecting his new creation. The frequent antithesis between Christianity as a hard-and-fast doctrine and as a life is a false one. Christianity is neither. It is the act, the gift, the grace, the creation, the communion of the God of Holy Love, if we take its own account of itself. It is not the infusion of a mere vitality, a mere colourless oxygen, which revives our native spiritual resources. The gift, the life, is something very positive. It is Christ, as His apostles were instructed and empowered to transmit Him—a positive Christ, as crucified for our guilt and raised for our life; Christ, not as a prophetic or revelationary person merely, but as Redeemer, as God in the act of Redemption.

Criticism of the more popular and amateur sort often suggests to the unwary that the continued belief in an apostolic Gospel is only possible to inadequate knowledge. But such criticism really represents a stage associated rather with Strauss and Baur (and, perhaps, Pfleiderer) than with more modern (though untranslated) work. It is unfamiliar with the work of the religious historical school, which holds the hour and the promise in that kind. One frequent statement alone gives such writers away. It is the statement that Paul and his doctrine were, as to the apostolic body, in a minority of one.

No doubt Paulinism as a system went under a certain

cloud after the first century, as Catholicism grew, till Augustine and the Reformation, each for its hour, justified Paul's truth as the truth in Jesus. But that is not the point for the moment, which is the existence of a solid apostolic Gospel as the creative thing in the founding of the Church. The other apostles did not hesitate openly to quarrel with Paul on occasion. They did so on an ecclesiastical question as to the terms of communion. But on his Christology, for instance, there was no quarrel. Nor on his soteriology. And, searching, provocative, as his creed was, they would not have hesitated to challenge it had they not held it. There were, indeed, different phases of the Apostolic κήρυγμα which made the Church; but they were preferential modes or idiosyncrasies—they made neither exclusive sects nor warring schools. If there was any man of whom it was true that he was " among the apostles in a minority of one," it was James. In the matter of the vital, creative meaning of Christ's person and death, Peter, Paul and John are all of one mind. Each stands on the shoulders of the other— John notably developing Paul, both in an atoning soteriology and in Christology. I add Hebrews and the Apocalypse. And I point out further that the Synoptics are so soaked in this apostolic, and even Pauline, Gospel that they create much trouble for the critics—trouble shown in able efforts like Professor Bacon's, to squeeze it out, and to present us with a dry-plate photograph of Jesus as He actually was.

What the great representative apostles held is certain; that Paul's irritants in his churches were their emissaries is a conjecture which loses ground. So far as we know, the Apostolate stood on the fact that Christ died for our sins according to the Scriptures. Paul had that from the other Apostles (1 Cor. xv. 3). And they were all at one in such a conviction as that God so loved the world that He gave His only begotten Son to be the

THE GROUND OF RELIGION 141

propitiation for our sins, whom also He raised from the dead, that whosoever believeth in Him should not perish, but should have eternal life. The specific Paulinism does not begin till after that point. A real atonement, which is now the *bête noir* of a " simple " or " lay " Christianity, is no mere Paulinism. It is incorrect to speak of the angles at which the common Gospel, so creative of the Church, was viewed by different men as if they stamped the New Testament with a warring subjectivity, instead of being our chief historic objective. (Unless, indeed, all history be a subjectivity magnified and projected, and there is no real revelation at all.) The most recent and competent work on the New Testament will not bear out this tendency to disintegrate the Apostolate, whether we turn to the more positive or the more negative schools. We may go to Schlatter on the right, Feine in the centre (*Theologie des Neuen Testaments*, second edition, pp. 689 ff.), or Weinel on the left (*Biblische Theologie des Neuen Testaments*, p. 437) —to name only the leading writers within last year, and we find the position to be admitted which I state. The whole work, also, of the brilliant religious-historical school in the last dozen years has gone to show a substantial dogmatic unity in the Gospel of the first Church. The object of the school is only to account for it ; which they do not by what issued from Jesus, but from what crystallised on Him from the whole atmosphere of current, and largely pagan, thought on religious matters. There was, of course, no universal theological formula, there was not an orthodoxy ; but certainly there was a common Apostolic Gospel, a κήρυγμα. There was no unitary body of Divinity ; but even Holtzmann admits " an approximate general average of theoretic content which became in course the base for the Church's doctrine." (*N.T. Theologie* II. 206.) And this theological κήρυγμα stands for us as the common chord in the three great names who represent the Apostolate—Peter, Paul and John. It was a fixed but elastic tradition.

The foundation of the Church in every age is not a common system, but this common Gospel; wherein Christ is neither the mere symbol of spiritual Humanity, nor the mere sacrament of God's love, but the full Saviour of the race and of its destiny by a divine act crucial for God's holiness and for all history. And may I add another obvious thing. We have a variety of opinions and sections in the first *Church*, but I am speaking of *the representative Apostles*, and of the New Testament as their register and index. The Church of the ages was not founded by the Church of the first century, but by the apostles as the organs of Christ. We are in the apostolic succession rather than in the ecclesiastic. It is not the first Church that is canonical for us Protestants, but the apostolic New Testament. Variation about that Gospel is not enrichment, like theological variety; it is disintegration.

Let us take issue where the hour stands and accept the battle offered. Let us face the crisis in all its clear force. Let us care a little less for liberty, and very much more for certainty. God will see to our freedom, and see that we see to it without *fanfarronades*, if we see to His Gospel. There *was* a common Apostolic Gospel and interpretation of Christ, right or wrong. It *was* the staple of the preaching which made the Church. It *was* the creative power which is still immanent in the Church. It may be true or false. That is, it may misrepresent Jesus, or it may give Him His true effect. But at least let us clearly see that it made, and makes, the Christian Church; and that to renounce it is to dissolve the Church and to paralyse its ministry. Gracious individuals may linger long with the way of the past on them. Another society may be started on the new

THE GROUND OF RELIGION 143

foundation. But the Church cannot go on without this indwelling creating Word. It must die of marasmus. For the Church the apostolic Gospel and version of the eternal Christ as atoning was creative, and must therefore be fundamental. It is our one protection from a destroying subjectivity, a groping temperamentalism, a fumbling futility. If it misrepresented Jesus the consequences must be accepted, and the Church it brought into being must go down. So be it. But let us be clear that in that case the whole Christian Church has been standing on a central and vital misrepresentation of its Lord, in a way that admits of no compromise now, if either side is to be faithful to Him as it sees Him. I do not know a more insidious or deadly principle for the Church than this—" make yourself beloved by your people, and you may preach anything." That is indeed "the poison and the sting of things too sweet."

We contrast with the Christ of apostolic faith the dry-point etching of Jesus, which is the thin critical redaction of the rich apostolic picture of Holy Love in the Synoptics. It is quite wrong and amateur to describe a theological exposition of God's holiness in His love as "an exaltation of the judicial and imperial aspects of God at the cost of the sympathetic and affectionate." The revelation in Christianity is not love, but holy love. The first thing in the Church is not the love in Christians, but God's love for Christians. And especially the manner of it rather than its amount and intensity—its manner as holy and atoning. The mark of our new and ethical construction of Christ's work is that substitution of God's holiness for His justice which entirely transfigures such a term as "judicial," and abolishes the usual associations of one like "imperial." We must arrest the current and feeble perversion of our redeemed relation to Christ into one of mere endearment. And the modern theology which is at once scientific and positive, is an attempt to take in entire earnest, as the rock reality of things and the undertow of all history, that holiness of God which has been dethroned in current religion; and dethroned with all the train of consequential ineptitudes which earnest minds on both sides deplore.

There, in God's historic holiness, and in its inextinguishable demands both as love and as judgment, is an objective and final footing. There is the last authority for all the certainty and obedience whose lack bewilders and shatters an age which nothing but such religion can save. If reality be not redemption, it is not moral. If it is moral it must be redemptive, considering the state of the conscience before a holy God; and if it is absolute, it has a foregone redemption. The whole message, promise, and destiny of the Church loses meaning otherwise. Its Gospel ceases to be absolute, ceases to be wholly divine in its reconciling initiative. It ceases to be wholly of God and His grace. And it becomes the mere convenience to which it has sunk in many who are active Christians, but who are losing the eternal background and the heavenly citizenship in the new materialism of social reform treated as the be-all of a Church, instead of a fruit of the Spirit.

The precious thing is not the historic fact of Christ, but the historic Word of Him, the apostolic Word concerning Christ, the interpretation of the manifestation, the supramundane burden and interior of the fact. It is the revelationary purpose, act, and effect of God and grace discerned in Him. It is the grace of God there. More, it is Christ as that revelation, as that living Grace, Christ as Himself the very presence and act of God. It is the entire fact, not simply as a speechless occurrence, a statuesque phenomenon, but with something to say for itself, with

THE GROUND OF RELIGION 145

its proper Word. The fact presents itself in the New Testament inseparably with its own interpretation of itself. The revelation reveals itself, expounds itself, and we have it no otherwise. But that is the same as to say that the fact is not simply the critical residue of the Synoptics, but their totality—the whole apostolic burthen of the New Testament, pervading the Synoptics themselves. The only fact ever offered by the Church is the total New Testament fact, where the synoptic figure of the Lord is self-interpreted by the same Lord acting as the Spirit. The New Testament revelation is the person of Christ in its whole and universal action, and not the character of Christ in its biographical aspect. The Gospels were not primarily concerned with Christ's character, but with His function; not with His personal type, but with His personal office. And Christ remains the personal providence of His own action in history, as Socrates does not. The whole action of that personal fact was not comprised in the impression made by its earthly appearance, nor was it closed when earth was left. The decisive thing was there done, truly, but its whole significance did not there appear. And Christ's apostolic revelation of that significance was a necessary ingredient, an organic part of His whole revealing act, an integral portion of the complete revelationary purpose and process in Him. The whole revelation was in the historic Christ *in petto*, but it was not yet *in power*. His earthly history had to become more historic still. It had to take command of the history in which it emerged by the history it started. He had not indeed to become the Son of God, but He had to become the Son of God *with historic power* in a Church.

The whole revelation, *i.e.*, the outgoing of God to man, was in Christ as a spiritual *fact*. " God was in Christ." But that it might become a *power in*

K

history, it had to receive an interpretation, as "reconciling the world to Himself." How, then, do we know that God's purpose in Christ was such a world-reconciliation?

1. Because it gathered up a whole nation which existed for that universal idea, and which broke upon its great refusal of it.

2. Because, practically and experimentally, the Bible built on it has produced that effect on the human soul though it has far from completed it.

3. Because the Apostles knew above all things else that they were selected by God, and dowered with the spiritual quality and experience which made them recipients of that revelation of revelation. They knew themselves, chosen, gifted, and inspired in such a way that all subsequent Christianity should but move within their finality and enfold it. Were they megalo-maniacs?

This interpretation of theirs, this exposition of Christ, was a providential, integral, and, we might say, polar part of the action of the total fact itself, and not a searchlight thrown on it from without. Christ's finality functioned through the Apostles in self-description, as it did not through the Fathers. "The Lord is the Spirit." The whole revelationary act included the manifestation *and* its posthumous self-interpretation included them in a polar unity. The fact Christ could act only by having a certain meaning, which was guaranteed as its own meaning by His own action in the Apostles. Socrates is interesting for the dialectic in his psychology, Christ for the theology in His psychology, the one for his method the other for His secret, the one as the agent of truth the other as the presence of God.

There is no reasonable doubt that Christ did promise to His disciples the illumination either of the Holy Spirit or of Himself, as the returning expositor and

THE GROUND OF RELIGION 147

translator into history of what He had done. But, when He gave them that promise it was not for their personal edification. His great word was not left for a little clan and its private uses. It was not left for single souls. The spirit was not to come simply for the Apostles' individual sanctification, but as their equipment and authority in declaring the Gospel to the whole world. " Little flock, it is your Father's good pleasure to give you the Kingdom."

When Christ, I say, called His disciples, trained them, and promised them the Holy Spirit, it was not as individual Christians. It was not as a reward of their deep peasant piety ; for their faith was outdone by that of the Gentile centurion. " I have not found so great faith, no not in Israel " and not even in His own circle. It was not simply for the good of their own souls. It was not for their personal salvation merely, as so many brands plucked from the burning. It was a special, corporate, and official vocation—that they might be select witnesses of His revelation to all the world, vehicles of His self-interpretation, and stewards of His universal salvation. He called and equipped them not simply *to* salvation, but *for* it, for unique position and function in the world's salvation ; and in such a way, not that every belief of theirs (like the *parousia*) should be true, but that their version of Him and His central work should be the true one. That was surely His object, as a matter of historic fact. Can His purpose here, then, have been a complete failure ? Their version of what His appearance meant did not place in the centre His words or miracles but His death and resurrection—His atoning death, absolute royalty, and eternal person. His words were not undervalued, as the Gospels show ; which were manuals of Church instruction for converts to the apostolic message. But they were written down in the interest of His consummation as crucified and risen, as the *memorabilia* of one whose value was not in a memory but in a faith, in his " finished work " and constant presence. It was the Apostles' supreme gospel of the dead and risen Lord that made the Apostles' Church (which is the only Church that has come down to us) ; it was not the precious Gospel of His teaching. If, then, this Gospel of the Apostles was not latent in His teaching, but is due to a gratuitous idiosyncracy of theirs—which we must discount as superimposed on the teaching from without, perhaps from some spiritual mythologies around—if that be so, what is the situation ? It is this. It makes Him to be one of the dreamiest ineffectuals of Time. The result of all His training of His disciples, and of whatever He meant by the gift of the Spirit, was such a failure that it left them at the mercy of a perversion which entirely changed His centre of gravity, and distorted His message. What a fiasco for Him, and for His work on them, if, as soon as He left them, they put the Cross, Resurrection, Atonement, and Redemption at the centre, where He put something else ; if they put these things above His words, miracles, and character ; if they foisted on Him and His teaching what it will not bear, and was never meant to bear ; and if they did this so successfully (though illicitly) that the ruling interest of the Church has been diverted ever since from what was His chief interest ! Did He teach so vaguely, train so badly, and impress so poorly that their central Gospel quite misrepresented His true message ? Did His promise of the Spirit to them and the Church mean nothing permanent and protective ? For, of course, it would mean nothing, it would be as futile as His selection and training of His Apostles were, if such a misrepresentation arose. It is impossible to believe in any presence of the Spirit in the Church if its whole history is based on such a perversion of Christ.

THE GROUND OF RELIGION 149

Are we not driven to see that this gift and interpretation was itself an essential part of the whole historic act, of the unitary revealing act of God in Christ. The revelation was to go on in the special and apostolic Word of revelation. The apostolic interpretation is an integral part of the revelationary fact, process, and purpose, a real though posthumous part of Christ's own continued teaching. In the Apostles took place a revelation of revelation—and a revelation of it once for all. That the revelation was in principle completed in the Apostles, I shall try to show a page or two later.

Thus the apostolic Word of the Revelation was not an invasion on the Revelation itself. It was not an interpolation, moving the Revelation away from us by all the diameter of the apostolic mind; whose very greatness would then but increase our distance from its source. It was not a drag, a *remora*, to be scraped off when the story was docked and cleaned in modern ports. But it was an engine and a propeller in the ship's first plan. It was the means of bringing it near to us. It was a sacrament ordained by the Revealer between the Revelation and us. It was a link and not a wedge, a bond and not a bar. It was integral to the Kingdom of God, it was no foreign enclave. It mediated, it did not intermeddle. It was not intercalary; it was organic between the revelation and the soul, between the person and the posterity of Christ. The central theology, the common κήρυγμα of Paul, John, and Peter was not a tentative inroad on revelation, it was not a gratuitous encroachment of apostolic idiosyncracy, nor an impertinent excursion of apostolic genius; but it was a sacramental function of the revelation itself, an integral function in God's complete gift of Himself in Christ. It was not insinuated, and not a guess. It is not otiose, and not a venture. It is an ordained mediator, a living and commanding mediator, and not an inert medium between the revelationary fact and all the spiritual future. It is not a wall that parts the two, but the great switch that connects. By the Spirit the Apostles are the living ligament and modulator in the whole revelationary process.

We gain in depth, therefore, we do not lose in purity, by having the revelation in the apostolic word and interpretation. The revelation becomes its own self-interpretation. It is Christ explaining Himself; it is the Saviour still preaching His salvation not only unsilenced by death but in the fulness achieved by its conquest; it is the Mediator mediating His mediation as an accomplished fact, through the Apostles that it made. The Apostles were not panes of bad glass, but crystal cups the Master filled. They were not mere mediums even, but sacraments. They were not mere channels but agents, not vehicles of Christ but members of Him. They did not merely take their departure from Jesus, they had their life, and function, and truth in Him always. We have no testimony of the fact but theirs, in which also the fact itself touches us. The fact works upon us only in their interpretation. If they are valueless for this interpretation, what is their value for the spiritual fact at all? No wonder the criticism which abolished the apostolic interpretation of Jesus has gone on to abolish His historic reality. Every dilution of apostolic doctrine does something more to dissolve the historic Christ. The Apostles were not like scientific experts or theorisers, who leave us the same access to the fact as they had, the same right to it, and the same command of it. We have no access to the fact but through them. If they are final for the historic fact, they are no less final for its central interpretation.

THE GROUND OF RELIGION 151

So we gain and do not lose by having God's Word in the Apostles' Word. And what we gain is not simply a historic link, due to their priority, but a historic sacrament due to their faith, and, still more, to their commission. They were not documents but sacraments. They did not simply contain the past fact, but continue it and its action—just as the Bible does not simply contain the Word but mediates it to our experience by the same Spirit that put it there. And they continued its finality in the polar sense I have named. They were within Christ's finality. They did not simply reflect it in the same sense as the Church does. They represented Christ more than they did the Church. They stood for Christ to the Church and not for the Church to Christ. And they were not simply the shining summits of the Christian range; they made a diadem in the proffering hand of God. They do not represent simply the first stage in the Church's continuity—its first few vertebræ (so to say). But, so far as concerns the marrow of their Gospel, they were for the Church more like a brain—creative, and therefore authoritative and normative, not as mere fellow-Christians, but as providential personalities, select agents of Christ and the Spirit.

At least they themselves so viewed the matter. They never distinguished their version of the fact from the fact. They took their interpretation (apart from details) to be given them specially by the Revealer Himself, of equal value with His prior words, and therefore as final. They laid, indeed, great stress on Christian growth and deepening insight (1 Cor. ii. 15, 1 John ii. 27); but they never contemplated that their interpretation of Christ would be outgrown, any more than that Christ Himself should be followed and superseded by another and greater revelation. It was His authentic Gospel as the action of His own person on them and in them still. He still taught through them, His spirit endowing them with the charisma of knowledge, in such a way that all the Church's growth in saving knowledge should be growth *in* their Gospel and not *beyond* it. Their interpretation of Christ's work (they taught) was part of His work. All independent conviction among believers was but a deeper and more individualised conviction of the apostolic truth that alone made them free ; it was not a freedom to round on that truth, criticise it, and leave it behind. Such was indubitably their view of their own theology—whether we think them inflated dogmatists for that reason or not. We cannot read John's epistles, for instance, without seeing that this is so. All independent certainty was but a deepened and appropriated certainty of that in which they corporately stood (1 John ii. 24). Such was the whole attitude of the Apostles towards the Church, whether to-day it seem overweening or not. Christ's words about another Stand-by never misled them to think of a more adequate Christ. The interpreting revelation to them was part of the action of Christ's finished work. Faith could only grow *within* the final word, not *to* it. In the word of that Grace they *stood*. They spoke, to be sure, of proving all things, and of independent conviction, but it was a conviction of the attained truth which made them free, not of the freedom in which they might attain the truth. Their truth created their freedom, and did not rise from it. They spoke of an anointing which needed not to be taught of any, but it was the indwelling of the truth they had in the beginning, and not an authority to criticise it, nor an insight to supersede it in the end. The conviction was an "unction," It was the Spirit's individualising witness, or warm assignment, to each soul of the same Spirit's special action in the Apostles,

THE GROUND OF RELIGION 153

for whom it was the endless energy of the saving fact. The base and condition of all independent certainty was the experience in the Holy Ghost of the apostolic Gospel. It was not an experience otherwise produced, nor a natural idea and expectation of God from a source outside the Gospel, to which their Gospel was led up for inspection and licence. The Gospel was certainly not true just because the Apostles said it was. If they or an angel preached another Gospel it would not be true (Gal. i. 8). But they said it because it was true, because they knew themselves chosen to be the organs of Christ's truth in its spiritual power. It was the whole revelationary fact interpreting itself through them (amid peripheral errors and misapprehensions) as select personalities, vitalised for the purpose with a real, intimate, and revolutionary experience of the truth. And whatever their posterity might see that they did not, it could never see anything which destroyed that truth, nothing but the more manifold grace of that light. The Apostles, unanimously, never thought of their Gospel as a subjectivity, as the product or the ward of human experience ("We preach not ourselves"), and therefore they never put it at the mercy of human criticism, or invited the winnowing winds of other teaching. They did say that their Christians were as responsible to the Gospel as they were, but never that they could have reached the Gospel without them. And they appealed, as I say, to that Gospel even against themselves. They said that all the members of the Church were equal under grace ; but they never allowed that this meant that they all had the same vocation for the community in that grace ; and certainly never that they all had the same authority as they themselves had as Apostles. The Church had no power to prescribe doctrine to these ministers as it has had to all since. They did not allow a right in the Church to be independent of their Gospel on the strength of any individual revelation, or culture, or spiritual freedom. Withal there must be personal, independent appropriation. It was no saving faith which only believed because Apostles believed. There could be no vicarious faith in that sense. "We have heard for ourselves and know that this is indeed the Saviour of the World." That *this* is the Saviour, that the apostolic Saviour is the only Saviour—not that there is, or must be, a Saviour struggling through their guesses and waiting to be disengaged from their mists.

We may not treat the Apostles as the Samaritans treated the woman who had spoken with Him (John iv. 42), with such independence, making them so intermediary, temporary, otiose. They were not merely the first witnesses; nor corrigible to the very centre. In God's intent their witness has a substantial finality for all time. What they testify of Christ was not just the product of ordinary religious experience in people with a certain temperament at a certain time. They were not just the first in the field with an experience of Christ common to all true Christians. They do not just anticipate an experience of Christ which every believer wins for himself anew, in a churchless way, without necessary reference to others. That was not their conception of Christian independence. They did not just stand alongside of us all and face God in a common but early attempt to express what we all feel as faith. As Apostles they do not simply head the Church, and form its van on the way to God; they stand on God's side, as the ministry must always do, facing the Church, and bringing to it a real gift from God ahead of their own experience, a more than tentative version of the Gospel. They were not "eminent Christians." They were elect souls for a special work, providential stewards of the truth aspect of the revelation which was in Christ

THE GROUND OF RELIGION 155

as person. We all own that the Gospel comes to us only as experience ; is it experience quite parallel to that of the Apostles, quite collateral, not to say rival, or is it experience of something final in theirs, which is ours only because it was theirs, only through the special insight given them in their providential place ? The revelation of the saving God was nowhere but in the Christ whom the Apostles preached ; and in their preaching of Him they bore a very different part from that which the woman of Samaria played for her townsmen. They were more than reporters of what Christ had done for their soul. Apostolicity is something much more than priority or forwardness in confession. Peter's impulsiveness was not his inspiration. Our apostle is not the first man that meets us with the news of Christ. There is nothing sacramental about a reporter. He is not a herald, whose person is sacred, but a newsman. What the Apostles had to tell was much more than their own prior contact with Christ, or intimate experience of Him. The possession of an individual experience and the desire to hurry out with it is not the apostolic call, the call to the ministry, however useful it might be to mutual edification in an experience meeting. The Apostles did not simply call attention to Christ, nor simply say what He had done for them, and then invite their hearers to repeat their experience, beginning where they began, and developing a fresh experience *ab ovo*, as if theirs had not been. They were called to be Apostles, and not merely saints, to be prophets, and not merely homilists. They had more than the word of exhortation. They were stewards in the household of faith. They had charge of the stores. They had a central place of their own, integral in an economy of the Spirit and the providence of the Gospel. They were providential personalities in such a way that our independent certainty can only be certainty of a Gospel which we have from God in their interpretation alone, and for whose central meaning we are dependent on them. The Holy Spirit that made them Apostles could but go on in the Church to open up their Word ; there was no idea of a later and parallel revelation, to say nothing of a superior, by which their Gospel could be judged and outgrown.

As a matter of fact, I have said we have in the New Testament no version of Christianity but the apostolic. We have none anywhere. The Gospels float in the Apostolic Gospel. Not only is Luke Pauline but even Mark. We have in the New Testament but apostolic Christianity, *i.e.* a theological Christianity, Christ interpreted in that apostolic way. And so the great question of the hour is how far this is final. Did the Apostles capture the subsequent history of the Church just because they were like other prominent Christians, but happened to get in first ? Or were they appointed and equipped for a providential illumination and stewardship ? All other forms of the Inspiration question are for the moment out of date.

This, of course, is a position of immense significance for the perpetual place of the Gospel, and of the Bible in particular, as has often been pointed out. It raises more than the Inspiration question ; it stirs the question of Revelation, and therefore of the final authority which belongs to Revelation always. It means that there was a close of strict Revelation, a specific revelationary period, outside which the word revelation takes another sense, inferior and expository. It means that in the interpretation of God's act in Christ we have from the Apostles the version authoritative and insuperable. The ultimate fact of Christianity is historic in such a way that its initial interpretation represents the moral element final and vital for

THE GROUND OF RELIGION 157

every age, and at bottom most active in it. The New Testament, taken as a whole, is perpetually and exclusively canonical for conscience, sanctity, guilt, and grace. It does not form just the first stage of patristic literature, and of the whole classic literature projected from Christianity, but it is the authentic revelation of revelation, and projected with it as its penumbra from God. It is the revelation as truth of that revelation which appeared in Christ as historic fact and personal power. The whole issue of the Reformation is bound up with the view that there we have deposited with us an authentic but indirect interpretation from Christ Himself of the revelation direct in Him, and one final, though germinal and not statutory. Apart from this view the Bible may be treated as a historic source, or it may be used as a manual of edification or a book of devotion (to say nothing of its literary worth). But it will then differ from other edifying books only in degree. It will not have a place all its own. We cannot then make it the norm of all possible revelation, and the great sacrament of it—coming in, as a sacrament should, to abolish time and space, and give us direct contact with Him in a mediate immediacy. And the Church is then not tied to it; and may at any time replace it by an anthology in which its finest passages are printed side by side with similar passages from all the religions or geniuses of the world. But the Bible of the race is not a volume of cosmopolitan selection, but the volume of a condensed election, the record not of our spiritual development but of our crucial redemption, declaring in the seed what it is impossible to exhibit in a bouquet—the whole counsel of God. And so also the Christ of man is the historic Jesus, and not the ideal spirit of a divine Humanity, in which we are all Christs according as we give that spirit free course with us.

So that the burning question about the Bible

is whether the apostolic version of Christ is an interpolation which parts us by all its ideal greatness from the authentic revelation, or whether it is the Revealer's statement of the ultimate Christian fact, God's own sacrament of the great Gospel and true creed. Is *der ganze geschichtliche Christus* a perversion of *der wahre historische Jesus?* What we say is that the Spirit is *in* the apostolic word, it is not simply *with* it and *in* us. Nothing we might call inspiration in us is of the Holy Ghost if it move us to revise the distinctive apostolic Gospel and relegate it to a mere initial and superable stage. As Schleiermacher said, any who feel it a relief to be no longer dependent on this Christ, who are thus redeemed not by but from this Christ, are outside the Gospel. That is an inspiration which is more of fantasy than of faith, and carries the mark of religious and rational man rather than of Holy Gracious God.

The question therefore as to the ultimate revelationary fact forces us on a wholesome choice in a deep dilemma. Is our final authority a residual Jesus or a compendiary Christ? Is it the Jesus found at the bottom of the crucible of synoptic criticism, or is it the Christ who interprets Himself in the plerophory of an apostolic Gospel? Is it a net Jesus or a gross Christ; an elemental Jesus, or the whole New Testament Christ; a nuclear Jesus, coated with a syncretistic Christ woven of parti-coloured moonbeams shining in from a farther east, or a total Christ, who is the essential " truth " of the historic Jesus and His consummation; who is the truth also of all the aspirations latent in those pagan ideas which seem most Christian?

One of these alternatives dissolves Christianity. It may well be that current Gnostic ideas played for Paul a similar part to that which Jewish ideas played

THE GROUND OF RELIGION

for Jesus, providing a mental dialect for his truth to use. But if apostolic Christianity is but a tentative interpretation by local formulæ of an elated religious experience which was in itself no more than impressionist; if it was a strong but dim dynamic and not a positive self-revelation of the eternal nature and action of God—then Christianity is but a makeshift or a stage, and we wait the real and final revelation still. If on the other hand Christianity is the direct gift and product of the superhistoric Christ, then we have found because we are found, we know in the strength of being known, and we love, because, being loved, we are loved to the end. We are not looking for a Saviour; our outlook is the vision of the saved. And we do not grow *to* Christ, but *in* Him.

B.—SANCTITY

VIII

THE OBJECT OF RELIGION

WHEN we say that psychology gives no values, that the Christian Gospel is autonomous though not indifferent to psychological form, that God is there His own authority, and that Christ, the Judge of all, cannot be brought to the bar of reason, nor made to depend on the permissions of our intellect, heart, or conscience—when we say that, we certainly do create a real difficulty, and one that it is not easy to surmount. It seems to throw us back on a crude external dogmatism, or at best an ecclesiastical positivism like that of Duns Scotus. It is especially hard doctrine for a weakened type of religion, unsure of itself yet enamoured of sanity, and accustomed to wait upon rational proof without the venture of faith. For many it is hard to realise that we may not apply to Christ the criticism which we must apply to the records of Him.

The difficulty is real because we ask at once, in the presence of such a σκληρὸς λόγος, " But how can I attach any value to Christ except as He appeals to something in me whose answer countersigns His claim ? Is there not an *a priori* in me with which He must set up a harmony, even if it is a harmony pre-ordained by Himself in my creation ? " This is a very telling point, and to examine it may be of much value.

First, I would point out that the action on a sensitive surface is not the same thing as the appeal to a judge. While Christ besought His disciples' sympathy, before Pilate's bar His silence was a King's. Response is other than proof. When light or colour falls on the retina it produces a response which has in it all the mystery of matter's action on mind, but it is an æsthetic impression; it is not a judgment, moral or intellectual. We may have a sensibility for God, equally mysterious and real, which is yet not a verdict on Him, and need not keep Him waiting upon our scrutiny and decision. The eye is *sonnenhaft*, we know not how. The artist responds long before he criticises, and mostly he is not critical at all. God has points of affinity and attachment in us which are not criteria. He does not appear before the bar of man; but the Father does say and we hear Him say, " My Son, give Me Thy heart." God is His own authority for the religious, and therefore at last for the race; and He is the only Authority we have in the end.

Yet it is quite true that our response to Christ is not a blind one; it is not impressionist, and not merely automatic. It does imply a judgment, or at least a preference (see next chapter). The point is that it does but imply it, it does not wait on it. The verdict is *in* the response, not *before* it. It is the verdict of the will in faith, not of intelligence. The verdict *is* faith, it is not a prior condition of faith. The judgment is latent in the act of faith, it does not precede it. We do not review God's claims and then admit Him as we are satisfied. Indeed we do not know how good His claim is till we have met it, and long lived on the surrender to it. We must taste to see. We must love Him to know how worthy of our love He is. We do not assent and then trust. That would reduce grace to persuasion, and faith to being talked over or argued down; and from grace and faith alike the divine element of miracle would disappear. The rational would be the only

THE OBJECT OF RELIGION 165

divine, and the licencer of the divine ; and only if things were ordered would they be sure. Religion is romantic so far as this, that the reality behind it is "irrational," or, if I may use an unfamiliar but apter word, alogical. But it is not an imaginative irrational, nor a metaphysical (which means Agnosticism), but a moral, as I hope to show.

But this point must be dealt with more fully later. For the present let us bear down on the question from another tack.

Religion is the root of all final certainty, all certainty on final things, on the things which make life worth while at last. What is it then that distinguishes religious certainty from every other ? What is the specific mark of the religious consciousness ? Is it something subjective to us and our make-up, something which marks it off functionally, something in the organ of apprehension, something at our end of the perceptive act, something peculiar to the psychological process, to religion as a faculty, and distinguishing it from other faculties like knowing or feeling ? Is the object of religion something reached, just like any other object of perception, only reached by the heart instead of the head ?

Let us here remember, first, that psychology has outgrown the "faculty" stage. We are not faggots of faculties. No "faculty" can exist by itself without the rest, or simply be roped up with them. They are all organised in the unitary action of the whole personality. It is the one indivisible personality that acts in each. In every function of it they are all involved. Scientific knowledge, we have seen, involves more than mind, it involves also an act and effort of will ; it does not come without a conative element, the passion and pressure to know. Belief rests not merely on evidence but on the will to believe. And conversely moral action is impossible without due knowledge. Each "faculty" implies the rest because it is the action of the whole person.

For religion especially this principle is of great importance. Faith is not a faculty. If religion were the function of one particular faculty, in a division of inner labour, it would claim but one side, or perhaps only one facet, of life. It would not cover life. It would have no universal value. It would have no ruling place in the sum of interests or energies. It would be much more tolerant of inconsistencies, two masters and a double life. It would just be one psychological phenomenon alongside of others, with no right to reign or to control life.

> Wer Wissenschaft und Kunst besitzt
> Hat auch Religion.
> Wer jene beiden nicht besitzt
> Der habe Religion.[1]

But we cannot explain the specific feature of religion as the action of a special faculty told off for this purpose. It is not knowledge of a province determined by the psychic organ, not the kind of knowledge appropriate to the faculty concerned, the knowledge, say, of the Unseen; it is not the approach to reality along one line of our action among several others, like art, science, philosophy, ethics, which converge there, and bring different people by their most congenial route to the same point. It is not a path which could be equally well replaced by any of these, so far as destination goes. Religion does not differ from these but subjectively, as a mere matter of psychological function. They have not separate provinces which they rule independently of each

---

[1] If you have science and have art
You have religion, too;
If you have neither, you, perhaps,
Can make religion do.

THE OBJECT OF RELIGION 167

other. There may be a primacy but no independence. Our attitude to each is an indivisible function of the whole rational man. The whole man is turned upon Nature in earnest science, and the whole man is turned on God in real religion. What makes the real difference in our relations to them, in what we call the faculties, comes from the other end. It is a difference in the objects themselves and their behaviour. And what makes religion different from science is not a difference in our subjective function, in our attitude to the same object, in our manner of approach, but a difference in the objects we face and in their behaviour. It is not so much a different instrument as a different object that is at work. The difference is not functional but objective. Without knowledge of a real objective there is no religion, but the kinds of knowledge due to our contact with the objective vary according to the object, and not according to the organ.

In religious knowledge the object is God ; it is not the world, it is not man. And that object differs from every other in being for us far more than an object of knowledge. He is the absolute subject of it. He is not something that we approach, with the initiative on our side. He takes the initiative and approaches us. Our knowledge is the result of His revelation. We find Him because He first finds us. That is to say, *the main thing, the unique thing, in religion is not a God Whom we know but a God Who knows us*. Religion turns not on knowing but on being known. The knowledge in religion is not absolute knowledge but the knowledge that we are absolutely known, in the sense of being both destined, sought, and searched. This makes more than a world of difference between religion and every other relation of man. There can be no mere theoretic, curious, or disinterested knowledge here. No other form of knowledge has such an object (except, in a modified way, our knowledge of each other). Religion, therefore, is different from every other function of the soul, not by a difference native to us or our faculties, but by the difference of its object, and the action on us proper to that object. In religion we know what knows us back again; and not only so, but His knowledge of us is the source of our knowledge of Him. That is not the case with science, nor with art. They are disinterested, religion cannot be.

It is not enough to say that in religion we are in contact with a living personality. That certainly is for religion both true and unique. Neither art nor science puts us in contact with a living personality. Religion does. And it is as essentially different from science or art as personality is different in kind from every other reality. But still a mere contact with personality, however great, does not give us religion. It may give us but our neighbour, our society. It need not give us more than ethic, or a certain impression, or a certain humanism. Religion is none of these. It is not mere contact with a great, and even immeasurable, moral personality. For such a person might be ignorant of us and our contact, neutral to us, heroic in his moral dignity but not divine in his care. Nor is it simply that we know one who knows things; but we know that He knows us, that we know religiously only as we are thus known by Him. It is a knowledge in which He does not simply take cognisance of us, but knows us, in a special sense, with such a creative intimacy as love alone provides. In religion the fundamental movement of the knowledge is in the reverse direction from that of science. In science we move to the object of knowledge; in religion it moves to us. We know Him, as we love Him, because He first knew and loved us.

THE OBJECT OF RELIGION 169

The several false conceptions of God are but variants of the fundamental error that He is for us a mere object of theoretic or disinterested knowledge.

1. Deism, for instance, is treating God as an object of knowledge Who is sharply delimited from the finite world, and is not Himself, therefore, really infinite. He is rather comprehensive than infinite and eternal. He envelops and supervises rather than pervades. He begins where Space and Time end. He stands over against ourselves, who are the subjects of this cognitive knowledge, as the object on which it is directed; He is, therefore, limited by the frontier of our cognisant selves, who reach him rather than respond.

2. Pantheism, again, treats God as a similar object of our attention; only now we invest the reality we so name with an æsthetic aspect instead of a scientific. What we do here is first to realise our soul as a harmonious whole, a closed symmetry, and then to transfer that conception to the whole of reality, and postulate a similar totality there.

Our memories and imaginations fall into a harmonious unity, especially in certain orderly and idealist natures made that way. And we take the bold step of transferring from the aplomb of our self-poised personality, which we do know as a whole, the aspect of symmetrical solidarity, so as to cover with it a universe which we do not know except in a section. Monism is the daring imposition of a subjective, formal, and æsthetic unity, which we feel, upon the whole of reality which we face. It transfers *per saltum* the unity of the soul, of individual experience, to the whole universe of which that soul is but a part. Yet, why should it? It is a huge venture of faith without foundation. It is an æsthetic fallacy, as Deism was a scientific. Monism is a closed combination of scientific and æsthetic perception, which we violently inflict on reality treated as a mere object of knowledge.

3. Theism, again, starting from reality as an object of knowledge transfers to it our moral qualities, and regards it as not only personal but humanely personal. It discards the remote and mechanical associations of Deism, it is more ethical; but it still begins with ourselves as the subjects of knowledge, and treats God as its object; only knowing Him as conscience knows, and not in the way of either science or art. It is quite possible to believe earnestly in a personal God of righteousness without arriving at personal religion. For such religion does not really begin till we know, above all things, that we are known and searched as righteous love does. It is not mere contact with a personal God, but communion with a holy.

The common vice, therefore, of all these imperfect forms of religion is that they treat God as an *object* of knowledge more or less theoretic, instead of treating Him as the *subject* of a knowledge, which is inceptive and creative, as searching as it is infinite, and as particular as it is universal. Each of them reflects but an objective perception more or less one-sided.

Religion is only possible by Revelation. It is provoked *ab extra* rather than impelled *a tergo*. Its root is deeper in God's moving to man than that in man's moving to God. We love Him because He first loved us. It is not aspiration, it is not a temperament, it is not a subjectivity; it is a certain relation to an object which takes the initiative, and which determines all. We only return God's visit. And, therefore, it is not a sense of monistic continuity or affinity with that object, but of confronting it, responding to it, or even of colliding with it. God is God by His difference, even more than by His unity with us. And religion confronts its object not in

THE OBJECT OF RELIGION

scrutiny or criticism of it, but in response, in welcome, in obedience to its visitation. We do not exercise authority, we recognise it.

This attitude is not ours, it is not of our ordinance, it is not at our arbitrary choice; it is created by the object, in its self-revelation, by its moral necessity. It is in its nature miraculous. For miracle is divine and spiritual necessity, acting directly from a person, and not indirectly through an economy. It is a necessity which can be felt by freedom alone. Revelation may or may not be associated with miracle in the external and empirical sense, but it is miraculous in its very nature as a new creation. We can give no reasons for owning God's authority. The will just knows its master, the heart its Lord. That is a fine and noble passage in Coleridge's prose *précis* in the margin of his *Ancient Mariner*: Part IV.

" In his loneliness and fixedness he yearneth toward the journeying moon, and the stars that still sojourn and still move onward, and everywhere the blue sky belongs to them, and is their appointed rest and their native country which they enter unannounced, as lords that are certainly expected and yet there is a silent joy at their arrival."

Revelation does not luminously continue into our particular case the spiritual substance of the world; it is not the assertion of a universal immanence common to us and the world. Its transcendence breaks through all immanence. Revelation is miraculous in its nature, like every access of the transcendent. In his experience of nature (including psychic nature) a man never gets out of the sphere of subjectivity. Science, with its boasted objectivity, is sheerly subjective. The experience it handles is founded in our notions of space and time, which are subjective contributions. A real objective, the certainty of a transcendent reality, we reach only by something in the nature of miracle, something donated and invasive from the living God. Only so do we reach the conviction, so essential for religion, of a reality totally independent of ourselves. No science can give that. To grasp that is to have the habit of mind which fits us for the discussion of the whole miracle question. Its axiom is the miracle of universal grace. Purely critical treatment of miracles, whether from the side of physics or literature, is quite inadequate without the miraculous experience of grace. It takes a miracle to make miracles credible. To science as such they are impossible.

Such is the view even of Troeltsch; who is one of the greatest experts of the psychology of faith, if only because he insists on the psychologist in religion being himself a man of faith, who carries much of his data in his own experience. He is very sympathetic with the immanential idea, in whose interest he makes considerable, and even grave, modification of the absoluteness of Christianity; but he is yet emphatic on this head. He breaks with the principle of immanence as found in Hegel and the Pantheists, and he plants himself firmly on the ground of the supernatural quality of real revelation. He does not, indeed, admit the exclusive supernaturalness of the Bible history; Christianity among religions is only supreme *inter pares*; but he does hold its inclusive supernaturalness. He holds and presses its revelation as the conspicuous summit, as the highest flight, so far, of all the supernatural which really makes itself felt in religious history. Religion is really made what it is by the authoritative *irruption* into the spiritual life of a transcendent and super-rational God. Eucken takes a like position. The deepest thing in human experience does not rise out of the depths of the soul, though it rises within the soul's area, but it descends from the depths of God. It finds us and stands

THE OBJECT OF RELIGION 173

over us, both to command, inspire, and stay us. It enters us, it does not simply blossom from us. It is not projected but revealed. Troeltsch calls it "Grace." It is not elicited but conferred. It carries us, we do not carry it "The history of religion is a chain of divine action and revelation to the spirit of man." And it creates the conviction, which could only be given by One Who saw the end from the beginning, and indeed already possessed that end, that all things work together in a final teleology of redemptive love.

But all this is no matter of scientific or objective knowledge. We do not apprehend the last reality, it apprehends us. What we know is God's holy, and loving, and creative knowledge of us. We do not reach it, it finds us. It is not a necessity of thought, it is a grace of revelation. The lines of human thought may seem, perhaps, on the whole to converge to a teleology as far as we can follow them ; but mostly they do not ; and we cannot tell what might cut across them in the unknown beyond our sight ; and we can, therefore, be sure of the divine consummation only if it is presented to us in advance by Him in Whom it always is—indeed, along with Him, in His gift of Himself, as at once life's Goal and Ground ; which gift is a miraculous thing, and is taken home only by the faith it miraculously creates. The last reason for believing is non-rational. It is not an innate principle to which we refer everything, but a new creation. It is a thing, as miraculous and inexplicable as falling in love ; whose daily occurrence cannot erase the wonder of it, and its invasion of our egoism. Nothing but a miracle can plant our consciousness on the centre of existence, and convince us of the paradox that all immanence is the immanence of the absolutely transcendent, and the humble visitation of the Most High.

The object of Religion, then, is One Who knows us far

better than we know, and knows us upon a universal scale, knows us altogether—*i.e.* absolutely. For religion, the question is not whether we can know the Absolute, but whether we know ourselves as known by the Absolute. We are offered analogies in those social relations which concern religion so much. Our neighbours know us in our act of knowing them; and it is this reciprocal knowledge that is the kind exercised in religion. We have here the point of attachment in natural experience for the knowledge we have of God, in so far as the relation is knowledge. It belongs to that order of knowledge where person meets person, rather than to the order purely and passively objective to our perception, where the percipient person meets a thing or a thought. But every analogue is limited in its contrast with the Eternal. Our own brother does not know us on a universal and eternal scale. He does not know us with the majesty of right and the intimacy of mercy which belong to holy love. He does not know our destiny. He does not make us feel that we know only because we are known with the infinite knowledge of a Creator and Redeemer, known in a way that not only evokes faith but creates it. Religion belongs to that order of experience—our experience of persons known and not of known things—but it is the experience of a person's infinite and creative knowledge of us, a knowledge of us which creates our trust of him. In religion I think; I think of myself; I think of myself as known; but not known by myself. I think of myself not by self-consciousness, not as an object of my own knowledge but of God's; Who knows me as a Will does; Who knows me as " finding " me, as soliciting me to see and not merely waiting to be seen, not merely watching, but bearing me and drawing me, searching and judging me, indeed, but unto salvation.

THE OBJECT OF RELIGION 175

Religion, Faith, is taking home the fact, and not grasping the mere truth, that we are thus known. That fact is the matter of revelation. In the faith that answers revelation we are more sure that we are known than that we know. God gives Himself to our experience as such a God. He does not prove Himself to us. He *comes home*. When a man comes home he does not bring credentials but just himself. He does not treat his family as a jury or a committee of investigation. It is a matter of alogical recognition rather than of rational satisfaction. Truly, if revelation were the communication of truth, it would have to make its appeal to some previous truth to authenticate it, to some rational *a priori*, with which it must mortise. That is always the way new truth comes. It must approve itself to the old. It must dovetail. The sitting judge must scrutinise and pass the commission of his assessor or supersessor. But revelation is not God's gift of truth, but of Himself. And there is nothing great enough in us to prove Him, to pass judgment on Him. We just wake up in our cell one day to realise that there is an eye in the ceiling, and, with a deeper divination, that it has behind it a heart. Our visitor is our helper. We apprehend that we are apprehended. We know nothing so much as that we are known. Revelation is not the presentation of something to be fitted to our prior knowledge; it is making us realise that we and all our knowledge are known, absolutely, eternally, lovingly, savingly known. It does not appeal to our active knowledge on the one hand, nor to our passive plasticity on the other, but to our receptivity. It solicits rather than stamps us. Yet it does not simply elicit a latent spirituality, but it creates something. From a moral freedom it creates a spiritual obedience. All God's direct action is creative. He does not work in an analytic way, opening or releasing the resources of our consciousness. As a mere warm atmosphere He might do that. As a telepathic influence He might do it. But His intimate presence and very self does much more. He is shed abroad in our heart. It is synthetic action. It brings something that was not there. It means a real gift. It is true Grace. Christ is formed within us. Something quickens in us which affects our whole natural constitution in a supernatural way, as a child makes a light girl into a grave mother. It makes us more than conquerors, it makes us redeemed in a new creation. And it goes on to make us creative, productive, in our turn and in our measure.

Revelation means far more than information. It means more than manifestation. It is in the same act Redemption, new Creation. It is not knowledge, I have said, but being known. And known in the special sense, in the sense of being chosen for a destiny. "You only have I *known* of all the nations of the earth"; where the history shows that knowledge is election, and an election to Redemption, to be redeemed, and, in another sense, to redeem.

The *a priori* is therefore not something which enables us to judge, but something which enables us so to be judged as to be redeemed. It is not a test, so that we can act critically on Revelation. Nor is it a germ whose innate resources Revelation develops. But it is a recognising power, a receptivity. It is not an activity, but it is as active as that—as the function of receptive persons, and not merely vessels. We are not as passive as clay to the potter. We are not dead, *perinde ac cadaver*. The knowledge in religion is not theoretic but personal. It is a person's intelligent response to a person. It is the personal power to know as we are divinely known. It is realisation and not discovery. It is more in the nature of sensibility than of knowledge in the scientific sense. Only it is

THE OBJECT OF RELIGION

not a passing sensibility to some aspect of a person, but it is the response of a will to a will, of the whole finite person to a whole person, absolute and holy. It is therefore ethical in its nature, and not merely impressive or sympathetic. It is certainly much more than merely objective, as theoretic knowledge in all forms is. It is far more intimate and reciprocal, more creative and universal. We know not merely *that* we are known, but *as* we are known, *i.e.* with that volitional and emotional knowledge wherewith God knows, *i.e.* wills, them that are his.

When we speak of faith as not of ourselves, but as the gift and creation of God, there is one difficulty sure to arise, even in the simple mind—if not, indeed, chiefly there, mainly because of its simplicity, and its unfamiliarity with more than the face of the subject. It will be asked why then God as prime mover does not create faith at once in every man, or at least in every man to whom the Word of His revelation comes. If He do not, is it not He that is responsible for unfaith and not man?

What seems to underlie the question is a naïve idea of what is meant by creation—as if it were a magician's power to bring out blossoms with a wave of his hand, or place coins suddenly where there were none. Beneath most of the more popular and obvious difficulties to faith will be found some form of prepossession by the magical idea, and an absence, almost entire, of any acquaintance with moral ideas, their peculiar genius, native action, and proper treatment (which carries us back, as most such things do, to defects in our system of education). Creation seems to be thought of entirely out of reference to the idea of moral freedom. It seems to be regarded as the production of a thing instead of a *soul*, and as the making of that thing out of nothing. But, in the first place, nothing could be made out of nothing. The original nothing was not there. There was always and everywhere the Being of God Himself. Creation out of nothing is a phrase with no meaning. It is unthinkable. It is that meaninglessness that has driven many into Pantheism, and especially into the crude form of it, which says that everything is made of God.

That view can become absurd enough when God is thought of as a substance. But if God be thought of as a subject and a soul it is not so absurd. We *are* His offspring, we hold of the Over-soul. We need not begin by troubling about created *things*. The problem and the secret lies with created *souls*. The meaning of creation is given there. When we settle it for the soul we shall not have insuperable difficulty in applying the principle to the world. The created soul is created by soul. Its life is in some form God's life. And if that be so, the real meaning of creation is the output of something which reflects its creator's freedom, and is therefore not a thing but a will. Faith is not a thing but a freedom. It is a soul in a certain relation, a certain state, a certain free act. It is a moral soul coming to itself. It is coming therefore to the freedom which is the unique badge of soul, coming to the higher freedom for which the lower was made. If it was a divine thing to create a man free, a free will, it is a divine thing to emancipate that first freedom—to redeem. But redemption does not abolish the first or natural freedom. It respects it. It can only work under its conditions. It can force salvation, faith, on none. The gift of the Spirit overrules natural character, but it does not obliterate it. It transfigures, but does not erase. The will God made so free that it can resist even Himself. It is free enough to resist even His gospel of more freedom and true freedom. To refuse faith is an exercise of the freedom which makes a soul a soul; only a soul can do it; and that native freedom is not

THE OBJECT OF RELIGION 179

put under coercion by any action of God (for that would destroy the soul), but under responsibility—*i.e.* under the only kind of pressure possible between the Free and the free. It is put under judgment.

There can, therefore, be no talk of God creating faith in us willy-nilly. That were neither creation, faith, nor salvation. There is no such thing as a faith which could be created and inserted in a soul. There is no such thing as a Spirit which comes like a rushing mighty wind, sweeps the soul of all its contents, and settles in as a totally new tenant. Converts are not changelings. Faith is the soul believing. Its creation can only be some action appropriate to soul—*i.e.* to freedom. Redemption is recreating a free soul through its freedom. It is converting its freedom, and not its substance. It does not change its natural psychology. As it is the production of more freedom it must be spoken of as a creation. As it is a creation it can only move within the lines of freedom, and act on its principle. And a freedom that has no lines or principles is not freedom, but caprice. The true line of freedom is positive obedience. Its condition is a positive authority. The old man becomes a new man only by receiving a new master. The new creation is a new obedience ; and the new Creator is one whose perfect service is perfect liberty, and who enables the soul in this submission to find itself and its destiny.

Indeed, in connection with the creative power of Christianity, we might go so far as to say that the revelation in Christ, new as it is, does not make an addition to our knowledge at all in the ordinary sense. It certainly does not extend the object, the area of Being. And the religious-historical school are fond of showing that Christianity did not add even to the stock of religious ideas, and they do so with much success.

That is not the form the new thing takes. It does not extend but recreate. It regenerates. It renews a lost moral power in the guilty soul, and removes the grand obstacle in the will to the realisation of our true nature.

The truth is that Christianity has little to do with our nature and everything with our will. I would go so far as to say that the chief error in the thought of our time upon the matter is the tendency to seek the relation between God and Man in our nature and constitution rather than in our will and state; to dwell on the godlike marvel and promise of that excellent creature man and ignore his attitude to the most godlike thing made known to him; to approach grace from nature instead of nature from grace; to prize grace only as it meets the best expectations of nature, or confirms its best achievements, instead of prizing nature as exploitable for grace; to treat the image of God as if it were the actual glory of our natural Humanity instead of its ear-mark and far destiny, slowly to be won, and not without a new creation; to magnify the æsthetic splendours of human faculty and feel nothing of the impotence of the human will for its grand destiny of steady and living communion with God; and, generally, to dwell on Humanity as an æsthetic quantity before its members, and ignore it in its ethical state before a holy God. We start with the first of Genesis instead of the first of Romans. We frame a great humanist, Christ, irrelevant to the miracle of Grace, and then of course we find nothing in the denial of all His miracles which need depreciate the value of such a Christ. We begin with a great human nature whose spiritual summit is symbolised in Christ, and then we trim the Christ of the New Testament grace and redemption down to the pattern of that mount.

What is extended by the revelation in Christ is not

THE OBJECT OF RELIGION 181

our human constitution and faculties, which have always been glorious, but our power to use them upwards instead of downwards. What is extended is our soul's moral power, and especially by a new creation of loving power, not of knowledge; and this by the gift of the divine Soul and the divine love, and not by truths from Him. It works by God's gift of Himself in His Son and Spirit. Certainly what comes is not out of relation to what it finds there. It could have no meaning if it were. But the relation is not that of truth which seeks licence and authority from truths, laws, or excellencies already enthroned. It is by no such means that God is realised in a distinctive Christian faith as Holy Love, but it is by a new output of creative power, lifting us to God's right hand, whence everything falls into a new scheme and a new perspective. All things then work together for the love embodied in the redeeming purpose (Rom. viii. 28). What is given us in the Christian revelation is rather the co-ordination, in a living and acting unity, of all the elements, even the contradictory elements, that make up our notion of God's creative power, moral freedom, fatherly love, and holy grace. These come with such convincing force as is exerted by a personality alone. Only a living personality in its native and redeeming action can reconcile in Himself the various and seemingly inconsistent demands that we make on a God, such as infinite knowledge, infinite power, infinite holiness, and infinite love in such a world as this. Only the direct action and presence of a living God, Who gives Himself in personal acts, enables us to trust and worship Him as holy Love. The new commandment is the old with a new power.

The mysticism which is essential to religion is not therefore a glow sent through a natural *a priori*, the transfiguration of a human postulate by a divine current, the elevation of a latent religiosity in us to high and ruling place. It is not hard to be content with a notion like that if we are thinking only of what is called natural religion, if we go, for our idea of religion, to its most elementary and universal forms, to the attenuated region where all men are religious and susceptible to some form of the spiritual in proportion to its lack of moral demand. That is beginning at the lower end, like the anthropology which looks for real human nature in the savage rather than the civilised. But the true idea of religion is rather given us in its classic forms. We must gauge the lowest by the highest, and not the other way. We shall not measure faith by religion, but religion by faith. The secret, the " truth," the burthen, the soul of natural religion is in supernatural faith. That was the holy thing that should be born of it. We begin with Christ, with the revelationary fact which takes command of us, and of everything, in Him. Christianity, as the eternal establishment of the Holy, has the key of all the creeds. It is not simply their analogue.

If then we start with the distinctive and classic Christian experience, we cannot, by any due analysis of its crucial cases and experiences, come out with the notion that the only effect of God's revealing action is to stimulate, or kindle, some innate *a priori*; as the contact of the outer world might stir to action the regulative resources or categories of the reason. There is something much more mysterious, incalculable, and " irrational " than that. Religious belief is not produced as rational belief is, by a must, but by an ought; it is not by compelling evidence which leaves the mind no choice in the face of facts. True, in religion, the fact, the object, like other facts, has a constraining power. But it is one that leaves us with a moral freedom they do not respect. In the face of the

THE OBJECT OF RELIGION 183

religious fact we are free. We are free to believe or not believe, trust or not trust, as in science we are not free, as we are not free with any theoretic knowledge of a mere object. Religion, faith, is not simply a fresh experience following necessarily on the stimulus.

The real problem when we close down on it, and do not hover round it, is this. These mystic movements of ours in connection with the object of religion—are they really impressions made on us by that transcendent object, or are they perhaps subjective illusions, rising from something only immanent to us, and deflected as they rise by all kinds of subjective error or circumstance? That is the question. And it is one that can never be settled by any psychology, or any theory of knowledge. We arrive at certainty and escape from illusion here, not by an act of rational judgment, but by an act of voluntary choice. Faith is at last a resolve; not a state of the self, but a disposal of the self. It contains a venture. The religious life is a great and standing decision, or a rising scale of preference. (Chap. IX.) We can refuse, or we can consent, to yield to the strongest evidence, when it is a question of practical religion, of living faith. It is our personality, not our rationality, that is at work—not even our sympathy. We can sympathise with a right we do not practically own. *Video meliora proboque, deteriora sequor.* We can answer the revelation of God in Christ only by a choice, a resolve, a committal. As Revelation is God disposing of His personality to us in grace, faith, if we are to answer in kind, can only answer by disposing of our personality to Him. We do not respond according to an irresistible law of our nature, but according to a free choice of our will. Any theory of knowledge, therefore, which is to fit the classic facts of the religious case must be a theory of the knowledge peculiar to faith—the sense of being known.

That is to say, theory cannot reach the ultimate nature of the act. For we believe in the grace of Christ crucified only by a miracle. Human nature is against it. Faith is something created in us by the nature of that act, rather than accorded by us on any kind of evidence. It is not only a free resolve but it is a created freedom. It is our moral freedom re-created by God's loving "knowledge." It is not the affinity of a personal section of the monistic substance with its universal movement, however we rarefy the substance. It is not the continuity of the great spiritual stratum with an outcrop at an individual spot. That is a kind of religion which may run out to Materialism, or to Theism, according to circumstances. It is not by any such pre-established harmony that we can secure the universality of Christian faith, and therefore of true religion. God cannot be known, like an object of disinterested knowledge, by our discovery or arrival at Him. We might so know a mere historic fact—even Christ. But that is not religion—not even if we regard the fact with the most sympathetic interest. God can only be known as the interested subject of knowledge, *i.e.* as the Revealer, as the Giver of Himself to our most intimate case and need, for a purpose which engages us and our whole self absolutely. He is known as our Redeemer into His holy Kingdom, Whom we only know as we are thus known into life and knowledge. Therefore, what we contribute is not that judgment by previous truth, whereby we test real discovery, but rather the sense of being judged and saved. Ours is the need and the receptivity, the choice, the owning, not of a *Must* but of an *Ought*, wherewith we meet a personal presence and a personal effect, and to which we surrender and do not merely assent.

In a plain word God does not appeal with His reve-

THE OBJECT OF RELIGION

lation in Christ's Gospel to man's native and general religion of aspiration, but to his actual concrete situation of guilt. The more natural factor is our sense of God's exigent and judging Will (especially in His revelation as holy) ; and the supernatural factor is His calling and saving voice amid the judgment (and especially from amid the judgment of the Cross). Again, Revelation is Redemption. His illumination is our condemnation. But nothing damns like what saves. Nothing gives such a blow to all our natural self-satisfaction and self-sureness. But also nothing produces such certainty as our knowledge by the searching saving God. And we can have no sound certainty in an age in whose central concern poverty has taken the place of guilt.

By nature we think religion real by its mediate congruity with what we know, or its direct remedy for what we suffer ; *by grace* we find it real through the immediate experience that we are known, known as holiness knows, known as love knows, and saved as grace saves. God is greater than our heart, than our consciousness, our soul, not because He knows more, but because He knows all things, *i.e.* knows absolutely, and knows *us* so—because He knows us as only the absolutely Holy can, knows us creatively, searches and judges, as only the Holy can, unto salvation, forgives as He only can who holily atones, loves us into love, and elects us into life.

So, in this point of view, the problem of the hour is not theological but psychological. It is not the problem of the Incarnation but of Faith. It is not " How could God reach man ? " but " How can man receive God ? " Not " How could God become historic ? " but " How can our faculties find God in history ? "

And there is no answer to it in academic psychology —none but in the religious and experimental—in the experience that we do find God only in being found by Him, and know Him only in the knowledge that we are known of Him. Faith is a real organ of such knowledge; and for religion, for God, for any personality, it is the only one. We are religious not as we ask " How am I to judge about God ? " but as we ask, and are answered, " How does God judge about me ? " Not " Can I believe with reason ? " but " Do I trust with my whole self, and strength, and mind ? "

But it looks sometimes as if men would be religious everywhere but in the treatment of religion.

IX

THE VOUCHER OF RELIGION

I REFERRED at the opening of the last chapter to the difficulty created for many minds by the necessary reference of a revelation to something within us. This inner forum, by seeming to act as the criterion of revelation, seemed also to rob it of a supreme authority. It seemed to make God's right wait on the permissions of human reason or the human heart, and man to sit in judgment on his Judge. Religion seemed to be kept waiting for philosophic or genial consents, and therefore to be a matter of rationality or sympathy in the final issue. Religion would then be preserved only in so far as it showed itself capable of being lifted, by a reference to the subjective *a priori*, into scientific certainty—which is absurd.

I ventured to deal with one aspect of this question in the preceding chapter. Religion is not knowing God but being known of God. But I recognise that it was rather a flank and turning movement than a direct engagement with the difficulty—effective, I must believe, but not conclusive. In many minds will still remain the double question : Is there not something in me to which any revelation must appeal ? And, if so, is that something not the authority which gives revelation its leave and its course ? So that the real revelation is in man rather than in Christ. God's supreme revelation, to which even Christ must appeal, is Humanity. Humanity is the only begotten Son of God. A conclusion this whose subjectivism would in due course ease God out of the picture altogether by first reducing Him to a merely synergistic place in the religious process. The main root of religion would then be the subjectivity to which all culture tends, and from which religion should protect us. We should be more interested in the kind of religiosity than in the kind of God, in our sincerity than in His reality—as many Christian people actually are to-day.

Moreover, Religion would then be regarded only as one among others of the great interests necessary for a Humanity fully and symmetrically developed. As science, art, or ethic arise out of the development of certain principles or impulses native to man, and could not but arise, given these fundamental laws of consciousness, so with religion, it would be held. Religion would be a product of that teeming Humanity whose evolution, under God's sunshine, made the course of civilisation. And it would have its charter where art, science, or ethic had theirs—in certain laws or tendencies of human nature. Everyone who had any share in the deeper interests of civilisation would then also share in religion and its sympathies, on pain of being declassed from the life of culture. Whereas religion differs entirely from these other interests in being much more a responsible matter of choice and freedom, and much less an æsthetic matter of necessary spiritual evolution. It stands under other criteria of truth and reality than theirs, other than logic or taste, or ethic. It has an autonomous life, a truth of its own, and its own authority. It places us, as these other interests do not, before an object where we are chiefly concerned not with knowing, but with being known, not with our certainty of God but with God's certainty of us, which to share is to own the Authority Eternal. There is now a wide recognition of the fact that the religious experiences form a group by themselves, with

THE VOUCHER OF RELIGION 189

a qualitative independence; that they are independent of their prehistoric and anthropological origins (which are of little value for a philosophy of religion); that they form an autonomous territory with a home rule that does not look elsewhere for imperial authority; that the appeal of Christianity must therefore be to religion rather than to reason; farther, that the investigator of religion must be chiefly concerned with the religion of the present, and not only so, but that he must consider a personal experience of religion an essential part of his scientific equipment; and that little or nothing can be done with those who start with the supremacy of our rational relations with nature or society, and have no religious experiences of their own giving a direct and even miraculous relation to reality.

Two things we must recognise. First, we must own the justice of that demand for some *a priori* in the soul to which the revelation comes, and on which it strikes its proper note. But, second, we must perceive that this *a priori* is not in the region of the reason but of the will. Its function is not criticism but obedience, not rational legitimation but moral response, not a voucher that the papers are in order, but an act of personal homage. It is not a case of new truth being fitly framed and built together into the truth we already possess, or a new process shown to continue the spiritual movement native to the soul What is so often overlooked is that in its highest forms revelation comes as a blow on the " old man " rather than a bloom. When it comes as the revelation of the holy, what it elicits is indeed response, but it is at first the response not to something congenial but to something contrary to us, or at least judging us, not to something which affirms ourselves on a great scale but to something which arrests us rather than promotes, which rebukes us more than it realises us, and which even condemns us utterly. How is the Word of God to approve itself to man when it comes with such a blow to human nature, when it humbles thoughts and desires that all go to magnify and assert the natural man at his best, to extend his egoism, and even to exploit God for the purpose? Truly such a word wakes a response to itself, but it is not the glad response of the eye which is *sonnenhaft* ; nor does Eternity here but affirm the conviction of an hour. It is the response of a will's penitent submission, confession, and self-committal. If the essence of all revelation is gathered up in the Christian revelation its nature is such as I have described. It does not ask our criticism, it begins at once by striking our weapon from our hand and criticising and judging us. If we attempt to base Christian certainty upon our natural certainty what we feel, when we grasp the meaning of the Christian Gospel and its approach to us, is not certainty but misgiving. Its first effect is to shake our confidence in ourselves and our certainties. If I am asked to credit a personal God revealing certain truths by the aid of miracle I can go a long way to challenge it, on the ground of things whose certainty seems an integral part of my legitimate self-satisfaction, my natural order, and my rational confidence in myself or anything. But if the revelation be the approach to me of the Absolute and Eternal Himself, in all His holy love—what is this that such my Lord should come into me? I am in no condition to receive Him—far less to haggle at the gate. It was all very well in my office or my laboratory. If one had come to transact with me the business I am used to there, I could meet him with my things and thoughts in order and control, even if he brought business from court and a commission from the King. But when he comes to me at my home in its very

THE VOUCHER OF RELIGION 191

sanctum, and to my conscience in its very adytum, comes in person as the King and Conscience eternal, when He comes to remind me of what no other being knows, what I cannot deny, but thought was dead and done with; when *I* am set full in front of the Holy One, and am put upon my mettle to answer, my mettle breaks and my spirit fails. His Word, which in the flush of my faculties I thought to evade, issues from the Great White Throne, and I am affronted, and speechless, and without plea. My response is but to confess, obey, trust, and worship. And it is not elicited, as if it were my native best, but it is created in me by the very power which reveals my worst. The supreme Authority of His grace creates a response of faith which His holiness alone would awe and benumb. When all is said, the reason why we believe in the miracle of Grace is a miracle. It is not of ourselves, it is the gift of God. It belongs to the region of what I have said it is now common to call the Irrational. The response is not elicited, it is created. The last Authority creates its own recognition. Our faith is the gift of God, given with a Christ whose nature it is to create belief. It has the mystery that lurks in every preferential choice.

The appreciation of religious value means an act of choice, and not a phase of sensibility, nor a mere verdict. Whether we say that religion is better than no religion, or that one religion is better than another, it means an act of preference. There is a collision and a competition for us; and the judgment we pass is according to standards which belong not to the intelligence merely but to the will. It implies more than a perception, it implies a committal, more or less, or a preference at least. There is a dilemma and a selection. There is a recognition of superior excellence. When the new fact is accepted, our former faith is not simply continued or enlarged, it retires.

There is a way of viewing the matter which says that the true Word commends itself to us as the prolongation and expansion of some principle we already have. Such, I have said, is the religion of Monism. The soul there is bidden to recognise in God the universal sum of its own being. God comes as soul made absolute. So with the religion of Humanity God is but man writ large, Man is God in the germ. Heavenly fatherhood is but earthly magnified, as if the holiness of it made no generic difference. Any revelation of God (like Christ) differs from man as God Himself does, only in degree. God is man taking fullest effect. In God man finds himself on the infinite scale. God is man's infinite continuity. The fundamental relation is one of identity. To be glorified we have but to be amplified. When God and man meet, it is but the fusion of the universal and the particular. It is the joining up and fitting in of the large half and the small half of a proxenic tessera. The design whose lines begin on my small end, I find completed when the large end is brought to it. And that bringing and fitting is revelation. What is revealed in God is a grand rational continuity of Monistic idealism, which we test by piecing it to the spiritual idea we already have. These patterns are thus prolonged and finished. They come to themselves. Our past receives itself, finds itself, feels justified in its infinite Self. It is pushed forward, asserted, vindicated, and realised.

But all this, while it makes an infinite extension of our horizon or our self-consciousness, is not religion. We may call it idealism, or what we will, but it is not religion ; and it does not produce the great fruits of religion, like dependence, humility, or at last, freedom. Its love becomes a kindly charity. Life loses its passionate content and falls to an evolutionary idea. In

THE VOUCHER OF RELIGION

true faith our past is not so much prolonged as superseded. Our "old man" is "put off." The old values are not so much enhanced as outbidden. The new thing overbears them. It comes with an urgency, a monopoly, a creator's right to reign over us, and not simply with a power to expand us. The past is not simply as good as the future only much smaller; it is inferior. Such is the nature of religious progress, and especially at its outset. And its course, its development, is a series not of expansions but of preferences. We do not so much realise our past, we renounce it, or at least we teach it its place. The new is not bigger but better.

This means a real difference in the function of the soul's *a priori*. It is not a rational test but a moral recognition. It does not accept the new in so far as the new repeats it on an ample scale, owns its laws with imperial range, and continues its natural principles into infinity. It does not go through a quantitative growth but a qualitative experience. It owns in the new something intrinsically *better and higher* than its natural principle. It recognises a new right over itself, and not a new range in itself. There is a new regime in its old world. It is not a case of greater extension, but of greater excellence. For its choice it could not always give a sound reason. It could not pass a considered verdict on the credentials of the newcomer. But it knows in him its master. "This sort of happiness often brings so much pain with it that we can only tell it from pain by its being what we would choose before everything else because our souls see that it is good."

There is then an *a priori*, but it is neither a rational test nor a spiritual germ. It is a moral potency and freedom. It recognises rather than contributes. It owns a right, but it confers none. We do not sit in judgment on the reasonableness of God's truth, nor do we develop our innate spirituality in the warm sunshine of His light, to find Him as our infinite self. Religion does not mean that human nature is enabled to assert its own principle on a grand scale. It is not our spiritual rationality. It is not the glorification of man's spiritual constitution, it is the redemption of his impotent will. It recognises Another, greater and better, Who is revealed ; Who comes to us, gives Himself to us ; Who does not give us to ourselves so much as enable us to give ourselves to Him, and to find ourselves only there ; Who demands our humble acknowledgement of His preferential right, and does not simply exalt our self-respect by affirming before us our larger selves.

Religion is thus at bottom a moral act in a mystic sphere. It begins in a choice between two conflicting values. We are religious because the divine comes as a contrast for our choice, and not as a continuity for our completion. Able missionaries tell us that the heathen (who are far from devoid of family affections) understand and prize more a God who delivers them from the evil spirits that they painfully worship than one who is a gracious Father to the prodigal. A God of redemption means more than a God of magnified fatherhood, forgiveness, or reconciliation. Christianity spread not because it was an enlarged and enlightened Judaism, but because it was different and better by all the range of a trinitarian God. And Paul kept reminding his converts of what marked his own experience in conversion, that they had not simply realised their past but rounded on it, and had not developed their better selves but condemned and put off the old man and his deeds.

It is, therefore, not a case of rational continuity as in Monistic Idealism, where we test the revelation or absorb it, but a case of moral preference, choice, and committal, in which the revelation tests and judges

THE VOUCHER OF RELIGION 195

us. We do not realise ourselves in Christ so much as submit ourselves. We do not accept Him on His credentials; we fall down dead before Him. We select; we have not only an influx of new life. Our will is summoned to its feet—to bow down and rise ennobled. We select higher values as we make spiritual progress; we do not only get more power and room. We receive not only something new, but something worth more. The comparison is not simply an act of estimate but of choice. We have to do with moral norms and not logical laws. The principles that guide are not only those of assessment but of action. We find in ourselves ready to hand certain native movements or directives of the will (as well as axioms of the logical reason). They work at first unconsciously or instinctively. But we cannot do them violence without denying and damaging our existence as spiritual beings and moral personalities. The free will has laws in its own kind. There are imperatives which are independent of our subjective whim, but which make themselves felt with a spiritual necessity in the deep interior of our personal will. They embody a certain intelligence, but it is the bystanding intelligence of the moral nature and not the outstanding intelligence of thought. The act is not magical just because it is not solely rational. The irrational here is not what is below reason but above it, as an exercise of that moral freedom which is not ruled by law or process (however influenced). To be rational here, in the narrow sense, would destroy freedom; it would be determinism. These norms of the will, as we may call them, by distinction from the laws of logic, emerge into action in the collision of different values. They emerge in the clash of lower and higher. And they contain a certain compulsion, which baffles our analysis, to prefer the higher to the lower. Both are motives, both are impulsive. They are not merely æsthetic. They are not there just to be seen and known in a scientific way. But among motives some are imperative and not only impulsive.[1] And what does that mean but this, that they rouse in us the sense that they ought to be *preferred* to all the motives that are impulsive only. They come with authority, but with moral authority, with an ought and not a must. And this is the region where religion has its seat and its appeal.

There is such a thing, then, as a religious *a priori* in us, though it is not an authority but the power to own authority. It is not a passivity but a receptivity, a loyalty, an obedience. Revelation does not come to us as if we were blank paper, dead matter, or blind forces. It finds something to appeal to, to stir, to evoke. But this *prius* resides in the will and its power, not in the reason and its truth. It is a voluntarist *prius*, and not a noetic. If we are to preserve the autonomy of the religious will we cannot reduce it to the action of a rational process and its laws. Kant saw that. But it is also true that there must be some nexus between what revelation finds and what it brings, if our nature is to be reconciled by grace, and not rent. And that nexus is found in the norms which guide the will and make it more than a blind elemental force. They are *a priori*, because they are not produced by experience, but, on the contrary, are there to receive experience and make it possible. So far they correspond to similar elements in reason. But they are not the same. Nor are they authoritative in the same way. Their authority, as I have said, is that of an ought and not of a must. It is a moral supremacy and obligation that is revealed. We choose on certain active principles, we do not simply continue on lines which passively prolong us,

[1] Wundt.

THE VOUCHER OF RELIGION 197

and which enable the Monist to integrate his atom of spiritual thought with the thought universal. Revelation has its influence on the heart and will and not on the perceptions. It makes a man choose, else it does not reach the centre of his being but leaves him cold. But it is a receptive choice on our part, it is not a creative. It does not dispose of the revelation but of the self through its treatment of the revelation. It does not, therefore, judge so much as it is judged. It does not know so much as own that it is absolutely known. The ground of the truth of a revelation is not its correspondence with some law of consciousness, or some general principle of the race's religion. It cannot even be traced in history without some prior standard to guide us. By the Spirit we try the spirits if they are of God. We need a revelationary point in history to give us a measure for judging the final tendency of what seem revelationary lines. If they only converge outside history perhaps they never converge, so far as we know. The revelation which is the measure and truth of all revelation is in history but not of it ; it is final there, if it is not completed—final but perfectible ; and it is accessible to the believer in its Word and not the diviner of its mere trend. An inductive law, gathered from a historic area not yet finished, cannot be allowed to act as a criterion of final revelation, or a means of its purification. The great revelations bring with them their own standard, their own sifting and purifying principle, their principle of self-elevation and preservation. The Lord is that Spirit. They are autonomous in proportion to their dignity. The inductive and scientific laws are not compatible with the moral freedom which is a first requisite of religion as it rises in the spiritual scale. The will, the moral man, must carry its ruling principles in itself. It cannot wait upon those of the pure intellect. We cannot wait to believe in Christ till a due examination of the religious psychology of the race, or of the metaphysic behind it, gives us leave; till we are convinced that Christ does not wound the general and fundamental principles of racial religion. There is no inherent and obvious necessity that the will should act according to the principles of the reason, and it often (some say mostly) acts in their despite. These principles of the will can be intellectually stated, but they are not principles of the intellect, of absolute disinterested science. Science must be disinterested, religion, conscience, can never be.

And especially when we are dealing with other religions, and comparing them, we have a standard here. We place a religion higher in the scale not as it integrates us into the All, but as it evokes in us the worship of the Holy, and stirs the energy of that moral preference. By such a standard Buddhism, with its absorption, is at the bottom of the scale, in spite of its humanist sympathies. Islam is higher, but its God is too much of a personal fate. Judaism is higher still because it stirs men with an ethical and national God. And highest of all is Christianity. And Christianity not as consummating the rest (though it does) but in even excluding and traversing them, as it does the tendencies which make Buddhism Buddhist. It is more of a religion that commands the rest than realises them—much as it does in that way. It can never master the other religions merely by purifying and extending their idea; it must bring them their King before it can give them themselves. It is not their evolution but their imperative. It has not only more practical value but more intrinsic dignity. For it brings the God not of mastering power only but of transfiguring holiness.

X

THE FOOTING OF RELIGION — THE REAL AS THE REDEMPTIVE — THE FINAL AUTHORITY OF THE HOLY

THERE is a liberalism whose badge is redemption *from* an Apostolic Gospel, and not *by* it ; and it is a frequent mark of its more popular forms that they seem to claim a monopoly of due knowledge, modern culture, and sound footing. It cannot help betraying its private conviction that any respect its opponent deserves is but the respect due to age. Hence it may be found in its more courteous advocates to acknowledge the æsthetic greatness of a positive theology, and the spiritual sweep of its purview ; but it treats it as a high or fine mirage, with no stable foundation. It regards it as it might regard a system of heavenly constellations laid out before the days of astronomical science—impressive but fantastic, grand on the heavens, but affecting earth only astrologically, with much influence but no footing (certainly none such as the critic's), with much poetry of its kind, but no reality. As if the minds capable of a great fabric were all the more likely by their greatness to be careless about a good foundation, and it were left chiefly to the critics, and not to the creators, to secure the stability of an ideal world, and found it for ever. It seems odd to do as even the generous critics are sometimes moved to do, to credit with a true passion for reality theological writers who, in the same breath, are declared to have everything but footing. And there is no charge more dear or easy to the amateur or the censor.

Underlying such charges is a different idea of what constitutes footing. Mostly the critic means that his is a footing in philosophy or reason, that there is no other organ of real knowledge, and that he is impatient of faith's demand for an autonomy which gives faith a first hand experience of reality. Religion is placed at the mercy of culture; or at least any positive religion is. Or if the critic do take stand on experience, he limits it to the experience of the modern mind instead of the whole soul's history. That is, he stakes off a recent region of experience according to his rational predilection, and erects there an assaying plant for all the rest of Time. And this is the real crux. Everything does turn on our footing, on our starting-point, our notion of reality. Do we find it in the *Word* or in the *World*, in a given Revelation or in innate thought, in the super-rational or in the rational, in the experience of supernatural grace or of natural culture, in the sense of the holy or in that of the merely spiritual?

The question of authority and certainty is this question of footing. Or, otherwise put, it is the question of reality. On reality, religion at least must stand, however it might be with other interests of mankind. If the besetting sin of religion is hypocrisy that only means that its cardinal virtue is reality—not sincerity, which is too subjective to be primary, but reality. Many sincere people have no footing on reality (hence their pathetic futility); but to have footing there is also to be sincere.

On what must the soul take its last stand, and where is built its everlasting mansion? It cannot be on experience in the sense of our own subjective impression; for that is too unstable, and does not

THE FOOTING OF RELIGION

secure us from earthquake, landslip, or bog. We do not stand on the fact of our experience but on the fact *which* we experience. The point of moment is not that we feel, but what we feel.

For a long time when the modern day broke the field was held by the principle that the real is the rational; that the last reality, the escape from subjectivity, is thought; that the movement, the dialectic, of absolute thought gave us the nature of our ultimate. Our real objective was a world process, kindred to that of our own thought, which at once placed us and absorbed us. This seemed at first to lend great strength to Trinitarianism, and to adjust it completely to philosophic requirements. Its end, however, was but to dilate our consciousness, and tie us up in a subjectivity enlarged and absolutised. Religion became a matter of ideas, whereas faith, being an obedience, has its only objective footing in a Will. The old reign of doctrine returned in a philosophical, instead of a theological form. Christianity became a grand fabric of dialectic ideas, where orthodoxy had placed juridical ideas, or another variety of dialectic. The incarnation became, then, the precipitation into personal form of the idea of the God-man, the idea of the essential unity of God and man as revealed in the nature of thought. The spiritual world was one of process, it was the explication of this polar unity, and theology was this rational process more or less mythologised. Idealism was Rationalism transfigured and ascended. Personality fell into the rear as a mere *Vorstellung*, a mere fleeting vortex, of the idea. Moral relations retired behind intellectual, and sin faded into a negative factor or a rude stage of good.

But thought is not an end in itself, and therefore not the nature of reality. It is only an instrument serving the purposes of that activity which we call life. " Knowledge is for life, and not life for knowledge." Life is the reality for which thought exists, life either on the human scale or on the divine, as the human spirit or as the Holy Spirit, life to which we do more justice when we seize it by faith than by any sight, even the sight of the mind. To this principle, of course, dogmatic liberalism is opposed. It founds on a philosophy. It does not get near life. Its faith must submit to the rule and not merely the dialect of modern thought.

We came nearer life when Neo-Kantianism taught us that the real was the moral. The will took the primacy from the intellect. *Bonitas est substantia Dei,* as Augustine said. The proper metaphysic is a metaphysic of ethic. It is the conscience that plants us on the bedrock of being. Morality is the nature of things. The diamond net of existence is a moral order and a moral movement of personal relations. Interest is transferred from the cosmic to the historic realm. The universe is not the key to man, but man is the key to the universe. Evolutionary idealism had placed man on the summit of things (and even made God to arrive at consciousness there); hence its last product should carry the secret of all. But if that be so, must it not mean that the supreme issue of history is not the dialectic of an idea but the assertion of a will, the action of a conscience, the purpose of a personality, the kingdom of a God. Our footing is not in the process but in the purpose ; not in the process, which is too changing, and even fleeting, but in the latent purpose, the goal, the destiny prescribed by the interests of the one good thing, great end, and final cause in the world —a good will. Existence is a kingdom of ends—*i.e.* of persons, of souls and not of mere movements. If we raise this to the Christian temperature we have the

THE FOOTING OF RELIGION 203

reality of things in a kingdom of moral relations infused with love.

But even this view was not final. Negatively it tended to produce stalwarts and stoics rather than saints; and it threatened to reduce religion to an exalted moralism, as before it had been reduced to an intellectualism. Religion became too much of a means for securing a heroic conscience against the onsets of the world, and too little of a redemption in which the whole world itself was involved. But positively also the soul had deepened. If idealism widened our range, and moralism set up righteousness, the supremacy of the moral in God and His holiness created repentance.

When we began to take in earnest the idea of the moral, when will began to discuss the situation with conscience, and we bethought ourselves of the conscience of God, a new height opened a new depth. The kingdom of moral affection cast us upon the King of holy love. And if the kingdom was interfused in all things, and if it was slowly rising through all things to its right and ruling place, still more so must the King be. As God passed from being the guardian and guarantor of the moral order, and became more of an absolute and holy God, He became more also of an immanent God. But it was the immanence of the transcendent. The holy, however intimate to us, has no meaning except as the transcendent. The real was not only as immanent as thought, intimate as love, searching as nemesis, but as eminent as holiness. The real became the holy. There must be our rest, our life. "Thou art our Holy One; therefore we shall not die."

That is all very well with the Old Testament sense of holy as meaning our own. "Thou art our own peculiar God, therefore we are secure." But the more holy holiness grew, so much the more it seemed not our own but our other. As holiness it blazed over us rather than glowed in us, or flowed among us. The great white throne was set up in each soul. It judged at least as much as it sheltered—and especially it judged its own, its believers. No man could have his eyes opened to such a God and live before that consuming fire. The day of the Lord was a day of judgment; and it began at the house of God; the sanctity was severest on those who owned it. The moral, raised to the holy, crushed rather than inspired. The more holy He, the more guilty we.

Where in all the universe is footing then? How dwell with the everlasting burnings? The holy reality of things, the white hot core of the moral universe, of the whole universe, is our judgment and not our joy, our doom and not our stay. Over the whole universe, and submerging it in burning light, was that awful throne whose pillars were in the deep foundations of the earth. If the real is the moral, and the moral the holy, what footing have sinful men on that sheer and shining face? That objective is as slippery in another way as our own subjectivity was. The reality we lost in our own soft sands we could not grasp on His smooth sides.

To be of all men most moral is thus to be of all men most miserable. It is an *impasse*. The last reality ends in a hopeless tangle. Our feet are helplessly caught in that subtle net of righteousness, of sanctity, in which all things are upborne. We rage, we are worn down, we die, shamed and cowed in the coil of that very moral reality, which we did think was to deliver us from slavery to a mere process of thought, and was to set our feet firm, and keep our head high. Conscience which, going some way, makes many heroes, going to the end, makes cowards of us all. It ends by accusing more than inspiring, and it cannot forgive.

THE FOOTING OF RELIGION 205

It repents, but the penitent conscience cannot forgive. The good man can never forgive himself. Conscience will give us sound footing up to a point, till it rouse the sense of the holy, and then it creates in us the passion for forgiveness as life's one need. But no conscience of ours can either forgive us or assure us of the forgiveness of God, the grace of the Holy. The reality for life's actual moral case, which thought could not yield, the conscience also fails to give.

That is the dark before God's own dawn, the chaos before the new creation. We are ready for the discovery that reality is only in revelation, life in a new fiat, and footing only in forgiveness. Our access to Him is only in His merciful visitation. "As is His majesty so also is His mercy." As high as His holiness is the depth of His grace. What is holiness to us toiling up is grace in Him coming down. The real is neither the rational nor the ethical. It is the redemptive. For Christianity, says Harnack, reproducing Weinel, " the essential thing is the moral ; and morality means life in God, in His redeeming power." The reality is not the redemptive process (which is no redemption of the soul into communion, but mere evolution of the character into excellence), but the redemptive person. Nor is it a case of redemption merely. The other redemptive religion of Buddhism means no more than the soul's release from life as a load; but Christ's is redemption from life as a guilt. Christianity is not the religion of redemption merely, but of holy redemption into holiness. And therefore it is the religion of atoned redemption, of a holiness that must be atoned, but is self-atoned, which is self-secured for ever. That is the last foothold of the soul. And that is the Cross of Christ. If man is the key to the universe, what is the key to man? What is his destiny, and what assures it? The only answer is Revelation, taken as the act of God and not His mere exhibition. It is Redemption, and Redemption by and for the Holy. It is the revelation which universalised Christianity—the Cross. The Holy Love is there at once the Reality and the Redeemer of all existence. It redeems in the only holy way, the atoning way. It is also the Redemption not of a soul alone, but of a race and a world that is involved. The Redemption is commensurate with the Sanctity, the Majesty, the rock Reality of things. For our sin brought us into collision with a moral universe; and our salvation can therefore only be by communion with the absolutely Holy, by the self-recuperation of that universe's moral Soul for our holy goal.

We may gather up our course thus so far as it has gone. Our footing must be on the eternal reality of things. Whatever is the reality of the world must be also the unity of the world. But the unity of the world, of such an evolving world as the modern mind conceives, must be a unity of its drift, and *nisus*, and goal. But as it is in its actual state as yet an unfinished world, we are put into possession of this goal only by revelation from One in whom it is already real. And that goal, again, can only be a unity of purpose; and, of course, of moral purpose, if we rise above mechanism, and if we give personality its key-place in an ideal scheme. The unity, then, is a teleological unity. The reality of the world can only be a teleological reality, the immanence, action and revelation of a transcendent Will, a Will holy and absolute, and therefore with an already accomplished purpose. If we contrast this invincible telic ideal so revealed with man's actual moral case, the action of such a holy will must be in the way of moral judgment and redemption. Absolute holiness must secure universal holiness; *i.e.* it must recover and sanctify personality everywhere. But as the underlying reality of the world, this unity cannot be merely an *effort* for redemption, it cannot be merely

THE FOOTING OF RELIGION

conative and tentative, with the result in more or less doubt. It must be, if it is reality, already accomplished in principle. It must be a foregone redemption, a redemption that has not now to be achieved but only actualised. The ground plan of an evolving Creation, and indeed of Being, is God's redemptive Will. *Heilesrath ist Schöpfungsplan.* We are born into a redeemed world. We are created for redemption, created by One who knew in creating that He had in Himself all the resources wherewith to deal with freedom's abuse of His creation. Beneath, behind, and above God the Creator is God the Redeemer. Our final footing in a moral world, *i.e.* in the universe, is the holy God of its salvation. The true metaphysic is the metaphysic of the soul, of the religious soul in a moral universe, of redemption. In a Christian faith we descend on creation from redemption, we do not descend on redemption from creation, on grace from nature, on faith from science. It is in the Grace of God that all our thought begins. In thinking of religion we must begin with what makes us Christians, and not simply with what makes us religious. The method here, as often elsewhere, is more than half the battle.

In a bold word, there is no access to the last reality, no final footing for the soul in the universe, no eternal overcoming of the world, no Rock of Ages for the race, except through the evangelical experience. The reality of a moral universe for sinful man's central experience is Grace. The holiness of God's love, and therefore love's elevation to be Grace, is the supreme revelation of the Crucified. Protest against theology is useless here, unless we are mindless. If our realism is thorough it is impossible for a religious soul to be real without being theological. Theology, in so far as it is a science, is *the* science of reality, of the Word which *is* God.

After the path by which we have come, is that a mere piece of dogmatism? Have we not been driven to it with a mighty hand? Or, if it is dogmatism, is it not the dogmatism of God, the finality of His self-revelation, the certainty and ultimacy of His statement of Himself, and the word of His world's last positivity? When we strip the hulls of beneficent illusion from every evolving dogma this remains, the dogma in dogma, the dogmatic God.

The supreme task for the last reality, if it be holy, is to assert and secure itself against the last challenge of it. It is to cope with moral evil, which is its absolute antithesis and mortal foe. If man can do that he is his own reality and his own God. If he cannot, his only footing is in the God who can—who indeed must, or He is not God. And his only footing in such a God is faith in His Redemption. We are not moral heroes with a noble record, who, with a shining face, go to meet our great reward and happy consummation in God. God be merciful to us sinners. Faith is footing in a world-Redeemer. Such is our world-Reality. God is God because He is holy; and the glory, the test, of the holy God is not in calling forth a world but in calling it back, not in its creation in love but in its new creation in grace. The last reality is realised by the metaphysic, not of being, but of mercy, the metaphysic not of ethic merely but of the redeeming conscience of Christ. Existence is not a quantity; nor is it a procession; but it is an act. If we think of it as a unity it is not an infinite substance (which can give no morals), but an Eternal Act, an Eternal Moral Act. And in our present moral case that can only be (as an absolute act, as an act of the Holy asserting His right by it), an act of Redemption. The God who is real in all is a God who

THE FOOTING OF RELIGION

by His very eternal nature is a God asserting and securing His challenged right in redeeming action; and that is the God of the Cross of Christ. The Cross is our footing, whether in history, or in an eternal and immutable morality.

Moreover, the only footing of the moral soul is a world footing. There is no salvation by private bargain, behind the world's back. We find our souls not in their isolated salvation, but in the context of a saved world, a kingdom of souls. Here again reality is in the evangelical experience. It is the only experience which places us in the whole moral tissue of a universe by replacing us in the communion of its holy God. There is nothing absolutely universal but the moral, the holy, absoluteness of God.

For [1] what is the test of reality? What distinguishes it from dream? What does so in our daily life? What should we require to do so in our religious life, our soul's life? What is to save us from the unreality of religious dreaming, descending into the unreality of religious hypocrisy?

How do we know, when we daily awake, that the visions of the night are not reality? It is not by their lack of vividness either in outline or in feeling. They are sometimes stamped upon our day more impressively than even its duties and interests. An impression is neither true nor real according to the sharpness or the force of its impact on us. So a religious experience is not true just because it is forcible and coherent, which would be a premium on bigotry. The most passionate convictions have at times been found to turn out dreams in the surer light of later life or history.

Nor is it that dreams are confused, contradictory,

[1] Much that follows here is due to a periodical source to which I regret that I have lost the reference.

or absurd. They are often much otherwise. But it is this—that they cannot be integrated into the practical context of life. What we find waiting for us when we rise is in that context. It joins up with the day before and the day to follow, and so with all our tissue of moral life.

Truth and reality must be measured by the way in which impression, view, or faith works into the whole fabric of our life, knowledge, or purpose. If we sail through the air on a broomstick at two in the morning, or inherit a legacy of millions at five, we cannot safely work the experience into the day's outlook or the day's conduct. Nor is there any cohesion between the exploits of one night and those of another as there is between day and day. If there were we should live in two halves, in two realities; we should live a double life ruinous both to sanity and to character. The test of a dream is not to pinch one's self, to get over one vivid impression by another, (as in religion people might seek to clear a nebulous faith by crowding new sensations on each other). The test is practice. The dream does not work—meaning by that not that it does not succeed, but that it is not in the context of our moral life. Such is all hallucination. But reality is in organic connexion with life's whole.

The reality in religion especially is something which provides in life's whole both a base for all philosophical footing, and a crown for all its spiritual effort. It makes our ground and our goal to be one. It is that which integrates the whole sensible and rational but sinful world into a solidary moral destiny which saves and completes it; and it makes it feel its best achievements to be but the promise of a collective life higher still, built on a foundation of redemption from its worst failure. And the only reality which does this is the holy, as the

THE FOOTING OF RELIGION

constitutive factor of all spiritual life in a divine kingdom, and the regulative factor of all its progress, the stability of each time and the strength of its salvation. It goes out in love, but it stands in holiness. It is the holy that makes love divine, makes it racial, eternal, sure, changeless, and invincible.

For the holy is not that in God which detaches Him widely from the world, though it is that which differentiates Him clearly from it. It is so real that it organises Him, as it were, into all the world. As holy love it lifts Him above the instinctive and passionate; and it draws Him down from the lonely majesty of Omnipotence, and Omniscience, and all the abstract purities that cow and crush us. It is majesty made intimate in moral mercy. But in doing so it makes the site of God's chief relation to the world to be those contacts which do most to bind it into one, the moral relations like love and righteousness. These, as they furnish man's true unity in himself, so here give him the site of his unity, and his world's unity, with God. It is an ethical thing in its nature; it is neither natural nor æsthetic. It is social and not solitary. It creates within the "old man" the new Humanity. And it certifies God's love as eternal because it plants it in the very foundation of His Absolute Being, unbeginning and endless, and makes it the *prius* and the creator of all our love to God. Nothing is more foreign to the Christian idea of the holy than that cold passion which tells us it is a piece of egoism when we love God to expect to be loved in return. Our love to Him is the creature of a love from Him to us which, because it is holy, is bound up with all His nature and providence, and flows from the springs of eternal reality.

The deepest reality of all my experience must be in such solidary connexion with the deepest life of things, the most universal life, the eternal life. It is eternal—for it not only works, it wears. It is 'placed' in the solidary organism of all moral existence, in the supreme spiritual history of mankind, in the kingdom of God. But how shall I, how can I, thus 'place' it? The panorama of that kingdom is not before my eyes. It is before no human eyes. Even the universe is not a completed system of reality; it is but becoming. This solidary and contextual proof of reality is not accessible to me. No footing is possible if I am to wait to see the whole fabric of history lapped in the peace and rounded in the glory of God. And yet I cannot wait, nor even hope, to see it without a footing that gives me such a commanding and eternal standpoint. This is a hopeless dilemma if we must *see* the integration, see it as in a map of the final good. Here again it comes home to us that the organ for the last reality is not sight but faith, not even the insight of genius and culture but evangelical faith—trust in the new Creator. We are real, not as we are integrated into the moral world, but into that world's Redemption. And for Christian faith, where man is not self-redeemed, that means integration into the world's God and Redeemer. " I am thy salvation." It is the evangelical experience that plants us, not only with our feet but with our home in the whole reality of things. " We see not yet all things put under man, but we see Jesus."

The whole nature of Christian certainty is dominated and determined by its Christology. And, among the many forms of the Christological problem, one dilemma points the issue most clearly of all. Are we to integrate Christ into an experienced system of guilt and grace or into an ideal scheme of the world and history? We may admit that He is central to either, but which is our mode of addressing the question? Under which set of categories—the soteriological or the merely philosophical—shall we work with most effect? Is Christ the source of our guilty confidence before God, or the symbol of all that is best in historic man? Shall we do more justice to Christ by pursuing the line I have been following, the line of moral experience as to Christ's value for the Church, or the other of rational, scientific, cultivated inquiry as to His value in Humanity, the place of Christ in civilization? Is He central for turning sin to faith, or only for changing negligence to diligence, and backwardness to progress? The former line is continuous with the marrow of the traditional way and its living power, the second imports an entirely new method, resting Christianity on something else than Christian faith and experience. The former is occupied with the weight of sin, the other with the range of knowledge or ethic. The former is more positive, the latter more liberal or modern. We need not pursue the one absolutely at the cost of the other, but the whole question will be pointed and clarified as we give the one the primacy of the other, and make the whole issue at last one of personal religion, of communion with God, and not congruity with ideas. The notion of a living world of grace and guilt is not a husk to protect for a time certain vital ideas of which Christ is but the symbol; but the ideas are there for philosophic analysis as collaterals or implicates of faith's true life in Christ. There or nowhere do we find our last authority and our last certainty. Christ as Lord means Christ as Redeemer. It is there alone that we can keep our certainty as that of a living world. And here our view of Christ is not the mere programme of a religious association's aims and ideas as integral to reason, but it is the personal confession of a Church's faith and experience integral to life.

If we are to face facts, then, for the *final* reality we must face *all* the facts. And the experience in which we face all the facts of the moral universe, the whole counsel of God, is the experience in which we are rooted and grounded in the compendious, germinal, and creative fact of the world's salvation. And that is not possible in a theism, however refined, or however reverential to Christ. For in no beneficent theism can God be truly, searchingly, real; because He is not, in all His mere improvement of us, repairing, but only ignoring, His own wounded holiness and the breach in reality there. In all our betterment He is not making good the past. He is softened to us, but not reconciled in Himself. His holy claim on the guilty is unmet, and He does not do justice to that sanctity which is the nature not only of things but of Himself and His eternity. None but Himself can do justice to Himself. None but the Holy can satisfy the holy and its eternal, *unquenchable* demand. It is only God as the Holy atoning Son that can do justice to the Holy Father, or satisfy the changeless conditions of a perfectly Holy God in a guilty world. And this is the God that we commune and live with, not by a lowly reverence for Christ but by a living faith in Him and His sacrifice; whereby we are not simply regenerated into a new life, but integrated into the New Humanity, and supernaturalized into the *Realpolitik* of the world-kingdom of holy Grace. To know Christ as the centre of an economy of grace and guilt is to understand Him as the centre of the world and history, if that history rotate upon the conscience. But to know Him merely as the symbolic centre of the world or man is not to realise Him as the supply of man's central need, where man is a guilty thing surprised by holy law.

Be I right or wrong, there is not here a word that has been loosely used or gratuitously set down so far as the writer's care can go. Nor is there one of these theological ideas that has not been thought out, without regard for any orthodoxy, in

THE FOOTING OF RELIGION 215

reference to the last moral reality of the world. Our relation to that is the root, the heart, the gold, the asbestos in all dogma. It is the irreducible life in it, the dogma in dogma. For dogma is the ethic of man and God, morals the ethic of man and man. The form of dogma does change. There were elements that belonged to its illusion, the beneficent illusion in it which made it of historic use for its age. But as we strip these elements away we go inward to something which is integral and central to the whole world of moral reality, and which has life in itself to produce new forms germane to each age. This central, fontal, vital, moral thing is neither sheer love, clear truth, nor pure being ; but it is the holy and its conditions. And the bane of liberal thought is that it does not grasp the idea of the holy as the changeless thing in God, God's conscience, the immutable thing in the universe, the ruling principle of religion, and the organizing principle of its truth as theology. Therefore it does not grasp the idea of sin. Liberalism refines all dogma away into a mere temporary envisagement of the general interaction of the divine and human, the infinite and the finite, with nothing at its heart which is positively given for ever as to God's holy will and purpose with our actual human case. It is looking for footing in the rationally real (which is a philosophic proceeding) instead of asking how a holy reality could find footing in us sinners (which is the procedure of religion). It deprecates the incessant reference to sin and sinners in such a connexion, it tends to treat the sense of sin as a ghost walking from a dead past, a bad dream haunting us from the Middle Ages—treatment which is an index of a blind spot in its vision, and its languor to the holy amid its zeal of love. For if God be first the God of the conscience, and if, therefore, the holy is supreme, we are sinners before all else ; and if we are dealt with radically, we must be dealt with as sinners, by all the resources of the holy and under all its conditions. If the real is the holy, its treatment of sin is the *locus* for our contact with reality, and our footing for all eternal things. And that *locus* is the cross of Christ in history and experience, as the crisis of existence both human and divine.

There is a whole system of religious philosophy which is known as Illusionism, and which resolves belief into a subjective system or process of great historic use but with no objective reality. It admits the spiritual utility of a belief in God, but it denies reality behind it. The whole world of thought, indeed, is fictive and regulative, but not existential. It is a mere piece of machinery necessary for practical purposes, a means to the end of business calculation and ethical action; but it has no objective or real being so far as we can say. This mode of thought fastens upon the modern theory of values as the proper method in a philosophy of religion; but it uses it only to prove that, as we count valuable only what is so to us and meets our desires, we are left with no more than a theology of our wishes. I jump to a conclusion as to the objective reality of a divine being out of its value for me as a belief. I create God in my image. I call my passionate project of a God a real object. God is thus for me a eudemonist need instead of a moral imperative. And, to be frank, there is no doubt the value theory is vulnerable here. For it has been overdriven in the direction of God's value for man, and under-estimated in the way of His right over men. (Chap. XX.)

The question of footing is not simply a question whether in any sound system of things there is room for *religion*. We find no escape from our subjectivity

THE FOOTING OF RELIGION

so. A whole scheme, which made not only room but demand for religion, might yet be only a vast dilation of man's subjective consciousness, only an æsthetic necessity; and about an objective it might fix nothing. And it might leave us with no security from illusion about the reality of any object for our religion, or any footing in the nature of things. We could not be sure that God comes, touches, seizes, and changes us. We are not sure whether our religion is a colloquy or a soliloquy. God might fit in with my rational world without a message for my soul; He might be the supreme concept without having the last word; and He might stand as a postulate but not as a visitation. He might be a valuable illusion for an early stage, so that we should discover, when the last conceptual hulls fell from Him as we got nearer the reality of things in the course of our development, that nothing was left, and that we were really carrying what we thought was carrying us.

When we are faced with Illusionism like this we must begin by admitting how much during our growth must fall from us as temporary and erroneous in our first conception of sacred things. But none the less we must react from the cynic notion that true growth is mere disillusion. We hear indeed from wise teachers about an education by illusion, as when we begin our march to a faith in fatherhood by a pathetic belief in the superiority of our own parent, holding it at school against all comers. The whole race moves in like way from *Aberglaube* to *Glaube*, from superstition to real standing, from belief which is less adequate to belief that is more. But were it all illusion, were it sheer delusion, were its proper treatment dense denunciation instead of wise interpretation, we could not talk of its educative effect or benefit any more. If no reality was emerging, if the faith were not slowly purifying the belief, if revelation were not subduing imagination, if we were but tearing off the hulls to reach Him, and He was not casting them off to reach us, there could be no education. As we drew aside the curtain of the God we should die, like Schiller's *Lehrling von Sais*. We should at every step approach the grand vacuum where we could not breathe, and not the great reality whose touch was life and stay.

We must admit, I say, that in religion and its tradition we are faced by a mass of thoughts, feelings, fancies, and experiences, which are, some normal, some abnormal; some healthy, some pathological, which all need great sifting and reduction. There is much that is anthropomorphic and individual, especially in the early stages. Comparative religion makes it its business to show us with great prominence this chrysalis of religion. And recent psychology comes to its aid. We are invited to pore on the subliminal side of conversion till we miss the sublime; and confession is made to the statistician with his schedules instead of to the priest with his powers. And even in the great Idealisms like Hegel's we are asked so to view the whole procession of being as the expansion of our rational selves that a real visitation from an objective God is but a way of putting things. That of course is fatal to religion. But these aberrations and superstitions have on the whole been a husk for a kernel. They have exerted a protecting and promoting influence on the process of evolution. And if there be any real revelation, one of its blessings must be that it puts us in the way of testing and sifting the form of religion that lies to our hand, and of parting between imagination and faith, or between what is mere psychology and what is the reality which no psychology, no science can give. Amid all the psychological conditions, however raw, fantastic, or confused, have we the authentic presence, touch, lift, and power of the living God acting from the

THE FOOTING OF RELIGION 219

deepest depth of things ? Have we in religion this real, personal communion with Him ? Is reality at last revelation ? Or is revelation the last illusion ?

One thing may be noted in this connexion. When we have recognised that very erroneous and obsolete views about the gods and their authority yet on the whole tended, amid all abuse, to exert the control and rouse the devotion in which civilizations are founded and the progressive process on the whole sustained, when we have owned, for instance, that a belief like Immortality, even if it were wrong, has done immense service in the idealizing of history, we may take a step farther. What man has to do is to secure his place in the world, in the vast and mighty evolutionary process. That world is at first in a conspiracy against him. The human infant has more against it than the young of any other creature. Man has to secure a footing in the world. But this can only be done by overcoming the world. The only place he can keep in the face of nature is the place of nature's master. He can exist only as a ruler. He must harness nature. He cannot run in the team, he must drive from the box. He can endure only by overcoming the world. He must have footing to cast it down under his feet. He must have footing outside the world which also sets him above the world. And that footing has been given him to a large, and on the whole effective, extent by his faith in those supramundane powers which he trusted so surely though he conceived them so poorly.

But there comes the question, If the idea of a supramundane God or a post-mundane life has had such a practical effect for man's chief end in the conquest of the actual world, can it have been a mere idea ? Must it not be an essential element in that reality where man and the world receive their life and course ? Is true life not the living out of that reality as a fact and power, and not merely as a notion? This life of society by conquest of the world—can it be quite explained or fed by the obvious factors of natural evolution regardless of what is behind? Is it not the ascent through evolution of something, some reality, which is more fundamental to it than any of its observed laws or more palpable forces? Is it not the continual emergence of something which stood by the cradle of evolution, and which always seeks to regain its source? Is it within the power of a sheer illusion to produce all the effects which such ideas have produced on the world? Could anything but the reality at their heart produce the effect upon life as a social whole which such beliefs have done? Is illusion not beneficent according to its core of revelation? That all is beneficial illusion may be the *reductio ad absurdum* of philosophic idealism; but religion is beneficent only according to the degree of reality contained in its revelation under whatever illusions of passing form.

There are two ways of answering the question raised by Illusionism. It is not illusion—some say because it fits to what was in us before, others because it brings something so new and powerful that it means a new creation.

Some say the reality makes appeal to an *a priori* in the soul which the mystics call the seed of the divine light, the rationalists call the spiritual reason of the race, and the moralists call the response of the conscience. It is said, by the rationalists in particular, that the appeal in revelation is through its congruity, its alignment, with the native organization or constitution of the spiritual soul; with ultimate ideas integral to reason, and as final as its light. They are such ideas as the conviction of the value and meaningfulness of existence, the unity and solidarity of

THE FOOTING OF RELIGION

universal reality, the spirituality and the exigence of the last reality, its creative originality and freedom. To such final tests a religion must conform, and it must be measured by the extent to which it continues and promotes these ideas. In the best and latest representatives of this position it is urged that this spiritual organization, which revelation fits as a key the wards, is originally the gift and signature, or at least the initials, of our Maker ; so that it is God's voucher after all. Thus faith has a value autonomous to itself, as against the *a priori* of common rationalism, or of logic, ethic, or æsthetic ; so that religion is not condemned to make its final appeal to some standard which is not religious.

I deal with such pleas more fully at another stage. I will only say that the other line carries more promise. I have been developing it. It coincides with the ethical line of the conscience, which forbids us to believe that what fits into the moral whole of life can be unreal, however it fail with the rational. The will owns the presence of another will not only greater but better, and the conscience feels not only value but right, not only an enlarged righteousness but a new creation by the holy. We are new born to a sense of God's holy right to us, and not simply to a sense of our benefit from Him. The conscience owns, in a sense of guilt, the approach of the absolute Conscience, His entrance, both on history and on the soul, with a sheer regenerating power, more miraculous in its action than continuous. The real is the creative. The most real is the new creative, the redemptive ; so that our last footing, which must be in the metaphysic of ethic and action, is in the central moral act of Humanity, in the historic objective of Christ's Cross ; which functions afresh in every regenerate soul, by a mystery intelligible to the Creator Redeemer alone, however sensible to us. There is no footing in reality except by a holy revelation, which, in its nature as a new creation, is more revolutionary than rational, and more of a paradox than a principle. The true Idealism is evolutionary, but it is so in an ascending series, not of ideals, but of miracles, creations. It is not a swelling process of thought but a ripening realm of will, not a more complex arrangement of existing spiritual matter but a series of new beginnings, conditioned each by the former but not contained in it. It gives us ever closer communication with the Absolute and Holy, as soul to Soul, and an ever closer harmony with the moral world, the world of human hearts and wills. It can be no illusion which does that, unless everything be illusion. And even that means surely that some one thing is not, by which we may call illusion everything else.

XI

AUTHORITY, HISTORY, AND DESTINY

THE question of authority emerges with peculiar force in connection with the philosophy of history taken together with the psychology of religion. What is the meaning of history—its drift and destination as distinct from its laws ? What does it all work out to ? To what are all its parts contributory ? What is the destiny of the race—not the manner of its action but its ruling purpose ? Is there beyond a science of history, a philosophy of it, and beyond that a religion ? If we *explain* history by its causation, have we a destiny which *interprets* it ? Is there any teleology in the course of human things. If so, where do we find the goal ? And is there any identity between the goal history goes to and the ground and guidance of our going ? Is the final cause the moving cause ? If there be such a ground and goal, that must be our Authority in chief, and our certainty is our living relation to it.

How do we get that living relation ? What is the historic object to which we are related as subjects of religion ? Do we find it apart from history by an intuitional experience of the world ? This would require the metaphysic of a monistic unity immanent in us as our *a priori*, but vaster than we, which, passing through our conviction, returns upon that vaster self, and reunites with its universal reality. To such a metaphysic the Kantians have some incisive things to say. Or do we find it by an induction from empirical history? That is the method of science; and science cannot give us contact with super-empiric reality. Scientific history cannot give us the super-historic in history. No induction can prove a miracle. Evidence could prove the fact, but not that it was a miracle, such as is God's creative relation to the world. Or do we reach it by an experience of history in another sphere than the intuitional or the inductive, by experience of a historic fact in the moral region which is central to all being, by response to a revealing Will in history, an experience which means a new creation by grace, and the revelation of a new order of things in which dwelleth final righteousness?

This is an aspect of the question of authority which I have already referred to. But it may repay more attention. And it may reinforce what has been said about the part our choice plays in connection with our footing.

When man confronts Nature, a dilemma is inevitable; Is he the product, and finally the victim, of Nature, which can unmake what it made; or is he the Master and Ruler of Nature? Does he serve some greater nature than himself, called the world, or does the world serve Him?

The arena on which this issue comes to a head is History. The spiritual destiny of the race is to be determined there. In History, man is at once dependent on Nature and above it, a product of it and yet a personality who descends on it from his partnership in the personality of God. In this regard a great change of interest has taken place during the last generation. It is no longer the natural sciences and their methods that dominate attention, but the psychological, and especially the historic. We think racially. The question of human destiny has largely taken the

AUTHORITY, HISTORY, AND DESTINY 225

place once occupied by concern about one's own soul. It is a change connected with the serious retreat of the sense of sin and the happy growth of the sense of sympathy. What of the hapless millions ? And it is a concern that emerges in the closest connection with the question about history, and its meaning. The purpose of history involves the fate of the race.

In studying history from this point of view, for satisfaction as to final destiny and not for the discovery of economic laws, there are two methods, which we might call that of induction and that of valuation.

We ask, of course, at the outset, what is to guide us in a maze so great, with what principle we shall start on our selection and examination of the mass of facts which the annalists and explorers throw down before us. What is to differentiate the historian from the mere chronicler, or the mere anthropologist ? What marks the partisan historian from the scientific ? In answer to this question of initial method, one side spreads before us the whole historic field as an area of induction, the other fixes our attention upon a luminous spot, or spots, which contain the standard of value. The former raises history from being a sectional interest, like chemistry, or a specialised form of scientific curiosity, and turns it into the autobiography of the race. History becomes the grand manuscript of the Soul, written in a difficult style, but still so that we can decipher the general drift. It is a field in whose survey we trace certain large and leading lines, which give us a base for all judgments about values and standards, according as events promote or retard progress on such lines. But when the soul really comes to handle itself and its destiny in religion this method leaves us in some difficulty. As history is unfinished there is no possibility of any absolute standard, and none therefore of any absolute certainty, and so none of any real religion. Moreover, there is

P

no history so hard to write as an autobiography. Of course, there are things known to the writer that another could not know. But there are also confusions, obsessions, deflections, to which he is pre-eminently exposed. To know ourselves is the hardest of all knowledge. And often the more we know the more we are silent. No one who has ever made the attempt but is aware that in many cases it may be impossible—and the more impossible as we rise in our range of consideration, as we come to handle our spiritual life and spiritual issues on the more complex and universal scale. In like manner the autobiography of the race by the way of purview, of disentanglement, of selected lines of tendency or guidance, may well seem impossible to a race which is not only not done living, but (for all we know) may not yet have reached its life's climax or done its great work, or come to its true self. Any such inductive survey always postulates for the induction some selective principle, which is really of more fundamental value than the generalisations that arise from the selected data. And these principles are mostly found to be certain intuitive ideas, like freedom, culture, or spirituality, whose assumed value really begs the question.

The other method I have called one of valuation. It does not begin with the panorama of history and seek by induction to construct a philosophy of it as a guide to all judgment. It begins less scientifically and more morally, by a method more appropriate to the subject matter, which is human life, will, and conscience. It starts from the idea expressed in Kant's axiom at the outset of his metaphysic of Ethic. " There is nothing conceivable in the world, or out of it, which can be called good without qualification except a good Will " The standard of history is given us in the moral personality. This might equally well be

AUTHORITY, HISTORY, AND DESTINY 227

called the method of revelation as distinct from induction. It makes a clear distinction between the natural life process, however rarefied or spiritual, and the action of the moral consciousness. It presents us, in the good will, in the development thereto of the moral personality, with a standard by which to assess the value of everything, either done or proposed.

And, of course, for religious, *i.e.* for the supreme and final, purposes, this method is of decisive value. We are at once cast upon the search for historic and luminous cases of the perfectly good will. And almost before we know where we are we are in the presence of Christ, having left all others behind as being of a goodness limited and relative.

But it is not as if our difficulties ended as soon as we faced this figure of Christ. In some ways they begin, on a new plane. Historic and other criticism has seen to that. By Christ is the Jesus of severe criticism meant—the reduced residuum of the larger New Testament figure? Are we to worship Christ or only to serve Him? Is He the creator or the symbol of man's best? And so on, in a series of questions which I have already illustrated.

In approaching such a subject as the place and function of Christ for history, and therefore for human destiny, we must keep clearly before us the two orders of interest, the two methods if you will, which we have named—the interest of history as an organism evolving on certain lines, laws, or ideals, and the interest of history as a supreme conflict of the good will to secure its goodness universally in collision with various forms of evil. We must contemplate Christ as the centre of one or other of two systems of history. We must construe history as moving in two possible schemes, and we must make a choice. For Christ can remain permanently at the centre of only one of these. Is He the centre and Redeemer in a system of sin and grace, or the apex of a system of historic evolution, crowning in his perfection the evolution of the humane world ? Is He the grand and final source of our moral Redemption, or only the grand influence so far on our spiritual development ? Is the world history in which he has played a part so supreme a divine conflict with evil, or is it a human escape from impediment and imperfection ? Is it the Lord's controversy with man, or man's with Nature ?

The Christian answer hitherto given to that alternative, is to place Christ at the creative centre of a system of man's guilt and God's grace. From Christ's point of view salvation is not a sectional shelter for the religious, but the ultimate spiritual principle of mankind. All that transpires in history is tributary to man's supreme destiny, to be redeemed by God from his collective guilt. With all history the purpose of God's goodness is to produce repentance (Rom. ii. 4). The real and inmost life of the race is the tragic conflict of man's egoism with God's purpose of holy love ; and at the centre of that interior, the crisis of that issue is the decisive Cross of Christ, decisive for all mankind and all eternity. The object of history is not the evolution by man of spiritual values through God's help fostering the potencies of the race ; it is the restoration by God of a communion with His holy self which was broken by our guilty sin, and the issue from that Communion of all the glorious image of God in man's spiritual attainment.

This is the feature which really differentiates the Christian point of view from the modern. There is no greater division within religion than that between Emerson and Kierkegaard, between a religion that but consecrates the optimism of clean youth, and that which hallows the tragic note, and deals with a world sick unto death. We choose the latter. Every

AUTHORITY, HISTORY, AND DESTINY

form of religion is less Christian as it retires from that centre where guilt and grace meet in an eternal and regenerative world-crisis in Christ. That treatment of the soul is the condition of living faith and its theology, all else is but religion and its philosophy. That faith is the foundation of the Church against the Gates of Hell for ever; the rest but fosters various affinities, fraternities, or associations, more or less fugitive. The one sets our feet upon moral reality, the other but satisfies more or less the modern hunger for activity. The one stamps Eternity on Time, the other evolves from Time what may be worth calling Eternity or may not. And nothing can really impress or transfigure Time but Eternity. At the Reformation (it has been said) this system of sin and grace (meaning less a dogmatic fabric, of course, than a spiritual construction of things) took the place of an organised system of sins and graces. It is a fact that has not been realised by many who are prejudiced against the arbitrariness or the triviality of what they have heard of grace. A new world was opened, and we carry on the task created by the open door. The work of to-day is to construe in this redemptive way, this justifying way, the whole moral order and spiritual structure of the world, in contrast with a mere ideal philosophy of things which may be more or less spiritual. We may for the time be more concerned about the justification of God in such an anomalous world than about the justification of man before such a holy God. But at least, either way, it is a case of justifying certain behaviour, and not of tracing and floating on certain ideal tendencies.. And if we return beyond the Reformation to Jesus Himself, it is only a minimist and not a productive criticism that can deny, first, that He knew His vocation to be the establishment of God's sovereignty for the world, and second, that the foundation of that sovereignty was the forgiveness of sin by God's grace. For the Man of men the moral meaning was the ultimate meaning of the world; and the moral problem was the adjustment of sin and sanctity, the reconciliation of guilty men and holy God. To read man's history otherwise is to depose Christ, and begin to excuse Him. And if such was the mind of Christ, we have only farther to ask if His apostles have totally misrepresented the manner by which He set up that kingdom on such a base, and offered Himself as the personal revelation and historic effectuation of this purpose of God for guilty man. Were they wrong in preaching Him as the presence and action of a holy God, in love regenerating the whole race to its divine destiny? (Chap. VI.)

If the one absolutely precious thing in the world is the good will then the Will perfectly good is the source and measure of the world's destiny. Has Christ such a will, on the scale of man's whole soul? Was the consciousness of Christ the battlefield of that decisive moral issue on which (as most own) hangs the destiny of mankind? Was His work the divine settlement of that issue, and the one guarantee of that destiny? Is the Father of whom Jesus was the Eternal Son the God of the whole world for ever? Does our faith possess in Christ the very authentic heart of God, His actual saving Will achieved, His final moral victory in history over every challenge and defiance? Then nothing in this world of God's creation can either arrest Christ's work or take precedence of it. That is the source of the New Creation, which lay with all its resources behind the exercise of the first. For God would have created no man free to sin had He not known himself to possess the power to redeem the creature He made. The whole resource of the Almighty did not go to create. The greater part was in reserve to save. To most salvation seems phantasmal compared with the power and reality of the creation. That is part of the illusive irony of the Cross, the conquering weakness of the Church. For as He was so are we in this world. It is not wholly our infidelity to the Cross, it is our partnership of it, that involves us in the scandal of the Cross.[1]

But are we shut up to a sharp dilemma between the two methods I have described ? If we begin with a philosophy of history are we debarred from applying it to Christ ; and if we begin with faith in Christ as God's grace to our guilt are we prevented from trying to articulate such a Christ into a system of history and the world ? Must either the philosopher silence the believer, or the believer the philosopher ? Surely that would be a poor and sterile deadlock, a schism between faith and thought which would be a continual irritant to both. It is impossible to arrest the gravitation of the historic thinker to a figure that has meant more for actual history than any other. And it is no less impossible to prevent the believer in such a Christ from speculation about Him which involves universal history and the whole cosmos. Even in New Testament times that was impossible, and Paul, to Romans and Ephesians, frames both a philosophy of universal history and a cosmic scheme of great grandeur. And he does this in order to provide a setting adequate to the spiritual reality he found in Christ. To be quite recent, the crusade against metaphysic which was identified with Ritschl has had a distinct set back of late years, and Christian thought is moving up to a cautious return upon ranges which are named from Schelling and Hegel. It is impossible to beat down the natural passion to unify the mental world—especially where the whole soul receives such an increase of vitality as a living faith brings. Faith itself gravitates to specu-

[1] For many suggestions in this chapter see an article by Günther in the *Zeitschrift für Theologie und Kirche*, 1912, 3. Heft.

lation on Christ. It moves to make its system of guilt and grace a system of the world and history. It cannot but so move. It is nothing less than coarse to ascribe such a tendency to a theological greed for territory. If in Christ we have found the heart of God and the secret of His action with men, we have also found the divine purpose for the whole world, the divine action in the world, and the divine principle of history. We have the ground of all things in the goal of all things. The total effect of Christ's redemption is not to be sought in the soul alone, as if it were only by His action on the soul and its exaltation to command a still alien and hostile universe (as the martyr does not feel the fire) that He secured the great consummation. For the whole creation groans for the Redemption, and is included in the process which works to the manifestation of the Sons of God. And the miracles of Christ show that His work is not simply to empower the soul to rise over an inferior creation and beat down Nature under its feet, but that it is also to involve Nature in the grand co-operation of all things in the everlasting kingdom. A historic Saviour of a historic humanity must also be the Lord of the whole universe, unless we contemplate a dualism more Persian than Christian at the close of all.

And we have this advantage, that we who believe are the inner experts of the matter; that we have a certain authority thereby, and not an impotence; that we have unique facilities for a judgment on the case, especially where it concerns the place and meaning of Christ for man's soul. We have been too susceptible to the imposing and monopolist claims of a science and a philosophy which have had enormous success with the world. And we ought to put aside this false modesty as leading to treason.

AUTHORITY, HISTORY, AND DESTINY 233

Let us not dread the charge of claiming infallibility because we are certain in our confession. In this region we ought to know with entirety, intensity, and passion. It is those who lack certainty, or any blood in it, that are most suspicious of infallibility—which must exist and be accessible somewhere. And where are we in contact with it if not in a faith which must be dogmatic as it catches its note of triumph from grace and its conclusive bliss? We need not be foolishly aggressive; but if we do not emptily assert, let us practically and faithfully use our special knowledge of the moral universe in an assured way. He that is spiritual, as a partner of the moral crisis and victory of the world, judgeth all things and is judged of none. If our faith involve a universe we must utter it in a universal way. We have been indeed something to blame in the respect that we have presented Christ too much as if He were but the Founder of the Church instead of the Arbiter of the race. We have spoken as if faith in Him had to do with a certain preserve called the Church, instead of being the divine principle of all high history and all the new mankind. The afterwash of a hard doctrine of election still erodes the banks of thoughtless thought, and ready writers, who write themselves down whenever they touch religion, treat Christ as a western Confucius or Buddha, the head of a peculiar set of people. We have induced a belief, among some who have but a literary acquaintance with such things, as if the martyrdom of the Cross were but a sectarian case, negligible among so many more, of the mighty tragedy of man, instead of being the whole human tragedy at its core, crisis, and crown. We must escape from that conventicle and provincial note, to see and to say that the secret of Christ is the soul of history, and that a truer and deeper philosophy of history spreads away from the theodicy of salvation than from the procession of an idealist evolution. It is in a philosophy of history as nowhere else that Christianity comes to its own.

But with all this said, let us be the more clear that the two methods are not necessarily competitive, and not exclusory. It is not a question of monopoly, but of primacy for the evangelical view of life. It is not that faith must despise thought and its wealth, nor thought despise faith and its power—so long as the historic order of guilt and grace appears as a deeper and more fateful order than that of mere spiritual ideas, so long as historic redemption becomes the ground of any philosophy of evolution, and so long as it provides those spiritual values by which alone we have an authority that can assess the world of ideas, or tell whether mere movement is rising as growth, or sinking as lapse. We can work together with great mutual benefit so long as we treat Christ primarily as the crisis of a system of grace, and only secondarily as the centre (so far) of a system of history. It is only as we know Christ as the soul's Redeemer from its guilt before God that we are sure of the moral (which is the final) destiny of men and things. Apart from Him we can have no such certainty as religion at least requires; for we have then but an unfinished area for our induction of tendencies, or an unsteady vision for the intuition of ideas; and we have not the final will of the Absolute God for our eternal destiny in a New Creation which leads but does not abolish the old.

Our destiny as an ideal humanity can only be our authority if our goal is given us in our Ground and our God.

C.—SOCIETY

XII

THEOLOGY AND CHURCH

No form of religion can live in modern society, with its growing education and its consequent rationality, unless it have a theology. A religion of the free spirit without the fixed word is nebulous, and trails off in vapours which only ascend and do nothing. A temperamental and romantic religion is doomed to a wide area, a weak effect, and a brief life. It revolves in a subjectivity which is the final ruin of real religion, because it is the destruction of authority. For religion is an obedience before it is a liberty; and its first requisite is an authority; and for authority the first need is a real objective which is at once the source of our life, the home of our soul, and the God of our worship. And it must also be an authority and an objective commensurate with the world. It must be greater than Humanity in heart, and soul, and strength, and mind—it must at least be no less. And the theology of it must be on the same scale. It must come home by our own experience, but it must far transcend it. We believe far ahead of our experience, even though we believe in terms of it. Experience is the field where our theology arises, but it is not the spring. The matter of such theology, its Word, is a Revelation which speaks the language of experience but with the voice of Eternal God.

Christianity at least cannot live without a theology which sets forth such a Revelation. It is impossible there to separate religion from theology, man from God's purpose, faith from grace. It can only be attempted at the cost of one of them. The object of Christian faith is a theological God, or else He is not Holy Love. It is impossible to separate the questions, " Whom do you trust ? " and " What do you believe about Him ? " For the latter only means, " For what do you trust Him ?." We only trust Him in a theological function—as our Saviour; not simply as our Father—that is not Christianity—but as the Father of the Eternal Son and sole Redeemer.

The word theology is here used with some care, and with particular reference to its historical base. It is the intelligible content, the inevitable statement (spreading out to the elaborate exposition), of the act and person given in a historic revelation. If we discard that historic base, and still pursue the scientific interest, the matter of religion may be treated in two ways. Either it is taken in hand by a Rationalism in which it is trimmed down to the laws indigenous to formal thought; or it is given over to a Theosophy in which the matter itself is provided by an intuitive knowledge somewhat intractable to logical control. So that while Rationalism ceases to be Christian, Theosophy ceases to be scientific. There is no doubt that the latter—an intuitive idealism—is the favourite resort of the hour. It seems to offer a generous escape from hard Rationalism on the one hand and from hard Orthodoxy on the other. And it does it in a way in which the individual seems to himself able at once to indulge his individuality of standard, to escape from external authority, and to preserve a mysticism of atmosphere and a stamp of reason.

Of course the word theosophy is not here used in the current sense which suggests India. It means any idealist creed whose subject matter is provided

THEOLOGY AND CHURCH 239

by present intuition, genial or intellectual, rather than historic revelation, and which refuses the limitations of the mere understanding in the freedom of the speculative reason. It claims for its ideas a reality which belongs to no mere abstraction or projection of thought but to Being as thought. But it does not escape the arbitrariness of imagination. Both Rationalism and Theosophy, logic and intuition, are too inward to be other than arbitrary. They do not release us from the ban of our subjectivity. We do not escape to a real object who approaches and seizes us, loves and saves. And they agree in their impotence for social purposes. They belong to single thinkers (like all culture), or to groups and schools at most. They do not create a Church; nor can they keep one alive. But Theology, on the other hand, is the statement, simple or scientific, of a living revelation given at a historic point, creating its own society, and persisting in a continuous social experience. It is not the science of the Christian experience, which would be no more than a Christian psychology, or a phenomenology of the Christian spirit. But it is the science of such a historic and self-communicated God as is given only in the region of our experience in receiving Him, and especially in the region of a Church's collective experience. It is super-historic in the field of history, and super-egoist in the field of our own experience. And its content is God's supreme act and deed of self-bestowal toward mankind in a racial Redeemer through a universal Church. In a theosophy (like Hegel's system) what we use is the intuition of thought by thought, in theology it is the intuition of a person by faith. In the one we have an ideal monism, thought discovering itself everywhere; in the other we have a moral dualism, in which a person finds another person by way of salvation and not mere discovery. In the one case it is the intuition of truth in a mind, in the other the intuition of personality in a community.

Without some theology based on a historic revelation Christianity cannot even be spoken of, and cannot live. And it must grow to be a theology on a scale corresponding to the centrality of the revelation, *i.e.*, corresponding to its finality.[1] For a revelation central to the *whole* of human history, past or future, must be final. And, if Christianity represent the final revelation, then the Christian theology flowing from it must be universal. That is to say, not merely empirically universal, but ideally—universal in its nature, and not simply in the extent of its recognition. It must be adequate and adjustable to the whole knowledge, action, and destiny of the race. It must at least have the aspect, not indeed of final form, but of final greatness and command. And the Church will always be inferior in a thinking world till it acquire and handle such an adequate creed with a dogmatism mightier, sharper, and sweeter than the world's own.

Theology in this large and expository sense does not belong to the individual but to something more universal, to the Church. It is not the product or the property of any single person, nor even of any single sect or communion. It belongs to the Church as a whole, and for that Church it is a necessity. It is the intelligent counterpart of its practical organization. It is a living product of the corporate self-consciousness of the whole community of Christian faith. A divided Church will always have a theology weak

---

[1] I have in my mind the frequent distinction between a prime theology which is the plain and fundamental *statement* of the revelation, and a secondary which is the swelling *exposition* of this central truth in terms of the Church's growth in experience and culture. It is the latter I have chiefly in view here.

THEOLOGY AND CHURCH

enough to justify even its own neglect of it—a neglect none the less fatal because just. As to individuals, it does not matter much what their form of theology is. With private members of a Church it does not much matter whether they have a theology or not, so long as they are respectful to those who do. It does not matter whether Messrs X, Y, or Z have a theology or not—except in so far as they may cease to be merely Messrs X, Y, or Z, and become teachers of the Church, use its prestige, and voice its Gospel. It is a matter that concerns the Church as a whole, and by consequence the public representatives and teachers of the Church in the degree in which they are its representative teachers, and not free-lances tilting amid spectators, or amateurs indulging a taste. A great theology is the rational and necessary expression of the spiritual content of a great Church. Without it the Church has no spiritual volume, whatever be the piety of individuals. And such a Church can make no spiritual impression on a whole age. Contempt for theology is the badge of a limited culture. And not only so; its real source is poverty of religion; and within the Church it may indicate more spiritual fluency than Christian faith. The due authority of a Church is in proportion to the authority of its Gospel, and not to its prestige as an institution; and it is no authoritative Gospel for any Church if it do not move progressively into a great theology, with a weight for the world according to the moral weight accumulated by the Gospel in the living Church.

But if the sense of a great Church is gone, what then? If the several Churches seek to justify their existence as protesting rather than ancillary, as a challenge instead of a service to the great one Church; if their chief attitude is polemical, sectarian, and not integral to the great federate household of faith? Must we not then give up all hope of a great theology and therefore of a commanding Christ? If we lose the practical sense and fellowship of the Great Church imperial or federate, as a part of our personal religion, must we not also lose from our Word the universal note? Is there not a real connection between schism and heresy—though we may not accept the old form in which that connection was expressed? A sect, which is content to be a sect (or even a religious club), or one which is ambitious to capture the whole Church for its egoistic sectarianism, instead of making its providential and sectional contribution to the whole Church's symmetry and its proportion of faith—such a sect cannot have a great theology; and it will soon cease to have a theology at all. It will despise its theologians in favour of its preachers or its patrons, and it will end in deserting these idols when one more engaging comes along. That is to say, its popular speakers will cease to have a voice that compels any attention from those responsible for the greatest affairs. It will not have the largeness of utterance that goes with divine authority in public things. It will tend to act either as a caterer, or as an irritant, rather than as a leader and commander of the people. Its activity will be more restless and forcible than controlling, or even guiding. It will not rule the intelligences that rule society. The deep reason why theology is ignored by many of our chief intelligences is not the existence of dogma but its hard poverty. The religious hunger of the age is felt by its intellect no less than by its heart; and it longs for a faith credible to the large and piercing intelligence no less than trusty for the eternal soul. With the divisions of the Churches and their mutual exclusions the Church's thought has grown thin and its voice small. The theology, even when it aims to be modern, does not express any commanding consciousness of a spiritual cosmos, nor the personality of a united Christendom. Or, if it goes back to the ages of a united Christendom and is not modern, it is untrue to a living Christendom which moves and grows. Where it is modern it is sectional and arid, and, where it is ecumenical it is antiquated and feeble. With such theologies, shut up to such an unhappy choice, Christianity must go down as a moral and social power. All its unction and sympathy will not save it, but will run into brotherhoods rival to the Church and without its staying power. With no sense of the Great Church there is no command of great truth; and with no command of great truth there is no future in a great and growing civilisation.

It is not for a moment meant that Christianity is but the religious obverse of an enlarging civilisation and its thought. That would indeed be making a present of the Word to the world, and secularising the Gospel to the measure of each age. It is not meant that Christianity must keep issuing a constant apologetic which adjusts its truth and claim to the spirit of the age. A Church of apologetics to men would be no Church of kings and priests to God. The Gospel confronts civilisation, and does not simply give it religious expression. Christ was neither a genius nor a symbol in history. But what is meant is that the claim must speak a language no less noble and ample than the best ideas of the time, and no less intimate and passionate than its moral need. It must face all the extravagant subjectivity of great mankind with One who is intrinsically greater than the ideal superman. And it must guarantee a salvation which is not more meagre than those vast conceptions of social weal or cosmic evolution which dignify but do not satisfy the modern mind. The Church of the Gospel as a society confronts two great rival authorities—Socialism and Romanism. Each claims to be the supreme authority for practical life. Each declares that human salvation is to be found in it alone—in it and its organisation. The one represents the new idea of the world State, the other the eternal organisation of the world Church. And the Evangelical Church must secure its existence and its ruling effect against both. This can never come about in the shape of imperial rule, never on the line of either of its rivals as a world organisation. It can come to pass only as a vast and universal moral power, as a federation of Churches, secured on the basis of a voluntary but collective confession, whose comprehension at once gives scope to the subjective, personal, and responsible side of Protestant Christianity, and makes room for the many varieties of national and other Churches.

It is another form of the antipathy, or at least indifference, to theology or corporate conviction to say that in a Church of a Christian spirit there should be unlimited latitude of belief. This is a quite impossible position, and I essay to deal with it in the next two chapters. It canonises liberty at the cost of truth. It makes liberty first and truth second. It reduces all truth to a matter of quest, and it leaves no room for final revelation. But for a Church at least there must be some fundamental truth or fact, something beyond a temper or ideal, as the creative source of all its liberty. This view we may take to be established among those who are most responsible for the Church's life.

But when it is said that there should be a limit to freedom of belief within a Church, the view is sometimes admitted in theory only to be dismissed

THEOLOGY AND CHURCH

in practice, on the ground that it is impossible to draw the line. If we recognize any necessary development in the Church's theology, any just variation from traditional belief, we shall be faced with the question as to a standard of authority to decide the justice of the variation or its limit. Many (it is said) of the views now called legitimate were at first treated by the Church as dangerous heresy. How do you know that what seems fatal to faith to-day will not be a blessing to faith to-morrow? Or, on the other hand, how know that what seems so natural and generous to-day may not, like the old Pelagianism, carry in it the destruction of the Church, and its reduction to mere natural spirituality, when generations have worked out the consequences on their true scale? How will you determine what variation should be encouraged by the Church as wholesome and what repelled as fatal? Now the first answer to that is this : Surely the Church has some criterion of truth other than the survival of a view in the agelong conflict of opinions. What is survival but the slow, and partly unconscious, action of some selective standard. Surely a Church possesses at its very source the principle of its own selection and comprehension, unless it is to be no more than the spiritual side of the world. Surely it has some test to-day which forbids it to fold its hands in quietism, leave truth to emerge far off from the scrimmage, and remit the whole matter to posterity centuries away. How will posterity be better off? When the hurly-burly's done that may be at set of sun. We may reach the great truth as history expires; which would be like waiting for future death to learn how to live to-day. For want of the vital truth while its truth was in the making, the Church, which should have been living on it, has sunk into the sand. The steed starves while his grass is growing.

And the second answer is this. It is not the case, in the history either of the Church or Society, that every new view once counted deadly has come to be welcomed as beneficent. There has been some other test than mere time and persistence. Some heresies have died out. Others, both moral and mental, have never made good their right to come inside, however useful as correctives from without. The future was not with the popular Arius but the persecuted Athanasius. What has made the distinction? It is not the case that each novelty needs but pertinacity to become an ingredient of the Church's faith. There must be some means of drawing an authoritative line, even if it is not always straight or clear. There must surely be in every positive religion some point where it may so change as to lose its identity and become another religion. There must be some principle which to surrender is for the religion to lose its own soul. There must be some positive message to try the spirits and protect us from the facile hierophant and the sweet *exalté*. There must be something which distinguishes inspiration from inflation, prophecy from hysterics, an apostle from a freak, a saviour from an ecstatic. Unless, indeed, we take the impossible position that the truest religion is the most devoid of characteristic features and cognisable notes; unless it be a religiosity which moves vaguely among the general features and aspirations common to all religion—such a religion as never actually existed. May the libertarians not be invited to say what is their objective touchstone of Christianity, whether they would draw any line besides good intentions, and if so where does it run?

I tried once in an article in the *Hibbert Journal* (January 1910) to indicate the difference between heterodoxy and heresy. I suggested that the former had a place permanent and precious in a Church of theological progress, while the other not only had no such place, but was made heresy by the fact that it destroyed the Church idea, that is, the social idea, and disconnected Christianity from a society. And as the Church was made by the Word of the New Testament Gospel, which remains its authoritative element, the Church-destroying thing was that which destroyed that Word, by stripping it of its unique quality, its historic finality, its absolute redemption, and by reducing it to be but the upper level of the other religions of the world, or the general religiosity of the race. It reduced Christianity to be one among many religions, *prima inter pares*, though one that did more justice than they did to certain spiritual instincts which they were all trying to express or meet. It made any form of religion but a tentative expression of something *in* man, something real however latent, instead of an authoritative revelation of something *to* man, final however progressive. To that article I might venture to refer some who may wish to raise questions here. I pointed out that there was a large and valuable range within the Church for a heterodoxy which yet maintained the evangelical continuity, and which declared the reality of a historic and moral redemption of the race in the Cross of Christ. Such a heterodoxy is still one with the Church in that solidarity of apostolic tradition which centres in the absolute Word and not in its successive prophets, in a historic point and not a historic line. Fixed there, a great Church, like a great oak, may be flexible everywhere else, and stronger against storms than a stiff tower. But to be loose there is not to be flexible but vagrant. It is to have no root, no revelation, anywhere, in the strict, true, and final sense of that word. And no liberty is legitimate which does not spring from, or consent with, the liberty that historically gave the Church its being—the evangelical liberty of the guilty soul in its experienced salvation by the grace of a holy God in the Cross of Jesus Christ, now risen and reigning in the glory He had before all worlds.

I would here approach the matter from another point of view.

Criticism has of late passed into a new phase which really makes its results a new religion rather than a new stage, a new ship rather than the old docked and scraped. And it would send the Church out with no hold of anything, with but only a progressive sympathy. We are presented with the religious-historical method. This is not an extension of the old method, but the creation of a new. And it is really less critical than dogmatic in its inspiration. The older criticism was, often at least, compatible with the recognition of a unique and final revelation in the Gospel of Jesus Christ. It left possible a liberal theology. It had room for the recognition of a final intervention of God at a point of history. It stripped away, indeed, a good deal that belonged to that historic moment, by its free handling of the Bible which carried the Gospel. Primitive Christianity was found to have been much coloured by the influences, and bound by the limits, of that age, that land, and the lands around. Pure revelation was muffled in many of the hulls of the popular religion amid which it rose. Inspiration was a challenge to current religion, and not its incandescence. But criticism did not feel that it must treat the trappings as the horse, or the curtain as the picture. It thought that it was possible and necessary to clear Christianity both of contemporary alloy and later accretions, and yet to preserve the distinctive, real, and final revelation of God in Christ. The secondary elements, the merely historic, could be detached, and the primary, the superhistoric, the evangelical, be all the more free and effective. There

THEOLOGY AND CHURCH

was a core of absolute revelation not traceable to, and not explicable through, any other influence than the actual and unique visitation of God redeeming in His Son. This was the foundation of the Church and the charter of its pulpit; and all its progress in theology or elsewhere was the expansion of this.

But criticism has entered a new and more dogmatic phase. The starting-point is not the objective Gospel of the Church but the subjective religion of Humanity. The general principles which form the precipitate of ideas in all religions are now held to account for Christianity also; which is but another and a finer mythology of them, accidentally attached to a certain Jewish Rabbi of whom little may be really known. Christ is a mythology built round Jesus, as a pearl upon grit; and religion did more to produce Christ than any Christ did to produce religion. The Church was not a creation by God's unique act in Christ, but a social product from certain redemptive ideas that seized the world with an epidemic force quite peculiar to those lands or days. Christianity is thus levelled down in authority, even while its refinement in idea is recognised. It loses in power as it gains in poetry; as in the modern representations of Macbeth, all the terror and sublimity of a deed brief but endless is lost in the effort to clothe it with intimacy and beauty. It is called more spiritual than the rest, but it is not therefore more real, not more sure as a revelation of God, or as a special act of His, to say nothing of a final, and one crucial for our fate. There is nothing wherewith to prove the spirits whether they be of God. It is but relatively different from other faiths. It is less original and independent at its heart than we were taught. We can at most speak only of the independence of religion, not of the independence of Christianity at all. And any authority of the Church is not only archaic but odious in an age of fraternal sympathy and individual liberty. All spiritual events are entirely and equally subject to the general laws of historical evolution. Historical science forbids us to allow any real branch of the evolutionary method in the most significant personality. All that happens in the spiritual region must be explained immanently, *i.e.*, from the nature of spiritual Humanity. And Christ Himself can only be reecived in so far as He conformed more fully to the laws of that nature elsewhere shown. His spiritual knowledge He reached along the same lines as other men. Christ is explained by history, not history by Christ. The Church made Him more than He the Church. He is the product of the Church more than its provider to this day. There is no history of redemption apart from the ascending history of the race developed with God's aid. Christ is more an expression of whatever revelation there may be in Humanity than of any revelation to it. The reality or the possibility of a constant revelation in everything we establish on other grounds, if we can, and then we go on to find its classic instance in Christ. Not only are miracles banished from revelation, but the miracle of revelation as redemption is abolished. It does not invade us and new create us. It only fulfils us and gives us effect. It does not regenerate. And the Church rests upon no initial miracle of the Resurrection, and upon no standing miracle of the Spirit. It cannot speak down to the old creation from the new.

That is the latest phase of historical and critical science applied to the origin of Christianity. Its treatment has gone far beyond the secondary elements of faith; it has plucked the source of Christianity out of its native heaven and made it natural to earth. But in doing so it has surely proclaimed another religion and dissolved the apostolic Church. It is

THEOLOGY AND CHURCH 251

not a valuable heterodoxy, but a fatal heresy. It has surely stepped over the line of freedom in any true Church, by dissolving the Church into a mere continuous vitality, stripped of the central, positive, and creative Word which keeps its vitality up, and reinforces it constantly by the Holy Spirit.

And to press the right of such a position in the teaching of an evangelical Church is to provoke a bitterness that was vanishing from mere theological difference. For heresy in itself does not now make trouble, except when it appears as treason. Attacks from without must be quite differently viewed from betrayal within.

There is one point that needs, perhaps, to be emphasised. When we speak of lawful liberty we do not mean liberty in the eye of the law. We do not mean it in reference to formularies, or trust-deeds, and their legal interpretation. We should all agree (I hope) to deprecate an appeal to the law to settle the liberty of the Gospel, or the invocation of Parliament to dictate to the Church her terms of communion. The Church alone has the right to determine its own comprehension, which it does by its selective Word. Of the liberty of the Gospel the law knows nothing. It deals only with the strict interpretation of articles of association and schedules of property. In respect of these the Church by consent may sit loose, antiquate the law, and require the law to stand on one side recognising her native right but conferring none. The limit we are concerned with in the Church is not documentary, not statutory, not subscriptional, but evangelical, descriptive, and declaratory. It makes a debt of honour. It rests on a positive tradition, a common understanding, hereditary in the Church concerned, presupposed in its postulants, and vital to its scriptural faith. The liberty which is lawful is made so by the law of Christ and not the law in ordinances. It is a liberty under authority, decent and true to that apostolic Gospel for whose sake the community exists whose advantages are sought or enjoyed. To renounce that Gospel would not be to reform but to reverse the whole current of the Church's past history. It would be the destruction of the community and not its correction, the abolition and not the modification of its reason for existing.

The standard of liberty, therefore, is one embedded in the authoritative Word of an evangelical Church, and not imposed or conferred by legal statutes. It is the kind of liberty whose honest limit would be overpassed if licence were claimed in an evangelical Church for Unitarian theology. The Church has no ground for its existence except the authoritative Gospel which Socinianism denies. Let it be once understood that any Church is indifferent to the supreme apostolic Gospel which finds the essence of Christianity to be grace to guilt in Christ crucified and risen, and from that hour it ceases to be worth preserving. All differences of polity will then seem incidental by comparison. They will not prevent many from seeking their spiritual home in communions where such a gospel reigns. And the preaching of a real gospel like that in a Church might even make people tolerant of a good deal they would rather disown. Were there no other alternative, Bishop Gore's gospel would make many put up, for the time at least, with his view of the ministry.

XIII

PLEBISCITE AND GOSPEL AS AUTHORITY

THE questions which hold the chief interest of the hour, even in the Churches, belong to the class which are capable of being solved by the decision of majorities. It is a fact less, perhaps, to be regretted than reckoned with. Naturally the majority are most interested in questions that majorities can settle. Most people are engrossed with the kind of issues and ills which they believe that Parliament can cure or societies mend. They aim, therefore, at votes or at funds. They tend to be ruled by the politic methods which secure them, by the considerations that tell in the whip's office or the treasurer's books. And the danger is that we should import these methods of strategy and haulage into regions where they are irrelevant and strange, regions hidden from the wise and prudent, where unwelcome truths and unpopular realities in the hands of elect minorities have always been the saving powers. Social reform, just because it is so valuable and so urgent, tends to swallow up soul reform, and the amelioration of conditions, or the rectification of belief, hampers the reformation of faith. The average voter believes in votes—their capture, their machinery, and their effect; and the average earnest Christian is apt to believe as a voter would. Hence the methods of appeal to him tend to be coloured by the atmosphere of the platform and of the press, and the arguments are often so adapted for public consumption as to lose reality and conviction. He is hard to convince that the public can seldom get the real and relevant truth of a difficult situation in either field. The public interest is not at every stage best served by publicity. Some of the subjects that most need discussion in the Church cannot be discussed, or vital aspects of them cannot be touched, if the discussion stage is reported. Hence our religious assemblies lose both point and weight. Do we not constantly find in practice that the real and shaping considerations only come out *in camera*, or in committee? The greatest public matters, especially in foreign or delicate affairs, are often decided by considerations which never reach the public, never should, never can reach it, and which, perhaps, we get at only in Memoirs a generation or two later. " The secrecy of the Cabinet is its strength. A great part of the weakness of Democracy springs from publicity of discussion," so insatiable, so suspicious, so premature often. Publicity by all means, but at the right and ripe stage. Public affairs demand such publicity as the safeguard of justice and freedom. But when we come to the Church it is not the affair of the public, it is no part of the public, it is not the nation, it is not the democracy, on its religious side. It is a family; and its note is not a watchful publicity, but the warm communion of saints.

My point here will be this. We have two democracies, a natural and a spiritual. The natural cannot survive without the spiritual. And the spiritual is only saved by that in its constitution which is not democratic, not brotherly but kingly, by an authority that does not proceed from the community, and is not amenable to its vote.

We are often reminded by the wise that it is the subtlest forces that are, in the end, the strongest, and the things least ponderable the most powerful. But at the present day, and to the temper I speak of, this is somewhat embarrassing; and it raises various questions about democracy with which the democracy has little patience. The deeper we go into conscience or soul, the finer the matter may be in which we work, the more subtle, penetrating (and therefore *formative*), the force is, so much the more urgent is something that no mere majority, no unprepared majority, can give, or wield, or even realize. Yet it is something that majorities need for their safety, permanence and beneficence. For power, truth and freedom, we need it. We need it for the protection *of* the majority; and we need it for protection *from* the majority; which, in the finer matters, can be not only inadequate but obtrusive and tyrannical. This is a consideration of immense moment for a society which deals in matters so great, high, and strange as the Church does. What protection does a particular Church system offer for a constitutional minority? That is a question of prime moment for any Church polity. It will be an evil day for the highest interests of the race when they are decided by those political methods which use but the rough arbitrament of numbers, which do not allow men to rebuke their constituency with unwelcome truths, whose power is in the big battalions or press notices, and to which martyrdom is failure. For current politics, indeed, and burning questions, it is hard to see what other weapon can be employed than majorities, duly educated, controlled, and safeguarded. I am not speaking of that region. But in spiritual matters, in the highest moral matters, in so-called academic matters, with the early stages of all great movements, with the pioneers, geniuses, thinkers and saints, it is otherwise. With the prophet, who is so much more than a tribune, who must at times judge his own people, and whose critical courage is not entirely kept for attacking the other side, it is otherwise. With the elect, who are the seed of the future in the greatest things, it is otherwise. And it would be establishing the Church with a vengeance, and putting it under the State in the most subtle and fatal of all ways, if the ruling political and prehensile methods were made the decisive thing in spiritual affairs, or those which approach the spiritual, such as art, or thought, or belief. For the Kingdom of God the public cannot be captured, but only convicted, convinced, and converted. Is it not putting the Church fatally under the public, and selling its spiritual freedom, if it agree not to discuss its most peculiar, intimate, and unworldly affairs in private, if it must have its own bitterness of heart published and canvassed in the press, or if strangers are invited to intermeddle with its inward joy, if its inmost counsels are flung out to be trodden under foot of men, if its proposals at the most delicate stage, its purposes at the most tentative, must be discussed with the gas lit, the blinds up, and the window wide, if its self-searching and its solemn vows take place under the observation and criticism of Assyrian and Philistine in streets and trains? And so also with the indiscriminate application to the Church of the majority principle. Majorities may decide a course of convenient action, but they have no divine prerogative, or even promise, in the region of thought, ultimate truth, and reality—on which at last the great concerns rest. In religious matters especially, in a Church, the majority principle is only adequate and safe if it be a majority in a society composed of people who care supremely for some given, settled, and final thing, which majorities have no power to decree or alter, and which neither the present nor the future has any right to control, but only the duty to obey.

I am constantly drawn, beyond the issues that

PLEBISCITE & GOSPEL AS AUTHORITY 257

promptly appear and appeal, to those that finally matter and are easily missed. Full of the delight I feel under the spell of the best orators of my side, or cooling down after some effort of my own to help them, I pass next day, from the things that flush platforms and rouse assemblies, to those ulterior questions which are, like death, so unobtrusive, yet so ubiquitous, so sure, so instant, so irresistible; and they sit with a fine, silent irony within and beyond the tumult and the shout, knowing they must one day inherit, control, and still it all. And I am urged constantly to ask myself, and respectfully to press the query on others, what the end of those ardent things shall be. I ask questions dismissed as obscure, on the scale, not of our congregations or our occasions, but of the whole Church, the whole world, and the whole Gospel. I suggest answers which hint that what is the matter with our Churches is their relations to the Great Church, and to that which makes it great. Questions force themselves on me which seem remote, but are anything but academic, which are only remote as the sun is which is the source of earth's life, and which are bound one judgment-day to present themselves in a way that will take no denial, and that will put us, our societies and our several Churches, on trial for our life. On our ministers kindly, on our laymen respectfully, I urge these questions—begging the latter especially not to dismiss them as unintelligible and irrelevant to practice just because, like the sun at midnight, they act from below the horizon of *their* daylight. They are bound to arise with a new day, and to create new demands both on duty and intelligence. We may make elaborate provision for our visible support, our palpable prestige, and our obvious influence on affairs; but what is it all if we grow less and less clear in our mind

R

about the ruling things, the things that must settle us before we can do much to settle society, the only things which are worth effort to support at last? Such matters are always unwelcome to those who are but officials, tribunes, or statesmen, or who know but business methods. The politician hates nothing like a Church question. But Church questions, for all the stir they can make when flung into an arena of zeal without knowledge, are yet the best type of those ideas which sit far behind the bloody edge of war, and really control the great campaign. And when we lose the sense of the Great Church, with its inseparable dogmatic basis, we lose the note of mastery with those commanding issues which, amid all perversion, still gives such a spell to Rome.

To illustrate these supreme but unpopular issues. A cellular and humanist religion, a mere concretion of the individual pieties or sympathies, loses the historic mind and the note of a universal Kingdom; it destroys the doctrinal intelligence and our grasp of a God as manifold and social as the world; it secularises faith, turns too readily to successive panaceas from a perennial and catholic Gospel; and it sterilises Christianity for the public future. So that we may mark, for instance, that the sense for the Church idea and that for the Trinitarian idea stand or fall together. The mentality which ignores the one tends to ignore the other at last. It is vain to try to spiritualise any particular Church without a real reverence for the universal Church that there meets in a point but is wholly there (Heb. xii. 22), and without a concern for it deeper than for any movement in society, or any issue of State. And how is this commanding and penetrating High Churchism to be cherished by us amid our fleeting moods, the vicissitudes of single Churches, and the

PLEBISCITE & GOSPEL AS AUTHORITY 259

tremendous importunities and secularities of the hour —religious and other? It is useless to talk of all life being equally sacred. The practical result of that notion is mostly the equalisation of temperature which is known as cooling down. We can only sanctify all life by the unique sanctity of certain parts of it. The keeping of Sunday is the means of hallowing all our days. We can sanctify Humanity only by the worship of One who is in it but not of it. We can hallow society only by hallowing within it the society of the Church. And the Church can take and keep its spiritual place as the Church of the living God only if by its living God we mean no glorified individual, but the Triune God who is the peculiar revelation of Christ. For the Christian God is not the Father, but the Father of our Lord Jesus Christ in the Spirit. It was such a God in such a revelation, such a self-donation of His in Son and Spirit, that created the Church ; and no other God can sustain it. The power that makes the Church a community of men is the same power that makes communion between man and God; and that again is the same power which makes the eternal bond of communion between Father and Son—the Holy Spirit. So solemn as that is the Church —no less unearthly than that—resting on the Word of a Reconciliation which binds in one the powers of Eternity itself.

Now this Revelation, constituent as it is of the Church, is the one thing that is withdrawn from its vote ; because a Church would unchurch itself that voted against it. And it is this sense, this faith, this Revelation, that must return to the whole Church, else it is bound to be submerged; because its principle of Reconciliation sinks to the level of the mere compromises of life. The impotence of which many complain in the Church of the hour is not unconnected with the relegation of the doctrine of the Trinity to a theological appendix, even when it is not denied (as it will be in the next generation). And, on the other hand, the joy and the uplifting that we have in meditating on the revealed depths of the Triune God is part of the blessedness which is the Church's consummation; and it gives us that self-possession of the holy which both inspires and preserves us among our best activities for man's weal. Such a doctrine, full as it is of difficulties for mere thought, when it is taken with serious depth by a Church of faith answers more difficulties than it creates. And such truth should be matter of adoration rather than criticism to an intelligence which is not merely exercised in speculation, but itself converted to the manner and movement of the Eternal Mind as it is revealed in Christ. The intellect needs conversion. As the theology of an age is, so is its Church life. When we ask what is the matter with the Church, the only radical answer must be *sub specie eternitatis*.

Now, with regard to the matter of public and authorised majorities, and with special regard to their relation to such eternal truth, there is something to be said which does not apply to the majority principle as the only possible method for practical and detailed action (even in the Church) in a democratic age. In the general challenge of authority, there must arise a challenge also of the authority of the majority on certain ultimate matters. It is a challenge raised within the common constitution of the Church, of course ; since it is no question of a minority of traitors or anarchists, but of those who join to accept the foundations of the society concerned. " Surely," says Mill, " when any power has been made the strongest, enough has been done for it; care is thenceforward wanted rather to prevent that strongest power from swallowing up all others."

PLEBISCITE & GOSPEL AS AUTHORITY 261

Again, "A centre of resistance is as necessary when the opinion of the majority is sovereign as when the ruling power is a hierarchy or an aristocracy. When no such *point d'appui* exists, the human race will inevitably degenerate; and the question, whether the United States, for instance, will in time sink to another China (also a most commercial and industrious nation), resolves itself into the question whether such a centre of resistance will gradually evolve itself or not." And questions offer themselves of a nature like these. To begin at the bottom. May an institution with a definite charter or articles honourably use the funds, even by a poll, for any object that a bare majority may at any time adopt? May a railway directorate subscribe to the capital of the British Association for Science, or of the Female Suffrage Society? May a trade union, by a majority, use its funds against the political party of its minority. Again, may a majority override the conscience? We hear it answered 'Yes and No. Quakers should be taxed for war; we should not be taxed for Roman teaching.' The ground of the distinction I think good, but to discuss it would occupy some space. But the point is, there is a limit. Where? Again, growing warmer, may a majority override the political Constitution? Has a majority the right of revolution? The right may be there. Does it reside in a majority as such? The old Commonwealth question (it will be seen) is still being fought. Could a majority on one election behead the King, or abolish the Lords, without destroying national continuity, and, therefore, the nation itself? Perhaps not. Yet, if one election should not do this, a series would. The point is, it can be done by electoral methods. Since 1688 the monarchy is elective, if the King is not. For the State, unlike the Church (as I shall immediately show), has no changeless trust from the past, even in the Constitution. Its ethic is utilitarian for the public good in the long run. It advances by steps which are valuable only as they serve a final moral ideal which is not in the charge of the State. But, how far could the Church do the like? In Church affairs, is it in the competency of a majority, for instance, to decide to abolish the existing constitution, and carry the resources of an Episcopalian or Presbyterian society to, say, a Swedenborgian or a Roman, or *vice versa* ? Could a law-court be expected to leave with the new body the property which belonged to the old? The men composing the congregation might be the same, but the *corpus* is not the same; the institution, the idea, the purpose has completely changed. But may the living Church, then, not settle everything about itself? Well, would you let the property of your Church go without a struggle if the members by a majority became Jesuits or theoretical anarchists — as many Protestant Anabaptists became at the Reformation—even if they were the sweetest-spirited men that ever stole a march or threw a bomb? May a point not be reached when it ceases to be a living Church, however occupied with religious, æsthetic, or philanthropic interests, and therefore ceases to have the right of settling things in defiance of the law which governs ordinary associations ? Does the vote of its majority that it is still a Church make it a Church? How far may a living Church, by any majority, modify its fundamental constitution ? " That," it may be said, " does not much affect those Churches which have very little in the way of statutory constitution." But they have something still more constitutive than a constitution, in the shape of their belief, which is spiritual organisation, and is the organisation of faith as the other is of works, the charter of the whole Church's existence. Christianity is not a religion of polity any more than a mere cult of conduct, but it is a religion of truth, and of the kind of faith that involves truth: and its Church, as it arose, so stands or falls by some theology; which, being involved in God's gift of Himself in revelation, cannot depend on any majority. Christianity is the only religion that has really developed a theology as a necessity of its existence. It does not necessarily preach dogma, but it cannot preach without it. Here its doctrine is like a man's family affections. The minister does not preach about his home, but it would be a very different preaching without it. He does not preach about his friends, but could he preach if he had none? Such a matter as the Trinity must be a postulate of Christian preaching, even if, by a reverent reticence, it is seldom its theme. Would a Church be a Church which by any majority denied that? Is a vote on such a question as the deity of Christ *intra vires* for a Church of the Gospel?

I have hinted that the Church differs essentially from the State in that the ethic of the State is utilitarian, or eudæmonist, while that of the Church cannot be. Let us examine this.

The State has not in trust any absolute truth, any creative deposit of a final kind from the past. It owes its foundation to no fontal and final act—on this side the Atlantic at least. It was not constituted by a specific and positive historic step, by a social contract, with inalienable features and principles of its own. It can do anything with the past which the public and national welfare seems to require, after due caution and free discussion, and much maturing. Even the American Constitution is not unalterable for ever. And even Conservatism, by its *penchant* for the Referendum, owns the political finality of the majority principle if it may prescribe its form. So much so that some have been prepared in this way to destroy the place of the House of Commons, as being a constitutional impertinence between the Monarch and the Multitude.

But the Church is totally different. Not that even in that home of the elect the minority must always be right. Which minority? There are usually several. A minority *quâ* minority is not the elect, and is not necessarily God's little flock. Neither the outvoted, nor the persecuted, as such, possess the future, nor should they control the present in the Church. Mere martyrdom has no divine right. Majorities and minorities are not the calculus of the Spirit. The Society of Friends takes no vote. We must look for a power which is immune from a mere majority. We look to an electorate in no form, but to an Elector, His choice, His historic gift, and His Holy Spirit in His Church; and no majority vote can guarantee His presence or His will. The Church has in its past an eternal charge and final Revelation, which it can never change by man's short estimate of social utilities without ceasing to be. It has a trust of the Gospel, and a work of the Spirit, which gave and gives it its being, and which to destroy would be at once parricide and suicide. It has in charge the historic panacea of Him who sees and secures the end from the beginning. For the Church to cut adrift from this historic source is to cut loose from its spiritual base and charter. It is to renounce what created it, and therefore to abjure its own right. It has a trust here compared with which its liberty is a minor issue. Its only liberty is the liberty to be faithful to that trust, or in it. Any liberty which destroys it ceases to be free, because it has ceased to be obedient. It is required that a man first be faithful and then be free. We have to be fair and to be free; but we have to be faithful most of all. Liberty, which is

PLEBISCITE & GOSPEL AS AUTHORITY 265

among the first interests of a State, is sometimes not even the second in a Church. " Liberty," says Burke, " must always be limited in order to be possessed." That is to say, it is permanent only under authority. Its right is derived. And this is truer for the Church than even for the State. Obedience may not be the first duty in the State, but it is in the Church. Faith is an obedience before it is anything else. The defiant and insolent spirit is much less tolerable in the Church than in the State, where humility is no virtue and no duty. Liberalism may be the mainspring of the State and its progress, but in the Church the historic base prescribes more of the conservative temper. Extremists have a place in politics which they have not in the genius of a historic faith like Christianity. Radicalism in affairs is on a different footing, is indeed a different thing, from the radicalism of such a religion (Heb. iv. 12).

And so between a Church and a democracy there is this fundamental difference and difficulty. No numbers can create a real authority for the conscience, such as we have within the Church; whereas democracy will listen to no authority but what its members, its majorities, do create. And its individualism and its subjectivity make it equally incompetent and indocile, at its present stage, for the supreme questions and issues of Humanity and of the Soul. It is too sure of itself and too full of itself, and it has no idea that it exists more for God's glory than God does for its ideals. The Church of Christ, with a living Christ for King, is no democracy, great as its affinities with democracy are. And it has a " once for all," a creed, whether foimulated or not, which is not simply tentative, temporary and regulative, but constitutive; not a matter of convenience, but of constitution, a matter of deposit and trust; not a matter of importance, but of existence;

not of concern merely, but of life and death. Its ministers are not seekers of truth any more than of power; they are stewards and spenders of both. And so fixed and final is the Church in this respect that a deep sense of the comparative plasticity, not to say fluidity, of the State has caused some great political thinkers to cling to a Church established in an organic connection with it as the only guarantee at last of the stability of the nation.

Now we may leave aside for a moment the question what part or form of the Church's traditional creed is such a permanent trust. But surely some part, some form, is. The Church has beliefs which are not mere beliefs but realities, the thoughts not of man but of God, beliefs which created it, which constitute it, without which it is no Church. Without a constituent charge, a positive call, a final and fontal gift or mandate from God—without such a constitution, the bottom simply drops out of a Church. And with a mere subjective constitution, not given as a charge but developed as a product of man's native religiosity or convenience, its foundation is desert sand or airy mirage. The Church rests on the given, the State on the achieved. The Church is not a mere religious assembly which could remove God, the historic existence of Christ, or the finality of Redemption from its belief, so long as it did all with the note of charity, and abolished Christ in the "spirit of Christ." A nation may survive regicide, but a Church cannot. In the State a revolution which thus renounced the past would not necessarily be treason. It might be but acute evolution. But in the Church that would be treason, and it would embarrass accordingly. A historic, positive, objective and final salvation in Christ is absolutely constitutive for the Church. It is not merely regulative, or valuable for a passing stage or purpose. The Sabbath was made for man, but man was made for the Saviour. His salvation is not a piece of the Church's primitive mythology, as some would Germanize it. It is of the Church's *esse*, and not simply of its *bene esse*. It is not useful, it is essential. The denial of it, or the relegation of it, has no more right within the Church than an alien in the Arsenal. The idea, for instance, that there is no more reason to believe in a living Christ than in a living Buddha is, within the Church, not free reason, but pure treason. It is a foreign and inflammatory body in the system. And the same with the denial of a historic Christ. " Religion," says a deep thinker, "has a meaning for men only if it find in history a *point* to which it can absolutely surrender."

The writer's argument throughout is that the Gospel of the New Testament forms (and for a democratic Church above all) that constitutional *point d'appui* which Mill found so essential. Only for the Church it is given and not discovered, not enacted, not evolved. Would any majority, then, have a right to vote away that constitution, and cut loose from that historic point ? Could it vote away the historical and final Christianity of the New Testament, which is not simply memorial and traditional, but creative for Christianity ? Impossible. It would be dissolving the Church in principle. A substantive belief in the historical Christianity of the New Testament, centring in the Godhead of Christ, is part of the Church's constitution, and not merely of its theology or polity. No Church, no majority in a Church, has the moral right to abjure that. It renounces the Holy Spirit of its creation and ceases to be a Church in the act ; and it is a mere matter of time when it shall cease to be a Church in fact. Here, then, is a limit to the powers or rights of a majority in a Church. And one of the most vital questions for a Church polity that goes seriously to work is how such a limit to mere voting power is to be secured in its right.

There is a serious limit, I suggest, to the power of these majorities by which affairs have settled so long among us that we may slip into thinking them final and omnipotent. What is the principle of that limit? Must it not be a dogmatic principle? Has a Church any basis at last, any principle, except a dogmatic? Must it not rest upon something that is not won but given, that is the self-statement of God, and that not only is true but can never cease to be true? With a mere sympathetic base we dissolve the Church into a mere fraternity; and with a base of free thought we make it but a school. Besides, where the majority principle is active in a Church does it not really rest on this dogmatic base outside its range? Did it not arise upon it? That principle was adopted as part of the Church's working machinery by dogmatic believers in days before any questions were raised like those that now emerge, or when those who did raise them went outside. Is it workable without that dogmatic foundation? Can majorities have any authority in a Church except as majorities of men who are made Christian by something entirely independent of majorities? Our right to be in a Church, or to seek a majority in it for this or that object, rests on something in the constitution of the Church quite withdrawn from majority control. That something may be expressed in a confession, or implicit as an understanding, but it is there as the gift which makes the Church, not as a regulation which the Church makes. The principle of trusting the people applies in the Church only with this extension—trust the people who trust the Gospel and confess it. Majorities may and should settle business in a Church only if it is composed of men who would be sure of the Gospel

PLEBISCITE & GOSPEL AS AUTHORITY 269

if it were in a minority of one, and who would administer it only by the votes of men whom the Gospel itself had made. The Church at the first was perfectly sure of its Gospel when it was in a minority of 120 against the pagan world and the Jewish Church. And the Apostles faced and ruled the Church as but a tenth part of that number.

Let us take an analogous question. Up to the eighteenth century the culture of Europe reposed upon the basis of the Church. The Church was the grand agent of Western civilization. But a quite new state of things has since arisen. Civilization and its culture have not only become independent of the Church but hostile to it, and even fatal. It could outvote it; it can certainly concuss it. And the problem of the age is whether the Church can recover in some new form its old guiding place for society, whether it can survive and repair the neglects or the attacks of the civilisation it set on its feet and started in life. Or we may put it conversely, and ask whether civilisation, its methods, and its machinery, can survive without this deep foundation of spiritual certainty and moral security which the neglected Church alone can give. In like manner we are coming to ask what place the majority principle of ordinary affairs has in a Church except on the Church's own distinctive base as a changeless condition. Is the new difficulty not one that the democratic Churches must some day face? Are they getting ready? Or are they content to live from hand to mouth on bustle, hustle, and tussle, on journals, campaigns and devices, on great speeches, special sermons, and the "last cry"! Is there no authority to be regarded by a majority except the prudential fear of schism? Is the risk of schism the only protection from a conceivable majority whose negations would take the Church's life?

We must come back to the question which it is so hard, so hateful, so essential to face—that of an authority and the discipline it exercises. Authority is the Catholic element in religion, which Protestantism must face and absorb—just as liberty is the Protestant element which, in Modernism, Catholicism must face and settle. Has a majority, in matters of religion, any authority of a positive kind above it? " Yes, there is its conscience," it is said; " even a majority has a conscience—certainly a Christian majority has." It is forgotten that some of the worst spiritual oppression has been in the name of conscience, and even of Christian conscience. Again, as the social idea comes to fill the air, conscience tends to grow gregarious and timid. Besides, conscience, apart from its content, is a mere formal idea. What is that content? What speaks in conscience? What is the word to it? If conscience is its own Word, then there is no revelation to it, and ultimately no revelation at all, and ethic swallows up religion. But conscience is not a legislator, it is a judge. It does not give laws either for action or belief, it receives them; it recognizes the authority of laws from another source, and administers them to the occasions which arise. It does not emit authority, it owns it. It does not give religion a constitution, it can but own the value and authority of a constitution given to faith by revelation from without. The value of salvation is not given by conscience but accepted by it. Otherwise salvation would be the gift of conscience to itself, not God's gift. And if we change the figure and speak of conscience as a witness, what is the burthen of its witness? What is it a matter of conscience that we should obey, defend, promote, labour for, sacrifice, and suffer? Surely not its own abstract liberty. That were (and has been) mere ethical egotism—just as the cult of unselfishness can become but altruistic egotism. We do not preach conscience, but something that inhabits, handles, kindles, suborns, and controls conscience. What comes to the conscience, speaks to it, imposes itself on it, extorts its obedience, and inspires its worship? Is that something the result of a vote? Is it of man or the will of man? Is there not something in the Christian conscience that is not of it, that creates it out of a guilty wreck, and that would be true were every man a liar? Has the majority, then, any authority of a positive kind facing and empowering it beyond the mere formal one of the individual or the contemporary conscience? Is there any promise of the Spirit to a majority as such, to any number of natural consciences? Has the majority any of the authority belonging to the objective content or matter of conscience, to conscience viewed in its power and reality, and not in its mere subjective form or psychological place in the hierarchy of the faculties? It is pleaded, perhaps, "We have the spirit of Christ." Again, as that phrase is meant, a mere formal idea, a subjectivity, a temper, a frame of mind, something that marks action but does not make it, something which may echo or honour Christ without needing to worship Him, and appreciates without necessarily appropriating Him—a mere simular of Christ, instead of Christ our food and life. The "spirit of Christ," thus taken, is no foundation for a Church, and no real bond. It is not faith, but only, at the best, a fruit of faith; at the worst, a mask for its loss. It is a spirit like Christ's, and not Christ the Spirit. Christ can even be pulverised in "the spirit of Christ." What is to save Protestantism from a "crass subjectivity" which tends to magnify self-will, and ends in the crank, theological, spiritual, or social—the mystic revolutionary? Can the Spirit ever come without a form, a body, a rational Word? Is man not a spiritual-bodily being? As God Himself concentrates the wisdom and spirit of the universe, and by His absolute personality saves it from being a mere diffused power or idea, so is there not a historic Word, a Deed, a Person concentrating and issuing the Spirit for human society, making its source, content, and perennial spring, and thus creating and constituting the Church? Is there not a Word which roots the spiritual in the evangelical, plants freedom in Redemption, and keeps in the centre positive faith, with its primacy of the objective, instead of Catholic or Humanist love (in Rome or Tolstoi), with its primacy of the subjective. Or does the Word vanish in a popular, mystic, spiritual, pantheistic serum, in which Bible history but floats, with nothing in it constitutive for faith, nothing inalienable, only something symptomatic for an age and stage? Is the true badge of spirituality what the Anabaptists who would have wrecked the Reformation thought it to be—a *lex insita*, an inner light, mystic individualism, and quietist piety, which is co-equated with the historic Word, and moves in socialist sympathies to anarchic demagogy? Or is it historic faith, founded on fact, energising in love, and working by constitutional progress? Which is the way of the Spirit—subjective illuminism with its shifting lights, or objective revelation in an ever-fresh and growing experience. Is it to-day's vagrant insight or yesterday's apostolic inspiration, good for to-day and for ever? Who utters the central Bible—Calvin, for instance, or Tolstoi? Is it the theological scholar and practical saint, or the humanist, littérateur, the individualist, anti-historic, anti-familist mystic—loving humanity and yet despising all it has most greatly done in the past, with insight into man but none into God, full of a love which knows neither repentance nor faith, and without a mean between naïve experiment

PLEBISCITE & GOSPEL AS AUTHORITY 273

and crippling tradition, "between plagiarism and revolution, between iron orthodoxy and a totally fresh start"? In the sixteenth century who had the keys of the future — Luther, with an open Bible, a live Church, and a free historic faith, or the spiritualistic anarchists who renounced Church and sacraments, and preached, from a Bible wrested and trimmed to their own atomic consciousness, the divine urgency of the Social Revolution?[1] Can the Kingdom come without the institution of a great Church ardently loved and served in its local Churches? Can any Church live, with staying power in history, unless it is organised round some spiritual authority? Can unorganised, brotherly, and *exaltées* groups endure, or can they deal savingly with historic society? Is the exit from Intellectualism, with its dialectic orthodoxy, only by spiritualistic coteries with a mystic heresy? Is Christianity dying in giving birth to another religion chiefly literary? Or is our way not through a historic Church organised round its final, moral, evangelical, and self-renewing Gospel? Can an organised Church live without a normative Bible, a formative Gospel, a positive Word? Can the renunciation of an organised Christianity take the external and highly-organised world seriously enough to affect it? I am supposing we do want to affect the world, and not to retire to a quietist, conventiclist salvation, remote from its concerns; which would be called other-worldliness. Farther, does a contempt for organised Christianity increase respect for the public interest, and for the authority of the State as the trustee of progress? Or does that public loyalty not suffer in the depreciation of all external authority?

[1] I recognise that Luther's language and his tactics with the peasants were as lamentable as his policy was sound and inevitable—just as it was Calvin that really saved the Reformation on Luther's lines, and made the freedom of the West, in spite of his enormity of Servetus.

S

Are our social sympathies serving us well when they ignore a social and historic conscience such as we have supremely in the tradition of the Church? Can an unordered Church of fraternal enthusiasms make any tradition, any loyalty, any foundation for the order of society? Does it not yaw and stagger in a locomotor ataxy? Is anarchy freedom, however purged of violent methods? Is it morally wholesome to treat order as a spiritual obstacle, co-ordination as mere officialism, and organisation as a necessary evil? And may the dreams of quiet and engaging mystics, like Thomas Münzer, not grow in other hands into social catastrophe? The " Friends of God " can equip with explosive ideas the foes of man, and the conventicle be no more socially fertile at last than the Church which ravaged it. The religion of still life and pious groups is but a cloistered piety, which is apt to end in unwholesome coteries, without practical judgment, and with an occasional fanatic, whose impatient, and even reckless, hope is some convulsive social *parousia*.

Is Christianity mystic love, losing self in God and then losing its way among men because it is at heart more set on its own perfection than on God's glory? Again, I am thinking of Tolstoi, so fertile as a ferment, so blind to history, so barren as a creator. We all love love; our great need and quest is what will create it. Martineau said most deeply that a truly catholic mind can never come by a volition; and it is truer still of the truly catholic heart. Religion is natural, faith is not. It is not natural to love human nature when it costs anything to do so. To love man as God does means a new creation. To love trying people like Diotrephes Shuvmináber, or Tabitha Gummidge is the fruit of the Holy Spirit, Who makes Christian love individual and miraculous. Is Christianity but a love of man, praised and prescribed, but never made possible, to me who am, perhaps, dying to have it? Or is it

PLEBISCITE & GOSPEL AS AUTHORITY 275

evangelical love, ever more full of God's sacrifice than its own, finding in grace the power to love which will not grow out of the mere love of love, and thus growing from a faith which commits self and society to Christ's historic, positive, and final salvation? Is Christianity illuminism or justification? Is it refining or revolutionary? Is it subjective saintliness, indifferent to objective truth, with a mood rather than a message; or is it objective reconciliation, with a positive Word from Eternity for all time? Is it a mystic spiritual liberty of rational feeling, or a positive moral obedience of experienced faith? Is the word of God something which goes direct from God to the individual soul, without any necessary ambit or agent in Bible, Church, or Sacraments, and which sets up to try them all? If so, which mystic soul or souls shall decide what it is? How large must a deciding majority of such religious atoms be to be the Word of the Spirit? Is the Spirit "the odd man on a division"? Such subjectivism destroys the outward means of grace in favour of casual inspiration, discards tradition as mere induration, and abolishes all religious institutions for fresh and casual groups.

The Word which makes a Church does not fine away imperceptibly into the World. It did not evolve in unbroken ascent from it. Therefore it is not at the mercy of what human nature, even in its natural spirituality, may by any majority decide about it. There is some point at which a decision on it un-churches a Church, and puts it outside the Gospel pale. About where is that point? Is it dogmatic in its nature, or merely pragmatic? Something that creates, or something that only "works,"—and is therefore uncertain till all the infinite returns are in?

These are questions which are not academic. Even if they were, what are academic questions in such a region but those that are already on the train, and due certainly to arrive? Is it not time to be discussing their arrival, and the preparations for it? It is useless to discuss the real merits of the greatest issues when they come to the hubbub of a popular arena. Burke, the chief source of our political wisdom, was called academic by the active nobodies of his day. But academic or not, these are questions whose ticket is taken. They are on the way, and they should be quietly prepared for among us, and much discussed under competent guidance, at those more private gatherings where opinion is really made. I mean that in the Church attention should, perhaps, be occupied less with the questions of to-day, which enrich our platforms, and more with those of to-morrow, which take the lead in confidential groups; less with *effects* to-day and more with *results* to-morrow; less with the questions thrust forward by the journalists and more with those compelled by the Gospel; less with such questions as ' How to reach the masses? ' and more with certainty about ' What is to reach the masses'; less with social problems and more with questions like ' What makes a group a Church and keeps it so?'; less with the prospects of the Church and more with the one foundation of a Church, if it have any; less with apologetic interests (on which no Church rests) and more with positive and dogmatic interests (on which alone the Church does rest); less with the action of Christianity on the society it finds, and more with its action in the society which itself created—the supreme society of the Church, which is the minister's first concern. These questions as to the Church have fallen out of the front rank of our interest, and Christianity is more thought of as an influence on human society than as the creator and inhabitant of a sacred society all its own. But the nature, base, and policy of the great Church are questions that will not remain always *in petto*. And their

PLEBISCITE & GOSPEL AS AUTHORITY 277

public discussion by minds quite unready or aggressively ignorant gives away the case in advance to a secularity which reduces our Church assemblies to mere parliaments. In proportion as that happens, the Free Church cause generally goes into retirement; because the freest Church becomes established in the subtlest way when it is dominated in its own affairs by the interests, problems, and methods of the State. Our mental habit becomes parliamentary instead of ecclesiastical (in the great best sense of that word). Practically, though not theoretically, we should then tend to believe more in the State than in the Church. Truly, that might be a useful passing phase, and less to be grudged than watched, lest it become a dominant habit and a final condition. For it might be at most but a wrong way of doing a right thing—of making up arrears of attention long overdue to things whose management (though not their inspiration) is very properly passing from the Church to the State. But were the tendency to get the upper hand it would mean that the Church began to reclaim its obsolete controls, that it claimed for social welfare the direct authority it has had to abandon in political affairs, that the State temper flowed back upon it in a stifling secularity. The conduct of the Disestablishment movement would then pass to those who take the Church idea more seriously and independently, who treat it as a matter of faith and not politics, of spiritual liberty and not mere political justice. It would pass to the growing number of High Churchmen in Anglicanism itself, who confess it as their hope, and who care more for the Church's autonomy than for political equality.

In a brief word, if we decide our last spiritual and eternal crises by majorities, are we to include in our counting of votes the dead as well as the living? And the living and present Christ in whom they all endure—

—for how many shall He count in the great division? I put it in this provocative way, to suggest how far the issue goes beyond our usual manner of presenting it, and how many questions are bound to arise as the logic of the position works itself out in practice. And in the same interest I would point out that the procedure or polity of a church, its form, is indifferent for faith, and that there is but one test for the machinery or action of any church; and that is its power, not, in the first instance, to win the favour of men, classes, or governments, but to confess, serve, and promote the Gospel which gave the Church birth, and forms a trust which is the one reason for its existence, whether men hear or forbear.

Finally, if those responsible for the affairs of any Church were to speak in this wise : " We have a large building we must fill, a large public we must attract, large philanthropies we must finance, and we are a large asset for the press ; the leader we need in our pulpit must be on these large and effective lines ; and if we find him we will ask no questions about his theology, nor be very inquisitive about his gospel, which seems to us pretty much alike in all successful preachers "—I say if the authorities of a Church so spoke it could mean but one thing (if the policy were long enough pursued). It would mean the destruction of those Churches that had their centre of gravity in such evangelical levity, and staked the Church on a policy that could be so indifferent to the trust of grace and history. And this particularly concerns those Churches whose centre of gravity is in the laity. The laity are in many quarters coming to be both ill-informed and indifferent to Christian belief, great as is their interest and value in the matter of Christian principle and temper. But credal indifference in the backbone of a Church is a fatal disease. Such a

PLEBISCITE & GOSPEL AS AUTHORITY 279

laity is not equal to the Church's trust, and can only create a reaction which might be sacerdotal. Not all the popular or angelic preaching in the world will save a Church that surrenders the theology of its gospel (Gal. i. 8).

XIV

LIBERTY AND ITS LIMITS IN THE CHURCH

WE are confused at the moment about most questions; but about none more than the nature of our theological liberty and its limits. Its cause was born in the seventeenth century. But as Puritan Independency developed into political Liberalism, the idea of liberty changed. And especially has this happened since the Revolution and the Democracy—so welcome and so hopeful in their line. An idea of civic liberty based on the assertion of natural rights has gradually replaced (even in the Church) the sense of spiritual liberty which comes by the gift of supernatural grace. The Church has been secularised by carrying the idea of natural freedom, self-achieved, into the spiritual sphere of Grace, donative and creative. Many a local church has been vexed and ruined by people in whom the natural aggressive freedom of opinion or action took the place of an experienced and humble freedom in Christ. Social righteousness has become with very many a concern practically paramount to being right with God. "Service is Faith," says some poet. And as in politics that is held right to do which the majority decree, the same authority, acting as the Christian consciousness, is held to settle truth. As if we had over the majority no spiritual constitution, and there were nothing that the majority in a church could not do or deny, and yet remain a church. As if we had from the past no

LIBERTY & ITS LIMITS IN THE CHURCH

more fixed criterion for Christian faith than we have in the present for political utility. As if the truth of the Gospel were at the mercy of an age's spiritual expediency. Accordingly, we have in many quarters become so politicised in our conception of the Church, we so treat it as a democracy with no other standard than the hour's majority of votes merely counted, that some (more Roman here than Rome) set its verdict above Revelation, or call it Revelation. They regard the modern Christian consciousness as the latest form of revelation, which adds a new region to revelation, and is entitled to challenge all that went before.

An eminent but orthodox and puzzled Congregationalist layman once said to me that if a Church became unanimous in rejecting an historic Christ, or an apostolic Gospel, in favour of " the spirit of Christ," it was difficult to see how it could be shown to have ceased to be Congregationalist. It did what it did in the exercise of Congregational freedom. The answer was that it had not ceased to be Congregationalist, as the Unitarians have not; it had ceased to be a Church. It had, in principle, renounced the Holy Spirit of the final Word for a spirit of charitable religiosity; it had ceased to be Christian in any positive sense, in any other than a courtesy sense; and it had left the Communion of Churches. For a Church is not made by a certain subjective temper, nor by long existence, nor by the will of man, nor by the unanimity of wills in a vote; but by a positive historic revelation of ageless Gospel, by a new creative act of God, and by the consequent presence and life in it of Jesus Christ, whose cross is the one source of the Holy Spirit. And no amount of subjective spirituality, in beautiful prayers, social sympathies, or inward light, gives any right to Church or preacher to abolish the outward and historic Word of the New Testament taken as a whole. This Word is not the book nor its facts, but its one divine Fact; its historic Gospel of the Grace of a Holy God to human guilt, effecting man's forgiven regeneration in a final way, through our faith in the Cross and Person of Jesus Christ, the Eternal Son of God. This was the Fact whose belief created the Church. There is no salvation for mankind apart from Christ's death.[1] This Word alone gives final value to the Church's polity, propaganda, philanthropy, and sacraments. They all collapse without it.

We are not at the mercy of the inward light alone. The Church was not created by the inward light. It was not created by the Spirit of God alone. It was created by the Holy Spirit through an apostolic Word of Jesus Christ crucified; it was created by the redeeming Lord as the Spirit. As a matter of fact, this was so. And its principle is given in its creation.

Its Creator, then, has, manifestly, the sole right to rule (which means to limit) its freedom, which is a derived thing from Himself. And this He does, not arbitrarily, nor vaguely, but by the regal nature of the creative act, and by its word of a redemption once for all but perennial in history. He does not do it simply by being an historic memory (however beloved) on the one hand, nor, on the other, by being an illuminating presence, giving divine *éclat* to our spiritual intuitions. Nor is He but the great historic symbol of humanity's spiritual reason and radiance. For He is neither the mere diffused Light of the World, nor its gathered focus, but its creative sun—as He is not God's sound merely, nor His echo, but His Word. He is not simply the burning point of the Logos or spiritual reason in the world; He is its personal and

---

[1] I do not speak of the conscious relation to it of individuals here and there.

LIBERTY & ITS LIMITS IN THE CHURCH 283

creative centre. He is not the divine soul-stuff out of which Humanity is made, with a doubtful consciousness and a difference from us only in degree; He is the increate Creator of the New Humanity.

So that if freedom must always be limited to remain free, and if it must be limited at last only by the principle that creates it, then the redemption of Christ must be the last regulative principle in the freedom of a Church, and finally of the world. The last authority of the redeemed is the Redeemer as such. Hence, surely, also, if the most venerable society in Christendom renounced as its fertile norm the apostolic Word of the Cross, which created Christendom, or, if it diluted it into an ideal process, a moral principle, or a sentimental sympathy, it would cease to be a church in that act. It would certainly cease to be free. It would renounce the Holy Spirit, whose source and matter and liberty are historically in that Word alone. And (as I have said) the renunciation would be no less complete, though it were effected in a quite solemn way, to the accompaniment of prayers and speeches of the most *exaltée* kind about the absolute powers of a church that cherished the Master's spirit. It would be a renunciation of its charter Gospel, which is the repudiation of the Holy Spirit, and the suicide of a Church.

The point in the present lecture is, therefore, this: Liberty is illicit which renounces its own creative principle. But the creative principle of the Church has historically been the Gospel I have described. (It confuses or evades the issue to say vaguely that the creator of the Church's liberty is Christ. Historically, as a matter of fact, it was *such* a Christ, the Christ of the apostolic Redemption.) Therefore the denial, or the ignoring of that Gospel is not lawful in a church so created. Another community than a church is then erected, upon another principle.

Vox populi vox Dei, if it ever be true, is certainly not true in the Church for its Gospel. The Church, here at least, is not a democracy; and the Cross is not the mere symbol or charter of the free rights of the natural spiritual man. The society of Grace has no rights or liberties but what grace and *its* freedom confer. In the Church, the *Vox Dei* is the continuity, not of man's spiritual insight or sense, but of God's creative act and historic Word, with all its perfectible finality, in the uncreated Jesus Christ. It is there, in the Gospel, that the inexhaustible God gives the final account of Himself, His will and purpose; and there He speaks and achieves the atoning, saving, and ruling word for all history and Humanity. There alone is the Word to the conscience that makes society morally safe and finally free. The best that the *Vox Populi* can do in the Church is to take home that gift and to unfold it; to confess, praise, obey, and serve, in all modern ways, a God really known as eternal holy Love only in that crucial Act and commanding Word. It is a Word that stands over the Church within it; and, so long as the Bible, with its creative record, is not wiped from the historic consciousness of the race, it stands fast if every vote in a church or council turned false. That renunciation would simply be the Church unchurching itself, and leaving the Communion of Saints, the evangelical solidarity, and the apostolic succession.

And, if it were said here that the Church is a mere name, and that the Christian society by any other name would work as well—that only betrays how far the self-unchurching has already gone beyond mere name. For what is lost (amid any amount of subjective devoutness) is the vital past, the evangelical continuity of that company, the legacy of the new creation, the social communion with the *Redeemer*, and the fellowship of the Holy Ghost. When any community ceases to care whether it is a real Church

LIBERTY & ITS LIMITS IN THE CHURCH

of the apostolic Gospel, so long as it is for the hour rationally free, pious and social, that simply means that evangelical liberty, the release of the conscience from itself by God for God, has been lost in the assertive liberty of the atomic, unhistoric, natural man exercised on a religious matter. Such a body then means nothing for the Gospel any more. To renounce the Word is, in principle, to dissolve the Church.

If this be dogmatism, it is only because the Church is dogmatic in its very nature, by the final Word of the Cross that created it, and by the Act of God that it has in trust to confess. (An absolute God cannot but dogmatise, however amply.) Its existence in the face of the world is the grand dogmatism of history, parallel (on a higher level) to the dogmatism of Humanity in asserting its dominion in Nature's face, or to the dogmatism of the reason in mathematics. It is the head and front of the new soul's godly self-assertion in the creation; and, amid history, it is its eternal defiance of time. But there is much religious levity and mental obscurantism in the prejudice and outcry against the dogmatic. It is the children of the mist thinking themselves wiser in their generation than the children of light. It only means that the intelligence of Christianity is to be limited to a criticism of its forms, and not applied to an exploration of its content, which then becomes a matter of the sympathies alone.

No Church, no minister, has any right to claim freedom *from* the apostolic word, but only *for* that word. The Free Churches, especially, have their right to freedom only in their prior duty to this Gospel. If it could be shown that an Established Church could better serve the Gospel, and better promote that spiritual liberty and fraternity of the conscience created only by the Gospel, then the Free Churches would have no case whatever. The politics of the matter would not concern them, however important for the mere voter. The politics of religion are those that are prescribed by the nature of the Gospel, and not by the ideals of democracy. If the Free Churches touched politics then as Churches, it would only be to declare that political machinery must follow the deeper ethic (which we do believe to be democratic), and must move to promote the final righteousness of the Gospel and the requirements of Christ's universal kingdom. As a matter of fact, we generally find that where evangelical liberty has given place to rational or political, the ardour of a Free Church soon abates. A Free Church can never live on free thought, nor on a free democracy as morally supreme. It can only live on a Free Gospel, that is, on souls whose guilty consciences Jesus Christ has made free by His Redemption. And all permanent liberty, whether of thought or democracy, rests on that evangelical release at the long last. *Between a Church and a democracy is this eternal gulf, that a democracy recognises no authority but what arises from itself, and a Church none but what is imposed on it from without.* The one founds on self-help, the other on Redemption.

As Harnack lately said to Jatho, "all freedom is but a means, and not an end"; except (he meant) the freedom we experience in being in Christ, our Redeemer, our Means and End. And that freedom is intrinsically an obedience. For we are His property much more than His brethren. Such is the only liberty the soul was made for at last; it is an end in itself; and every limitation of freedom is lawful and needful for a Christian which can be truly shown to be necessary to that obedience. Such was the limitation that the free Grace of God Himself took in Christ. It is the very principle of

LIBERTY & ITS LIMITS IN THE CHURCH 287

Incarnation of the Son and His humiliation of the Cross, the principle of its strait gate, and all the liberty therewith. It is moral Redemption as the supreme exercise of God's liberty, and its historic principle. Much popular talk about our absolute freedom is long out of date, and as hollow as it is stale. Let us turn from it to seek into the inner grounds of things. Let us toil for truth, and not pick it up. Let us read matter in which every word is weighed and which demands that we shall linger and attend. And let us ask ourselves, and stir others to ask, why we want any freedom. What is its content? What is its principle—its source—its goal? That is the question of the hour. What right have we to any freedom? Have we any rights that are not gifts, and lay us under obligation? Are we still floundering, a century to the rear, among the natural, inherent, undonated rights of man? Whose freemen are we? Who gave us our freedom? What is the nature and manner and obligation of the gift? Is it not a gift? Is it but an instinct; or, perhaps, the captive of our own spear? Has it not a witness in it? Does it not speak of a giver, more even than of the gift? What or whom do we serve by it? What is the binding duty that creates our right to be free? Is it duty to self, duty to truth, or duty to Christ?—to our self-culture, to philosophy, or to the Gospel? The free Grace of God means that before Him (*i.e.* at bottom) we have no rights. If we had rights before God, we should have deserts, and grace would not be free. We have nothing we have not received. That is our true spiritual equality. It is an equality before God of nothingness, of impotence, an equality of absolute indebtedness, an equality of a common perdition but for the saving Grace and Gift and Liberty of God. It is the equality of the Reformation, and not of the Revolution. On nothing was

Christ more explicit than on this equality of Grace. To every man this penny. The more we live in Christ with the best of our race, the more we realise that man has no liberty at the long last but what His finished and funded Redemption gives us. Let us think and speak less of our liberty, and more of our Liberator. Let us be more concerned that *He* should have free course in the world than that *we* should, or our liberty, or our independence, or our propaganda. There are many Christians with whom liberty is more practically potent than Christ is.

What was it that made the tremendous strength of Calvinism? What makes some form of Calvinism indispensable and immortal? It was this, that it cared more to secure the freedom of God than of man. That is what it found in the Cross. That is why it has been the greatest contribution to public liberty ever made. Secure that God be free. Seek first the freedom of God, and all other freedom shall be added to you. The Calvinistic doctrine of predestination was the foundation of modern public liberty; and, deeply, because it was an awful attempt to secure God's freedom in Grace at any cost. And we must retain the perspective in that doctrine (though we need not feel that it must be done in precisely the same form). We must put God's free grace first—far before our free thought or action. It is the creative centre for thought's freedom in the realm of Christian truth as for man's action in a world. To secure a long freedom, let us be more concerned about God's freedom than man's (for we have made Him to serve by our iniquities). Let us be more concerned about the freedom of the Word than the freedom of the Church, or the pulpit. Let us care first for such a free Word as secures God in His freedom. Let the historic Word of Grace have its way with us. Then the Church must be free. But a Church freedom which, in the name of free-thought individualism, or spirituality, feels itself free to abolish that apostolic Word and succession, is destroying Word, Church, freedom and future, all together. And to despise such prophesyings as meaningless is to announce that the destruction has already begun.

Surely there is a point at which evolutionary Christianity ceases to be Christian. To include all is to care for nothing but inclusion—which is an empty circle without a circumference, a void and formless infinite. There is a point at which the modifying of faith must cease its accommodation to the time, and limit its wholesome reduction of the ponderous fabrics which descend to us out of the past. A liberal theology properly enough claims that as belief develops in one direction it shall be reduced in another. But how far may that go? That is the great Church question of the hour. And liberalism totally fails to answer it. It is not: May we modify and revise? That is long settled. But how far modify? That is the question. What is the use of the old fustian about a right to liberty which we have now got? Let us face the actual and exact question. What is the point at which reduction becomes extinction, and modification transmutation, and re-statement another Gospel? Where shall we rally and stand? Just where does a modified Christianity become another religion? There is no question so serious for the churches to-day. And there is none that, as they become mass meetings, they are less disposed to face, few that they resent more being compelled to face. It is not a question of liberty, but whether we have liberty to believe as we please in a Church of the Gospel.

Now there are some extreme people even who are ready to say: Yes, there must be a limit. There is a general and fundamental truth of religion. We must stop there. We must apply that. We will boil down all the religions to an essence, and this pemmican will be our test.

Well, if our object is to get in the greatest possible number in the quickest possible time, we may be tempted to pursue this method of a minimal religion. Cursed with the crowd's impatience, the fatal impatience of unfaith, we may increase the supply of believers by reducing the demand for belief. We may offer people their least common denominator. But if our object be to glorify God's gift in Christ and His salvation, with a secondary interest in His popularity (which He does not court), we shall seek a maximal religion, the fulness of Christ, and let people come in not as *we* bring them, but as *that* does. We shall offer them their greatest common measure. The Church will offer the world something worth the scale of its great reason and imagination And that is the fulness of Godhead, the amplitude of the historic and apostolic Gospel, which has room to carry us all, and power to rule us, and is not small enough to go into each man's pocket like a tame creature and lie still.

The question crucial for religion at this present hour concerns, above all, historic Christianity. It is the question whether direct soul-certainty (and with it the spiritual future) is certainty of something fontal in the past, or only in the present. Is it a faith or a gaze? Is it the will's answer to a divine act historic for all, or a vision of the inward eye with temperamental facilities in some? Does it depend on faith in the past or intuition of the present—on an inspired faith working back historically through the Church's living line to rest on an eternal Christ and His claim of right, or on a congenital insight which discerns with sufficient clearness and force the whole spiritual idea immediately present in experience, enriched, of course, by a Christ merely historic but much out of date. It is a question of historic (in the sense of apostolic and evangelical) Christianity; of a Christ always equally mediatorial, and of such a Christ as the sole condition psychologically of the directness, fullness, and certainty in man's experience of a loving God. It is a question of the prime (and not merely ancillary) function of history in faith, of the authority of something historically done and finally given, which is the marrow of the Church's living tradition, Roman or Protestant. And to that question our answer is that the centre of gravity and source of authority for any Church is Christ's person and act, historic, yet immediate. We cannot throw it over, and start on a fresh, and perhaps revolutionary, revelation arising in the modern consciousness. It is something divinely final for the destiny of the race, something which emerges in the past, and has a miraculous power (by the Spirit) to convert itself from past to present ; which has been doing so in the history of the Church for two thousand years; and which lives in to-day's experience as surely and directly and authoritatively as it did in that of the first century. It is a ceaseless Act, Word and Gospel—not an infallible Bible nor a complete theology, but a continuous act of Gospel, pointed once and present always; which has done so much to create Christian civilisation that to throw it over for a mere continuity of the " Christian spirit," or " the ideal Reason," would cause that civilization to collapse in course of time, or be lost in the sand of a subjectivism which has begun to silt up and choke us already. And for the sake of the Gospel, our first social duty is to repair the great neglect into which we have allowed the unique conception and function of the Church to fall.

What, then, is the principle of the historic Gospel which made the Church, and modern society as affected by the Church? What is the apostolic and New Testament revelation, God's central, final gift, the gift which is the source of the soul's release, the creator of the Church's life, the secret of its society, and the principle of its theological freedom and progress? For that is the principle which forms also the limit of freedom within such a Church. More remotely, it is the condition of freedom everywhere else. And we cannot profitably discuss the old miracles, for instance, till we settle the miraculous nature of that present grace.

I look forward to see the whole Church confessing but one Article, stating at once the source of her life, the principle of her action, and the warrant of her freedom. I mean, of course, that it should be the collective message of the Church and not the exacted subscription of individuals.

First (in preamble), she would recognise, by virtue of the revelation which gave her being, that the central question of practical religion for men as we actually find them is one of the conscience—How shall Humanity stand before its righteous Judge? How shall man be just with Holy God? All constructions and interpretations, whether of the world or of the soul, are secondary to that. And to that question God's answer is the message of Grace, that the Judge inflexible is already on our side, that our Lord is our Lover, and our Holy One our Redeemer.

And second (in substance), that that holy Grace, on which everything turns, is not mere graciousness, not mere beneficent favour, and not fatherly kindness, but is consummate, final, and effectual only as the self-donation of God to guilty man, at a point crucial for His Kingdom and for human destiny, in the justifying, reconciling Cross of Jesus Christ the eternal Son,

LIBERTY & ITS LIMITS IN THE CHURCH 293

our risen Lord, who in that Act creates His Church by His eternal Spirit. God gives Himself, and the Holy One is Redeemer, only there.

This is not an article of theology, nor a tentative interpretation by apostles of a vast, vague spiritual impression that they felt, without positive features of its own; but it is their inspired statement of the Gospel of God's act and gift, the marrow of Christian religion, the object and content of faith. To leave that living tradition and experience of the Spirit is to adopt another faith. Some may prefer, according to their idiosyncrasy, to develop the sanctifying influence of such a faith rather than the justifying. That matters less, so long as they do not deny what they do not prefer. And it is not a question whether we hold these things as truth, but whether they hold us as power. Faith is not faith in truths, but in powers. Such limitation of freedom is really its concentration, and therefore its power.

Some minds marvel that all this pother should go on about such truth over their heads; and they discharge themselves of trouble by reflecting that one theology is about as good as another; meantime, to work for man's good! But the same people, if they had been present when Peter healed the lame man at the temple gate, would have insisted that he should tour the town and cure every invalid in Jerusalem instead of turning to preach theological sermons about the Cross and the Resurrection. If these things are true, they *are* man's good. And if all men heartily believed them the power of healing would be a social power in daily use. All human help or history is in their interest. All Christian work, all human good, is only the expansion of God's redeeming work in Christ for the whole creation. What they call theology here is not man's scheme of God but the will of God; it is not only for man's good—it is man's one life and hope, it is the burthen of all being (Rom. viii.). We need not wonder that some Christians would lay life down for these truths, which others have yet come to think it the essence of Christianity to give them deadly liberty to deny. To discard such faith is to cast away the soul's one foundation. For what we find we have to do with, when we have graduated in well-doing, when we have not only played with it, when we have not only done much good but really been educated by it, what we find stopping and foiling us and making our work waste, is not simply human backwardness, nor is it the untowardness of fate, but it is human guilt and perdition. We always run up against that dead wall. Christ is not the crown of man's optimism ; He must be the Saviour of his despair. What the Cross must save is not human nature, but human lostness. Human nature is great and wonderful; it is human will that has the blight and the doom. And we find in such a creed as I have named not a mere article of belief, but the statement of the one power and work of God to the will's salvation. It is a matter both of obedience and honour to His Holy Name, as He reveals it, and it is also the one hope for stricken Humanity. Nothing gives us the whole Christ but our despair. (Matt. viii. 23-27.)

Out of such a principle questions easily arise, such as that concerning the relation between Christ and the Spirit. But these are matter of theological thought and progress, under the guidance of a living faith and a personal religion revolving on the Gospel I name. They are matters of liberal, experient, and scientific theology, starting from the historic Word and taste of salvation. They are not at the mercy of theological liberalism; where theology is not an intelligent confession of grace but a section of culture and a depart-

LIBERTY & ITS LIMITS IN THE CHURCH 295

ment of the rational man, resting on his rational claim to be the final arbiter, and to make the sanity of modern men the chief test of apostolic inspiration, and the final measure of any possible Christ.

The issue raised by our present mists and low temperatures is a much more serious matter for the Churches, and therefore for Humanity, than any of the political questions which engross passion for the moment, and which, if allowed to monopolise the Christian soul, would sterilize it. We are at a parting of the ways and a crisis of the Spirit which involves the Church's whole future, and, what is more, the future of such a Gospel as the world most needs. The Church cannot act in the name of a toleration to which nothing but toleration seems supremely dear, nor can it tolerate in the name of a charity which has no fixed truth at its source. The Church cannot be asked to treat as otiose the moral (*i.e.* evangelical) Gospel that created it, and which is its supreme trust from a holy God—the Gospel of an atoning Saviour and His Kingdom. Its decay among us is a disease from which our extremities have already begun to die. Our foreign missions will never cease to welter and dwindle, while we bustle with cordials round their swoon, till we have settled this issue, and made our choice with heart, and strength, and mind, so that our creed is not our burden and problem, but our stay and power. Too many are occupied in throwing over precious cargo; they are lightening the ship even of its fuel.

It seems to some that, if the matter is left by the experients of faith to the amateurs of charity, and, if the issue is not sharpened to a clear alternative which subdues the heart to the will, and the intellect to both, we are about to glide into the same condition as was produced by eighteenth-century Arianism. And we can be saved from it only by some evangelical movement, if not as emotional, yet as large, positive and fit for the time as was that of Wesley and his peers. For, when Paul's Christ goes down, the Churches certainly follow.

The Church was created by the resurrection and victory of the crucified Redeemer, and if it discard for any liberty the principle of its creation it parts with its life as a Church.

XV

AUTHORITY AND INDIVIDUALISM

THE chief question on the horizon, especially for the ministry, is not concerned with the State but with the Church. It is our question in these discourses of the religious, *i.e.* the fundamental authority.

Of course, since the ruling interest and the raging war is economic, the form of its approach may be economic, as before it has been political. It might be forced upon us by the common inquiry why the Church can do so little to prevent the economic anarchy threatened by either rich or poor who are without sense of a responsibility to a Master or to Humanity. Why is the Church so powerless where we need such help most—with those to whom indiscipline is a passion, or those to whom power is a lust, who have nothing above themselves but a class egoism (rooted often but in selfish comfort)—or with those who have only a dim and thin idealism over them, unable to cope with the vigorous egoisms of nature? Is it fatal to Christianity, whose first and central appeal was made to the central and sinful conscience, that it fails to commend itself to masses of men who have no other ideals than those passions prescribe, whether they be employers or employed? Must it commend itself to people who look even in an authority for something they can exploit? Must it appeal promptly to men engrossed with their utmost rights and negligent of their best powers, who are more concerned about status than righteousness, or about autonomy than competency, who are more sure they are right against the world than that they were ever wrong before God? So that the social question raises the whole issue as to the nature of religious authority and what is to be expected from it, the kind of claim or promise the Gospel makes, and the kind of work its Church should be expected to do. The Church has disappointed many in the promotion of brotherhood; but was it just to promote brotherhood that the Gospel came, or was it to establish a higher relation, which makes brotherhood almost automatic, and as inevitable as permanent?

The great question, being the Gospel question, is the Church question. For the State, divine as it is, is ideally but the basement of the Church, the groundfloor of the New Jerusalem. And the ministers of the Church would become demoralised if they were so dominated by the State as to accept its definition of Church membership, or its prescription of their duty (as in divorce); or if, on the other hand, they became so engrossed with political and journalistic interests as to lose the Church idea, or if they grew warmer in attacking its wrong form than in promoting its right. The Church that becomes more of a democracy than a Church is doomed. It takes all the loftiness of a great Church to keep the State high and enable it to resist the gravitation of human nature to pagan dust. Nothing but the liberty whose secret is with the Church alone can serve or secure the liberty of the State. It is foolish, of course, to say the Church has nothing to do with politics. But are we to debase the Church to a political lever or a servant of society, so that its public action should be chiefly as an organ of political pressure or a tool of social reform by egoists who have scope on behalf of those who have none?

Now that the battle for outward liberty is substanti-

AUTHORITY AND INDIVIDUALISM 299

ally won, the prime question of a Church is that also of the civil society so far—it is the question of its use, the question of an authority rather than of a freedom or a sympathy. Because the free centre is not in man—not even in his love or faith—but in God and His Grace. And because the supreme revelation of Christianity is the *holiness* of God's love even more than the tenderness or largeness of it. In Christ we not only have a vital relation to God, we *belong* to the God He reveals; we are not only His inheritance but His purchased inheritance ; and we belong absolutely: and especially our freedom so belongs, belongs absolutely to that revelation.

The danger of many is to have inverted this order of importance. They have neglected the matter of authority in their passion for sympathetic liberty, till the due authority of the Church by its Gospel suggests to them only reaction, priestism, prelacy, and popery. And they thus reduce the Church to impotence, by toiling after a fraternal sympathy which the true paternal authority would produce of itself where it is now manufactured. They can even at times ridicule the great idea of Mother Church in the name of brother man. If anyone demur at this, and protest that the cult of Mother Church has left mankind with but a grandmother or a stepmother Church, let him, unless he renounce all Churches, stop to consider this. Let him consider that the world needs a benign and holy authority more than aught else, an intimate and yet majestic authority, and let him ask if his own Church is providing it. Let him own that the idea is among the great ones of the earth, and that the New Testament brings it on its front. Let him ask whether such an aspect of gracious authority and merciful majesty is that which his favourite Churches present to the World. Is it the note of their preaching? Do their sermons wield authority, gracious or other? Are they as bent on nobly bowing men as on loudly rallying them, assiduously pleasing them, or kindly cheering them? Are the reformers of their mode of worship as much bent on the expression of moral humility in the ritual as they are on æsthetic reverence? Do they always exhibit the mind of men who are themselves palpably under authority, and more concerned to obey than to be graceful or free? It is a true and lawful joy to rejoice to be free; but what is inside the freedom? Is the Church but a stabling for religious free lances? What do the people understand by freedom to whom the free lance glorifies it? Is it a humble freedom to confess from the repentant soul a holy God in His Grace, or is it a stalwart's freedom to take our own course—with a certain willingness to listen to God if He treat our freedom respectfully? Is it freedom to go wrong if we like, freedom to be our native selves, untrammelled by other men, untroubled by greater, and unbroken by the Greatest? Has current religion not more freedom than power in its freedom? Has it freedom to control its freedom? Have we the art to pacify men who are now too free for their own peace, or to fortify men who have now more liberty than power? Can we do as much to feed, fill, and guide the liberty around us as we can to egg on its gnawing unrest? Have we a *Word* for the hour or only a *cry*? Which are the Churches multiplying most—subjects to Christ or rebels to tradition, victors of sin or opponents of wrong, makers of repentance or pursuers of the ideal, cleansers from guilt or soothers from care? What is our principle of education, when we can be induced to look at the hateful thing? All the best wisdom of the world's best teachers bids men who are set on the highest things begin with the acceptance of authority, and thence work their disciplined way to freedom by appropriation and development, more than by rebellion or by criticism. Is this the modern idea? Is it what our youth is encouraged to do? There is need and place at times for both the rebel and the critic; but they should be masters, not tiroes. Order should only be broken by those who have learned gratefully to revere it. Have we not gone far to invert that fundamental principle of education in the moral and religious realm? Are we not too early and too often taught to begin by whetting our wits on a challenge of the finest and profoundest traditions, the greatest and most venerable institutions? Are we not constantly encouraged to suspect the past, and distrust those that rule? The kind of conscience so produced—which mark does it bear? The mark of our native self-assertion on its best side, or the mark of our disciplined self-conquest? We are fond of military metaphors; have we the inner spirit of the soldier?

The error of recalcitrance is made plausible by the plea of developing our own individuality; and some never escape its results. They must be themselves, their native, it may be their impracticable, selves. Even women, under certain literary influences, are coming to discard the idea either of duty or sacrifice, and cultivate an ethic whose first principle is that they must be free to be themselves, and live out their own life before all else, and in scorn of all others. By premature criticism and aggression men doom themselves to moral and spiritual barrenness just when their powers, if duly nurtured and admonished by the past, should be ripening to true, effective, and progressive purpose. Liberty is sterilised. The air of our time is full of aspirations, vague but barren, not unworthy but often hopeless; and cries for some lordless but futile freedom bleat, like sheep in the ruins of Nineveh, amid the downfall of the controls and authorities under which civilisation has slowly grown.

The question of a real authority is the prime question of the Church because it is the prime question of religion—or at least of Christianity; which first came, and chiefly comes to the conscience, to men who are seeking to know how they shall stand before their judge, and what they must do to be saved—they and their kind. Our peril, both in social politics and in religious belief, is self-sufficient and self-conscious individualism, ignorant of history and unequal to affairs; which the passion of conflict often hardens into a dogged recklessness, smouldering volcanically, and moving to anarchy. Its representatives are the crank or the mutineer. Its true prophet is Nietzsche, and its Messiah the merciless Superman. The most hopeful thing about it is what sets Nietzsche and his age so far ahead of Strauss and his—the sense of a tragedy in things instead of a mere backwardness—a tragedy that calls on religion for redemption instead of rationality and sanity. I know that the demand of the modern hour is for a theodicy rather than a theology. We demand from God a rational justification of Himself in presence of life's anomalies, rather than a tragic justification of us amid our guilt. But the latter is the more fundamental and permanent note of the soul. So that the soul's authority is its Saviour rather than God's Advocate. And while we have no guarantee that a theodicy would erase our guilt, we are sure that our justification would be a theodicy for all life. For the saved conscience is integrated into the justice of the universe.

Were the present hour the time to sing the praises of individualism the pæan could be strong and long. But

AUTHORITY AND INDIVIDUALISM 303

it is not the time. We have now too much individualism; what we have not is character. Individualism has for a season done its needful work. It has gone its fussy but useful way, like the tug that tows the *Temeraire*, and we are suffering from what I have already called the erosions of its afterwash. The tide of a radical individualism has retired and left us on the mudflats of life. It was an extreme and necessary protest. And in its place it will always be required. But only so long as its egoism is not set up as the plan of the world and the principle of human life. For, if supreme, it is anti-social and anti-Christ. It arose in the eighteenth century, and it became the source of its thin old optimism, of the doctrine of self-help in getting on, and of our more recent subjectivism with its zest, intimacy, and mobility, its vagrancy and restlessness of life. It was the moving spirit of much of the old political Liberalism, passing into Radicalism, with its impatience and its extravagant faith in Parliaments; and of the old Rationalism, passing into Unitarianism or Agnosticism, with so much now discredited confidence in science. It did much to produce modern constitutionalism, with its protection of the citizen from the ruler; much to foster political liberty in its early stages; much to develop economic enterprise and all the success that belongs to that level of civilisation. But it has now more than done its limited task. Both political and theological Liberalism now require some more positive and social ideal to preserve them from disintegration—the one asking for social reform in the interest of a ruling Humanity, the other for a great Church to give effect to a final Gospel. Individualism, taken strictly, means that the individual is enough for himself, and an end in himself; and that he makes all social unities by his will and its compacts. But, however natural such a view might be as a reaction from a feudal state of things in thought or life, it can be neither a philosophy of the world, a bond of society, nor a religion of the soul. It flourishes still in the populous levels of those who are but where culture was a century ago, with the aggressive dogmatism of the self-made and the rationalism of the unschooled. Its final brood is, in society, the crank; in civic life, the " cit " of Villadom, the *Eigenbüttler;* in politics it is the axe-grinder; in Church life, the mere critic and separatist; and, generally, it is the atomist, anarchist, and wrecker, whose ethic is the truant's—to avoid school and be himself at any price. But it is no longer the ruling note or need of the time; and the anachronism of it is often the plague of the time. While we may recognise its utility for a stage, its value grows less as we rise in the scale of moral and spiritual interests. When we discuss such things as conscience, faith, the Church or Humanity—or indeed anything in its height, and depth, and length, and breadth—it seems the more narrow as our thought grows the more wide, and it looks more common according to the distinction of our cause. In Christianity it is, taken by itself, an alien and an outlander, a Gibeonite and a Helot. Truly Christianity must develop, sanctify, and perfect the soul, meaning the whole man. But it does so only in a Church of those who are in loving, absolute, and corporate obedience to God in Jesus Christ, the Saviour of the race. Individualism there issues upwards into personalism of a far more moral, social, and religious sort. Certainly reform, progress, and fullness of life will always owe much to those active and original spirits who are dissatisfied with the past and who round upon it. But that must not mean that they despise it or destroy it. They must react on it appreciatively and constructively. If we come into our

AUTHORITY AND INDIVIDUALISM

inheritance by parricide we are very likely to squander it in riot. None should depart from tradition but those to whom it is dear. None should be entrusted with the destruction of the past but those who love it. There may be room or need for a law-breaker at certain rare junctures, but he must not be a law-scorner. We shall have the best laws from men who most feel the majesty, sanctity, and continuity of law; and the best beliefs we shall have in those who appreciate the authority, power, and fertility of the historic past.

The cure for individualism, in faith as in practice, is some real authority interior but superior to the Ego itself. The best recipe for making men is to give them a Master. The future can only be saved by some influence, from Church or State, with power to make an authority for us which shall be at least as real and effective as our liberty, a power, too, which shall be an authority not merely over base selfishness but over our natural egoism and many of its reputable and even religious forms. Many victims of egoism are afraid of selfishness. We can always have our audience with us in denouncing selfishness. What searches, and irritates, and repels people is the exposure of their subtle, prized, and deadly egotisms, even in trying to be unselfish.

Why should the German Emperor speak as extravagantly as he seems to us to speak about the monarchy? He is neither a fool nor a freak. He is in a place high enough for wide vision, with power to feel what he sees; he is central enough to Europe not to be insular; and he sees that the Protestantism, the religion of his country, orthodox or Liberal, has lost the inner note of authority, and has therefore lost control for the modern mind. Yet the great public authority must be religious; and, as he is no Catholic, he is driven, rightly or wrongly, to invest the head of the State with the religious as the only effective kind of authority. That appears to be the psychology of the situation. It is, of course, a forlorn hope. Emperor has even less intrinsic authority than pope. But it is eloquent both of the need of a religion for authority and of the loss of authority from religion.

Many earnest and forward people to-day are concerned with the repudiation of an external authority. Some are as passionate about it as only those can be who do not gauge, or even grasp, the situation. Often they are more concerned to repudiate the externality than to own the authority. They are not always quite clear what externality means. An authority must be external, in some real sense, or it is none. It must be external to us. It must be something not ourselves, descending on us in a grand paradox. We might well for a little relax our recalcitrant animus against the externality of the authority and bestow more anxious pains upon the reality of it. Is an obedience the groundtone of Christian life and action? Some vehement antagonists of external authority lose all influence (except with the crowd) because their type and demeanour of mind show that their groundtone is not obedience, not historic continuity, and not competency, but mere autonomy, mere recalcitrance, extending occasionally to intellectual turbulence. They do not impress us as habitually and palpably living under any authority higher than their better instincts, or their conscience at best. And their very conscience often does not impress us as either a ruled or an instructed conscience. It is but a phase of their self-will, it is their self-assertion turned on moral or social subjects. Their obedience to truth is only to such truth as commends itself to their atomic judgment, is verified by their sectional experience, and is clear to their undisciplined understanding. " I

AUTHORITY AND INDIVIDUALISM

know what I like. I know what satisfies my need or my mind "—the mind having never been stirred by any knowledge of a large world to problems hard to meet. They eat what is tasty and fills a hole comfortably, no matter if in the night it rouse the house and the doctor. Even Christ they bring to this bar, and every Word of God. They do not believe it because it is God's; for them it is only God's in so far as they understand and agree. They may expatiate more freely in the spirit of Christ than they live on His Work or His Word. As if we could ever have the Spirit of Christ except by His Work, or keep it except by absolute submission. But does all this not mean that such a frame of mind has really no religion—not more at best than a subjective, sympathetic, or even sentimental religiosity, combined with a rational and intractable individualism. It is a temper which would sacrifice the whole choice experience and deep revelation of the past to views limited by a man's own horizon and personal equation. Such minds take more pains to be true to themselves than to reality. 'Be true to yourself' is no Christian note.

To be delivered from this backwater we must come to be much more concerned about our authority than about our independence. If we properly see to the authority the independence will not fail. In Christian religion independence is not the way to authority, but authority to independence. We do not first become our own moral masters and then accept the Saviour. We do not cultivate the spiritual virtues and then mark and admire their consummation in Christ. That is Stoicism patronising Christ. It is Christ's authority as Saviour that gives us to ourselves, and His service makes us our own freemen. Christian obedience means actual obedience to an authority we have found, and found only because if first finds us; it is not merely a willingness to obey if our authority could be found. To obey Christ thus is better than to be free; it is the only way to be permanently free, individually or socially; and without such obedience freedom is a curse. *Absolute* obedience is the condition of *entire* freedom. We must be more concerned about our God than our religion, about our Gospel than about our sermons, about our Word than about our liberty, about the Church than about Society. And if we are really to revere and serve Humanity—really and intelligently—we must not be so contemptuous of tradition as we may have been tempted, or even taught, to be. We must escape from the superstition that the traditional is the conventional, or the authoritative the reactionary. For what is the soul of tradition but the rich and select experience of the largest and most precious part of Humanity known to us—the Past. It is the old Gospel in its eternal youth. Is there any other spiritual freedom to be found to-day than that which spreads its golden wings in Augustine, Athanasius, Hooker, or Thomas Goodwin. I do not, of course, speak of what is often, with much poverty of intelligence, called breadth of thought; I speak of the grand vision and plerophory of the soul, ranging from one end of heaven through earth to the other, mightily and sweetly ordering all things.

An individualist democracy, which believes only in the moderns and subjects everything to the private judgment of the living, is not truly democratic. It leaves out of account the great mass of mankind—the dead, to say nothing of the unborn. It is an ochlocracy. It sets up " an oligarchy of those who happen to be alive, and it robs of their franchise those who happen to be dead." It throws about words it has never stopped to interrogate or striven to command. It sees no difference between tradition and convention, between conservatism and reaction;

AUTHORITY AND INDIVIDUALISM

and it dubs as a mere traditionalist the man who becomes the tribune of the dead, the mouthpiece of their dim, dumb millions, and the champion of the great memories most precious to a noble race. It calls the conservative a reactionary if he turn to take the opinion of the past, and urge the inclusion of the past as a power in the active life of the race. It is very necessary to protest against the dictatorship of the day in those vast questions which affect every day and every age of history alike, and which go to the bedrock of human faith and destiny. For in such matters it is never the spirit of the age alone that can deliver us from the little circle of our individuality, turbid with all the prejudices, passions, and interests that ferment in our raw egoism. The spiritual entail of a historic deliverance cannot be broken. And the deep problem of any age can only be solved by that which solves the problem of all the ages.

Surely no one can take due account of the disintegrating tendencies current in society without some misgiving, whether he overcome it or not. The old authorities are fading much faster than new ones arise, and modern individualism runs down on its lees to choke society with its dregs. Is it only cowardice to fear the strength of the visible forces that make for anarchy in faith and life, and their rapid progress when compared with those that invisibly make for real order and power? It will be said, perhaps, that the forces of religion are very strong, in this country at least; and that the mark of the age compared with the generation bygone is socialist rather than individualist. But let us look into this.

And first, as to the religious influences. The trouble is that so many of these simply represent, not a personality created by religion, but an individualism applied to religion. It is applied to religious subjects, or baptised with the religious name or sentiment, but it is not regenerate by the positive message and corporate power of religion. For, as I say, the spirit of religion is first a spirit of humility and obedience to divine authority in some form as concrete as God's action always is. Whereas the impression left by very much of our religion is that of an immense confidence in the present, and a ruling temper of challenge, or even of mutiny, to tradition, of contempt for things held most divine in the past, of an ignorant " I know better than the past," or a reckless "I don't care, it does *me* good." Much that is prized as religious liberty is but natural egoism in the religious realm. A man who so wasted his education as to have learned nothing which subdued his pert, glib intellect to reverence for the great and wise, naturally finds nothing to prevent him, as soon as he gets a platform, from banal attacks on those truths and powers from the past which embody the deep experience of many generations, absorbing and correcting each other, and founding on a close and profound knowledge of Revelation at its sources in history and experience. Religious liberty is in peculiar danger of becoming more free than religious, and more fractious than free. It is in danger of losing the unmistakable note of having been mastered as the condition of having been set free. Men, for instance, are all too ready to rise to the tocsin of popular No-Popery polemics, destitute of the historic sense, or of any history with more insight than a demagogue's. And when they are reminded that sacred tradition is the true mother of liberty, that freedom must have its Jerusalem which is the mother of it all, they are apt to suspect the subtle influence of Rome. They scent a Jesuit. They are so obsessed with the fear of an official hierarchy that they renounce a hierarchy of competency, sanctity, and moral sovereignty.

AUTHORITY AND INDIVIDUALISM 311

The Roman curia as a political or strategic force, eaten up with ultramontane ambitions for every other state, is the tyrant of some nations and a menace to all; but let us treat with something else than either assault or hate the Roman Church—unless we are to deny its right to the name of a Church. Mere anti-clericalism is a poor foundation for Protestantism. It is French and not English. It beats the drum, but it cannot order the battle. Let us watch the priest; but let us also be more vigilant that our Churches and ministers are priestly enough in the better way. Let us protest against the Mass; but do we go from the Lord's Table as moved, edified, certified, and exalted as the devout Roman when he goes from the altar with a sense that something has been done that really matters, that affects both God and man and the world unseen. Our complaint should be not that Rome makes so much of tradition, but that she makes so much of the wrong element in tradition and allows a Pope to say, " I am tradition." If Rome has made a tyranny of Church continuity, have none ever fetichised Church atomism? Have no Churches turned continuity out of doors and lost entirely the sense and allegiance of a great historic Church; so that the Word often whistles shrilly in a waste when it should trumpet the crowd to their ranks, or make them hear the bass of Heaven's deep organ blow? Because we reject the historic Episcopate must we refuse the historic Church its true motherly place in our spiritual education? We throw into the arms or avenues of Rome those who do cherish that great idea. There was much said at the Edinburgh Missionary Conference of 1910 about the need of stripping from the Christianity we carry to the East the hulls of its Western form. That was proper enough. But equally proper was the reminder that to strip the true Catholic element from Christianity is to carry round something which is not Christianity at all, and certainly not Christianity with missionary power. There is an irreducible Catholic tradition, with a right not only to interest us but to command us. And to drop that tradition would be like emptying the tanks and bunkers to lighten the ship.

The first Christianity had very definite and uncompromising convictions which made it as a sojourner and a stranger in the midst of the Græco-Roman civilisation. And this was the attitude upon which it throve. Truly, elements from Paganism crept in, but they were comparatively peripheral or superficial to the faith, which made its irresistible way by its native power. The great liturgies witness this more than the great creeds. As time went on these foreign influences came much nearer the Christian centre. The Church came to terms with the world both in action and thought. And it meant a more rapid extension of the Church, but a Gospel more shallow, hollow, and worldly. The Church no longer conquered the World, it went into partnership with it. All this is as true to-day as it was two thousand years ago. For the modern man is still at bottom the old Adam; and so he remains, with his egoism merely turned pious, until he is more than modernised, till he is renovated by the second Adam and becomes the new man in Jesus Christ. Christianity can do little for civilisation till it is extirpating that egoism on which all the civilisations play fantasias, and till it is absorbing civilisation in the kingdom of God. The Church as such need have little direct effect on current culture. It does not act on it by pressure. It brings no formulated answer to its problems, and no policy for its affairs. Its first condition is the new birth for a soul or a people, and its first work is to bring that to pass. All things else are added to that. All doctrine and organisation grew out of that. The light must come from the fire, not the fire from the light. Christianity made modern Europe by coming to the old Paganism, not as a culture but as a regeneration. The Gospel and the world, Christ and the civilisations, have little common ground though very great mutual influence. Christ is not another King, but the King of Kings; and His Word is not an influence among others in the world, but the true moral principle and sceptre of the world. And the anxious effort on the Church's side to leaven the manners, tone, and laws of a civilisation whose egotisms still remain its ruling morals—such an effort always means at last a compromise where there should be at least a co-ordination —a compromise in which the Church succumbs to the world, and of course earns its neglect and ridicule. There is a tradition and a continuity in the existence of the Church which we cannot abandon for any prospect of missionary success. Here let us deceive neither ourselves nor others. The arrest of the Church's extensive effect is due to the decay of its intensive faith, while a mere piety muffles the loss. The prime object of the Church with its Gospel is neither to sweeten, spiritualise, nor rationalise the civilisations and religions; but it is to conquer them. All, of course, with an intelligent and sympathetic regard to the precise problem they present. And all with care that the Church do not preach herself more than her Gospel or her Lord, as she still freely does.

We may now pass to the socialistic influences of the hour which are looked to to temper the old individualism. Is it not the misfortune of many socialists that they are socialist (as many Christians are humanist) on individual grounds which destroy both socialism and Humanism? The socialism has not leavened their intellect or tempered their will. They are still incorrigibly critical, aggressive, unconquered, atomist. They love putting men right more than they love loving them. Their sympathies, indeed, are of the twentieth century, but their mind represents the thin rationalism of the eighteenth century, or the ideal rationalism of the nineteenth—in either case being intellectualist still, individualist still. They are socialist largely because of an individualist reaction against tradition and the order represented by tradition, because their ideal society has no past. Socialism is the policy of the disinherited, and the self-disinherited. It appeals to many not so much by its own merits but as a chief challenge of the social tradition. If their cause won and they lived one hundred years hence they would be opposed to socialism for the same reasons as now lead them to embrace it—if you can call an embrace what is often but a hold. They are drawn to the socialism suggested by present facts, which are seen or felt but not construed, not interpreted, not " placed " in a great historic context. They are not taught to realise, what would alter their whole habit of mind, that the past is as truly a part of human society as the present, if we believe in the unity and solidarity of the race at all. They do not realise that tradition is the crystallised experience of the social past, the choice spiritual legacy of the race, the distilled elixir of onward life; that the more permanent it is, the more it embodies that select experience. But if, on the plea of appealing to experience, they will concern themselves only with the present they make the true individualist mistake. They do not really believe in experience but only in impression. They are impressionists, as individualists always tend to be. But experience is a slow, considered thing, sifted and verified, a thing weathered by stress and matured by time. And impressions are not experience, just as sensations

AUTHORITY AND INDIVIDUALISM 315

are neither knowledge nor life. They are not experience till they are schooled, organised, corrected, and matured by a long process of contact with a world of men and affairs. Yet nothing is more common than for the light-of-nature individualist, who went straight from school to business, with some instruction but no education, to offer his impressions *sans gêne* as experience, or his experience as a measure of his whole age, or his age as the standard of all history, or history as the canon of all Revelation. Such people represent the cardinal error of the thorough individualist which is to suppose that their solitary feeling or opinion can get at any truth higher than that of the street. It is to suppose that their opinion is worth anything without passing through a real discipline, without self-knowledge, and all the humbling and purification which a sound self-knowledge means. How can we ignore, for the sake of the experience of to-day, that which ought to be the basis of all evolutionary education—the experience of all the days that have produced it? How deep, how ubiquitous, how tough the distrust and dislike of education is, and sometimes in the name of religion! The ignorance of the priest is not held to affect the value of his sacraments. The ignorance of the orthodox pulpiteer does not discredit him with the crowd he tickles. And the ignorance of the crude heretic makes him but the more intelligible to an audience of fanatical libertarians.

Is it good or seemly that we should sacrifice to the autonomy and self-sufficing of the living individual the continuity and competency, the weight and majesty of the whole human past? Would it not take all the earnestness out of our individualism if we were sure that most who come after us would treat us and our effort with the neglect and contempt, with the perversion *in malam partem*, that many of us expend on the experience of the past? Is there no such thing as the autonomy of the race, with a tremendous call upon the reverence and deference of the individual and the present—especially in connexion with those great moral and spiritual issues where progress has but a secondary place and the vital is the eternal? The best in us to-day is the distilled, fructified experience of bygone time. We have learned to speak of the subliminal present and its subconscious influence. Well, I have tried already to show that that is not all. But it is much; and the more we go into the psychology of the matter, the more we shall probably find that the subliminal self is the funded past, making us before we were made, and fashioning us in a secrecy long before to-day, while as yet there were none of us.

My present point is that in the social region it is the intractability of individual freedom, the mere spirit of revolt, rather than reverence for the solidary race that moves many to socialism. But in so saying, of course, I do not wish to obscure the fact that far other and higher motives are at work. Some have their intellectual impatience stimulated by deep sympathy for those afflicted by the evils of the old society. And others, finer still, make this observation. They note that, in an age wild with the passion of individual freedom, there is a growing lack of character and conviction, a growing weakness to stand up against the impulses within, the demands around, and the fashion without, a growing tendency to court popularity and seek votes. Character succumbs to candidature. Individualism kills individuality and liberty. Autonomy destroys personality. Men have not a resource which protects their liberty from becoming the victim of " collective suggestion." Either their freedom is hypnotised by the loud mass of similarly hollow free-

AUTHORITY AND INDIVIDUALISM 317

dom round them. Or, when they are not hypnotised by it, they rush to take refuge in it as a counterweight to the hollowness and limitation they feel in their now masterless and burdensome autonomy. Often, when we try to escape from ourselves, and even when we think we escape, we succumb in another form. We become the victims of a crowd of individuals too like our vagrant selves, victims of this "collective suggestion." We are worn down by the incessant dropping of dilettantist modernism, by journalistic corrosion. The soul, friable instead of firm, more sensitive than steady, and yearning for a freedom which is often little more than nervous greed, is concussed by voluble majorities and epidemic levities. It yields to mere magnetisms. Or it is brow-beaten by the form and pressure of a crowd who are themselves not free, but only units in the mobile mass and mode of the hour. Men do not stop to consider that their own defects multiplied by socialist millions can provide no substitute for that mighty authority which fills the race with the purpose of God, and thus provides the one thing needful to make its freedom free. How can Humanity be truly or permanently free if it find its freedom anywhere short of the absolute God and His salvation?

It is the same thing substantially with religious belief. For it will be found that it is the historic world-religion that is the social secret; and, conversely, that the wreckers in religion have seldom the true social soul. Our creed should be the distilled and advancing expression of a corporate life, faith, and experience (that is, of a social life) stretching through a long and living past back to the fountain-head of a Revelation given in history, in the act of a universal soul, and not merely in the recesses of the single soul. It is there that our growing freedom must have its birth, and school, and food if it is to gather weight and ripen to a beneficent power. But if its first concern is to assert a prompt, private and indocile judgment, and to claim the right to thrust that upon public notice, unschooled and unabashed, then it is neither of grace nor of power but of egoism and contention. If our first joy is to break from that corporate tradition, and start to make everything over again from the beginning, then freedom becomes a prickly, boyish, freakish, and powerless thing, weak in itself and as weakening as every irritant is. The truth that is to rule and bind the race is not to be come at by the *tours de force* of an individual intelligence which strains at every leash. It is but in the school of a great and old authority that we lose our egoism and find our soul and our brethren.

XVI

AUTHORITY, FREE PERSONALITY, AND FREE THOUGHT

WE ought here to consider a difficulty in some minds entitled to respect. They have been brought up with a great regard for the right of *private judgment* as one of the chief conquests of the Reformation. And they ask if no room is any longer to be left for such a palladium of Protestantism. But there are ways of putting the claim which are against common sense. And there is an easy confusion between freedom of private opinion and facilities for public influence. Is the private judgment of a Protestant youth of any doctrinal value beside the public judgment of a Catholic theologian? Did even Kingsley come out of it well with Newman? What would be the value of a novelist's private judgment against Lord Acton's in a matter of Church history? Or a No-Popery preacher against Döllinger's? Or a village evangelist's against Bishop Gore on Church, Sacraments, or the Ministry? Again, what is the worth of a pure scholar's judgment on theology? Or what is the worth of my private judgment about the date of a psalm, or the Aramaisms in the Gospels? Is the private judgment of Smith, who does not know the subject, who never took pains to know it, who wasted the time in which he was supposed to learn it, of any value against the mature judgment of Jones who does know it by trained attention and experience? Has it any moral right to a public appearance? What has been the moral effect of the popular cult of private judgment? A certain sturdiness, no doubt; also, a certain freedom, which is of prime value when we are but keeping a ring for the struggle of opinions that the competent may have scope. But what of some of its most popular by-products —the premium on ignorance, the aridity of judgment, and the loss of humility and moral weight?

But, as a matter of fact, the unlimited right of private judgment is not a fruit of the Reformation but of the Renaissance and of the Revolution with their wild individualism. It is Socinian and rationalist, it is not Protestant. The Reformation certainly made religion personal, but it did not make it individualist. The Reformation, if it destroyed the hierarchy of the Church, did not destroy the hierarchy of competency, spiritual or intellectual. In a political democracy we speak of one vote, one value; but in the intellectual and spiritual region all opinions are not of equal worth; nor have they all an equal right to attention. What the Reformation said was that the layman with his Bible in his hand had at his side the same Holy Spirit as the minister. Each had the testimony of the Spirit as the supreme religious Expositor of Scripture. And, since for that age the whole Bible was equally inspired, the witness of the Holy Ghost was held to bear upon everything in the Bible. (Even then the ministry, being especially appointed by the Church, had an authority in worship and teaching belonging to no layman who was without such appointment.) But now that we do not so read the Bible, now that we distinguish in the Bible much that belongs only to knowledge or imagination from much that belongs to personal faith, much that is outgrown from the things that cannot change— now the region where the layman's word is as good as the minister's, and the ignorant equals the expert, is much circumscribed. It is confined to the

AUTHORITY AND FREE THOUGHT

testimony of personal experience under the Gospel, and to the witness of what God has done for the confessor's soul. That is the only region of the entire liberty of prophesying. It does not extend, without special discipline, to points in the Bible outside that, where preaching becomes teaching, and individual confession becomes the theology of the Church. Any one can qualify. The due knowledge is not confined to any class or order. A devout miner may be a valuable preacher, but as a teacher he must qualify. He must dig in the history and mine in the books which enshrine greater souls and greater experience than his own. The intelligent, nay, the ignorant, layman is entitled to an opinion, and more than an opinion, as to whether Christ is risen, because it is part of his faith as a Christian to have dealings with the risen Christ. But what is his opinion worth as to the raising of Lazarus, now that the Bible is not swallowed whole? That belongs to the whole thorny question of miracles, of the fourth Gospel, and of Bible criticism. In the one case he has qualified by the relevant experience and knowledge, in the other he has not. He is morally entitled to a public opinion (*i.e.*, a teaching opinion) only where he has qualified and is competent. Let him preach his *faith* and put it into works; but it is better to reserve his *opinions* till he is competent, or till the competent substantially agree.

But an age or a race of individualists unbroken to any yoke is too suspicious to be docile; and I am very conscious of stirring here all the popular dislike for the expert. It is a suspicion which is largely due to the self-confidence of the amateur, who is unsteady after all, and uneasy and touchy for that reason; but it is also much justified by the pretensions of the professional expert in certain levels. We are distrustful of experts as they appear in the courts, or of specialists in small and outlying subjects, which are easily magnified by their pedants so as to destroy relative values and hide everything else. There are those who are red-hot on the theme that the whole future of society depends on due care of children's teeth. But, as we rise in the greatness and dignity of the subject concerned, it is more difficult to exaggerate its range and value for life. And the more we so rise, the more trusty and valuable for life the expert in the universal subject is. The height of his subject gives him range, perspective, and footing. He is less likely to immolate life to it because it becomes co-extensive with life; and he is more qualified by it to see life steadily and whole. In subjects like philosophy, ethic, or theology, the expert is balanced and steadied by the greatness and gravity of what he handles. He partakes of the stability of life's centre as he nears it. And he acquires for human life and destiny an authority very different in its value from that of the biologist of bacilli or the zoologist of beetles.

It is a common charge against any form of authority that it interferes with *free personality*, and especially *free thought*.

As to its effect on free personality.

We are in this world to acquire for ourselves and promote in others a moral personality, in which freedom is an element, but only one. And the effect of a real authority upon personality is the most kindling and educative influence it can know. In the interior of the soul authority and freedom go hand in hand. For here it is soul that acts richly on soul, and deed produces noble deed. Moral influence is entirely a matter of personal authority. It is the effect of a good will on one less good. There can be no greater development of personality than that represented by the slow conversion of a rude fisherman to a great

AUTHORITY AND FREE THOUGHT

Apostle, of the Galilean pilot to the writer of 1 Peter. And that was done entirely, not by the development of private judgment, but by growing subjection of every thought to the authority of Jesus Christ. On the other hand there are many instances where a premature and unbridled independence of opinion has ended in wasted years, moral sterility, personal futility, and spiritual desolation.

It is often to be remarked how the tendency to a ready assertion of the natural self destroys personality. Egoism, while it may produce "characters" for a time with a racy tang and a literary effect, is the enemy of character and the death of freedom. For it is but a part of nature, and the soul that was made for grace if it live by nature is a slave. It is arrested and stunted. Nature-worship is moral bondage. Nature does not develop soul in the long run. It only develops up to soul; and it rolls over it at last. The egoist, as he multiplies, grows less and less fit to assert himself against the crowd, which is only himself enlarged and inflated. More and more he becomes but a unit in a mass of similar units, all tending to one type, all the victims of the prevailing mode, all determined to inflict it on the rest, and all infected by the kind of servility which lives for tips, doles, or bets, and which cares little for what it can earn by its powers compared with what it can win by luck, cunning, or flattery. Personal values are overwhelmed by the fashion of the time and place. A class morality, which is no morality, but only the custom of a set, interest, or trade, becomes the rule of life. Class war invokes from either side the moral support of the Church, though the same people may sneer when it is invoked for national wars. Or, on the other hand, to be inoffensive, agreeable, popular, becomes the chief wish. The people tend to become like the houses they live in—to exist in rows, each exactly like his neighbour, and as dull. Individuality itself becomes erased—for what is idolized also grows debased. The man who does not rise to be a person becomes an item. He has none but a party conscience, a class interest, and he votes as the boss bids him. He does not live; only some gregarious force lives through him; and he does things not because he will, but because he must. He knows nothing of action, only of incident. Incident engrosses him; and action as it grows great grows unintelligible. He is the slave of his heredity, his environment, his disposition, his mates. He knows nothing of responsibility, of guilt, of sin; and his only goodness is goodness of heart, because he is built that way, and that is the way of least resistance, and is always popular. He resents nothing but a master, he hates nothing but an authority that makes any demand on him, shows him what a slave he really is, and tells him that a good fellow may be a poor creature. An individualist age is one in which at last men tend to be as like as blackberries, and as cheap. So that they can make no resistance when some larger egoist sees his chance and breaks away to become dictator of the situation. Our safeguard from the tyrant is not intractable individualism with an average of happiness, but moral personality with an ideal of perfection. Self-will is not manhood. Men who lose the moral power of acting together loyally under a true leader end by only herding together under a few dogs. The flock that will be led by no shepherd invites the dogs, first to drive them, and then to worry them. For the very dogs that round up slaves become demoralised. And so a non-moral, a non-Christian democracy goes to the dogs, and both to the abyss.

As to the effect of authority and its discipline on

AUTHORITY AND FREE THOUGHT

free thought, I will here take up what I have touched on more than once—the discipline essential to freedom.[1] Are we always quite clear what we mean by free thought? The thought we start with is anything but free. It is loaded with prejudice, passion, fashion, and all the bonds of ignorance and inexperience. An immense amount not only of study but of self-discipline is required to make thought truly free. Freedom of thought is a hard-won power and glory whether in generations or individuals. It does not come like flight to a bird, or love to a boy. It is not its emancipation from the past, nor its escape from tutors and governors. But it is thought emancipated from the prejudices and passions of the common natural man, or from that "collective suggestion," which makes a man the victim of his most ordinary environment even when he tries to escape from himself. Do we reflect when we sacrifice everything to renounce tradition, that we may be only choosing one tradition for another, and one less noble? In the early years of life especially we are least of all free. We are mostly what we have been made by a series of mental legacies and spiritual impressions descending on us, which we have not yet enough power of personality or intellect to react upon, to select, measure, correct or assimilate. We have not worked our passage into freedom (and there is no saloon on that ship). The pilgrim must foot it with Bunyan; there is no "celestial railway," as Hawthorne delightfully pourtrays it. Youth is a great coward in matters of form, propriety, or ritual, as practised by his school, his set, or his class. Traction-engines will not drag from the schoolboy treason to his class, which may yet be owed by duty to his teacher. There is no social ritualist like the undergraduate. From that early

[1] For this point (and others here) see Förster, *Autorität & Freiheit*, 1910.

stage most uneducated people, and very many who pass for educated, never emerge. They are simply indices of the tradition or *milieu* that lies nearest them at their plastic time—at best, of the spirit of their own age. And, even when they assail the long tradition of the past, it is mainly as the organs of the inferior tradition called fashion. In the name of a contemporary tradition, brief and ordinary, they renounce tradition old and venerable, which is much more experienced, and full of genius. There is really no free thought possible but by an amount of self-knowledge beyond most people, and especially beyond youth. Thought truly free is an accomplishment and privilege of maturity—not of youth—whether we speak of the individual or the race. And its aggressive exercise in public may come to be in the same category as brawling in church.

Let us frankly realise that the interior of the public mind has gone through a great change since the sixteenth and seventeenth centuries, owing partly to the influence of the Reformation in personalising religion, partly to the effect of the new scientific conception of the Universe, and partly to the new Humanism of the democracy. This is bound to affect the form of our faith. The type of faith (and I am not speaking here of the form of belief) could not remain the same amid such changes in our ethical, æsthetic and scientific views of things, and our relation to them. The monotheistic idea, *e.g.*, has been deeply and happily affected by the immanence idea; and the Christological idea has been similarly affected by the ideal of Humanity, and especially of personality. And our ideas about the origin, integrity, and authority of the Bible are almost revolutionised by scientific criticism. Such changes go deeper than views of the world or of man; they affect the psychology of the soul itself, the type of religion, and the quality of faith. If Christ remain central, it is to a very different world; and so far it is a different Christ. It is a Christ who must stand a greater strain than the mediæval Christ, and approve Himself the Saviour of a far vaster world, a more subtle, more difficult, more self-conscious world, a world with all the play and intimacy of the new subjectivism, with its cross-currents and swift mobility, a world more exacting and independent than ever before. Revelation and redemption are both vaster, in so far as their problem is a vaster world, a world much more complex, and a prouder Humanity. They have also to be adjusted to historical evolution.

And one psychological change I have named should be noted in particular. The idea of personality, the more it has been challenged by naturalism, develops the more, and steps to a commanding place. The person is ousting the old idea of the individual. The moral person we grow to is replacing in our interest the elemental instinctive individual with which we start. Moral personality is sending wild egoism to its own place. Discipline discredits mere growth. And the prime object of society is less and less to make a ring for the individual, and give him room to make a mess or a success of his life as he likes; but it is to develop (that is to say to create) moral personality. The individual with his egotism is born, but the personality has to be made. It grows; and some weak, violent, or obstinate people die without it. The individual is the necessary product of natural evolution; but the personality grows only through the exercise and discipline of moral freedom, judgment, and responsibility. It grows through moral freedom trained by social culture, but still more by super-individual, supernatural powers; which are gathered up into a creative point in Jesus Christ, and flow down through history in the mighty stream of His Church, and all the Church connotes for the world. It is only as we acquire this personality that we really experience God, and the freedom, the largeness, that such an experience gives to thought and life. If a theistic experience give much freedom and range to thought, how much more a Christian. (Judaism has no dogmatic, no theology. Its thought expands in every direction but this.) It is the morally-educated personality that owns the true authority, and feels how spiritual it is and yet how influential upon mental conclusions, how inward it is yet how beyond us, how real it is, how inevitable, how blessed. We believe best, repent best, love and obey best at the last, and not at the first. The first love has the romance but the last has the reality, the kingdom, power, and glory. And we then learn that external authority is only mischievous, not when it comes to us from without (for all authority must), but when it represents a kind of pressure which cannot evoke and cannot nourish our moral soul.

Thus freedom of thought is really part of something much greater—free personality. What an inversion and an anomaly, then, that it should be claimed with most passion by people (of whatever age) at a stage when their egoism, their natural forceful individualism, their instinctive smattering self often posing as reason, still has the upper hand of their personality, when their individuality has never gone to school with a wisdom that comes down from above—from history in knowledge, and from heaven in grace ! How archaic, how primitive, how elemental it all is, how aggressively resentful of challenge ! How a Christian culture is bound to invert these natural values and orders ! The true school for thought and its freedom (especially if we still believe in that Grand State Secretary of heaven on earth, the Holy Spirit), is that great living tradition of which we are but the fringe, and which is so much more than dead convention—being the choice experience of the past, its select knowledge and faculty, acquired from *life*, distilled by *genius*, and founded upon *Revelation*. This is the great *Aula* of the highest education. At its moral height it is the grand evangelical and catholic tradition of the Church, whereof the Church itself, in its various forms, is not simply a vehicle but even a part—for the Church is inseparable from its vital Word. The Gospel and its fulness of explication in thought, word, and deed is the greatest tradition in the world, as the Church is the greatest product of history. The authority of the Church is but the weight of its experienced Gospel in a vast plexus and long series of regenerate and corporate souls. And so the true authority of the true Church is a leading condition of thought truly free. If the first authority be God in His salvation renewing the soul, the distilled elixir and ordered experience of ages of that salvation must be an authority in the second degree. True freedom of thought is therefore not merely emancipated from the past but as certainly from the thinker and his present; not from the beliefs of others but from our own egoism, or from the vagrant views and dilettantist impressionism of the hour. It is delivered by self-discipline, luminous because laborious, from the natural passion or levity in which we all begin. It escapes from the common assertive self whose freedom is a mere instinct (it may even be mere temper) and not yet a principle; whose very conscience may be but a crude moral instinct. And it is an instinct soiled by admixture with other instincts more base, instincts debasing and deflecting thought itself by an infection of our whole solidary nature—of our head and not only our heart. The naïve beliefs of individualism are mainly the intellectual expression of the elemental man, which to impulses is fire, and to impressions wax. And they do not really become free except in an educational process, in which we grow while we learn, which is moral self-emancipation as truly as it is an extension of the intellectual horizon, and which is self-empowerment as truly as it is mental enlargement. Surely it is clear that for free and just thought there is nothing our society so much needs as an education which a youth gets far elsewhere than in free-thought prints or coming up in the train with a handful of his passionate peers—and his paper, written by his like for his like.

There is another plea which deserves some respectful attention. ' Is it not part of my duty to God, Christ, and conscience to be true to the light in me, to develop my mental idiosyncrasy, to be myself intellectually, so that I may bestow upon Christ my best mind, and subject Him to the reverent criticism of my highest reason? Will such a tribute not honour Him the more? Does a regard for authority not destroy my intellectual conscience, its duty, and its service to God? ' That is a mistake which deserves appreciation. But it is a mistake. Christ did not come to take the tribute of our honour or the resultant of our assent, but to take possession of our soul. We do not elect our Eternal King by any judicious process. No man is a Christian who has not got beyond criticising his Saviour as such. Whatever He taught or did is true and final in the sense in which He taught or did it.

Of course I am not here speaking of criticism of the Bible, of a selection among the things there attributed to Christ in word or deed. That has its own good right, rightly used, and it may go far. We allow duly for our critical reductions in the record, and for His own kenotic self-limitations in the fact. But

AUTHORITY AND FREE THOUGHT 331

I am speaking about criticism of points where we are agreed what Christ said, did, and meant for His central, His total, work. For the Church to take an utterance of Christ about which scholarly criticism does not arise, or where it is agreed (as His canon against divorce in any circumstances within His ideal Church), and to say, ' I can accept this as divine only in so far as it commends itself to my rational judgment, in so far as I understand it, in so far as it fits the truth I already have, the ethic by which I already live, the theology I already believe, or the social expediency of the age I live in '; to bring the clear teaching of Christ, who lived in the centre of the ideal Church always, and from there saw to the heart of the whole moral and spiritual world, to the bar of our individual vision and its poor insight ; to judge Him by our individual experience or that of our century; to make Him wait at the door of our notions of right and true, and to reject in Him what we cannot assimilate, or what our age would not regard as sane, normal, judicious, Wordsworthy or archiepiscopal—all that may, in cases, not be far from the kingdom of God, but it is not necessarily in it. It may be one phase of the ' I know better ' spirit which is the baneful conceit of the intellectual age, and part of our worship of good form or of the spirit of the time. There is nothing so great and mighty in all the tradition of the past as the personality of Christ active in its true train and succession ; therefore there is no moral truth so true as his; indeed we call both his person and his truth absolute. And to treat Him as I have said is to turn our rejection of the past into the rejection of God. It is to reduce revelation to the service of reason, and of contemporary reason besides, which is but a phase or stage. It is to misunderstand Christ's claim, which is a claim not to our assent, or sympathy, or help, but to our surrender. He makes a claim upon our reason only when we have already submitted and consigned to Him (once called mad) our whole personality—of which our rationality is but a function. It is not liberty thus to outgrow Christ. It is bondage to what our natural man, our native self-respect, our national ideal, our sectional experience, our current society, our practical training, and our favourite reading have made us. Our mind cannot work freely on Christ till our whole self is His absolutely and for ever. Nothing but moral freedom can give us power to understand a moral greatness like Christ's; and in the end nothing can understand Him or His words but the moral freedom which is His own new creation in us. Therefore it is no part of the Church's own true freedom to work critically upon Him (as distinct from the record) and to judge our judge. A true freedom works critically *from* Him. It accepts His Word against our own judgment in obedience of intellect and not its sacrifice, and so wins the power of deeper and deeper insight into His wealth of originality *credo ut intelligam*. I trust myself to His Person that I may understand His truth. That is so in the whole region of personal relation, and most of all between us and our Saviour. But the plea which I am examining reduces Christ to be the patron of our free thought, or even its beneficiary. He then like any favourite preacher, owes His position with us to our agreement with Him. He is not then the author and creator of our thought's true freedom. The Christian freedom in regard to Christ is freedom in His grace, the freedom with which He sets us morally, experimentally free by setting us in communion with God. It is not a freedom by which He benefits at our hands, but the freedom which is our benefit in His, the freedom of which He is the absolute donor, creator, and

AUTHORITY AND FREE THOUGHT

authority. It is in His worship; giving to thought that unique range, penetration, and liberty which we find chiefly in the great theological saints. His work on us is to create the profoundest moral inwardness and insight the world knows, through the evangelical re-birth of the sinful conscience to the spiritual world. There is nothing in all our modern and analytic subjectivity so intimate and searching as the evangelical psychology of sin and faith in the great new birth, as these are found in their greatest exponents. There is nothing so poignant, nothing that goes so close to the core and passion of moral reality. And this regeneration quickens the whole spiritual intelligence from our moral centre. The moral liberty we receive through the epistles is the one charter and security of the critical freedom we exercise on the Gospels. As Christians we have no freedom *before* Christ, only *in* Christ.

And we may profitably ask ourselves every time we assert our liberty whether it is given us by our Christian authority, or brought to it from another source; which then, of course, becomes our authority. For that is our authority which gives us our freedom. The Church, for instance, will be the authority of the world in so far as it gives the world its liberty. And it can only give that by giving the world an authority, and a moral authority, which destroys guilt in forgiveness. Let us ask if we receive from something in ourselves leave to trust Christ, or leave from Christ to trust anything in ourselves; if we are exploiting God for our liberty or our liberty for God; if we are using our liberty chiefly for divine worship or for humane sympathy and natural progress; whether the prime passion with us is always to find and deepen the authority over us; or whether we delight rather to go on from point to point of freedom for its own sake, like the scientific huntsmen who care less for truth than the pursuit of it, less for the quarry than for the quest. That is very well in sport; but this is no sportsman's world, with the Saviour on the Cross, the kingdom at stake, the Judge on the great white throne, and Eternity at the door.

There is indeed no plea that should be treated with more respect than that which urges the need for intellectual honesty. It is one of the best gains of the modern time; and it is largely due to the scientific age and the scientific spirit. But are we always clear about the meaning of that ideal? We suffer much from idealists who are made martyrs, not by the idea, but by their own confusion about what it means, and their wrongheadedness about serving it. Especially may they become victims of a morbid and (shall I say) egoistic scrupulosity about their own fidelity to their own ideal instead of to their historic situation and its actual duties. It is a part of the subjectivism which finds in religion its greatest opportunity. Intellectual honesty means a due regard to the facts of the case. But to *all* the facts, to the *whole* situation. Is it such a regard if a man ignore his duty of consideration to the great deep past with its reverend claim, or to the young and immature who need gradual education? Does intellectual honesty justify the heartlessness of fracturing their spiritual world? Is that speaking the truth in love? And Christ did not come just to teach us to tell the truth, which can be heartless enough. Again, is it such honesty to ignore the specific nature of the class of fact most concerned, to treat commanding spiritual realities with a mere critical inquiry, to apply to morals the methods of biology, or to settle the merits of the theological case with the apparatus of the textual scholar or the historian of dogma. But the plea is still, ' I

AUTHORITY AND FREE THOUGHT

have a duty to myself, I must not do violence to my mental and moral nature.' No doubt that deserves respect, though, as I say, it may sometimes betray the ethical egoist. But let us take it. Is it not part of our intellectual duty to know the limits of our intellect?[1] Is that modesty not a part of the mind's science of itself, of its honesty with itself? Is it not doing wrong to our intellectual nature if we refuse to recognise its limits, if we force its function, especially in every individual, and if we set up the individual intelligence, or even that of an age, as the last bar to which the great legacy of the race's experience must be brought? Intellectual honesty has as much to do with the acceptance of the right limit as of the right method. It urges that we should measure our powers at least as carefully as our rights (for our powers determine our rights), and criticize ourselves as carefully as we do the past. The more truly we measure ourselves in the face of what has come down to us, the more we rise in the scale of culture. Criticize your competency as well as your ancestors and your superiors. It is essential to a broad and honest science, which takes count of the whole situation, that it should discuss its own organs and methods of knowledge, discover their carrying power, and take the range of its own weapons. It is a poor artillery that knows more of the target than of the gun. A true science requires such intellectual honesty, and it protests against a conception of honesty which isolates an individual and sentimental rationalism as the fit instrument for the handling of the greatest tradition of life, the legacy and continuity of a new moral creation. It does not ask the sacrifice of the intellect but only of the self-sufficiency of the intellect, either as undisciplined, or as overweening when disciplined, because disciplined only by a half-culture which may ignore

[1] Förster.

the fundamental morality of the world. It protests against the detachment of the individual from the corporate intelligence, of the intellect from the actual state of the total soul or person, and its consequent despiritualisation and demoralisation. It bids it have the courage that audacity never knew —the courage to be humble. It prescribes a greater reverence for the past, more residence in it, and more assimilation of it. The most violent critics of the past are but tourists in it. Great historians are seldom revolutionaries. Progress does not come chiefly from criticism of the past but from appreciation of it and fulfilment of it. " My Father worketh hitherto and I work." For mere individual or intellectual criticism the problems are too great and subtle, too moral and complex. They need to be handled by a social organization both of action and of knowledge, by a Church of faith or a school of mind. Our tradition is our inheritance, not our burden. And it is a corporate legacy; therefore we have not to sacrifice it to a man or an hour, but to reconcile the race's hereditary wisdom with the fruitful inquiry of a whole age or society. Progress must be social on the scale of that great socialism of a solidary Humanity, which recognises amid the affairs of the present and the prospects of the future the citizenship also of the past.

It will be asked, perhaps, if I suggest that the religious and moral safety of civilisation requires that at its centre there must be a Church as a single, vast, and powerful institution, forming the authority for belief and practice, and protecting us from the narrowness, eccentricity, and anarchy of the individual and the sect. And the answer is, first, that the suggestion is a piece of mediævalism, with a dream of the Church which fell

AUTHORITY AND FREE THOUGHT

with mediævalism ; second, that however valuable in some ways such an ideal might be, it is impracticable for two reasons. It is impracticable because the Roman Church is the only possible reversionary of such a position, and Modernism has shown it to be either too honeycombed and rent with fatal divisions to act as a spiritual authority, or too spiritual to lend the despotic curia moral influence, or too weak to get rid of the curia. And it is farther impracticable because, even if it is meant that curial Rome should be replaced by a sympathetic Rome, which gathered into one majestic and impressive organ all the Catholicity of all the Churches, yet that event is too remote to be in time for the purpose in hand; which is to save civilisation from anarchy by a moral, spiritual, and theological authority it would respect. The need in civilisation grows much faster than the prospect of such a Church.

And yet vast is the authority of the whole Church in the world if only it will court an authority moral and inspiring, and not statutory and coercive. If we are to be saved from sheer Paganism and anarchy it must be by some influence, some form of authority compatible with a federation of Churches equal in their right, one more likely than the Roman ideal to be available when wanted, more ethical in its nature, and more spiritual in its note than is possible to one vast institution in such a world. The vaster the institution, so much the harder it is to keep truth supreme in it. " Der Mächtige lügt immer," says Nietzsche—" power always lies." And the more prone it is to act on affairs by intervention instead of revelation, so much the more it tends to put work before faith, to sacrifice spirituality to action, insight to shrewdness, belief to benevolence, and ethic to sentiment. The authority, though inseparable from institutions, must be more religious than a mere institution, however valuable, can be. And it must be more directly an action, and even a part, of God Himself, bearing upon the individual soul in its personal experience. It must be a kind of authority with that profound and unique moral inwardness which belongs to a Christianity truly evangelical. That means a Christianity where the moral soul is delivered from itself in a way not only radical but absolute. Which again means delivered through an experienced redemption by the absolutely Holy from a state of moral perdition. Which means, farther, saved from that moral helplessness through sin and guilt which used to be misunderstood as total corruption, and which feels, not indeed that human nature is rotten, but that the soul is morally forfeit, and the will impotent to regain communion with God till saved by that God's initiative in a holy salvation of the whole conscience of the world. The only moral authority that can save society is one that thus asserts itself in the individual conscience by its saved experience of a universal Redeemer; who therefore becomes our spiritual feoffee with His absolute gift and new creation of eternal life. The authority is thus religious and personal, and more than rational or institutional. The Church is authoritative only as it has the power and note of this Gospel. The authority is this Redeemer in this experience, changing, ruling, and normalising every conscience, acting through the message and confession of a historic Church of such consciences, which is the witness of the Gospel and the social agent of its principle, yet not the vicar of Christ nor the Judge of the world. It is the authority of grace saving the guilty conscience and not only the miserable heart, and saving the conscience of a race, by the power of a society, into the obedience of a kingdom.

The Gospel, thus experienced, has the secret of the

AUTHORITY AND FREE THOUGHT

salvation of the future only because it has the authority before whom we are not our own at all, to whom we owe our delivery from perdition and impotence and not from mere backwardness or waywardness, and to whom our absolute obedience is our only freedom. Faith is such a delivering power because it has within it such a gracious authority. Everything else, Church or Bible, is authoritative for us in the proportion in which it is sacramental of this final and absolute authority, of the Creator as Redeemer, the authority not merely of God but of a God of grace. Authority reflects a dying King.

And about this authority there are three things more particularly to be said.

1. It is in its action miraculous or "irrational." All absolute authority must reveal itself in a way of miracle. It does not rise out of human nature by any development, but descends on it with an intervention, a revelation, a redemption. It does not evolve from human nature, it invades it. An authority, which has its source in ourselves, is no authority. In us authority can have but its sphere and its echo, never its charter. The blight of democracy is that it will own no authority of which it is not the source, and believe nothing the light of genial nature does not understand. The great authority over us is miraculous before it is rational, and external more than intrinsic to our soul. It is not foreign, but it is other. It is mastering to the soul before it is perfecting, the soul's conquest rather than its fruition. It is rational so far as this, that it is the authority of a spiritual *nature* kindred to our own. On each side there is a person with a rational constitution. But it is not the rationality of its nature that makes the person or makes the authority. (There is the question how far a free person can have a 'nature' and remain

free.) It is the freedom of its conscious *will*. The action of authority on us is not the action of a truth or an ideal of the reason, but of a will, which is free as we are free, but whose free grace is a mystery greater than any freedom of ours to sin. There is no greater miracle than our freedom, except the authority which is its source and salvation. That grace is a standing miracle, in command of all the rationality of the world.

2. This authority, so super-rational in its nature and action, is yet in its method so rational that it emerges only amid psychological conditions. It is not magical. Conversion baffles intelligence, but we cannot be converted against our will. It wears the garb and speaks the tongue of our spiritual and conscious experience. Its externality is real, but it is such that it acts inside the soul and does not go round it. One feels here, of course, how our whole discussion of these subjects is vitiated by the introduction of spacial metaphors of extension and mutual exclusion, which are quite foreign to spiritual action with its inter-penetration. But we may perhaps use such language failing a better if we are vigilant against being misled. The point is that this authority visits us, faces us, and graciously constrains us, and does not merely continue, complete, and express us. The Christ who stands over us is the act of God and no mere classic achievement of man. Were He but the best of a divine Humanity, to revere Him would make Humanity too egoist to remain divine. This authority does not indeed impinge upon the soul's surface, it wells up within the soul's centre. But it does well up. It does break through. It lifts its head in our most secret place, and asserts its influence most in our inner castle. But the castle well is fed not from the rocks' subliminal depths, but from a reservoir far higher in the eternal hills. This authority truly has a power over us such as nothing that was not of

the soul's nature could have; but it is a power that could never arise from the soul's nature itself, however glorified. It speaks in the midst of our most intimate experience (else it could never be mistaken for a higher phase of it); but its decisive word is not drawn from our experience. Its note of authority, right, and possession was not learned there. And it does not come home to us merely by examining the experience of others. It must emerge in our own. I might put this technically by saying that while it is psychological it is not phenomenological. You may review all the psychological phenomena offered to observation by the religious experience of others, but you are not yet properly equipped to give an account of the whole matter till the authority speak in the Christian psychology of your own experience.

James and Starbuck examine with great effect such varieties of religious experience as are accessible by biographies, circulars, and schedules. But they make no use of what is so indispensable to the true psychologist of Christian religion—their own personal share in that experience. They are happy in their analysis, but the chief datum of the serious inquirer in this region is, first, his own experience. But in any case his work is synthetic. He must not simply dissect either others' experience or even his own. For he will not find the great thing, the *mirum quid*, by dissolving experience into its psychological constituents. He must know that supreme synthesis by which a man ceases to analyse his religion, lays hold on his God, and realises how his God holds him. For this is a God who does not treat men hopefully, according to a deep analytic vision of their hidden excellence or resource, but graciously, by a perfectly synthetic gift to them of Himself and His salvation, a gift so synthetic that its secret is with Himself alone.

The authority at the head and centre of the religious experience, I have said, is the authority of God's will of free and absolute grace in a new creation. This is the final authority the soul has to reckon with, the principle of the last judgment. For by grace we are saved and by grace are we condemned at last. And the psychology we need most is not an examination of the conditions of religion as a phase of human nature, but a psychology of that religion which answers God's grace with an active note as unique and positive as its own—the note of *faith*. The need and promise of the hour is a psychology of religion by the true experts of sin and faith. It works with a faith, in the positive Christian sense of a miraculous new creation (whether startling or not), that feels and owns practically the last authority of life. It is the miraculous authority in grace that makes religion into faith, by making it the last and inmost obedience. The final authority is a gracious God in salvation—miraculous, because if we could explain this act He would cease to be an authority, and the authority would then be the explanatory principle.

All other authorities for the soul stand ranged in a hierarchy as they are near to this God, necessary for His purpose or full of His action. The authority of the first degree is therefore religious. It is God as actually and historically experienced, God in Christ, Christ in the Holy Spirit, through a Church. The authority of the second degree is theological. It is the witness, not of our soul's instincts or our heart's voice, but of the experienced nature and action of the prime authority. And it is given us first in the Apostles, and second in their prolongation in the sifted and select experients of the Church. Apostolic authority rests on the fact that in the Apostles we have something beyond ideas which grew out of their faith, ideas making them, at the lowest, tentative interpreters

AUTHORITY AND FREE THOUGHT

of their subjective faith, or at the highest, classics and no more. It rests on the fact that we have in them interpreters of God's revelation, who had this for their unique vocation, and were equipped by God accordingly, to open up Christ's wealth of significance once for all time. And the authority in the third degree is ecclesiastical, though not officially so. It is the Church of the experients as the social creation of the Gospel, the Church of the worshippers, of the hymns and liturgies, the graces and virtues, the saints, martyrs, and blessed ministrants, rather than the creeds. It is not the Church as an institution prescribing faith, but as a community confessing and giving effect of every kind to faith. It wields an ample and intimate experience, and not prescriptive knowledge or impressive thought. Its power is felt in our heart and conscience, and owned in love, service, and patience. Reason is no authority. It is but the power of discerning authority, whether it judicially weigh evidence or faithfully own personality. It only co-ordinates, it does not commend. It registers, it does not value. And as we grow in our power of reading the psychology of this faith in grace, and the metaphysic of its spiritual history, we shall grow also in our sense of the authority in it as the be-all and end-all of human life and life's concern.

3. We then find that the supreme authority is that of our Judge and not simply of our ideas. And our salvation is salvation not from our Judge but by our Judge and Father. Salvation means acquiring a new and final authority, an eternal Lord and Master. The prime question of religion is not, "How do I stand to the spiritual universe?" but "How shall I stand before my Judge?" The last authority must be the authority owned by the conscience, and required by the sinful, guilty conscience of a race. It is the authority of a Saviour; but of a Saviour who is

final, as Saviour from *absolute* perdition; the Saviour of our moral helplessness and not merely our backwardness; One whose absolute property we are, therefore, by this absolute redemption and this gift of a new-created life. It is the authority of the moral absolute, of the holy, which stands over us and changes us from self-satisfaction to self-scrutiny, self-knowledge, and self-humiliation in the presence of the righteousness loving and eternal. It saves in the Cross, regarded not as a sectional palladium but as the crisis of all moral being, the world-crisis of the holy and the evil. It is not love that makes the authority and has the last word with the world. For in itself love has no authority, as instinct has none; and it needs constantly to be braced by an ethical verve, fixed by a moral bond, and taught in a moral school, to be preserved from its own perilous fondness or passion. The note of authority in love is given according to the holiness of it. Nor is it love that is so wonderful. There is nothing wonderful in our love of the race's beauties, heroes, and darlings, who overflow with a splendid, kind, genial or magic humanity. It is the formidable holiness of Christ that is our eternal hope and glory, that makes His love so wonderful, so miraculous, so subduing, commanding, authoritative for ever. The endless wonder is the conjunction in Christ, and most in His Cross, of moral majesty and spiritual mercy, of infinite holiness and intimate love.

XVII

AUTHORITY AND HUMANITY

THE idea of Authority is one which thus far at least has been found indispensable to human history and progress. It is bound up with order and therefore with freedom. So far as we have gone there has been no liberty without an authority which it had either to bring as an idea or to create as a power. It is the one thing that saves equality from becoming anarchy. And for the existence of fraternity it is as necessary as fatherhood. There could be no brotherhood without a father, or some shadow at least of the authority that fatherhood represents. Authority is a factor as essential to the economy of things and the order of society as either liberty, equality, or fraternity. And indeed more so. For it is the foundation of them all. And it is what makes them most worth having.

Moreover, it is especially connected with one element that tends to vanish from a society which resents it— the element of distinction, the aristocratic element. This is the necessary complement of the democratic. It drives faith to the worship of Christ, the world to the worship of genius, and women to the worship of the gentleman. There are many who are democratic in principle but not in taste. And may we not go farther? Politically we have a Monarchy which is now but the titular head of a substantial democracy, and a Conservatism which differs from its opponent rather on the rate of progress than on its reality. And the thing which casts many to the aristocratic or royalist side, now as in the Civil Wars, is less snobbery than the craving for some form, high or low, of that element of spiritual or æsthetic distinction which is the truth underlying the doctrine of a hierarchy on the one hand or an elect on the other. No democracy of principle should destroy hero-worship. None should abate our reverence for a moral *élite*. None should tie us up in the sphere of the elemental sympathies, the natural kindnesses, the domestic affections, the common equalities, the obvious truths, in such a way that the fine, the rare, the remote, the subtle, the illustrious, the commanding should cease to move us, or even rule us. No fraternity will continue to hold us which is not the product of prior loyalty. In the divine brotherhood each one resembles the children of a king. The predominance of the hearty, the genial, the kindly love as distinct from the holy, lofty, fine, and severe, is but contemporary, and is not permanent. It has a vast popularity, but not a posterity. The holy God Himself is not popular. The genial Jesus is a fiction of Humanism in search of a patron. Beecher's influence is fleeting compared with Newman's. A beloved disciple like Norman Macleod brought but a flush to the skin, while Bishop Wilberforce brought an irritation, when compared with the solemn effect of Maurice on the soul. The retiring saint, who may take up no 'cause,' may wield a spell both on present and future as the genial brother or champion does not—and we owe much to both. It is much that is demanded from us by those to whom the great tasks are given. They may fascinate our soul more than they delight our hearts. As in the Saviour's fidelity in the dereliction on the Cross, the greatest sacrifice may be the sacrifice of love's joy, comfort, and fellowship in the service of love's holy faith when of the people there are none with him. And,

AUTHORITY AND HUMANITY

if we review the whole history of the Christian Church (which embodies the spiritual distinction of the race), do we not find that the men who have made and saved it, who are its stays, its saints, and its deliverers, its prophets, priests and kings, have been those in whom the note of distinction took the lead of the note of geniality, and gave it its immortal spell. They were more at home with God than with men, and they loved the holy even more than the poor. "Good fellows are bad officers," says Lord Kitchener. It was what St Francis had in common with St Bernard that gave its best distinction to what was his own. The compassionate love of the one draws its permanent distinction from the holy faith and obedience common to both, from their being men under authority rather than fraternity, men who reveal the kingship rather than the brotherhood of the Redeemer. In the great judgment the real value of compassion was that, however unconsciously, "ye did it to me," more than to men. Fraternity can only rest on fatherhood, and men are loyal to men only as the children of a king at the long last. All the brotherhoods are but side chapels to the great Church.

It is the principle of authority, in whatever shape, that must save democracy from becoming easy, casual and corrupt, from mean, grey, and gritty mediocrity; as it is the democratic principle that saves authority from the inhuman superman. The principle of authority is the foundation of education and of religion. And no ethic is possible without it. An ethic of pity and sympathy substitutes the sentiments for the conscience, and the pliant affinities of love for the sure obedience of faith. It is an ethic of the popular Catholic kind, which presses lightly on human nature, however exacting it may on the few.

All wise men agree that authority is necessary for the

propædeutic stages of progress. It is essential (as we have seen) for education, which passes us on from one authority to another, and dignifies our freedom not by the wider range of it but by its higher kind; and this it measures by the spiritual quality and searching intimacy of the new authority's control. The stages, through which we are thus passed, may be described as the rude, the rational, and the righteous. If obedience is purely passive we submit to what is in its nature brute force. We are under the authority of the strong man. We yield to mere coercion. We are weak, and nothing but weak. We are helpless to resist, or perhaps even to react. But when an active element begins to enter our obedience it becomes rational. We not only *feel* the force of our authority, we *see* the force of it. We see reason for it. We assign ourselves to its control with some consent and freedom. We have the kind and degree of freedom that goes with rational perception. It is not indeed true moral freedom. It has laws instead of norms. Rationally we believe as we must—as the evidence compels. We are still under compulsion to a law lower than will. We are made to see rather than choose. But it is an inward perception, and so far free. It is not mere outward pressure. It *is* reason, it is not force. Our strong man is then our wise man. We acknowledge his superiority in knowledge or thought. He has the prestige of a scientific leader or a captain of the understanding. And we may treat him even with a certain reverence, or with the æsthetic admiration drawn from us by a vast system in which he construes the whole of existence, from a principle or a movement, as Hegel did.

But this is not a final authority, obedience, or freedom, after all. The sage's thought can be revised, his wisdom enlarged, his prestige excelled. He has mastered us not by his will but by his intellect. We

AUTHORITY AND HUMANITY

pass to recognise the social authority, the authority of the State. Schoolmasters deliver us to laws. We own the authority of other wills, of the collective will. If we have no religion this becomes our final authority—and our supreme interest. We worship the Emperor. That is, our public is idolised. Without real religion we succumb, even Socialism succumbs, to political Absolutism. If, on the other hand, we have a wrong religion, we put the Church in the place of the State as this final authority, and we have ecclesiastical Absolutism, with the Pope for perpetual dictator. But with a true religion the final authority is not a collective will but still a universal; it is a Will personal and absolute, to which our first relation is personal and final faith, in direct response to his native action on us; and it is not dependent on a prior and rational conviction that His authority can be proved. True authority, final authority, is personal. As it acts on wills, it must be a will. It must have moral quality. It must be good. It must be the one good thing in the world—a good will. At last it must be the will absolutely good—the Holy. We yield to the holy man; and to the absolutely Holy One (if such there were) we should yield nothing less than our whole selves—not our preceptual or statutory obedience, not our assent, not our admiration, nor our reverence, but our whole selves without reserve and without end. Our attitude is neither assent, admiration, nor reverence, but worship. In this region we recognise neither the volume of will nor the range of perception, but the will's quality, not its edicts but its norms. We are not simply convinced but mastered, not only mastered but won. We know it is good for us to be there. To be there always is our endless good and eternal life. And we yield not only with joy but with all the power of our soul as found and perfected. In such a Will is our peace. At last we are ourselves. We live and love with all our heart and soul and strength and mind. The authority which is the foundation of all superiority is not an intellectual, imperial, or ecclesiastical power (far less is it a physical); but it is a moral power, a spiritual person; in such a way that the completion of our moral self is in yielding to it. We love beneath us when we serve anything less than a person. We choose this Master and His choice of us. We do not simply recognise, we choose. We feel that our Master does not rule as the continuity of our best self but by our act of preference, by our miracle of freedom. We choose Him by a moral reciprocity as One who first chose us for His own holiness. We answer His choice in kind. We are free chiefly that we may freely choose our authority as a free grace choosing us. Our response is as miraculous in its way as that grace. Our obedience becomes a communion, and our subordination is not inferiority, as the obedient Son is not inferior to the Father.

It is a deep remark of Höffding that if there be an absolute authority he can only express himself in miracle. If He is absolute He can be founded on nothing outside Himself. He is His own norm. He can be proved by nothing. There is nothing more great, true, or sure by which He can be mediated to us, or tried by us. He must reveal Himself less by an appeal to rational order than by what seems an invasion of it. His supreme revelation must be the supreme miracle. Revelation does mean miracle. And Rationalism in rejecting the miraculous is confessing its lack of religion. The absolute is in history (if it is there at all, and wherever it is) only by a miracle. This is what we worship as the miracle (and not simply the marvel) of the person of Jesus Christ. To renounce miracle is to renounce an absolute revelation in history, and therefore a sure

AUTHORITY AND HUMANITY 351

eternity. And that is at last to renounce religion itself; which has no final place or positive meaning if we have no access and no relation to an authority absolute, and final, and historic.

Men are mostly agreed as to the educational necessity of authority, but they are not agreed as to its place or necessity in our final stage. They are not agreed that man's perfection is for ever absolute obedience to an absolute Lord. Is there really an absolute authority for the moral adult, or for the adult stage of the race; or is the free man the superman, monarch of all he sees or knows? Is the freedom of our ripeness perpetually conditioned, as was the freedom of our adolescence, only how by holy love and not by stated law? Is it secured by an authority whose right to reign is the ground of the free soul's right to be, to obey, and to worship? Here there is a great gulf fixed between the modern world and antiquity. And not only so, but between it and the Middle Ages. The attitude of antiquity to the gods was resignation; and the gods themselves were powerless against the Fate or Fates that loomed behind them. It was the same with the mediæval Christianity, except that the resignation had changed, through the nature of Christianity, from a passive to a comparatively active. That is to say, the obedience was accompanied with a willing joy or a warm peace. But for the modern world of civilization and culture the idea has changed, with the discovery of the individual and the tremendous assertion of his individuality and its freedom. The ideal is no more submission, or even obedience; it is self-realization. The ethic is not heteronomous: it is autonomous. The whole note of extra-Christian ethic is the moral autonomy of Humanity. It does not contemplate in an adult Humanity the recognition of any final and absolute authority. The ripe man (if he can be said ever to become ripe) is his own authority. He knows, but not as he is known. The superman has no moral limitations. And where the limitations are admitted they are only such as are needed for the equal autonomy of every other unit. It is, of course, hard to base Society on any such view, and the problem of atomism and anarchy yawns before this modernity, till the superman arrests the career by a relapse to the despotism of force. Without force no authority, then. Death to the weak, and licence to the strong. And the principle even finds its way, disguised as an angel of light, into Christianity, where certain forms pursue into religious anarchy an unlimited freedom of belief and atomism of faith, while yet sheltering in a community created by a real and absolute authority alone. In the case of Nietzsche this autonomy means the rule of the moral monster, and at last the dominion over him of the most elemental instincts. And in the Christian parallel it means the dominance of the average man—the superman of multitude—and the prevalence of those feeble sentiments, fickle ardours, and mediocre interests of religion which raise the impatience of strong men everywhere.

It is a fatal fallacy of all such autonomy that it must regard virtue not as the principle of action but only as its result. Virtue is no check on the strong man; he has but the code which is found to serve his rise to the top and his remaining there. And it is the standing curse of all such heroes of force that they must perpetuate a revolutionary state of things. By the relapse on elemental force they become the great reactionaries. And they not only provoke a reaction equal and opposite but a reaction in the same kind, opposing force to force. And thus it must come to be wherever authority is sought in the right of the

AUTHORITY AND HUMANITY 353

stronger instead of in the right of righteousness, the majesty of moral personality, and the supremacy of the Holy — the King of Saints. The ground, the right of authority is at last not the demonic force of will, nor the mere mass of a majority, but a certain quality of will, which appeals to a free and thinking will as its superior in kind: in whom our will yet finds its good self, its freedom, power and peace; and without whom progress has no goal, rest, or Sabbath, but goes on and on—over Niagara.

Few challenge the relative need of authority in the social region. But when we come to the region of belief, and, indeed, whenever we go inward upon the spiritual personality, many aspire to leave the sphere of authority behind. We escape, they would say. And the very use of that word betrays their conception of authority. It is not a power for them but a force. It is a burden to be shaken off. It is coercive. It is not the source of liberty, but its load. It is something which sooner or later must produce impatience and not bring peace. It is something to be renounced as men pass to spiritual maturity. The more spiritual they consider themselves, the less they like to feel, think, or speak of authority. And where such spirits appear in the society which is peculiarly spiritual, in the Church, they are apt to think that the rejection of authority is the badge of adult faith and the measure of moral culture. So much so that in cases the Church is entirely detached from a controlling Gospel, and it is retained simply as the sphere of liberty to believe anything which feels a divine impulse, wears a religious complexion, or goes with a " Christian spirit."

Whereas the lessons of religious history go to show that spiritual freedom is deepened only in proportion as authority is exalted. We are to prove the " superior " spirits, spiritualities, and mysticisms by a given Gospel. (1 John iv., *cp.* 1 and 10.) We can profitably escape one form of authority only by being more deeply pledged to another. A real authority is the first condition for that which is the Christian end of society and its true freedom—the development of moral personality. And the first duty of a religious teacher is not to encourage the *instinct* of freedom, but to press the necessity of an authority as the only source of a *gifted* freedom, to bid his flock take care of this authority and the freedom will take care of itself, to ask them if they have found such an authority, and to urge them to go on to inquire with much self-examination whether their dearest freedom is the fruit of their nearest obedience.

Let us try to clear up some loose or casual notions on this subject; remembering chiefly that any society is doomed at last in which there is spent more talk and passion about liberty than about authority. No liberty is worth the sacred name which grows under the shadow of a hatred and contempt for authority. It is but a mask for self-will. And freedom can only be truly dear where authority is dearer still, and an obedience the first and noblest concern.

What we usually mean by authority is this. It is another's certainty taken as the *sufficient and final* reason for some certainty of ours, in thought or action. And that is what we are apt to ban hastily as external authority. But surely (as I have said) authority has no meaning at all unless it is external. No moral individual can be an authority to himself. Nor, collectively, can Humanity be its own authority without self-idolatry. If we are to retain either the word or the thing authority, it must be as something which

AUTHORITY AND HUMANITY 355

does not depend but descend upon us, either to lead or to lift.

The sphere of authority is not in religion alone (though its final source is there). In all the affairs of life it has its action. Most people live under what they hold to be the authority of *all*. They do, or seek to do, what everybody else does. They are most secure in those things which are the universal fashion, in the primal unities, customs or instincts of society, in immemorial convention. In the religious sphere we are familiar with the principle as " *Quod semper, quod ubique, quod ab omnibus,*" or " *Securus judicat orbis terrarum,*" or the " *fides implicita.*"

Some again are satisfied with the authority of *most*. They live as the politicians do—by majorities. They court and follow the multitude. Their ideal is the popular. Their standard is the general. What they dread most is " the heritage of a speckled bird," to make themselves singular or unpleasant to their side or party. They habitually obey its demands (and they have the *flair* for them), but they make none. They ride, like the strident sea-fowl, on the crest of the wave. They are never laden prophets to rebuke their own, they are only racy tribunes to champion them.

Others again follow the authority of the *few*. It may be a minority of experts, as in the case of science. Very many people accept without further question what their favourite paper tells them is the opinion of the scientific leaders, even about things where a mere scientific training does more to disqualify than to equip. And here we are growing " warm," as the children say. We seek more worthy shelter under another form of minority—that, for instance, of the Church as God's elect and militant minority on earth, or that of the Apostles, Fathers, and Bishops, as men specially commissioned and fitted forth for a special truth or task. As we have those whose authoritative minority is an *élite* of culture, so we have those for whom it is an elect of grace.

Narrowing the issue and growing "warmer" still, most Christian people would take Christ's certainty as a perfectly sufficient ground for any certainty of theirs. His word and teaching is for them the supreme authority in the world. And these pages are written in the belief that Christ is indeed the supreme authority: but it is Christ in His Gospel more even than in His precept; Christ as present, powerful, and absolute Redeemer rather than as past and precious teacher; Christ as breaking our moral ban by His new creation of Eternal Life, giving us to our forfeit selves by restoring us from perdition to God's communion, and leaving us with no rights but those so given, to rebuild faith, creed, and action from a new unitary centre and a monopolist throne. It is Christ as King in His Cross.

Wherever we have authoritative belief it stands or falls with the belief of the other, of the authority—whether that authority is single or collective, a man, a school, or a church.

Now, to begin at the bottom, let it be owned that such authority goes a long way. For a strong and quiet life we all owe much to the organised instincts, sympathies and conventions of Society which are elemental and universal. *Nomos*, as Plato says in the "Gorgias," is a great god and king. And it is not good for any man that he should not be with the majority in many things which make the broad base of social security. The man who is always against the government may be neglected—unless he take to *sabotage*, when he should be secluded—into eternity if need be. There are also countless matters daily where we must trust the expert, and even put our lives in his hand. There are more matters than most people own where we can have no opinion, and

AUTHORITY AND HUMANITY

are entitled to none. We can measure our wisdom by the number of things where we consent to have no views. For more people need an external authority than are willing to own it. And the whole period of adolescence is ideally covered and reared by some form of authority. Parents deliver us to schoolmasters, and these to laws and to conscience. The area grows very small where our certainty is absolutely our own. The range of the individual conscience even is limited as questions grow great. The great matters are those that most concern the whole; and the individual is not the whole; and he is at a disadvantage compared with the whole. It is only in connection with the most intimate and personal affairs that we have much *locus standi* as individuals, and are free of human authority. It is only at the inmost shrine that the soul itself stands or falls with an absolute personal certainty. There we cannot depend finally on other men, nor on a whole Church of them. On the last issue of faith our certainty must be relatively independent. Our only authority here must be God Himself, or Godhead, Father, Son or Spirit—God who is at once the most external yet the most intimate and the most absolute of authorities. Here the source of our certainty must be the object of it. To put it somewhat technically—the content of our faith must be constitutive for it. That is to say, the object of our faith does not simply regulate its form but create its existence. For faith is not a condition of salvation, but part of it; it is salvation; and salvation is God's gift. God, as the object of our faith, does not simply prescribe its form by a commissioned Church from which there is no appeal, but He creates the faith, the salvation itself, directly, by the very nature of His self-revelation, for which a Church is sacramental to us. And the creator of faith must be for it an absolute authority. Faith is our response with our whole selves to God's absolute gift of Himself; it is not our assent to His edict or information. It is our answer to His grace and not to His Church or its creed as such. We believe *in* His grace, but only *through* His Church. Our authority, the object of our faith, is Himself in His grace—yet not His grace in founding a Church for us, but His grace in redeeming us into a Church. No Church can found our faith, or accept our faith; but only the Revelation can which founded the Church. My faith and the whole Church go back equally for this direct foundation to the same grace which, by the Spirit, is as present to-day as in the first century. We each are what we are by virtue of the same direct yet mediated salvation—a salvation in the one aspect corporate, in the other personal. Our faith is a faith in the historic and saving facts, and not in their transmitters or guarantors. We believe (according to the familiar phrase) in the Church because of Christ and not in Christ because of the Church. The Church is the historic medium, but the Spirit is the historic mediator, whose organ the Church is. The very meaning of the Holy Spirit in history is a mediated immediacy of our relation to historic fact. The Church, after all, is but the creation, it is not the continuation of Christ, and we live on Christ, and not on His creature. That were idolatry. And its nemesis appears in the Roman obedience. The apotheosis of the Church by Rome has come to this, that that Church has now practically but one article of belief. Its Gospel to the world is all in this, " Believe in me." It arrests on itself the faith that should pass to Christ. It is sensitive really on one point only —its own authority. It will be patient with many heretical views or movements which do not attack that, which are willing at due call to submit to that. And then, when we inquire as to its right, the only ground on which that authority rests is the Church

AUTHORITY AND HUMANITY 359

itself The Church is the warrant for its own authority. It is the authoritative Church that guarantees the Church's authority.[1] Which is true of Christ and His Gospel alone.

For Christianity is an absolutely personal faith. That is to say, we are judged and saved eternally not by our relation to the Church but by our relation to Christ the Redeemer. In the last resort this Christ is the authority to our soul as directly as He is to the Church. The spiritual immediacy of the relation is as real as its historic mediation, and its reality is higher. The function of the Church is to introduce Christ and the soul, that He may do for that soul His work for every soul; it takes no responsibility for the soul, which is the prerogative of Christ alone. The soul's saviour is the soul's King—being absolute Saviour, absolute owner. Faith in Him is not a means of certainty, but it *is* the certainty dominating and organising all. The soul's certainty at its centre, the guarantee of all other certainty, is the certainty of salvation, into the new Humanity, given directly by the Saviour Himself in His Spirit, Who, in redeeming us from the instability of absolute perdition, made His redeeming Gospel the absolute moral certainty of a race which is either moral or meaningless. That principle is the very meaning and marrow of the Reformation. And one

[1] Leibnitz, at the end of the seventeenth century, asked if the Catholic dogma of tradition rested on the notion of a complete revelation of truth, exceeding what was in Scripture and was conveyed to the apostolic age, or upon the hypothesis of a continuous inspiration of the Church in regard to such Scripture truth. In the latter case he said it would be very hard to define the features required in such an infallible organ of tradition; in the former case all the traditions of the Church could not be traced to an apostolic authority. Tradition is either an exposition of apostolic doctrine or an addition to it. If an exposition, how is it to be shown that the Reformation branch *of the Church* was wrong; if an addition, what becomes of the claim for the apostolicity of all Catholic doctrine. Since the time of Leibnitz papal infallibility has been defined indeed; but in the forty years since 1870 it has never been exercised. It is an invention that is specified and patented, but does not work.

of its applications is that all Christian truth (which is finally all truth) grows, however indirectly, from personal certainty of Christian salvation. The theological authority is Christ as our active and experienced Saviour—not the impressive inner life of Christ, not the superlative character of Christ, but Christ crucified, the regenerating salvation of Christ *experienced*, experienced on the scale of the salvation of a Church and a race.

XVIII

AUTHORITY IN CHURCH AND BIBLE

WHEN we have passed inward, with the Evangelical Reformation and its central, searching, saving treatment of the sinful soul, inward from obedience of the external Roman type, where do we find ourselves? Are we then but denizens of the spiritual wild, vagrants in a mystic uncharted land, ramblers at will on some high plane and shining tableland, the sport of winds on the heath that blow as they list, whose freaks but match the irresponsibility we feel within? Did we go out from venerable Rome but on a vacation, to turn boys again for a while, to forget the moral manhood we had reached, and escape in individual solitude into the pranks of spiritual youth? Did we abandon the hoary experience of the old Church just to kick up our heels in moral juvenility, and fantastic opinion, and casual creed? Was the release worth all it cost and all it lost if we did not pass into a region of obedience more intimate, searching, and absolute than before, the obedience of the soul's total self to its new Creator, instead of its mere assent or submission to the old vicar? The Kingdom of God, in this new avatar of the Gospel, means a righteousness (*i.e.* an obedience) exceeding that of scribe and pharisee, who dream of an æsthetic or institutional salvation—exceeding them, not as being more punctilious, but as more intimate, universal, and absolute. It follows us where no Church can come, and dominates us as no Pope can, and peers where no Inquisition can search, dividing joint and marrow, and piercing the very subliminal thoughts and intents of the heart.

Escaping from Rome we do not escape from external authority but from one such to another, and to one whose externality and claim make themselves real at depths where no mere Church can rule, subtler than all the psychology of sin, and surer than its perdition; with a penetration whose search is sharper than fire, and its grasp closer than law. The liberty of the Non-Roman Churches can only be permanent under conditions which as yet but partially exist—only if it endure in an obedience more deep, real, and hearty than that of Rome, and serve an authority more absolute in its daily, practical, unashamed recognition. All questions of State and of public liberty fade for a Christian before the question of the Church and the experience of its obedience of faith. And all devotion to such public questions and liberties, inseparable as it is from corporate Christian faith and life, may yet do great mischief if it indispose us to the severe self-scrutiny, self-humiliation, and self-submission which the Gospel entails on the Church, or if it blind us to the serious condition of the Churches—the more apparent the more inward we go. The most urgent questions for the Free Churches, for instance, concern not the condition of the State, nor of Society, but of the soul, and of the Church. What is lacking is religion, Christian religion more than Christian work. The lack of certainty is not due to lack of intelligence nor of energy, but to lack of religion, to decay of experience, and poverty of soul. And it is much easier to be optimist about the actual State than the actual Church, about the voter than the believer. But it is the condition of the believer that counts at last for the voter's fate. I do not doubt, for my own

AUTHORITY IN CHURCH AND BIBLE 363

part, that the dullness to spiritual issues in an unideal people like ourselves, and therefore the spiritual lassitude and dubiety of the Churches, is in part connected with our absorption in political and social issues—not our interest, not our devotion, to these momentous issues, but our absorption in them. I speak of the de-churching of Churches, their reduction to religious groups, their loss of the sense of the great Church, the great guilt, the great Gospel, and the solemnising creed. And I carefully do not say that this is *due* to our keen and overwhelming passion to end public wrongs and realise social ideals. But I do say there is a connection, that that preoccupation helps to distract and blind many to the secularising influences,[1] that it is withdrawing attention (which should be a first charge upon us) to the case and the kind of our religion, withdrawing it from the more practical and intimate questions of experience, certainty, obedience, and authority, and putting our duty to the community, practically though not theoretically, in front of our duty to the Gospel.

Do our Churches really, practically, *i.e.*, consciously and experimentally, rest on an obedience, a certainty, and a security which they *feel* to be deeper and graver than their sense or claim of freedom? Social ardour is not necessarily the zeal of the Lord's House, nor is fraternity the communion of saints. Brotherhoods are a fruit of the Church, they cannot replace it. The danger in social service is that it may become the victim of a mere hunger for gregarious activity, and of an extreme passion for the actual at the cost of sustained contact with the soul's

---

[1] By us I mean chiefly the laity of the Churches. A minister, by his study, his responsibility for worship, and his contact with spiritual woes and with aches that no reforms can heal, is protected as most laymen are not. Let him not forget that he is set apart by the laity for this service, and that he sanctifies himself for their sakes.

reality. "Every age is really impressed by what is more than the age—by Eternity." Enthusiastic religion is very well, but it is not the same thing as obedient faith. It is far behind it. The passion of great assemblies, hot on burning questions, is not the same as the hearty faith of a Holy Church, though it may not be incompatible with it. The ardour of occasions is not the habit or principle of life. Assemblies constantly and lightly pledge themselves to grave resolutions with which they take no farther concern. This is moral levity. The quantity of religion is often inversely as its quality, especially in crowds; but for wear it is quality that tells. What is the condition of the Churches between the periods of excitement? How do they behave in the trough of the waves? What is their chronic temperature, insight, and action? Have we an experience of obedience deeper, more searching, more subduing, and more fertile than the obedience of Rome? Are we mastered by our better authority as Roman Christians are by theirs? If we are not, might we not leave popular polemic and No-Popery alarums alone till we can outbid Rome in this cardinal matter? There is no hope for liberty at last except in the power of an external and absolute Master, in whom we glory more than in our liberty, and whom we feel more, and confess more. The real bane in all that is mostly known as external authority is that it is not external enough. By which I mean not different enough from us, not heteronomous enough, not absolute enough, not chosen by us as far beyond all other worth, for which we could count all as dross. The powerful Churches may be too worldly to master the world, and the popular Churches may court the people's suffrages too much to subdue them to their Gospel. And I especially mean that the authority of a Church that seeks swift and wide effect by Parliament or Pontiff must

AUTHORITY IN CHURCH AND BIBLE

grow weak. Its power is not equal to its claims. It is a valuable guide, tutor, and governor, but it is not capable of providing the *sufficient* ground for the freedom and the certainty of an *eternal* soul.

The vulgar solution of the problem between freedom and authority is the previous question. There is no problem at all. Authority is simply rejected. Men or groups become their own authority. We go as far to the extreme of freedom as Calvinism, or even Determinism, ever did to the extreme of sovereignty. And of the two the Calvinistic end is far the less dangerous. It is better that a Calvinist God should rule men than that they should be their own authority. He is certainly a greater and holier power than the superman, in whose dictatorship all extreme liberty ends, and all the native divineness of Humanity falls with him. Nothing worse could happen to man than that he should be absolute lord of himself and all besides. Nothing would so surely reduce his dignity to the swagger of the cowboy hero.

What does make a true problem, and sometimes a very grave and fine one, is how to pass from one authority to another *upwards*, both being external, and therefore real. It is not how to pass from a human authority to a divine in the common meaning of the phrase. For the divine authority always reaches us in a human form—uniquely so in the case of Christ. It is how to pass from an authority which is not sufficient and final for the soul's last certainty to one which is. All true progress in life is registered by the kind of liberty which accompanies the ascending scale of our successive authorities. All true education is the refinement of liberty, and at the same time its metamorphosis, by an effective authority. And the great step in life, the great qualitative change (corresponding spiritually to the psychic change which passes the growing youth into the responsible adult), the change in which salvation transcends education, is the discovery of a final and absolute authority; one which is sufficient for the soul as eternal, and which is the experienced base of all certainty on the last things, on the moral issues central and royal to life. To pass from one authority without finding another of more spiritual and intimate quality may be more of a fall than a rise. Indeed, it may not be a rise at all. It may be merely an extension of knowledge. It may be merely a widened horizon. It may be merely an increase of the area and the scale on which self-will can expatiate and its mischief extend. Merely to know good and evil is for man to be more evil than good. The Reformation was an escape from one authority to another. But the Illumination and the Revolution represent a totally different movement, an escape to no master at all. In so far as the Reformation was an escape from mere membership of an institution to personal contact with a spiritual Saviour, it was a rise. But in so far as this faith faded, and was replaced by the Intellectualism of ecclesiastical, orthodox, or rationalist interests, by pure doctrine or pure reason, it was a fall. The faith of the Mediæval Church was a finer and more exalting thing than the politics of the German princes, the orthodoxy of the seventeenth-century theologians, or the rationalism of the eighteenth-century philosophers. That Church was the greatest tutor that Europe ever had. And largely by its penitential tradition, which flowered in the Reformation, and shed its husk. It is only this line of the evangelical faith, in its experienced intimacy and moral greatness, that represents the real rise. Much as we may value the breadth of the rational movements, there is something much more precious than breadth. It is depth and height, moral power, penetration, and intimacy of soul. The great white throne is a more precious vision than horizons of moor or sea, the light of setting suns, the wind on the heath, or the sense of something far more deeply interfused. And if He who sits on that throne deals effectively with human sin, His judgment comes nearer the heart of the human problem than all the criticism which corrects but does not create, or the ethic which but enlarges our duty, or altruises our action, to the scale of the race.

True faith releases us by passing us upward from one authority to another. The faith that caused the rejection of Church authority as direct and final has no real worth except as it is the discovery of an authority both final and direct in God and His redeeming self-revelation carried home by the Spirit. To this authority faith does not simply involve submission; it *is* submission. The obedience of faith is not an obedience that flows from faith; it is faith as obedience. Our plague is to have come to regard obedience as a by-product of Christian faith instead of its genius. So that we have many Christian homes which are hotels of liberty and not schools of obedience or even respect at all. Faith is nothing except as an obedience. The authority we own in faith is greater than that of conscience. It is one that saves us from conscience. For it forgives, and conscience can but accuse. It new creates where conscience can but approve, and mostly condemns. In any faith which is more than theistic we commune with an authority which is not simply God, but God as He has bestowed Himself on man, God as actual to historic Humanity and its evil case, God in history, God holy in guilty history, God as He gives Himself for man's sin in the historic Gospel, God our eternal Redeemer in Christ. That Gospel and grace has an authority not only historic but absolute in the experience of Christian men. It is a new creation in which *we* do not live, but Christ lives in us ; and we are the property, as absolute as persons can be, of the Person who took us from perdition to eternal life.

He is therefore our authority for everything in proportion to its place in the perspective of that new created world. We *must* believe everything in the degree in which it is essential to the Gospel of our new life and absolute Lord. And if sin and guilt be denied, sin in any sense that calls for a new creation, it is difficult to get farther with the denier. For we are up against an ultimate, the soul's sense of itself and its case, the verdict of conscience upon its own moral condition. And if any conscience, recognising the centrality of moral issues, can place itself before the absolutely holy Power, with whom it has finally to do, and yet feel no sense of hopeless guilt, there is no more that men or books can do. It is temperamental defect or moral hardening, and it must be left to another influence, another experience, and another light.

There is, it will be seen, no final authority for thought, or science, or statement of any kind simply as such. That is at most theosophy, while the sphere of authority is religion, theology, in the sense of life, *i.e.* of positive experience. There we do have finality; we have the God of grace, the Redeemer, certain to us as no human agency can certify. And the influence of this authority on thought or creed, though powerful, and even creative, is but indirect, as the action of life on knowledge is wont to be.

In so far as the Church is expressive of that Gospel, and created by it, it shares in its authority. But only as the Gospel's new creation and moral organ—not in the sense of a miraculous, hierarchical, statutory, prescriptive, institution, whether curial, conciliar, or consistorial, which has come to be a thaumaturgic

AUTHORITY IN CHURCH AND BIBLE

shrine for the Gospel; only in the evangelical sense in which it is created (one might almost say secreted) by the Gospel, as the experient trustee of the saving word, as its offspring and organ. It has immense prestige, and, for the catechumen stage of young or old, real authority. The riper we are the more reverent we must be to the Church—but only as the ambassador of the imperial Gospel. So it is also with the authority of the ministry. It is that of an office and not an order. And it is drawn entirely from the Gospel for whose sake the office is there.

But great is the moral and mental authority of the Church of the Gospel, tempered and matured by an age-long experience of human life in contact with the last, the Eternal, Reality. Let us never in the name of a personal Christianity so reject the authority of the Church as to do despite to the great communion and conviction of saints. Christianity can only exist in the world as a Church and not as a mere spiritual movement in the midst of society. If the final authority is God in Gospel, the Church shares in that authority as the expert of the Gospel and the soul. Let us not, under the influence of any *Zeitgeist*, begin our spiritual career as rebels to our spiritual stock, or seethe our wild liberty in the blood of our spiritual mother. That can only mean a curse, a pinched individualism, a prickly independence, a starved freedom, an ignoble self-will. How are we to escape the little ban of our single selves if we own no authority at all in the voluminous and corporate experience of the Church? How can we preach to any purpose with nothing but our own experience to declare? What right have we to obtrude our small experience on the world of our own fellows, and even expect their silent attention? At our best we but *share* the far vaster experience of those who have made us what we are. We are *members* of a great spiritual corporation. We but focus, reflect, and prolong, even in our most vivid experience, the vaster faith of the great Church. We do not possess a rival experience to whose bar we can drag the faithful certainty of the Church as a whole. Luther did not do that. He disentombed the New Testament, and brought to light the supremacy and autonomy of a kind of faith which, however buried, was always the Church's inmost life. He had no idea but that he was rescuing and prolonging the true Church in the evangelical experience, that in him and his movement the Church was recovering itself. He was not setting up a new Church. To own a Church authority duly, to own it as real though not absolute—rather derived from the absolute, just as Eve was taken from Adam in a mystery of the Church and the Cross—to own this authority is to enlarge oneself; it is not to stunt and enslave. The Church of faith is one of those limits to our individuality which neutralize our limitations and exalt our obedience into loyalty. The Gospel Revelation contemplated a Church; therefore only a Church could grasp the whole compass of the Revelation. The great truth was delivered and promised to a Church, and not to any individual or group. It could never be grasped by the individual, who must, therefore, allow great authority to the competent in correcting facts and to the Catholic tradition which runs through the Churches and braces them in eternal unity. We have no right to repudiate elements in that tradition merely because they are as yet beyond us, so long as they do not contradict the evangelical principle of the Revelation itself. And there are some such elements that we must recover.

And this relative authority of the Church is shared by the theologians of the Church as distinct from the schools. It does not belong to the academic or scientific theologians of a philosophic religion, but

AUTHORITY IN CHURCH AND BIBLE 371

to the exponents and interpreters of the Church's capital of positive faith, who do not claim to make learned research the foundation of a certainty which faith alone can give, nor substitute an erudite priesthood for an ecclesiastical. It is impossible when we are dealing with the last reality to separate knowledge into theoretical and practical. All theory roots and rises in practice; and the practical reason needs positive knowledge if it is not to found on the sand of mere wishes or postulates.

I have said that the final authority must be external in its nature. In its nature, be it observed. For we have much need here of Bergson's caution and protest against the intrusion into such a region of spatial notions of externality. A large part of the reaction against authority is due to its externality being treated in this abstract and almost literal way, instead of being realised as within the nature of spirit or will itself. Externality here means otherness, and not outwardness or foreignness. This polar spiritual authority is not something which lies upon us with a pressure, but it interpenetrates us and completes us like a paradox; which is really the wealth of the soul, and not its oddity, and which is heterogeneous in its form, but not in its content. The soul resents pressure, but it welcomes paradox as essential to its own kind of action; which is the reconcilement in one personality of what were otherwise fatal contraries or antinomies. Authority and Freedom, however antipathetic for abstract reason, are conjoint and inseparable both in the nature of a Godhead which is Father and Son, and in the nature of a spiritual soul, which cannot have a history except by the reciprocal action and progressive union of both freedom and authority.

That is to say, returning to what has also been advanced above, the final authority is not only external, or other, in its action, but personal. It is a relation of person to person in holy love. The great certainty is a matter of direct personal contact and assurance, *i.e.* of religion (so that uncertainty is due to poverty of religion). That is, it is an assurance not simply mine as a person, but of my personality as face to face with Another, and finally a communion with Him. It cannot be the relation of a person to an institution like the Church, nor to a group like an Apostolate, nor to a book like the Bible. The institution or book is valuable, but it is as a medium. It is not indeed mediatorial but it is intermediate. And it is only saved from being intercalary by being sacramental, by acting on us in no atmosphere of trance or magic, but in a way which draws upon our whole moral personality. It knows nothing of a sacramental action or order which is magically independent of personal character and conscious experience. Power of a kind may reside in the subliminal, but not moral authority. It is what Wundt would call instinctive motive and not imperative. It acts by pressure and not by influence. But in religion, in faith, in the soul's last stand and supreme action, we are in direct contact with the last, the absolute, the holy reality, with a person subliminal even to the subliminal, but One who saves us not merely into His own Being but into His own holiness. Our Saviour is our authority. The soul takes both its order and its peace in the last eternal resort from a living person whose direct action is the source of its new life. Our mediatorial Christ leaves no room for a mediatorial Church. He is so much the direct presence of God that no Church could take the part Rome assumes without sharing Christ's relation to God; without prolonging (rather than answering) the Incarnation, in a way to obscure

AUTHORITY IN CHURCH AND BIBLE 373

Christ rather than reveal Him, and to impugn His new creation rather than to give it effect as a new *creature* should.

But here arises a difficulty for us Protestants. If the last authority has its seat in experience, what is the place for the authority of the Bible? Do we not put the Bible in the same obstructive place as was held by the Church? If the Gospel is the supreme authority, and its nature is fixed normally (though not formally) in the Bible, is not Christian experience superseded by the canonizing, the absolutizing, of this very early (not to say crude) stage of it? Is a real recognition of the finality of the Bible revelation compatible with a certainty based on our experience and realised there?

Here we are in some danger of being misled by an ambiguity in the use of a word like experience. Sometimes it means the mere subjective consciousness, sometimes that consciousness cross-examined, sifted, and organised. Sometimes it means the action on us of an objective fact which emerges *in* experience but is not *of* it. We discussed this more fully elsewhere. But, if we take it in the subjective sense (whether instinctive or organised), can it really be that we are to bring the Gospel in the Bible to this natural or inherited experience of ours as its bar? Do they compete for our obedience? Are we to believe only what commends itself to our individual experience, or even to the experience of the Church so far as it has gone? Is the authority the Christian consciousness up to date? Is that what gives us our Saviour, or does our Saviour give us that? Is the witness of Christ in what we become, or in what He reveals to us? Is our actual condition His great revelation, or is that revelation a great historic and creative fact, to which our present condition is due, and which it but imperfectly reflects? Is our faith up to to-day's date—is that God's great witness of Himself, or is it but the response to His great witness in nature, history, Christ, and all that stands over us as given reality? Can the revelation of an absolute God be authoritative in a relative stage of its history, except in so far as it is so in the continuous creative source of that history?

For instance, if the Bible teaches that the nature of Christ's revelation involves the necessity of a propitiation or a satisfaction to God's holiness, are we to reject that, if the experience of most Christians should be flattened to demanding no such thing? Should we reject it if even the great body of the Church's opinion at a given date were as much against it as at a time it was against Athanasianism? A reverent and rational son of the past will not begin by proposing to do in his own soul all that has been done by the Church, to start *ab ovo* and run through the spiritual history of 2000 years on his own account, as if the Church had never been, as if he were at the very beginning and not the end of a long spiritual age, and must be as original as Adam. He will not begin by discarding a real atonement just because it may be offensive to the sympathies of the modern mind. But he will accept its principle, and seek to co-ordinate it with the ethical ideas that mark our moral progress and to adjust its form to these. As Anselm co-ordinated his Gospel to the ideas of his age about monarchical honour, or Grotius to those of his time about the moral order, so we adjust our theology to the more spiritual ethic of holiness which the Gospel has brought to pass, and to the new reading of the New Testament. We construe it in terms of holiness, confessing in the act the growing effect on the Church of the Holy Ghost, with His Word for every age, and His deepening of them all.

Again, we are sometimes urged, in default of authority, to *try* Bible Christianity and the results will verify it; the effect, it is said, will make us sure of what is presented for our belief in the cause. But the problem is still there: How can an individual experience prove a universal cause? The Bible claims to be truer than we, or the race, or the Church, have yet experienced. And we believe the Bible for other reasons than the mere subjective reason that it meets our " felt need." The Bible claims to have in it the salvation of the whole world—which the whole world has not yet experienced, nor as a whole feels to need. And the mere fact that its Gospel satisfies me does not warrant me in believing offhand that it has the power to satisfy and crown Humanity. Besides, the greatest need that the Gospel meets is not felt till it is revealed in us by our certainty of the Gospel coming as a fact with a right and claim.

What a helpless confusion is revealed by such an appeal as I have named! Try Christianity! How can I try it without believing it? Can the effect of a provisional hypothesis, however useful for Science, ever be for the soul that of a real cause? Can a postulate create penitence? The Gospel only has its effect if we are sure of it. How can any man verify the Gospel in experience till he is thus perfectly sure of it? And by then verification is not needed for certainty. Only a certainty can save; and you cannot try to be sure. *The* results of the Gospel are those of an absolute faith in it. You propose to experiment for a certainty which is absolutely necessary for the experiment. The verification in experience cannot be the ground of our certainty since it can only be the sequel of it. Experience is the fruit of faith, or its medium, more than its ground.

Again, and chiefly, a faith which only allows what it has itself verified in sufficient detail is no faith, but sight. An authority which only goes on to a point where we pull it up is no authority. Doubtless there are corrections which the modern Church, as the society of an evolutionary faith, is able and bound to make on the traditional *statement* of it. There is even a parallax to be discounted as due to the refraction on the far horizon of the first century. There are adjustments to be made as to the range or periphery of the conscious theology of the New Testament. And it is one of the delicate tasks of a skilled and equipped theology to make these. But it must be the theology of faith; it must be the Church's faith acting as theologian; it must not be philosophy, nor science, nor the mere amateur religious consciousness turned upon a theological topic. The Gospel can be handled by no experience but that which it really creates—and creates as mysteriously as is the way of all creation, so mysteriously that no experience of it, and no psychology, has yet been able to analyse to the bottom the process or reason of our decisive faith. We can no more explain our second birth than our first.

In the Bible we are in a region where the matter expands from faith to inspiration; and it takes vast dimensions which we might expect would, in magnifying the process, clarify it. But instead of that it grows more subtle and miraculous. There is some new factor there, carrying faith as much above itself as itself goes beyond ordinary experience. For, as we saw in an early lecture, we cannot regard New Testament theology as mainly made up of ideas which grew upon the apostles out of their personal faith, their private and tentative interpretation of their religiosity; so that they became, as "eminent Christians," the mere classics of such faith. The Bible reflects more than the first fresh stage of Christian experience. Rather, the apostles were

AUTHORITY IN CHURCH AND BIBLE

heralds of God's revelation, elect and providential personalities, who had from God a special vocation and equipment to receive and display the central genius of the Gospel by a new departure germinal for all Christian time.

In regard to the Bible and its authority, therefore, the great question is this: "Have we here men's thoughts or God's Word?" It does not matter for this issue whether the formal ideas are those of a Paul or those of some religious movement or society of the time, Jew or Gentile, taking effect in Paul. Have we at their heart the suggested and tentative speculations of men, or a final revelation of God? Have we the ideas of men who were trying to set down the contours or the conclusions of their personal religion, or were these men in some peculiar way living channels of God's gift and heralds of God's Word? Were they only examples of the way faith ripens into insight and insight takes form in thought, or had they a positive vocation and unique gift from God thereby to open in principle the wealth of His thought and His revelation once for all time? Were they there to encourage us also to trust and formulate our religious experience boldly, even if it should dethrone the creed we have from them; or were they there to lay down once for all the true meaning of the Christian fact and the sole principle of positive belief, which a true Christian experience could only ripen and explicate but never outgrow?

The latter alternative in each of these pairs is here viewed as the truth. There is an autonomy and finality in the Bible for faith. Experience in this region does not mean a prior standard in us by which we accept or reject the Gospel's claims. It does not mean that the Gospel submits to be tried by the code we have put together from our previous experience of natural things, even in the religious sphere. The Gospel is not something which is there for our assent in the degree in which we can verify it by our previous experience either in the way of need or of rationality. Our very response to it is created in us before it is confessed by us. It creates assent rather than accepts it. The experience in which our final authority emerges and is recognised, as the servants know their true lord, is the soul's leap to its touch. It is not a conclusion but a venture of faith. The Christian experience is not something we bring rationally to the Bible to test scriptural truth; it is something miraculously created in us by the Bible to respond to divine power acting as grace; and it can therefore be in no collision with the authority which makes the Bible what it is, the authority of the Gospel, of the Redeemer felt and owned as Redeemer. It is not our independent verification but our appropriation and completion of God's gift and revelation of Himself by faith of the most intimate, and therefore mysterious, kind. It is the assimilation of this by our hungry personality—without the hunger being the test of the value of the food, which might satisfy the mere hunger equally well if it contained an infusion of slow and tasteless poison. To such experience the authority in the Bible is no more antagonistic than the action of a free and gracious Creator in any shape need be to the free and growing creature. Christian experience is the experience of the authority of the Gospel; it is not an experience which becomes the authority for the Gospel; whose authority can be most mighty when every reason drawn from human experience is against it.

Allusion has been made elsewhere to this confusion of *appropriation* and *verification* in our treatment of the Christian claim. The two things are very distinct. In the one case we begin by *owning* an autho-

AUTHORITY IN CHURCH AND BIBLE 379

rity *in which* we " place " ourselves; in the other we either begin by *scrutinising* an authority *in front of which* we place ourselves till it convince us (or fail); or we accept it as provisional till it is found to work (or not). In the one case we make personal surrender of ourselves to a real creative object, in the other we accept a hypothesis till it approve itself as more, till we find it works.

The ideal Christian development is by way of appropriation. Youth is meant to appropriate the authority of others, and so we gain power at a later stage to judge and make it our own. And as adults we appropriate Christ, we do not simply appreciate Him; and we grow and expand in all judgment as we do so. His true saints shall judge the world. We recognise, moreover, even as mature, a great, common, and catholic fund of faith, from which the individual draws, at which he feeds and strengthens his own soul's life, by which he measures and orders his own faith, till the very strength and lucidity of that faith so reared may even compel a revision of its traditional forms. Our true attitude to the Church and its belief is appropriation of it in a growing personal and evangelical certitude. The faith we are born into must become personal, and that is only done by its appropriation in a moral act or process. We do not take it on the strength of external authority; *i.e.* the belief of others is no sufficient ground for ours at last, though it is an essential school. Nor are we content to treat the Gospel æsthetically, impressionally, appreciatively or judiciously. But we live on it. It is the spiritual and moral world in which we thrive and freely move. And our vision grows more clear and true by such trust; so that we are able to adjust some of the forms in which it reached us to fit the faith to which we, and especially the Church, have grown.

We cannot treat it as mere hypothesis, for it did not simply help, or fill a hole; it created our personal Christianity; and it did so by being, in those before us, not a hypothesis but the supreme life, certainty, and reality.

But verification works otherwise. It is vigilant and critical, or at least judicious, about what it inherits. It treats it but as a hypothesis or a postulate. It is always bringing it to book as new tests arise, and always accepting it only in so far as it meets them. They are tests of nature and not of faith, tests of feeling rather than insight, tests of empirical experience instead of soul experience, of success rather than of devotion. We withhold full committal till we have tested things in life. We make no inspired venture of faith, but we put Christ on His mettle to see if He is effective in thought or practice. We turn pragmatists and trust Christ because He works; which may come suspiciously near to trusting Him because it spiritually pays and enhances our spiritual egoism. We may grow in certainty or we may not, but we do not work from a certainty, but from a temper of wakeful probation. We keep the certainty as a luxury, or as idle capital. We do not appropriate an initial life vaster than our own, and surer to us than our experience, living on it as the soul's true capital and source of certainty. We work *to* Christ rather than *from* Him, to the Church rather than from it. And we pursue the instinctive curiosity of nature (which gives us tentative science—critical or other) instead of the inspired insight of faith (which gives us normative theology).

And it is the misfortune of much of our religious education that we are encouraged to begin with the verification instead of with the appropriation. Youth is encouraged, by way of exercising its powers, to be more tentative and critical than sure and docile.

AUTHORITY IN CHURCH AND BIBLE 381

There is no " venture of faith " to exercise the soul. We are urged to treat religion in a scientific way instead of in a religious way. Verification is the scientific term and process, appropriation is the religious. And the poor and sad results that so often accrue from addressing the subject in the hesitant way are due to the perpetual sterility of scientific tests for soul realities, to the substitution of experiment for experience, and of theology for religion. It is the error common to Orthodoxy and Rationalism. Whereas spiritual things are spiritually discerned, and their moral soul lies in personal relations. It does not even lie in the success of an empirical morality. That is to say, faith is not conduct. Christianity is proved by the conscience, not according to a moral code for its carriage in life, but according to a personal experience of the Gospel as its Saviour.

The whole question of the relation of authority to experience has another aspect when we keep in view the fact that God's revelation did not come to extend the margin of our religious knowledge on easy terms. Nor did it come to provide a test (by the amount of it we could swallow) of our readiness to obey whatever a god might command. In either case we might well find in Rome the one vicar of this authority on earth. It did not come to men as rational beings nor as sympathetically humane, but as sinners; to touch and seize them with the regenerative power of the holy, and lift them to communion with Himself. Hence it has its effect only in so far as it enters our inmost experience ; where it teaches us to be so engrossed with the authority that recreates us that we forget about the freedom; which yet grows, we know not how, day and night, till it surprises us in some hour of self-realisation which was never achieved by ourselves, and reduces us to a silence whose solemnity may be even desecrated by the pæans of the proudly free.

XIX

THE THEOLOGY OF CERTAINTY—ELECTION

THE question of Christian certainty is the deep root of all human certainty, and it carries us beyond the psychology and the religion of the matter to its theology. Or rather it extends the area of the religion over the theology. When religion rises to Christian height it must become theology. Its theology is intrinsic. Christianity is the only religion that has produced a great theology. Its truths then are no more merely true, and no more but a part of the science of religion, rather of the science of God. And more. They become part of man's footing in eternity. They enter the region of creative forces shaping history; they are part of the action of God; they belong to God's own account of Himself and not merely to the realm of our guesses; they are bound up with adoration, and constitute its inseparable intelligence. What we adore (as in the Trinity) is not a mystery, it is a revelation. It is not the mystery that is the object of religion but the light; nor is faith but a flash, it is a knowledge. We do not "worship we know not what." And a worship that knows what it worships is not religious merely, it is theological religion. Those who devote their lives to the science and culture of religion (unless they take their souls casually) continually find themselves compelled by their own spiritual necessities upon theological faith. The simple and elemental pieties may suffice those who are aided by a ministry, but they will not carry

THE THEOLOGY OF CERTAINTY 383

the minister who has to carry the people. And the great certainty on which the minor certainties hang, whether in priest or people, must rest on a theological reality and a theological conviction.

There is a danger set up here for those tendencies which chiefly develop the impressionist influence of the Church, and whose authority is unction. It is the danger of neglecting the truth of religion for its effect, and cultivating an aversion for all those problems and aspects of faith which, while they enrich it, and give it real weight, yet seem, or threaten, to arrest its direct impact on the public. Truly the moving preacher is a great gift of God to any Church; so long as he does not become the supreme power in it. For the faculty in such preachers is mainly temperamental. Grace is passed through a temperament, and can even be lost in it. Temperament counts for more than character, and for more than insight, with the modern public, which suspects originality. Would, indeed, that there were far more temperament and far less sentiment in our type of faith; but it would subvert the idea on which the Church rests if its grace were dominated by a gift which is really a nature-power. The Apostle should lead the Church, and not the hierophant; and the preacher is made an Apostle by no temperament but by the matter which the temperament handles, and the Spirit which hallows genius by an anointing from the Holy. The mere preacher is tempted to cultivate what will gather the people in swift and mobile crowds (not necessarily to himself) rather than what slowly makes them the people of God. The immediacy of religion engrosses the whole field of attention, apart from its reserves of strength and its staying power. The young preacher especially is beset in almost every newspaper with the *éclat* of the successful artist in his line; and in spite of himself he is deflected from the reality of his message to its results, through influences that may care more for copy than for creed. Further, those who in the churches are responsible for their organisation, finance, and practical effect add to this pressure. Most churches are loaded with more impatient ideals, practical work, and pecuniary responsibility than their living faith will now carry; and it becomes a *sine qua non* that the preacher should be able to maintain the going concern. The effect of the sermon is apt to replace the effect of the Gospel. They fear most a little flock. Their kingdom is given but to the large institutions. The action upon the ministry of this pursuit of effect is often unhappy. The preacher may be haunted by cares and fears which do not really belong to the Gospel, while he is blinded to things which in its interest he ought greatly to dread. He is tempted to be preoccupied with the success of the Church as a business, and proportionately blinded to the issues that make the life, or the problems that threaten the life, of the Gospel itself. A man might be a most successful preacher who does not show a trace of impression, or even contact, with the challenge to faith raised by the intelligence of his day. Biblical criticism, for all that his utterances show, might have no existence. Philosophic questions, which in a crude form trouble even the youth in the pew, may seem unknown to the pulpit. The finer questions of personal or social ethics in a complex society may not emerge over the horizon; though there may be reference to the ordinary social problems connected with grievance and affecting the vote. The points where philosophy or ethic abuts on theology, and often pierces it, may be entirely avoided. And the atmosphere may be that of an effective pietism rather than powerful truth, of the spirit that delights rather than of the quick, subtle, and searching spirit that hallows and abides. And though all this may be the proper thing for this or that man according to his idiosyncrasy; though, also, the pulpit is not primarily for the discussion of problems, yet it ought to betray a due knowledge and conquest of them if it is to bring to the age the Yea and Amen; and it is serious when such a cloistered message sets the fashion for a whole Church. The autonomy of faith is not its seclusion. It is serious when the whole Church is led so to discourage the less marketable interests that it is felt to have no luminous or influential word for the society that counts. A Church must be pious and it must be philanthropic, but if it exhaust itself in its sermons, or its benevolence, or its missions, at the cost of a piercing gospel, and a discerning eye to read the time, it will not lay Christ's hold on society, as the spread of knowledge and ideas is making society to be. The message to the human will will fail because of the indignity done to human nature. Discourses may then be as powerless as they are interesting, and the digestive system of the Church may grow atrophied because people are fed with pre-digested food, and are not taxed for their natural powers. Hence we have from other lands criticism of the Free Churches (who are much exposed to this peril) that as a rule they are indifferent to theological knowledge, or hostile to it, for fear of the mental unsettlement it might produce. (One British critic has said, with more smartness than sympathy, that the Free Churches are living on their wits.) The symptom may be rightly stated but the diagnosis is wrong. For the unsettlement is there, and its worst and most intractable forms are due to the lack of proper theological training and not to its presence. Theological knowledge and depth, truly conceived and wisely used, would be the cure for it. There was a time when the Free Churches were the theological Churches—the time when the foundations were being laid on which they now stand, and the capital stored on which they still live. The aversion to theology, and the consequent unsettlement, come rather from a too close association, not to say identification, of the Church and the democracy, and the submersion of the Kingdom of God in the progress of man. It comes from the necessity of being popular at once (as the holy cannot be), and from the aversion of the popular mind to anything but impression. So that a Church's first duty is apt to be regarded, especially by its laity, as being to impress the people, instead of to confess heartily the Gospel of a living Lord and leave its results to Him. This is a burden which the preachers often feel very keenly. They are driven by their duty into such a contact with the slow, unwelcome Gospel as makes them feel it. They may even be torn with the contrast and the strain between the eternal demand the Gospel makes on the public and the passing demands the public make on the Gospel.

And the appetite for success, for numbers, for effect, grows as it feeds upon the democratic philosophy of Pragmatism, with its note of American business and efficient bustle. A harder time than ever would seem to be awaiting the conscientious preacher in a popular body as the Pragmatist definition of truth comes to prevail, that it is what " works." Our truth does work, no doubt, but in very large orbits; and not always in time, within one life, to let us make up our minds about its results with that certainty which alone enables it to " work." The vice of Pragmatism, so understood, is that, where absolute truth, or any faith, is concerned, we must begin with a belief in the absoluteness of it before we can set it to work with its native might. We must begin working with that conviction of its absoluteness which its working is

THE THEOLOGY OF CERTAINTY 387

supposed to provide. We must begin producing with the product in our hands. We cannot make an absolute truth work in which we do not yet believe. The world can only be converted by a Church which believes that in Christ the world has already been won. And without a theology treated as a religion that belief is impossible.

The tendency (and danger) I am criticising is also enhanced by the modern stress upon experience. It is a proper stress. But experience is not the whole of faith, as I have shown. We can go on to make our experience of Christ universal only by a faith which outruns all experience. For we believe in the reality of a Kingdom of God as it has never been experienced yet. A very large section of the public hates and fears to be made to ask questions about its religion, even when these are not hostile but friendly, and meant to enrich the religion to itself and strengthen our grasp of it. Newman found that the Roman Church was indifferent or suspicious towards that apostolic interest which seemed to him a chief debt of the Church to the age. Indeed people are more patient of challenge from without the religion than of problems raised from within. And the cause is twofold. First is the cause which is at the root of so much of our rational shame—the lack of education its early arrest before ideas have been acquired (to say nothing of the taste for them), the suspicion of education, and the consequent torpor of the intelligence where there is not the sharp stimulus of immediate action, *i.e.* of the minor problems, the minor convictions, and the tactical expediencies. Even shallow souls are not to be mastered by shallow powers. And, second, because the great issues of religion for Humanity, and the great demands made by Humanity on a Gospel, come home most to those who spend the whole of their best powers on their faith, and who do not give it but their exhaust steam and their recreative interest. These things come home to the ministry rather than the laity —to the ministry, that is, when not itself laicised by the serving of tables, or unduly pressed by those who do. It is one of the gulfs between the minister and his charge that while their best and most strenuous hours are necessarily spent in carrying on the immediate business of the egoist world, his are devoted to things which are not of the world, and which have another centre and principle, and yet are of prime concern at last for the world itself. The difference is bound to breed a corresponding difference in the habit of mind. The principles of the two regions are extremely dissimilar, not to say sometimes mutually subversive. And it is bound to make a great difference between two men if one give his fresh and ruling energies to the one, and the other to the other. If one man give his morning time to religion and another but his evening time the difference will work out in several ways. The one will move to feel that religion is to be taken with all the seriousness of an eternal business, and therefore more seriously than the business whose pressure is near, urgent, or clamant; while the other will be influenced to think of religion as an interest to be postponed to more obtrusive things, treated as a luxury, relegated to his spare time, and thrown down to the level of recreation, or near it. He may resent it if in religion (which, no doubt, must be there for help and comfort), anything be presented as a tax on his intelligence; as if that were not tried enough by the combinations or perplexities of business to need at church rather a milk diet and a warm bath. It means more than appears on the surface that the control of the Church should be in the hands of a laity for so many of whom religion fills the relaxed and marginal hours of life. And, while it is proper that it

THE THEOLOGY OF CERTAINTY

should be so, it is also proper that such a laity should seek and welcome, with less suspicion than they often do, the due guidance of the experts of the Soul. Otherwise we must not be surprised if, as culture spreads, many should be disposed to seek in a hierarchical Church that safeguard for unpopular or incipient truth which is really secured by due respect for the authority of an educated ministry, whether it fill the press or not.

I return from this detour to what I began to say, that the question of religious certainty, wherever it is taken seriously and rises above mere religious effect or impression, is bound to become a question of ultimate truth, *i.e.*, of theology. And faith will never have its native effect unless it do. I ought to protect myself by adding that the certainty which concerns us most is not so much the sporadic certainty of individuals as the continuous certainty of the Church. The very greatest matters of our faith cannot monopolize an adequate attention, experience, and passion from individuals every day or hour. It is enough that in the great and formative or luminous hours they should be sure to us, and should spread from such reservoirs for life's daily supply at a lower pressure. But they must form the standing matter and ruling note of the Church's corporate testimony. The Church should not contemplate dormant winters for them, or banked-up fires. Which means of course that theology is less the property of the individual than of the Church whose living consciousness it expresses of its perennial trust.

When we say that religious certainty is impossible at last without theology what is meant is this—not that it calls in theology but that it is theology, luminous, warm, and dynamic—theology risen from its grave in the resurrection power of holiness—theology as Luther knew it when he said, "Theology makes sinners," not pedants, and not sages, but sinners. Theology is not the interest of a certain guild or craft in the Church, whose object it is to enhance its own consequence by pressing its services, or manufacturing exigencies which it can exploit. Theology is the expression or the exposition of the Church's fundamental consciousness of what makes the Church the Church. And the Church's certainty is certainty of its theology, and not of something else by the remote aid of its theology. It is the certainty of salvation—a word which has no meaning but a theological one for the soul. Faith is salvation; it does not lead to it. If the object were to show that theology had as good a right as any other science to the scientific name, then it might be said that the Church was calling in its theology to acquire a reputable place in the scientific world, or a good footing on the platform of the British Association, as it has secured it in the faculties of the modern universities. But that is not the Church's interest in theology, which is not an aid to the Church, or an advantage, but an essential—the statement for each age of its central life and distinctive certainty as grounded on objective reality. In theology we have to do with certainty, in the sense of objective reality and not mere subjective certitude. In the Gospel the object is not that I should be certain, but that I should be certain of the Gospel God, and at least as certain of Him as He is of me. The Church was created by a theological God in a theological act, by a power and a deed which cannot be described except theologically. And if I would be quite specific and concrete in what is meant I would take one provocative illustration, and say that the certainty which makes Christian faith is

THE THEOLOGY OF CERTAINTY

the certainty of something very theological and objective, indeed, of what is the last ground of our being —of our election by God in His eternity. Let me develop this illustration.

Our certainty, security, and peace in the Gospel is not a certainty *about* such election but our certainty *of* it and *in* it. It is not scientific but religious. We may experience justification and regeneration, but such experiences are precious, not as mere experiences but as experiences of acts historic and divine. And these acts again have their eternal value as expressions of the divine will and purpose in its fundamental eternal act. And it is our security in that eternal purpose that is our certainty. It is our election by God. That is the eternal divine act which is the ground of every historic act of His in Christ and kingdom. My point is the connection of that act with Christian certainty.

The source of so much uncertainty on the highest things is that religion in becoming personal has lost its balance and become too subjective. Faith ceases to be a certainty and becomes a piety; which loses its interior stay in reality and becomes a frame of mind. People ask how they should feel instead of what they should trust, believe, and serve. And this subjectivity acts in two ways. First, it weakens character in the religious, so that the man does not really press and wrestle through; he does not fairly face questions, and insist on answers from himself at any cost of labour and patience. But he takes refuge either in mysteries with one section of the Church, or in pieties with the other. One end falls back on sheer authority and the other upon sheer experience; and between them faith suffers, in the great, sure, and powerful sense of the word faith. In the next place, a subjective religion has nothing to say to the man whose questions are of an objective nature, and who asks for anything like a scientific solution or action on a large scale. It has nothing to say to knowledge, or thought, or the *Realpolitik* of things. Thought is suspected and banished by current religion. Even literature at this moment may be searched in vain for any light on the last problems, or any but an amateur interest in them. But when thought returns either to faith or art the great verities will become again engrossing and mighty. Of course it is not contended that the Church should become a dialectic arena, or lay itself out before all else to answering questions in the science of religion or the niceties of economics. Nor is it meant that its prime duty is the quest of intellectual adventure, or the exercise of philosophical gymnastic. But what it is not fashionable to remember is that faith, by the very nature of its relation to the God without and the world without, is committed to a perpetual fight for its existence. It can only keep its conquests by continually regaining them. It has continually to face the warfare involved in making itself good to itself in face of the challenges that it not only meets but feels in the mind and fashion of the time. The man of faith cannot descend on the conflicts of opinion with foregone solutions given as a bolus. Solutions have to be worked out. What he comes with is foregone certainty, confidence, and power. He has solved life, solved the soul, in advance by his trust in God's practical and final answer in Christ; but he has not solved in advance the questions addressed to that potent and prolific answer by the public need. And it is useless to offer to such questions his own experience as such. It is indeed a great gain that in these modern days faith should be grasped and construed in terms of experience instead of mere thought. But in the price we pay for the gain must be counted the tendency to offer experience for faith, and to answer the inquiring soul with a subjectivity

THE THEOLOGY OF CERTAINTY 393

instead of an objective Gospel. An audience will hang on a sincere man who describes in a *causerie* his spiritual and often sentimental adventures on the way to a mystic peace, but it complains of theology in the passionate exposition of an objective Gospel which is the moral crisis of the whole world. Nothing produces more uncertainty than a constant reference to subjective experience alone. It is detaching the Spirit from the Word, and the hour from its history. Some of the experiential Churches seem almost as much bewildered with Modernism as the authoritative Churches, when one gets below the surface. And when a question is put as to objective reality, and it is answered by a reference to the respondent's subjectivity, such a reply is not only ineffective but it may be irritating. Nothing is less effective or more exasperating than to be asked to note how happy a man is in a certain belief, and therefore how true it must be. To say to a questioner about the grounds of faith in the Gospel that "it saved me" is not necessarily to make him covet its fruits. And it need mean no more than that he was saved in connection with it, not by it.

In various ways religious uncertainty dogs the steps of an excessive subjectivity, such as marks an age that has just discovered the value of experience and can think of nothing else. If we care more for piety than for faith we increase that unhappy effect. We court the facile, temperamental, and warm forms of religion, we worship *Gemüthlichkeit* (which indeed is a precious and blessed thing), and we are indifferent and impatient towards everything that does not attract us, move us to give, or do us immediate good. We think we are not set upon the eternal rock unless we feel good. Which (as I say) is like measuring the value of our food only by the sense of immediate well-being on eating it and before digestion. We are apt to be more interested in the inspiration of an incalculable spirit that blows as it will than in God's act of justification, which sets us for ever at the Spirit's source in the final act of His saving will. Yet to put spirituality in the place of justification is to vaporise the Church. It is to detach the soul from the one decisive, final, and eternal act whereby it is placed within the eternal will of a God whose holy love founded our destiny and our peace before all worlds. The spot made intensely luminous has round it a corresponding gloom; and it is not strange that the area flooded by the lime-light of subjective religion should deepen the darkness of much that is not in it. A Gospel mainly experimental and subjective, one which culminates in the Christian consciousness and allows nothing to historic authority and tradition, is bound to have its obverse in a greater uncertainty and a freer challenge by contemporary society, which sees the weak side of current religion as it does not that of the past; which challenge is not therefore to be set down as an assault on faith. What it asks, and does not get, is that established contact and life communion with the first and last reality which is the commanding differentia of faith from piety, and which must involve a theology. If a theology be repudiated, such as sets us upon the rock of our election, our faith is little better served by the temperamental pieties which praise it than by the objective criticism which challenges it. Our piety may enable us to feel that we walk with God amid trees in a garden before a fall; but it is our faith that plants us where we know that our dark life is yet hidden with Christ in the counsels and decrees of God for ever. The certainty of Christian faith is inseparable from a revelation of

THE THEOLOGY OF CERTAINTY 395

our predestination to that faith as the consummation of human destiny.

It is a matter quite peculiar to our evangelical type and experience of Christianity—this idea of faith as the certainty of our election. It is challenged from several sources. First by an Agnosticism which tells us that we can have no certainty about God of any kind; which uncouples our relation to him altogether, and lets us run free by our own weight (*i.e.* really as determined by the coercion of a mere force). Or it may be challenged by a humanist and sentimental type of religion which pooh-poohs the whole region covered by theological terms in favour of a heaven expressible only by the sympathies of social life or the endearments of the fireside—a religion less Agnostic than Unitarian, and, when it escapes from the nursery, often nobly Theistic with the Theism of the Psalms. Or it may be challenged at the other extreme not by a deprecation of theology, indeed by an elaborate theology, but a wrong theology —it is challenged by Roman Catholicism. The Roman Church repudiates the idea that the Christian can be perfectly sure of his salvation. It says dogmatically there is no salvation outside of itself ; but it cannot say dogmatically that any individual is saved within it; while it was just such certainty that the Reformation brought.

The two ideas of certainty are different. The Pelagian element in the Roman view does something to reduce the certainty on that side. For, as has been said, if you must contribute to your own salvation you cannot be certain of it, unless you presume to be certain that you have done everything you are required to do in the case. Which means a self certainty not quite congruous with the humility implied in any true Christian faith. The Protestant position is that we contribute nothing; that our salvation is wholly and solely of God's grace, with which we are placed in direct contact, and are sure at first hand; that it is quite undeserved by us, and on God's side absolutely free. In which case the lack of certainty is lack of faith, lack of direct personal contact, lack of communion, and, by so much, lack of Christianity, which is entirely the communion and trust of a saving, forgiving God.

Besides, in the Roman view salvation, grace, is something comparatively external. It is a *donum superadditum* to the native power of man. It is attached to the rest of his life by the supernatural agency of the Church; and he might become isolated from the Church, and put out of reach of the addition required. His security cannot become an inward, direct, and permanent certainty. But in the Protestant faith man was made for Christ and His salvation. That is human destiny. And his faith is to trust and to act Christianly in the occasions and vocations of life as thus created. It is in that medium that the experience comes home. And especially in the moral life and its experiences. Eternal life is moral renovation, not mystical merely, and not magical at all. It is moral certainty of the absolutely righteous and holy as the Saviour. It is certainty of the Word before it is certain of the Church —of the word of reconciliation which makes the Church, rather than of the Church thus made. And it is absolute, and it abides. It is the certainty of God's moral and eternal will of love for us, and of that alone. Faith can be confounded only if God fail.

> "I steadier step when I recall
> That, if I slip, Thou dost not fall."

It seems a singular thing to declare that Christian certainty is the certainty of our election when we remember how many would say, and have said, that the

THE THEOLOGY OF CERTAINTY 397

doctrine of election was just the thing of all others which destroyed any religious faith they had, or even any desire for certainty on such things. But before we go further it is worth remembering that the trust of this election has made the greatest religious certaintists (if the word pass) that the world has seen, some of the loftiest, deepest, most learned and acute, most influential and beneficent men that have ever turned or moulded the course of history. I need but name Calvin himself, to say nothing of many of his note or in his train. To the banal suggestion of narrowness it need only be noted that Christianity did not come with a broad creed as the grand means to give effect to its universal kingdom. The universalism of modern missions was started by a group of narrow theologians and not by the liberal thinkers of the time. The gospel is not chiefly concerned to be broad but high, deep, intense, holy and creative. It was not a genial glow but a consuming fire. Its gate was strait if its realm was wide. Faith was life, and the way to life was narrow; and if it was before all else broad it was not the way to life. To be truly Christianly broad means a great struggle; I have already quoted Martineau, " A truly catholic mind does not come by a volition "; nor is it the indulgence of a natural tendency to expatiate, or an inborn hatred to submit. And if appeal be made to the expansive and comprehensive instincts of love, let it first be remembered that divine love is holy love which has a severity of its own. And, second, love is quite as much concerned with the sorting of the fish as their netting. Love itself is selective—at least monogamous love is. And I will stop at this stage with a fine phrase from Joseph Roux, " Aimer c'est choisir." We select one, we narrow down on one, from all the world. Has love not a necessity of its own? Its true freedom lies there. For the soul to be unchosen is to be unloved.

There can be no such certainty in life as that which grounds us and our destiny not simply in God (which might be but mystic) but upon the eternal will and absolute act of God, the will which is the final principle of all other action of His, and the power and purpose which nothing can unsettle or withstand. It is the one compendious *actus purus* of God, the act whose participation makes all action divine, the act of incessant free choice, wherein His will is not simply mighty but absolute. And that is what we are established on by faith. That is the certainty and freedom of faith, the certainty that we are objects of the eternal choice before and beneath all the foundations of the world, members of a creation whose ground plan is its movement to the everlasting Redemption, and destined for the kingdom against which no power can prevail. To be settled there is to be on eternal rock. One may question whether we *are* so settled, but surely it cannot be questioned that, if we were, it would be a certainty and a security incomparable. It would be one of far deeper value for human destiny than all the sympathies that comfort and cheer us without it, only perhaps to fail and drop us at some crisis in the far future too great for their cohesive or their sustaining power. Without the certainty of such a faith the very sympathies might well distrust themselves and their own permanence, and by such misgiving be slowly eaten through. Humanity might well lose confidence in itself in the face of Great and Holy Eternity without such a stay. And for Humanity to lose self-confidence for eternity, when, by the hypothesis, it has none in God, would be to crumble, however slowly, to a doom as great as its faith and triumph would have been. If our light be darkness, how great the darkness is. Man cannot face eternity except in the strength of the Eternal, by being made to partake in the Eternal's certainty of Himself, which is the certainty of all

THE THEOLOGY OF CERTAINTY 399

Being. Nothing less is the meaning of our Christian faith by the Holy Spirit. It is the certainty both of an eternal security and an eternal perfection at last. It has been pointed out that Calvinism fell into decay through its invasion by pietism, *i.e.* by giving up the anchorage of its faith in its idea of God and fixing it in a subjectivity of man. Hence the incapacity of Low Church to provide either footing or command for a great but distraught age. It is possible to believe in salvation very heartily without taking it home as the personal certainty which the doctrine of Election conveyed. And one result has been a welter and a haze in which the soul turns for assurance from itself and its piety to seek in the sacraments a stay and comfort which the elect found at a higher source.

Now for this tremendous certainty there is no other foundation than the historical revelation and salvation in Christ as the eternal and comprehensive object of God's loving will and choice, the Captain of the elect. We have not sufficient ground outside that for believing or trusting such a God. We cannot start with a view of God reached on speculative or other similar grounds, and then use Christ as a mere means for confirming it or giving it practical effect. That would mean a certainty higher than Christ's, and the superfluity of Christ when the end had been reached. Which is not the Christian Gospel, be that Gospel right or wrong. In that Gospel our final certainty can never be detached from what Christ did, what He is and does for eternity. The eternal election is in Christ, "Mine elect in whom My soul delighteth"; and only in Christ does faith at every stage realise it. Hence it has been well pointed out that we must not preach election to produce the certainty of Christian faith, but preach Christ and faith in Him to give us the certainty of our election.

Theological as election is, it is not most valuable as a piece of theology but as an exercise of our personal religion. For it concerns the individual, else it has no religious value. Saving faith rises to saving certainty as we grasp our personal place in the election of a personal God. In His will is my peace. God chose me from eternity. That conviction sets a man above princes, and inspires him to beard princes. God chose me, of course, as member of a great whole, a great community. In that and for that I am chosen—gloriously doomed to fraternity as to sonship. So that the final and direct object of God's choice is the Church, is Humanity as a Church, the New Humanity, and, indirectly each soul as a cell thereof. What is chosen is no Church regardless of single souls, but a Church with the very hairs of its head all numbered. All history exists for the Church, but for a Church of living souls as the distillation of history. The saints shall rule the world, but just as the world is translated into saints. Apart from these souls the Church is an abstraction, and any election of it is out of relation to personal faith. Truly election contemplates a vast totality of souls as the direct object of God's choice and work, but the election (if its object is not a mere idea or abstraction) is apprehended by individual faith, sure that the believing soul is thus in the eternal thought of God. There alone have we due ground for realising the unspeakable value of a soul; which will never come home to us from any wonder over its psychological structure, or any æsthetic admiration of the excellent creature called man. It is precious as the Church is holy—as being ear-marked by the Holy for holiness, as having such an eternal destiny, without whom the Kingdom of God is not perfect. And there is no soul for which this is not the last and the most

THE THEOLOGY OF CERTAINTY

practical question of its being. That choice by God is its authority and its charter for all the best it can ever be.

If each man could be made to feel himself equally entitled to say, "I am chosen and elect of God," it is hard to see why any exception should be taken to the idea, by any lover of his kind, however hard it might be to realise the tremendous fact practically and experimentally. The theology would then cause less difficulty than the religion. The ideal would be welcome; the task would be its realisation in personal experience—which is always the hardest thing in connection with Christian faith.

Now this is just what each man is entitled through Christ to say. "I am chosen and elect of God." There is no man who has not a right to say that with Christ's cross for his charter. The sin of unfaith is refusing to say it, *i.e.* refusing Christ and the God Christ brings. For that God is the Saviour of a world which has its concrete existence only in its souls. He is the Saviour of such a race, and not of a section of it. In the Cross Christ became absolutely final, and universal, and particular. That is what faith says, and what it ensures. And it is surely something we should wish to believe. The world is badly enough in need of salvation, of reconciliation, of the kingdom of God. Salvation and a saving God, as I have conceived them, make an ideal that surely comes home to every worthy mind. The question of uncertainty then arises not about this ideal of faith, but about its reality. Has God so chosen? And has He the means to make such an ideal good? It can never be demonstrated that He has. But we can still be perfectly sure of it. And that certainty is the differentia of faith. Faith is faith because it assures us of the fact, because it is in contact with it, because conscience is in personal union with it. The certainty of faith is that the salvation of the world is assured by no arbitrary choice of God's, nor by a passing *tour de force*, but by the eternal act and nature of His holy will. The holiness which condemns sin would be but a negative thing if it did not go on to destroy it, *i.e.*, to destroy its power to come between God and man, and thus to thwart the universal empire of that holiness which makes the universal and infinite power to be truly God.

The revelation in Christ, therefore, is the salvation of a world of souls, a new Humanity. We each touch by faith in Christ the one true human universal. Each man has the right to call himself God's elect, and to find his security in the changelessness of the eternal nature and the indefectibility of the divine purpose. How then can there be talk about a will of God for the perdition of any? Faith realizes the will of God in Christ as pure salvation—and my salvation. Damnation is not preached enough, but from a Christian Gospel eternal and destined damnation is excluded. If every man did as God willed there would be no damnation. God willeth that all men should believe. If man heartily believed in God's salvation there could be no perdition. And that is what he must believe if he believe in Christ.

" Yes, if he believe in Christ. But how if faith be itself a gift only to the elect? How if faith be the consequence of election? " Faith is neither the consequence of election nor its cause. These are mechanical categories. It is simply the personal receptivity of it, the response to it. It is not its cause. For then grace (which is the one thing faith answers) would be destroyed, and faith with it. It would not be grace if it were caused, if it were bestowed as the divine response and debt to faith, if it were not free and absolute. It would then be deserved and bought. Nor is faith the effect of grace, the consequence of

THE THEOLOGY OF CERTAINTY 403

election, and given only to the chosen. For that would make it but a psychological (*i.e.* a natural) sequel in man of a certain act of God—an unfree process like logic, resulting from a divine initiative or decree. It would not be an act, it would only be a reaction, a process, and therefore not free. Certainly it would not be as free as the grace which produced it. Therefore it would be no answer to grace, whose freedom must be answered with ours. Therefore it would not be faith at all. Personal relations would cease. And the soul's prime certainty would be lost.

We cannot lay too much stress on the fact that a doctrine of election is only reached as a religious or theological thing, by personal and evangelical faith in Jesus Christ the Saviour. He is the authority for that certitude of ours. But is that not the same thing as to say that in God's intention and use any discrimination is in the interest of salvation, and that the suggestion of perdition is imported from some other quarter. The certainty of election is always a certainty of faith. It is the discovery that what Christ did for us was rooted in the eternal changeless being and purpose of God. And what He did for us was to save. Let me follow up this point.

This matter of method and procedure is of first moment here. The Christian view of election does not arise out of an attempt to explain the world and account for its two classes, the good and the bad, like some theories of it; but it is the explanation, nay, the revelation, contained in Christ—who (and not the world of history) is the source from which Christianity starts. It sees all the goodness of the world in Christ, and is compelled by Him to carry it back to God. But it is under no compulsion, nor has it the power, to explain the causation of the mischief in the world.

For it the source of goodness is God in Christ, but it has nothing to say about the causation of the bad beyond referring it to the mystery of human freedom. All we can do with the bad is what we must do with our own souls—commit and trust it to God, and to the merciful God, the God of a final, consummate, and holy salvation. The religious and Christian course is to trust the wicked to the mighty mercy of God; it is certainly not to explain them by His eternal, arbitrary, and absolute decrees—for which there is no Christian authority whatever. Paul's references on this head are not to the eternal fate of souls, but to the providential function and order of races in history. The certainty of revelation and faith is that in the universal Christ the world is chosen for salvation, and is saved in principle, and shall be saved in fact. The lost are lost by refusing that gospel in their mysterious and incalculable freedom. And then the question is removed to be one of eschatology rather than predestination. For freedom is well within the scope of a divine election. The self-determining power of the individual is part of the ordered predestination of God, and of the necessity felt by His love to endow man with a freedom like His own if He expected man to respond to His own. Only a fatalist predestination, not a personal, excludes such freedom.

When the question as a question of freedom becomes eschatological we may then discuss, among other things, whether a race can be complete with any of its members missing, whether for a species to continue and fulfil its nature every individual must be conserved that it ever produced. But even such a consideration could be very misleading, and it can form no analogy. It might be importing a natural law into the spirit world, whose principle is not nature, but something which so subverts nature as grace does.

THE THEOLOGY OF CERTAINTY 405

Does it not become probable that the most of the difficulties and doubts which beset faith, and especially in connection with the central certainty of election, are due to a false method, and especially a false start? We start with nature, or the observed course of history, or our empirical experience, what we call our knowledge of the world, instead of with Christ and the new creation. And from nature, or the natural man, you can only get a God who repeats upon a vaster scale those anomalies of experience from which a God should deliver us. We only get a natural God of preternatural scale. We cannot get a spiritual God, a God of Grace, from a natural world. And the transfer of the analogy means also the transfer of anomaly, as the fate of Butlerism has shown; when the great argument that told so well against a mechanical deism is ineffectually transferred to the conditions of an age like our own of Vitalism, Agnosticism, or Monism.

We start wrong, in dealing with grace and the miraculous altogether, when we start with our experience of the world. We quickly mark of course its two vast classes—the good and the bad. And if we are in quest but of a divine causation of the world we refer to the same cause the goodness and the evil in it. We conclude from the two irreconcilable phenomena a twofold cause, a double predestination, one election of some to life, another of some to death. We practically assume two causes in this act, two wills, two gods. And, in so far as we remain Christian with such a reading of the world, we regard Christ as a mere provision of God, or even an engine, by which the happy lot of the one class can be brought to effect.

It is a procedure totally wrong. It is constructing a natural God who works with a spiritual machine instead of receiving a spiritual God in a moral redemption. It casts Christ down to a place from which He is bound to sink lower still in popular regard. Hence it is a false orthodoxy that is largely responsible for the popular debasement of Christ, and for current heresy and unbelief. For our Christian thought and faith of God we have but one source, which is Jesus Christ. And His revelation is to our faith and not to our inferences. And what our faith answers in Him is election as Love's mode of action, God's election of the world to salvation, and its effective and solidary salvation accordingly. It is the salvation itself that reveals the principle of salvation; it is not a natural principle, with which salvation but complies. And how could salvation reveal any other principle than itself ? The Saviour could reveal no equally divine principle of perdition. Certainly He implies responsibility and judgment; but that is not perdition. In so far as faith is our source, personal, experienced faith in Christ, there can be no talk of God's damnation of any. For our one source of knowledge is a knowledge only of salvation. We can never be as sure of the perdition of others as of our own salvation, *i.e.* we can never associate it with the absolute certainty and the eternal will of God. Faith knows much of predestination, but nothing of a predestination of some to bliss and some to perdition. And when the Bible speaks of election it is never the election to heaven or hell.

" But if He did not doom them out, did He not leave them out? And is not that practically the same?" Indeed it is not. And very far from the same. The doomed out must stay out, the left out may yet come in. No doubt there is *preference*. That is in the divine order of the world. God is responsible for it. That is His election, His predetermining choice. And it is impossible for us to reach the divine reasons

THE THEOLOGY OF CERTAINTY

for the order of its action. Predestination of some kind is an absolute necessity for religion. But while relative predestination is a tolerable mystery, absolute predestination is intolerable. And the relief is that it is a case of priority, it is not monopoly. The chosen are but preferred, not secluded. The left are but postponed, not lost. Every man in his own order — in a historic process not ended by death. The whole world plan is a teleology, a perspective, a hierarchy, of salvation. Some races have a hegemony, some individuals have a start. But for what? Not for privilege, not for prerogative, not out of favouritism, not for immunity, not for dominion, but for leadership. And divine leadership means service, sacrifice, help, uplifting, redemption, the Cross. The elect are there for burden. Burden is the badge of the best—not to exploit and exterminate, but to lift and rescue. If any are higher on the hill it is that they may turn to redeem and not to rend, to carry and not to devour. We are elected, individually or in races, not to primacy, but only to priority, and to a priority of service. That is the election of the captain of the elect in his cross. It is an election in love to obedience, and service, and even death, for the rest.

The error of the bad old way was in construing the case as if it were an election by power for power, instead of an election by love for communion and service—chosen in Christ. No wonder that such a fatal start has produced so much confusion and uncertainty. We should expect it when a principle so pagan is thrust into a world whose moral movement and destiny is revealed and determined by Christ. There is no such heathenism in the Bible. It is an election of love—to be redeemed or to redeem. It is an election by love for love. And we have seen that love is selective in its mode of action. Love has a necessity of its own. It is preferential in its nature, but not exclusive. If love be the surest thing in the world, the ruling thing, no less sure and dominant is the principle of election, as the mode of action of God's holy love. It is love working in a historic and evolutionary perspective, according to the moral principle and order prescribed by absolute holiness and human freedom. But it is an election of some from others *for* others, to bring others in, and not leave them out, far less cast them out. And what we have at last is a doctrine of the election of Humanity to the Kingdom of God which believes that everything really valuable for man has its ground in the free and sovereign, the gracious and giving will of a loving and holy God. This alone makes life religious and humbly sure. There is no earnest, personal, experimental religion at last without some faith in predestination. And it not only accommodates it, it founds on its authority all our certainty and all our security at last.

XX

THEOCENTRIC RELIGION

THERE is a question which may have arisen to some out of certain of the considerations which I have been offering in the last chapters. God is God to us not as a mere fact, however vast, but as a value; not simply as an objective fact, as our *vis-à-vis*, but as a spiritual value. But does that not involve a risk which carries much danger to religion? If He is chiefly God to us because of His value to us, does that not tend to fix our interests chiefly on ourselves, and lead us to prize God in proportion to the service He renders either to our egoism or to spiritual Humanity and its consummation? Over the God with a supreme value which we enjoy is there not the God with an inextinguishable right which we must serve? And is this latter not the conception of God which is final for faith as an obedience? Faith has no meaning without authority. But if we treat God as our supreme asset, do we not destroy Him as our supreme authority? He may be much as a mystic value for our feeling; is He not more when invested with moral right for our service? We may use that mystic value to enhance our own subjectivity, even to minister to our spiritual egoism; and so God may serve us more than we obey Him. We may exploit Him rather than worship Him. A mystic value, moreover, does not protect us from the risk of illusion. It gives us a tremendous impression or impulse, but it does not necessarily give us foundation; it does not give us fact and footing. It does not give us the truth, the reality of the matter. It does not protect us from the risk of illusion. It may only serve a high spiritual utilitarianism, minister to our self-respect or sense of well-being, and fade, as many a fine belief has done, when it has lifted us to dispense with it.

Do we not need something more moral, something with an ultimate right, an absolute authority, inexplicable because the source of all explanation—do we not need that to defend us from the risk of illusion, or at least the suspicion of it? Does religion not turn at last upon reality—not on spiritual value we use so much as on moral right we serve? Is it notthe moral justification of our experience that preserves us from illusion in it? Is the reality we worship not an authority which asserts itself to our moral experience as more than spiritually valuable, as one who makes good to us His royal right whether it seem to enhance us or not? I will trust though He slay. Only that can be the ground of our faith which becomes, by experience, a fact of our moral life, which acts there with moral compulsion, which does not simply do us good but which rules us, and does not merely bless but redeem and use.

But I may be told that I am using the word value in another than its usual sense in this connexion when I make it mean only value to man. It really means more (I am told). It means intrinsic worth. It means, not God's value to man but His value to Himself. It means the one good thing in the world made absolute—a good will.

With that definition we not only have no quarrel, but we have everything to do. It carries in it all for which we need contend—moral rights which we must absolutely serve, and not merely spiritual power by which we endlessly profit. It lands us with the absolutely Holy God as the one Authority. It removes us from the subjectivity of our Idealism, and teaches us that our higher self is imperative only if its ideals are the immediate and urgent presence of the Holy One. God as Love might be our servant, but God as Holy Love is our absolute and eternal King. A religion of love alone has no authority and no power—as the hour's religion shows. It is loving Holiness that makes our rightful Lord, our true worship, and our full freedom. Our freedom is the conscious submission of all we are to a righteousness made absolute in the freedom of the Holy. It is not a power to act without a cause, *in vacuo*. It is the autonomy by which the single soul makes the Holy One the principle of all its action and life.

Certainly we can have neither judgment nor religion without a valuation. Whenever we speak of reality we make a valuation. We select. True knowledge means a selection that we make from the whole mass of our experiences and fancies by some standard of value. It is really a volitional thing, and at bottom a moral thing. It is ruled by a standard of moral value. Even science acts by selective will, which implies a nought. We do not simply recognise laws at work, we prefer one line of law to another. And in the end we come to the transcendent Ought, where the must is not a rational sequence but a royal Word, which all that is within us rises to worship and obey.

I have urged throughout that the question of authority is a religious issue when we go to the bottom of it. But it is a religious question which has regard to the primacy of the moral issue. It is the question of the moral absolute, the holy. It is the question of the supreme and final right of the holy. Its focal point is where that issue concentrates which places the holy not only in the moral realm but in the sublime command of the whole world, as a goodness which transcends goodness and creates it. And if Christianity be *the* ethical, and therefore *the* universal, religion, it concentrates for the whole world in the Cross of Christ, where the right of holiness was, by God's gracious love, secured in man's salvation into holiness, because into communion, for ever. It is then that we know what holiness is, in the supreme act of worshipping it. Our sanctity is to worship holiness from within it, with heart and soul and strength and mind. Mankind was redeemed in the Cross not for its own sake but for the sake of the holiness of God, for the sake of His Holy One, for Christ's sake. The gospel of Christ's Cross is therefore the final centre of all Authority, because there alone the Holiness of God—the absolute sublimity, transcendence, and victory of the God of the Conscience—establishes itself for ever in the destruction of both guilt and sin. We transcend mere immanence only morally —by Redemption.

The Cross of Christ is thus not the centre of an orthodoxy, nor of a theology, nor of a religion, but of the racial soul, of all history, of the moral universe, of the Eternal Holy God. This is a position which can be demonstrated to none. It is a religious realisation. The root and source of all other authority, of all formal authority, is the holy Authority set up by God through His act of Grace, in the moral soul, in the soul as guilty, in the new and holy Humanity, in the experience of faith. The last authority is not demonstrable, it is only realisable, as *the* religious experience of the conscience. It is the moral imperative of holy love acting upon our moral experience in historic grace. That alone can be our authority which has none, which is its own authority, which makes its own sufficiency, its own satisfaction, its own complete atonement. That which makes for us the grand " Thou shalt " is

THEOCENTRIC RELIGION 413

that which has no "Thou shalt" over it. It says, "Be perfect" to all but itself. It is the Will eternally and absolutely good in itself—where will and nature are in perfect, sublime, and eternal accord, and goodness exists, throughout innumerable souls, in and for itself alone. That which for us is duty is for the Holy One not duty but a nature, which makes our duty and is our sovereign. Our holy is the absolute of all those things which have no price, because nothing can be their equivalents, but they have an intrinsic worth and dignity—things like justice, love, and faith, which rule us from themselves and not from boons they bring in their train. All such things were secured to mankind for ever, as its divine and certain destiny, in the Cross of Jesus Christ. And the holiness revealed there is the worshipful End of a realm of ends, the person in all persons, the *God* of all *souls*.

Truly, as Kant says, "How the imperative of morality comes to be possible is a very difficult question." And he ends with no solution of it, but with its absorption upwards into a worship by the miraculous action on us of personality. He ends with the famous apostrophe to Duty, which we may with even greater effect transpose into the still higher key of sanctity, and make the alogical ground of all religion and obedience "Holiness! Thou great, thou exalted Name! Wondrous thought, that workest neither by fond insinuation, flattery, nor by any threat, but merely by holding up thy naked law in the Soul, and so extorting for thyself always reverence if not obedience—before whom all appetites are dumb, however secretly they rebel—whence thy original? And where find we the root of thy august descent, thus loftily disclaiming all kindred with appetite and want? To be in like manner descended from which root is the unchanging condition of that worth which mankind can alone ascribe to themselves."

The distinction between a God of value for us (in the wrong sense) and a God with right to us contains the whole issue, so vital to-day, and so poorly grasped, between a religion which really centres in man and one which ought to centre in God; between a faith which exploits God and one which worships Him; between a God who is only love and a God whose love is His outgoing holiness, and whose grace is His holiness going down. The great spiritual task for Christianity at this hour is to replace its holiness in command of its love.

Let us look into this.

There is a certain religious lack which many feel more or less and deplore. They feel it in themselves, and they feel that it is eating the interior out of many Churches—even the most active. And it is the lack of power.

And there is another thing that they feel about this defect—that it is not so much a lack personal to themselves, or one for which particular Churches are culpable. It is a defect in the religion, the type of religion, common to us all, and to the age.

What is the source of this defect? We lack power in our religion because we have too much lost the idea of power, greatness, and majesty from the object of our religion. We have lost God's holiness in man's sympathy. I do not mean that it has fallen out of our theology but out of our working faith. It has not fallen out of our thought of God, for we still think of Him as the Almighty, correctly enough as far as that goes. But it has fallen out of our practical, our experimental relations with God. His practical relation to our soul has become more sympathetic than commanding, more indulgent than controlling, more of liberty than discipline. We experience Christ as Brother, or as Ideal, or as Master, but we do not experience Him as Saviour; or, if as Saviour, then

THEOCENTRIC RELIGION

not from perdition, not as absolute Owner, King, and Lord. Even when we think of Him as Brother, we are apt to think of Him as the Brother of the right minded, or of other people more needy than we are, the Brother of the strugglers, or of the proletariat. And when we think of Him as Ideal, we may be thinking of Him entirely in relation to ourselves and not to God, as our Ideal rather than God's Word. When we think of Him as Saviour it seems to be mostly as a Saviour from lovelessness and unkindness and not from guilt; from what comes between us and our poor brother, rather than between us and our holy Father. And he steals sweetly into our spiritual imagination rather than rules and lifts us with a mighty hand.

It is a religion of permeation, spreading on the level, rather than of power descending from above. And as a consequence the action of the Churches upon the world is low—though Church interests permeate Society in a growing way, and religion of a kind has more notice in the press than ever it had before.

But our faith can never have its own effect in changing the world unless it effect a very great change in us. And this it cannot do unless the object of it be more of a ruling power over us than of a mere infectious influence within us—to say nothing of a mere interest round us (and to some religious people He is not more than that).

It is the happy mark of a modern Christianity that we refer everything to the test of experience. This is the grand difference between mediævalism and modernity. Experience is the modern court in which our faith has to justify itself and prove itself real. We claim to be done with a dogmatism that must first be accepted as such in order to give religious experience any worth. As evolution or gravitation are dogmas because they explain facts, so the only dogma that can expect to be received is one that gives an adequate account of personal experience or passes its muster. Experience even becomes a tribunal, and not merely an organ, for God.

But all this throws upon us a much greater burden than ever before. It is true that it gives a certain advantage to the facile religionism where bland piety easily seems to the public to be superior to a more arduous faith because more easily experienced. For most people readily confuse sensibility with experience, rapt enthusiasm with spiritual excellence, and a religious temperament with godliness. But a true evangelical faith grows not easier but harder. It must be lived. We all readily believe, it is a pulpit commonplace, that it must be lived out. But it is more important that it should first be lived in—that we should feel all the range and force of the natural world, and yet command it in something more than a bloodless, facile, and instinctive sanctity. We have to see to it now that our actual experience is adequate to our real moral case before God. And it is much easier to elaborate doctrine about the experience than adequately to cultivate the initial Christian experience itself. This *is* the work of God, a mighty work—not simply that we should believe, but that we should believe in such a Saviour of such a world. We are compelled to ask at once questions more cosmic and more personal than before, and questions therefore more unwelcome. We must ask those who plead their experience if it is a regenerate experience or a natural. If we are to fall back on experience we must ask the religious leaders, and especially the religious critics, what their own experience is. We must ask them, " What is religion, what is God, what is Christ, personally to you? These mean a new creation in me. And you have not a *locus standi* with me till they

THEOCENTRIC RELIGION

are new life to you." We may put it as urbanely as we can, but that is what we put.

And when the question is framed like that, what are we to do if we discover that much pushing religion and pungent criticism has no real religious experience at all ; that the public proposes to become the tribunal of the Church and of Christian truth, and the press of Christian conduct and charity? Many have religious impressions, and keen religious interests, and busy religious activities—but religious experience, a life habitually at close quarters with God as He has revealed Himself, with a judging, saving God, a life therefore familiar with His inmost principles—that is another matter. Christian experience as a life superior to religious impressions, influences, and interests, as a life spent at close quarters with God, in much thought and prayer nourished constantly on the Bible and lived steadily in the Holy Spirit, in spite of failures and even sins—that is another matter. And for the ministry it is a tremendous matter. While for smart criticism it matters not at all.

What is our faith so often but a religious subjectivity? We are preoccupied with ourselves in the very act in which we should lose ourselves, make ourselves over and sign ourselves away. Our soul is not so much engaged with God as with its own condition, its appreciation of God, its utilisation of Him. Religion is courted and cherished either as a stimulus to a beneficence worth much more, or as a sense of inner harmony rather than of reconciliation with God, of happy calm rather than sure confidence, of a soul disburdened and freed to be itself rather than forgotten in a walk humbly with the living God. It may become a religious egotism, an *uti Deo*, an exploitation of God's value rather than a confession of His right.

What most endangers our public freedom at the long last is the fact that we are more concerned about our freedom than about our authority, about man's freedom than God's. Our freedom can permanently rest on God's freedom alone, and on our dependence upon it. The greatest power of Protestantism, of the world, for public freedom has been Calvinism, and the supreme concern of Calvinism was the freedom of God. Its great stumbling-block, predestination, was one effort to sacrifice everything to God's freedom of choice and grace. The effort was sound. It belongs to the very essence of religion. God must be free, if every man turn slave. There may indeed be other forms of securing that freedom besides predestination as Calvin taught it. But, by what ever form, that object must be a first charge upon faith. And our liberties are threatened whenever human freedom or human piety becomes the first concern.

So also with our concern for justice and righteousness. The old theories of Atonement had it for their leading interest to secure the righteousness of God before that of man—as the only condition, indeed, of man's righteousness at all, or of any divine value for it. This is the nobler side of the error we are now striving to undo—the separation of justification from sanctification in theological thought, and the demoralisation both of theology and religion in consequence. Man could only be set right with God (which is his true and final righteousness) by something which first did justice to God; whereas till quite lately modern theories have gone to the other extreme in protest, and have concentrated on the setting right of man in an ethical way without reference to a satisfaction of a holy God at all except what He might find in their improvement. But it is still true—seek first His righteousness and all human goodness shall be added. And it can hardly be said that, since the old theories were discarded without being

THEOCENTRIC RELIGION

re-interpreted, since the effort to do justice to God's holiness has been simply dropped for the cultivation of human goodness, the new anthropocentric theories have had the success of the old in making righteousness the ruling thing in character. That place has been taken by sympathy. The passion for righteousness has given way to the enthusiasm of Humanity. Singularly enough with this has gone a decay in our sympathy for small and struggling peoples. And it is uncertain to many if we are increasing the number of men who care more for righteousness than anything else. And while it is true that there is more stress on experience than ever, and on personal kindness, it is not the case that there is more sense of power; just as, with more stress on conduct, we are not more productive of character. Rather there is less. As the sense of God's power became merged in His love, there came a loss of man's power to stand up against the world (especially the world of his fellows) and to take moral command of it. We can help men to every good thing more effectually than to God. Yet if we cannot establish God in men's hearts what hope is there of the grand fraternity, the new Humanity, the kingdom of love ? The kingdom can only rest on the Church, and the Church rests on more than sympathy, on something which creates the true brotherhood, and outlasts all the brotherhoods that work with kindness alone. These have great value, but for their permanence they must be agents of the Church and its holy salvation.

An experience of something which is also our life's power is what we lack. Now in the Bible God is before all else the power over us, the moral power, the spiritual, holy majesty of life. Even as love He is so. His love *constrains*, it does not simply inspire, elate, and enlarge. When we expound fluently and eloquently that "God is love," we are too easily prone to take from the "God" what we put on to the "love." The King and His authority is lost in the kindly Father, who overrules not so much us as what is against us. But God is love in absolute power, not only over our enemies but over us. We are His redeemed property. It is not the love of equals between us. It is the love of grace, which loves beneath it, and comes down to the lost. It is love with a consequent royalty which descends with demand, of holy majesty which must be not only served but adored. God is only God as absolute, eternal, holy love; His love conquers; it is the absolute power over us, and the final power over our world. All things work together for good to them that love God *in His universal, royal, holy, and final purpose* (Rom. viii. 28 fin.). Such is the God of the Bible. He reveals Himself, but it is of His absolutely free and royal choice for His own holy end. He commends or reveals *His own* love to us (Rom. v. 8); it is not done by proxy. He is not discovered. He is not forced into the light, even of love, by any power outside Himself, not even by our misery. For that would be but pity, and grace is a world more free and mighty than pity. And God ceases to be God when He ceases to be such a God—the absolute, miraculous, personal, holy, and effective King and Lord of us and our world. To curtail His power is to infect Him with weakness; that is to say, it is to make Him a mixture of power and weakness—which again is to make Him part of the world, and destroy Him altogether as God.

This power of God to secure the empire of His holy love is not something that we arrive at by thought. It is not a theme of scientific theology. It is revelation. We experience it in our saved life by faith. What we experience is not merely an invincible Being who confounds man's device and compasses man's death, but our own true King and Lord, in whose gift we find ourselves and our destiny and all our aspirations for our kind. From the pages of the Bible especially God bears Himself in upon our new experience as such a God. He makes the Bible His Sacrament to reach us in that way.

And what He gives us first in this donation is not ourselves, or our souls, or our progress, destiny, and perfection, but Himself, His holy self. We are more sure of him than of our experience. Truly, he comes in our experience, yet so that we forget it, and we live only to the sense and reality of Him. The first content of my religious experience is not myself as feeling so or so—*e.g.* dependent (Schleiermacher)—not myself in a certain frame, but God in a certain act, as giving, as giving Himself, as thus grasping, saving, new creating me. The old-time word, or thought, turns *Spirit*. The living God is more than the old Creator to us. The Lord the Spirit is the historic Christ and more. This presence and power is the most sure and real thing we know. The absolute mastering power of the holy, loving God becomes our supreme reality. We do not simply feel Him in life—that is but religion; He takes possession of us; and that is conversion. It is faith. He belongs to us and *we to Him*. He belongs to us—but it is as our King; therefore we belong to Him. *He has not only a value for us but a right to us.*

This latter point is what we most need to have carried home to-day. We belong to Him—and not simply as His favourites for comfort, nor His friends for company, but as His subjects—for our obedience; as His servants — for His purpose. Perhaps both Japan and Germany have something to teach us as to the meaning of royalty and loyalty which we lose in a long peace. This is the kind of faith that lasts longest. It has the staying power often denied to tenderness. The people who have really known God by way of obedience chiefly have a faith that wears better than those who know Him by way of affection only. And there is no real proof of God but that experience by which He proves Himself not merely as a presence, nor simply as a help, but as a power; and as the power that does more than pervade life, that is enthroned on it by what He has done. If He is our Saviour it is that He may be our King. If He is our Father it is a fatherhood holy and royal. He certainly tends, nourishes, comforts; but He has the right to call on us for extreme service, sacrifice, and suffering, and no reason given whatever. In Dr Dale's last illness he said it never came home to him before as it did with his extreme pain that Christ was not only his Saviour but his King, who had the right to exact anything and everything from him at His silent discretion.

What is true of God is also true of Christ. He is not only Saviour but Lord. The same Bible that becomes the sacrament of God's present reality and power becomes the sacrament of Christ's also. Through the Bible, God, with all His power and claim, comes in Christ. But we know for what Christ lived, died, and rose. If God save us in Christ, he saves us not first for our happiness or comfort but first for His kingdom, for His holy power, purpose, and service. We glorify God before we enjoy Him, as the very Son did in His agony. God and Christ come to us in the Bible as one and the same absolute power over the world, and therefore as its goal and rule. The Jesus who once lived and conquered becomes in our experience our conqueror, our present Lord and King. We are more than conquerors for Him, we are conquered by Him. The historic Saviour becomes our living Lord, with a claim not simply to our conduct but to our soul and will. The Bible, and all the Church's testimony of Christ, becomes but a sacramental means for this translation of the earthly Jesus, not simply into the heavenly Christ, nor even into the precious Saviour, but into the unlimited Lord. This alone is full Christianity or the fulness of Christ—namely, the faith in the Lord the Spirit. Christ seizes us, " apprehends " us, as present Lord, not as Master only but as absolute Owner. He is all that is most resented when men refuse to say master, and say employer instead. He is indeed Saviour and sole Saviour; but what he saves us into is His own absolute and holy Lordship. Personal Christianity is not simply being saved from ruin, but being saved into that active obedience. It is not being saved from hell, but saved into heaven. And that is our destined heaven—to be in this Kingly Christ. God's real grace is not taking us out of despair but taking us into His service. His mercy is not simply in sparing us but in letting us glorify Him, even in our pain. It is a theocentric more than an anthropocentric salvation. We are saved into an obedience before we are saved into a liberty. We acquire our soul only by glorifying God. The goal is not Humanity, but God's holy purpose in Christ with Humanity. It is a new Humanity. God's greatest gift to us is a master and not, simply, a manhood. It is as we get a new master that we grow to new men. This kind of theology is the religion that our present preaching most needs.

And all this is true in such a way that (to sharpen the issue by an impossibility) if Christ clearly said one thing and every conscience in the world clearly said another, it is with Christ we should have to go. The best consciences were against Him when He came saying that it was the goodness of His day that most needed repentance, the religious that most needed saving.

And men became His true disciples as they saw the truth of that paradox. It was the core of Peter's great confession of Him as Messiah. For one brought up as Peter, with his Jewish ideas of goodness, and his inborn respect for the religious leaders of his society, it was a tremendous thing to hail as Messiah one who said that. It was something taught him by no flesh and blood. And the same perception tore Paul out of Pharisaism, and left Judaism behind for the human soul.

But if Christ said one thing and *my* conscience said another—not the Bible but Christ? It may be doubted if such a case could really arise in a Christian man. But if it could, he would remain a Christian man only by going with the Christ to whom he owed the salvation, the eternal life, of his conscience, and waiving its momentary verdict on a point. Many of our puzzles arise from not realising that an evangelical salvation is the salvation of the moral man in Christ, and not the plenary inspiration of his moral judgments on Christianity. The new creation is a re-creation of the conscience and not of its conclusions. If the conscience is well saved its verdicts will come right in due course and congenial company. Even from ourselves we shall judge what is right.

The chief sign of salvation, I have said, is not a sense of freedom, but an experience of mastery and of obedience. Hence a passion for liberty is not the first equipment for the study of Christ, or His God, or His salvation, or His kingdom; but the first thing is the enthusiasm of obedience. How far is it encouraged to be so among those who begin the Christian life? We must first be faithful and then free, and not simply faithful to freedom.

If we may distinguish where we cannot separate things joined by God, " Man for God " is a deeper note than " God for man." And it is the dominant.

THEOCENTRIC RELIGION

Christianity is not anthropocentric but theocentric. God is for man only that man may be for God. Man is not there to exploit God but to glorify Him. Christ is not there to enable Humanity to be all that it aspires to be, but to effect in Humanity the Kingship of God. Faith is realising not only that we are there by salvation, but that we are saved for God's absolute service and God's holy honour. Faith makes us servants more than beneficiaries, and trustees more than grantees. And we have no rights but by His gift.

In this connexion we must revise the modern idea of the *Werthurtheil*, or judgment of value. God is not God simply in virtue of His value to us, but in virtue of His right to us. He is not worshipful because of His service to Humanity, but because of His holy nature and claim to Humanity. True, we begin with what He does and is *for us*, but we do not end there. God is for us that we may be for God. His greatest service to us sets up His deepest claim. We are released into the — bondservice of Christ. God's blessing to us is the revelation of His absolute re-creating holiness in Christ's Cross, and our redemption from the judgment of that holiness to live within it in a joyful communion of its entire obedience.

This idea of God's right, as the highest form of God's value, needs to come back to both theology and religion. Both the greatness and the graciousness of Christ have blinded us modern men to His *glory*. Our new sense of greatness in His character has obscured the glory of His person, and we admire and copy where we should worship and fall down. The love of God has ousted the glory of God, and the grace has been declared at the cost of the holiness. We are shy of an atonement, and we do not preach about heaven, or the saint's everlasting rest. And in the champion's boldness for humane causes we may lose the prime place of humility as a Christian grace. " It is the joyful sense of God's holy omnipotence, especially in forgiveness, that makes us so willing to submit ourselves in service to the people we have to do with. And that is the humility which is the peculiar stamp of the Christian Church " (Herrmann). Both in the Church and especially in Society there is an appalling absence of the fear of God.

Owing to this preoccupation with the beneficiary side of Christ's work, with the " for us," faith does not issue in service so much as in sympathy. And a religion of sympathy will always end in being a religion that expects more sympathy than it gives. Christ is Saviour to it rather than Lord. The Father is not the King so much as the loving confidant and guide. Religion becomes subjective, psychological, absorbent, the recognition of God *in* the plexus of life and the soul rather than *over* it. It becomes more intimate but less effectual, less influential; it grows more persuasive but less authoritative, more suggestive but less imperative. The idea of God grows more urbane and less majestic. He is more of a friend and less of a power, more dear perhaps but less worshipped, more of a good and less of a glory.

But the grace of God in Christ is the grace of an absolute Lord, else it were worthless as grace. And all the gifts of His love do but the more extend the claim of His holiness.

Once on a time the justice of God was everything, and love and grace suffered. Then by a reaction the love was all. Then love to the sinful was felt to be another thing from love to the lovely, and grace regained some of its rights. Now the holiness of God has to come to its own.

The love is not merely sympathetic but redemptive. It is not the love of equal hearts. It is grace, mercy, forgiveness, not simple or mystic affection. It is love adjusted to sin. And the object of the grace is not simply to reclaim us, but to reclaim us for God's glory and His holiness. The Jesuits and Calvin are so far right.

The grace, to be sure, must never come short, but it is there for the sake of the holiness. What is God's gift in Christ? Is it simply a donation of help to us, a dole of mercy? Surely it is very much more. The Almighty Lord, the Holy One, our Judge and King, gives Himself up in Christ, and submits Himself to his own holy and unsparing judgment for pure love and grace to us. It is more of a gift for us than to us—for us, but to God, for blessing to us, but honour to God. Thus the Kingdom of God is not a subsidy to man, it is not simply the development of Humanity, but wholly a gift to it. It is the practical self-hallowing of God's name, its actual establishment, in history and society. God comes in Christ to meet our needy case; but it is to give us power to do the thing Christ alone did—to meet His holy will. It is rather to place us on His road than to help us on ours. If grace blunt our sense of the Almighty Holy Lord and His absolute claim to us it is received in vain, and it becomes a judgment. He has a loving right to us, our work, suffering, happiness, everything He chooses to take.

So also with Christ. We can, we constantly do, pervert his grace to our religious egotism, and we think of it as having for its grand object our needs, instincts, aspirations, ambitions, rather than God's Kingdom. Truly all these are hallowed, but it is by their subordination. The chief effect of grace is to give us that holy Lord and Master of whom I say so much, and the liberty only of those who are absolutely mastered by Him. It does not so much release our latent power as make us confess His. All the Churches complain of the difficulty of getting service rather than funds. It has also been complained that while recent worship does not omit the note of thanksgiving it lacks that of adoration. And it is worth considering whether one chief reason why religion does not produce more service, reverence, and godly fear, is that we have come to look on Christ and salvation as ministering to us, as chiefly there for our sakes, as for us first instead of for God and His holy Lordship. We become consumers of His mercy, rather than producers of His kingdom. We think of the kingdom of God only as man's *summum bonum*, as the consummation of his latent possibilities by God's help, as an order of things where we shall be secured and happy, instead of regarding it as the new creation of a personal relation and a purpose that we obey. How can we promote the spirit of service when we are wholly preoccupied by a religion of being served, when we cherish a God whose great worth is His value *to us* ? It is a conception which, when it gets the upper hand, puts man on a pedestal, and makes him the spoilt child of a doting God. How can it be otherwise if our very religion insists, in and out of season, that we are the objects of divine service rather than its subjects, and if we hear oftener that God is there to wait on us than that we are there to wait on God ? It may be said that we are called to be imitators of God as good children, and are therefore committed by a serving God to serve. But it is not found that a fond father who has no other idea but waiting on the pleasure or the advancement of his family is readily imitated by them in that respect, whether we take the old Lear or the modern Lear—Père Goriot. A Cross which is nothing but a revelation of divine sacrifice and service to us is an indulgent and demoralising Cross. It is a piece of indiscriminate charity. It makes sacrifice divine for its own sake, and descends till it canonises the most weak and wilful forms of sacrifice. It produces in the long run more egoists than imitators. The call to imitate a God who is solely a serving God will always be neutralised in the long run by the self-consequence generated in us by the notion of a God who has nothing to do but wait on man. If all His feeding, sheltering, and promoting of us be not there to make us the more absolute servants of His, it is not wonderful that the last product of Christianity should be a spiritual egoism which punishes its God by renouncing faith and refusing to worship Him, when He thinks it well to send us along the dolorous way. "Why should I praise Him if He do not prosper me?"

It is not ministering love that is the supreme Christian ideal, but holy love as forgiving love. Ministry is the outflowing love of the forgiven. When our religion ceases to be theocentric and becomes anthropocentric, it means the retirement of the holy. That means, farther, the decay both of the sense of guilt and of the sense of forgiveness; which then does not saturate our prayer, but is tucked in frequently as a decent after-thought at its close. And with the life-sense of forgiveness sinks Christian love, which is proportionate to the forgiveness, and is the spring of true sacrifice. The lack of the sense of sin, *i.e.* of the supremacy of the holy, means the lack of Christian love, the love most distinctively Christian; we lose therefore the note of Christian service and of the new Humanity. It is penitent faith that is the faith most truly and practically human at last. It is not the genial, liberal faith, but the evangelical and redeeming faith that serves Humanity most divinely and deeply. If we are not forgiven much we do not love much—as God prizes love.

The Kingdom, through a mistranslation,[1] has ob-

[1] "The Kingdom of God" will often yield a better sense if we say "the sovereignty of God."

scured the Lordship. It becomes a realm of fraternal love administered by God, instead of a realm of obedience, faith, and worship created by God. It becomes practically more of a fraternity than a kingdom. Very precious things may suffer from being so misplaced. Reparation takes the place of repentance, charm of grace, geniality of holiness. Sympathetic, cordial, brotherly men, of vague belief and human charm, may preoccupy us more than the holy and gracious Lord. He is in our theology, but they are in our religion. Fidelity dissolves in fascination, communion with the living God may be lost in a haze of Christian disposition; and our response to God is impressionist not moral—or, if it is moral, it is not the ethic of a new life but only of better conduct, a new way of life. "For us" takes precedence of "for God." So also it has become with the work of Christ. In such interpretation of it as we do give, the "for us" ousts almost entirely the "for God," the side which for Him was always uppermost. Ritschl, who made most of the *Werthurtheile*, does not recognise a real "for God" in Christ's work—the effect was but on us and for us. But the same thing has also happened in less degree with many who do admit some real atonement in Christ, but keep it for their theology rather than their prayers.

The idea of a God who is chiefly a God of value rather than of right and rule really canonises Humanity He is a "God for man." God is made to serve. We are not provided with a power over us but only in us. We have not a real ground provided of "man for God." Religion becomes gratitude rather than worship. And gratitude will not keep up service. Grace taken alone, taken as mere graciousness, might even become the servant of a moral and spiritual egoism. On the national scale this was the vice of Judaism. The pride

THEOCENTRIC RELIGION

and confidence which broke Israel did not rest simply on the nation's pride in its good works, but on its call by God's grace. The race was rooted and grounded in this grace. It rested on circumcision, the law, and all the sacraments that came freely and graciously from God, and pledged its troth with Him. God's grace gave Israel such a pre-eminence in the world that the nation held itself to be indispensable to His purpose, however bad and impenitent it might be. That is, the grace was severed from the holiness of God. It was not the pagan pride of achievement that wrecked Israel, but the religious pride of an elect of grace. What precipitated the disaster of the Exile was an overweening confidence that God's grace would never leave Zion nor permit an invader's foot on it. And a similar idea wrecked Israel for good and all at last. Their grace was perverted from God's holiness to feed their religious egoism. Hence the central thing Christ had to do was not simply to convey grace but to secure its holiness. And the religious vice of Humanism, when Humanism is religious at all, is Israel's vice raised to the universal scale. Humanity tends to think itself indispensable to God's holy purpose, whereas it is God's holy purpose that is indispensable to Humanity. The development of moral, and even spiritual, personality, though it were on the scale of the race, is not the one goal of society; and if we make even that the one direct object in life, for which all the grace of God is to be used, and which we are always thinking about, we become prigs, potterers with our own moral perfection, artists in sanctification, and *virtuosi* of virtue. We can really develop our spiritual personality at last only by thinking about it less, and by being preoccupied with the realisation and confession of God's holy personality. The object of ethics is the development of personality, but the object of religion is the kingdom and communion of a holy God, which is the only means of securing, through a new creation, a personality worth developing at last.

Ever since the Reformation there has been this danger of its personal religion developing into spiritual egoism. We have had forms of Christianity intensely craving for peace, or for some ultra-subjective holiness, or some individual certainty, and *arrested on these things*. Even in our deep confession of sin the Ego may preoccupy the attention and honour due to God. We may come to think we repent best when we brood almost to madness on some deadly sin instead of dwelling on that loving holiness of God in our salvation whose worship and communion alone are well pleasing in His sight. There is such a thing also as egocentric renunciation and selfish self-sacrifice. "Work, serve, it will do you good." We may serve men with an eye on the main chance of reflexive benefit to our soul. We may have a God Who is only our helper and consoler in domestic and business affairs, Who sanctifies our human ties with boon and balm, Who guarantees our eternal happiness —a tutelary God, a God who only consecrates our natural affections and affairs, so that the soul dreams to the evening flute and is dead to the last trump, a bourgeois God, pent in the family pew. Is that not one peril of the Protestantism which took God out of the monastery, and infused Him into the relations of life? It is the danger that God, and Christ, and Kingdom, are apt to be reduced to means for securing the single or family Ego either in a condition of prosperity, a mood of peace, or a state of perfection. Or they may serve but for the stoic fortification of the moral soul against the onset of the world, or for the consecration and consolidation of natural society. But what saves us from religious egoism is our spiritual service to the Kingdom—the

THEOCENTRIC RELIGION 433

Kingdom which is really God's personal lordship, with a lien upon all natural relations. And all our humanising of God, and our preaching of brotherly help, will not bring about anything but a laborious *corvée* instead of Christian service, unless the very soul of our faith is God *the Lord*, Christ *the Lord*. Our salvation must be grasped as salvation into that Lordship, with its life-passion of absolute obedience and reconciled communion, whether in having or losing every friend, lover, or possession beside.

Let me approach the matter from another side. When we speak of God as God to us because of His value to us, is there not an ambiguity which may far mislead us?

1. We may rightly mean a God Who makes His way with us through impression and not pressure, through our joyful and reasonable consent and not by sheer power—a sympathetic and not a domineering God—a moral God, and not a nature God—a God Who satisfies us, as moral response and obedience does satisfy the soul and give it peace.

2. Or we may wrongly mean a God Whose grand concern must be those ideal interests of Humanity which seem at the moment supreme—and Who is exploitable to that end, a God Who is valuable only in so far as desirable—a contributory, propitious, auxiliary, ancillary God.

Now the radical difference between natural and supernatural religion is involved in this difference between the two senses of the word value. Of course there is a region below either, where there is no religion, because the notion of value does not come in at all. God is not in all their thoughts—except perhaps as a vast power in the dim background, with which they have nothing to do till it sweep over them in death. He has no value for them. But if there be

2 E

some religion, some real reference to God, then it is either to a God available for man or to a God prevailing over man ; to God as an ally or God as a Lord ; to a God with the value of utility, or a God with the value of royalty ; to a God valuable as serving and helping man's ideals, or to a God valuable as being of intrinsic dignity, and commanding and using man thereto ; to a tutelary God or a sovereign God. Religion, then, is either an alliance or an obedience, with God as either a Colleague or a King of Humanity, the predominant Partner or the absolute Master.

Now to a great mass, even of Christian people, it is to be feared the value of God is but as tutelary or auxiliary. But the true Christian idea of God is not what is found in the experience even of the majority, but in the classic experience of the elect—especially in that of the Apostles and saints, under the grace of Jesus Christ.

If, then, we turn to such experience, what do we find?

At the present moment great and fruitful attention is given to the psychology of religion, and especially to that of conversion—where a belief in conversion remains, and is not ousted by the belief that we are born good, and only need to grow. We have all been attending to the fascinating book of the late Professor William James on the "Varieties of Religious Experience," including the psychology of conversion. But I have pointed out that it is a principle in a wider philosophy of religion than James's that we ought chiefly to examine the psychology of the converted experience from within and not from without, with the knowledge and sympathy of one who has gone through it. The only direct object of religious inquiry is the religion of the inquirer. All religion is subjective in the mode of its approach to us, however objective that is which approaches. And it is quite inadequate to apply to such a matter the

THEOCENTRIC RELIGION 435

methods of a psychology merely objective and observatory—like the statistics of Starbuck or the analysis of James. We cannot understand religious experience unless we have it, unless we understand its *truth*. What the psychologists tell us is that there is in conversion a powerful eruption into light of the subliminal consciousness. No doubt that may be so phenomenally and empirically in many cases. That is what an observer would see in the creature under his lens. And he sees (if we may vary the image) that the whole aspect of the surface is changed, and permanently changed, by the lava of that eruption. If we go no farther we are apt to get the notion that conversion is after all but a subjective convulsion, in which the hidden interior of the soul is flung mysteriously and permanently to the surface, and that is all. And when these psychological works are read by curious people who have no real experience of religion as the life of their life, or who are the voracious victims of their last book, they very easily come to think of conversion as a mere subjectivity, a phenomenon, abnormal, morbid, febrile, or even corybantic ; or, at least, they may think of it as a raw and crude stage of subjective religion, which we grow ashamed of in course, and which must disappear as religion becomes more educated and mature. Or perhaps they take another line, and they are led to think that the deepest and truest union with God is to be pursued in the direction of the subconscious (but still subjective), amid the darkling, mystic, and monistic recesses of our being, in an impersonal and non-moral region where all the gnostic occultisms lie in wait for the soul. They may even find there the key to the union of God and man in Christ, or at least the place where the key is hidden. Whereas the principle of the Gospel, of a historic Redeemer for the *conscience*, is this—that it is in the exercise of our highest and most conscious personality, in the region of moral conflict, choice, and change that we reach the secret and communion of the God of Christ and the Cross.

But is the convert such a victim of commotion and obsession that he has no voice equal to his observer's in this matter? Nay, indeed, his voice weighs most. And his mature account of the matter from within goes far beyond what I have named. He is not simply turning himself inside out, or bottom side up. It is not a somersault, and not a mere upheaval. For him it is not simply a new experience of unprecedented force. Were that all, it would simply be a deeper and more insurgent self-assertion than ever before. It is an experience which affects his whole life—both his way of judging his past, his way of disposing his present, and his of way expecting and ensuring his future. And it introduces a new power, not himself. It is a new creation; and self-creation is absurd. It affects him so much because he (who knows it best) knows that it is much more than a terrestrial convulsion (so to say). It is much more than a subjective explosion. It is much more than the conversion of a subliminal consciousness into a sublime. The thing that matters is not the experience, nor even the subject himself; not the experience but its occupant, not the whirlwind but its rider. It is an invasion of the man's whole sphere by God. Within the earthquake is His voice. The experience is produced by God. It is not volcanic but celestial at bottom. Its deep foundations are laid in heaven. It is God that announces Himself to the man, and not his own interior.

If that be denied, he has no more to say; argument ends; for religion as Christian faith is an ultimate, a creation—a last judgment and a new creation. The experience is not a mere thrill or commotion. It has a content. There is a moral power moving in it, and a voice speaking which removes the convert beyond

THEOCENTRIC RELIGION

man's judgment or challenge. What the man realises is not himself in a new mode of experience, but a God, holy and not merely immanent, Who comes to him in and through that experience. At the lowest it is a power not himself that emerges in it, a power greater and better than himself, and a power that would do him good. It is a tremendous addition to his own life. He has got an immense subsidy and even ally in this new Suzerain. He receives power to be himself against his lower self, against the whole world. He acquires new and infinite value in his own eyes, not because he is deepened in soul, but because he is loved; not because he knows more, but because he is utterly known; not because he rests on subliminal depths, but because he is called and borne to celestial heights. He is so set on his feet that he can stand, and walk, and even run, and sometimes fly. He is changed, besides. What has invaded him is not only an energy but a value. It does not only press on him, or through him; it enhances and transforms him. It is not only mighty but auxiliary, not only full of force but of blessing. It is there to give him to himself, to make the spiritual most of him, to develop his best nature by the new nature's gift. And it does the same on the scale also of the whole race.

But even that is not all. Nor is it most. That is but the beginning. The mighty power which announced itself as blessing announces itself with the same voice as ruling, judging, creating. He not only serves and saves; He exacts and commands. He is not only love, He is holy love. He appears with a right which we have been flouting or impugning. The more religious the man grows, and the more he reads his experience in the religious light, the more he finds that the supreme value in the precious power that has seized him is a value not of mere assistance, but of obligation; a value not of force, but of right; a value which not only aids him, and lifts him, but judges him, condemns him, leaves him forfeit, yet claims him—and takes possession of a new creature. It not only blesses but uses him, gives him not only a freedom, but more—an obedience; not only works conspicuous among other powers, but takes command of them all, and triumphs over the man and all the resources in him or around him. God is then valuable not only as desirable but as imperative— as an imperative Who judges our desires. The supreme value then felt in God is not His utility. If He slew us we should praise His holy name. It is a question not of His utility to us but of ours to Him, not of His service to us but His right and glory over us. Our repentance is not merely seemly or salutory for our soul; it still more justifies our holy Judge, glorifies our loving Saviour, and confesses our absolute Lord. His greatest mercy is not in sparing us but in seeking and accepting our praise and service. His last word to the soul is not only " I save," but " I claim." It is not simply " I am yours," but still more " You are mine "; and mine not for caress but for worship and obedience. It is less a fond love than a faithful that he seeks. The new power a man receives in conversion is not balance, nor moral symmetry, nor self-realisation. All that is finely Hellenic and nobly pagan, but pagan still. The gift is not chiefly the power to be his full self but to be God's, not chiefly to expand and be free but to surrender and obey, the power of the Incarnate to shrink, die, grow and prevail —all in one great Eternal life-act, to which God does not only move but makes human nature move. The final meaning of conversion is not deliverance merely, but surrender and service to the uttermost. Justification is meaningless without sanctification in the same act. Forgiveness is but the negative side of the gift of Eternal Life. The God of absolute

THEOCENTRIC RELIGION

deliverance is also the holy God of an absolute demand that will not let us go. The One God does nothing by halves. If He is One, He is actively One, He is the Unifier always, and the Reconciler, the Perfecter. So that if He wholly frees us, He wholly claims us and remakes. But He demands nothing which was not involved in our redemption, nothing for which He did not give power when He saved us. The demands of the Kingdom can only be met by the children of the Spirit. The unbroken young Stoic says, with a fine moral pride which is sure sooner or later to have its fall: "When duty whispers low 'Thou must,' the soul replies, 'I can.'" But the action of the Spirit is the other way. God first turns a man's sense of values upside down. He shows him that what nature puts first, grace puts second, if not last. He shows him that he is a profitless servant. He teaches a man to put duty, righteousness, first, and the purest pleasure, second, or tenth, or twentieth. He comes in aid of the new moral ideals. And then, when much failure has shown a man that a divine ideal cannot be reached by God's help merely, but only by God's new creation, not by the old man subsidised but by the new man made in Christ, when the demand of God has become, by the way it was met for us in Christ's Cross, a source of new life and not of crushing obligation—then he comes to say I can do all things through Christ. Then also, and then only, he comes to say "I must." And duty whispers low "I must" when grace has said "I can." The Stoic says in strength "I must, therefore I can"; the Christian says in grace, "I can, and therefore must. The new power I have is given me by a God who claims it again in my surrendered, adoring, and serviceable soul. By God's grace I feel a new power—to do what? To develop all the best in me? No, that is making God my tributary. But to put myself and all He has made me at His absolute disposal, whether He make much of me or not ; to seek first the Kingdom of God and His righteousness." The *must* of the old conscience, which was always being flouted by the natural man till we were in a state of miserable civil war, is fructified anew. It can now take effective command of the natural man. That is the true moralising of religion. Conversion is a moral experience at bottom. It is the enthronement of the holy "must," and not simply the emancipation of the human "can."

To moralise religion is to make it personal as the Reformation did, and yet to rescue it from the subjectivity of Modernism and its collective egoism. And, however truly the empirical psychologists may describe conversion as the upcast of an underground reservoir, the religious experience, when it gives a matured and considered account of itself, goes beyond the mere method to the nature of the transaction. It says that it is the visitation of God. It is an invasion even of the subliminal. God came to the soul before it came to itself, and its darkness and its light, its subliminal or its conscious, are both alike to Him. And He came not as its servant (its Jesus) nor as its ideal (its Christ), but as its *Lord* and very God. What we really get in our conversion is not only a Saviour but a Sovereign. So many converted lives go wrong and relapse because their conversion has not given them a Sovereign but only a Saviour. And the Christian life is not only gratitude for blessing received, but absolute obedience to a claim that we must own as holy just and good, whether we feel it is our blessing or not. Christ felt no blessing on the blessed Cross. But, on the other hand, He did much more than endure to the end. He never saved the world by mere endurance or perseverance. He obeyed absolutely, when every human reason for obedience was gone, and there remained only a reason entirely private to Father and Son and to their knowledge and trust of each other in the face of all that man or nature had done or could do against Almighty and All-holy grace.

There are many to-day, though fewer than yesterday, whose hopes for religion are fixed upon such a revision of Christian doctrine as shall make it more welcome to the mind of the age. But infection from the age is one of the weaknesses and dangers of current Christianity. And what is more urgent for religion as well as more potent than a change in creed is a change in the religious type, in the direction of the soul's movement, however it is to come about. The Church needs to recover not now from an Orthodoxy but from a Subjectivism in its spiritual cast and ideal, which, having lost the objective power that Orthodoxy did have, runs out into spiritual softness; and being subjective and therefore problematical, is not authoritative, and has no firm hand to lay on the age's passion, and no firm footing to stay its wavering doom.

"Erit igitur veritas, etiamsi intereat mundus."

EPILOGUE

EPILOGUE

I

MAN is not man by his power rightly to reason, so much as by his destiny duly to obey. The question is grave enough at any time, but with the bond of control so relaxed as to-day it is ; with the traditional creeds and sanctities so shaken ; with the public mind so hungry and yet so poor, so interested and yet so distracted upon final problems ; with the rising generation tutored in independence till, in an evil sense, the child is father of the man ; and with the rising classes so ignorant of responsibility, affairs, history, or human nature—it is a question more urgent than ever. Criticism has established its own right ; so far so good ; but is Christianity, is anything, left by it with any positive authority ? And the inquiry is all the more urgent the less it is felt to press amid the multitude of problems, passing and passionate, which fills an outworn age trying to narcotise with mere energies its moral fatigue.

The question will not bear to be lightly handled. It is deeply implicated in the nature of human progress ; and the law of progress is that from the great deep to the great deep it goes. Only quackery assures us that, as we move onward, the answers to the great questions grow more simple, and that the litterateur is now, by the spirit of the age, in a better position to deal with the old enigmas than the philosopher or the historian. Simplicity is not the test of truth. It is not the badge of progress. The simple solutions are the most suspicious. There is much preaching of simplicity which is no more than a sop to spiritual indolence. The immediate affections are indeed always divinely simple. But to transfer these affections to the object of worship and the ground of existence, either without more ado or on the word of some saintly soul ; to say that it is one of life's first and clearest simplicities to think of the ultimate reality as Father, and trust Him as sons—is to trifle with the subject and with the heart. It is no sign of real progress to settle to-day by the prompt intuition of a genial but impatient heart questions which have taxed on a time the greatest intelligences of religion and of the race. The doves have indeed got into the eagles' nest when pulpit poets, with more taste for abstractions than faculty for reality, can blandly close questions which Jonathan Edwards had much ado to stir.

It is in the region of theology that this greatest of questions must be fought out. It is there that all such questions must be decided, if they are admitted to be real questions at all. And in the region of Protestant theology this must be admitted. For the question is hardly real, it is but leisurely and academic, in a Church whose decision has been, ever since Duns Scotus, an ecclesiastical positivity in default of a rational or evangelical base.

But it will be said, on the other hand, that even in Protestantism the question can hardly be real, because in Protestant theology there can be no real authority since the collapse of Scriptural infallibility. Any authority that may be set up is so inward and so subjective that it quickly becomes individualist, modish, and decadent. And thus (it is said) theology here becomes no science of reality, but merely a science of religious phenomenology. It may discuss the idea of God as it appears in psychology and

EPILOGUE

history, but it has nothing final to say on the reality of God or Gospel. We may explore and admire the consciousness of Christ so far, but we are in no position to say anything authoritative about His Gospel. We may own (it is said) the extraordinary spiritual influence of His person, but we cannot dogmatise about His work. The only thing approaching finality in Christianity is the Spirit of Christ. And "the Spirit is the emanation of His consciousness" (Sabatier). Under that influence we find rest, so men speak. But is it more than rest we find there? Is it footing? Is it more than a mood, a lenitive for life? Is it reality? Is it life itself?

In a brief compass one can do little more than state, in reply to such remarks, that for Protestant theology the authority is not so much the historic, or the ideal, or the spiritual Christ as the moral, holy, historic Gospel of the grace of God in and through Him and His Cross. It is not Christ as mere historic figure, as ideal symbol, or as spiritually infectious, but Christ as Redeemer.

Protestant theology is founded upon authority as much as Catholic. It starts from something given. It is not the discovery of new truth so much as the unfolding of old grace. Christian truth is as unchangeable in its being as it is flexible in its action. Surely this is so. Surely Christian truth *is* something fixed. It is not just what every man troweth. Individualism there is mental anarchy. There must be authority. And by authority is meant something outside our personal opinion, will, vision, inclination, or taste. It is something which takes a place we never give. It imposes itself on us. It comes with power. It compels submission and obedience as the condition of weal, order, and progress. One form of it is essential to family life, another to civic life. Another is the source of all salvation. It is so in our personal religion. Faith is meaningless without an object, that is, an authority. Everything there turns on the obedience of faith to faith's authority. Is our theology, then, to have a different foundation from our faith? Is faith submission to a positive God, but theology so detached from faith, as to be submission to nothing?—is it mere opinion? What scepticism, what a fatal schism in our soul and creed that would be! Again, a Church must have an authority of some kind (even if it be no higher than the authority of a majority). But if theology own no authority, the two fall hopelessly apart, just as they would if theology had an authority but the Church had none.

"But," it will be persisted, "if theology have an authority it can never be a science. For science is absolutely free, and with an authority that is in contradiction. A free science owns no authority?" Except, of course, the authority of the facts it founds on; to say nothing of the axiom that we can trust our faculties. "Oh yes, of course, that is different." But is it different? Is it not the very point? Theology founds on certain historic facts, on the one revealed fact of a gracious God in particular. It founds on a fact with a particular nature and power—on Christ and His Cross, and the action of the Cross—as chemistry might found on the qualities and effects of things. The authority in theology is not external to the matter it works in. It is spiritual. It is inherent in the fontal fact, and connate to the soul. It belongs to the revelation itself as such, and not to any voucher which the revelation created, like a book or a church. It is an authority objective to us in its source, but subjective in its nature and appeal.

If we are not sure and clear about an authority for

faith or thought, we can have neither Church nor theology. But if faith has no Church, it has no contact, no affinity, with society, and so religion is hostile to humanity. And if it has no theology, it has no relation with science. Religion is then even hostile to science, because a science of our religion is impossible. No religion is friendly to science if it disown a science of itself. The fundamental relation of faith to science does not depend on its attitude to physical science, or even to philosophy, but on its capacity for a science of itself. A religion that despises a theology declares war on science in the act. We may of course shut our eyes and abjure any interest in theology. Instead of regarding it as a precious gift of God, and a necessary element in a great Church and culture, we may look on it with amused but vulgar patience as the hobby of certain maundering minds, impractical and ineffectual. We may choose the better part, as we think, and bury our heads in the sand of practical activity. But practical activity, though a supreme function of a Church, is a poor foundation. To found on it looks plausible, and wears the air of Christian business. But it is of Philistia, not of Israel. And it has no stay. The Churches with a theology must carry the day. No theology, no Church; and no Church, no kingdom.

Protestant theology is as much dependent upon authority as Catholic, but the form of it is different. We have something over our thought as commanding in its nature as the Church or Pope is for Catholicism—nay, more so. The great matter in Catholicism is Christian truth, Christian doctrine, Christian system. That is really its supreme object of faith. Faith means assent to certain truths supernaturally conveyed and guaranteed. They were conveyed by a revelation which included the standing guarantee of an infallible Church. Revelation is the supernatural donation of theological dogma, secured for all time by a Church fixed at Rome. Faith, of course, is always the answer to revelation, and corresponds to its nature and source; and here it is the acceptance of revealed truths from the Church as their responsible voucher. The Church takes the responsibility for them, and takes it off each member. So faith of that kind really means faith in the Church, and acceptance of its absolute authority. And wherever revelation is understood to consist of a body of truth we have the Catholic habit of mind, and, in the long run, the Catholic result in the way of Church and Pope. There is much of it in circles violently anti-popish. The enmity is a family quarrel. Orthodoxy means intellectualism. And as most people are not intellectual enough to deal with such truths for themselves, this means that they must leave them to experts. And Romanism is simply the greatest apotheosis on earth of the expert, the specialist, and his dominion. It deifies [1] the specialist in sacramental grace and truth.

But orthodoxy is foreign to the genius of Protestantism, where the supreme matter is not dogma but grace, and grace understood as the Gospel, as God's redeeming act in history, and not His sacramental action under nature. It is a revelation, not to one side of the man, the intellect which grasps truth, nor to the subliminal man whose defective substance needs a sacramental food or drug, but to the whole moral man, whose need is forgiveness, redemption, and power. It claims from him a different kind of obedience from Rome's, namely, faith in the sense of personal conviction, personal surrender, and personal

---

[1] In the Roman catechism the priests are described as *sicut dii*, pars ii., cap. vii., quest ii.

EPILOGUE

trust in a gracious God. It is an obedience of personal response, not of assent. It offers up the man as a will, and not as a mind. Faith becomes really religious. It means an acceptance of grace, not as the sacramental capital of the Church, but as mercy, forgiveness, and redemption in a definitive act of God which enters our experience because it is *ejusdem generis*. The authority is neither primal truth, developed dogma, nor chartered institution, but this act, power, and person with whom we have direct dealings. It is the Gospel in the Cross, conceived as the moral word and deed of God, and not as any human version or report of it.

The see-saw of the old supernaturalism and rationalism is interminable, because both started from the same fallacy, that the content of revelation is truth as statement or doctrine. The one found it in the Bible, which demanded acceptance through an external guarantee of prophecy and miracle; the other found it in the reason, which guaranteed truths not necessarily different from Bible truth, but held on a different ground. It was really a question of the religious authority, vitiated in its discussion by the notion, still popular and fatal, that religion is a thing of beliefs rather than of faith and revelation, a matter of truth rather than grace. Both sides were enmeshed in the intellectualist conception of religion. And supernaturalism fell (as it always must fall) before rationalism, through the contradiction that the Gospel was essentially a doctrine while yet it was withdrawn from the criticism of the understanding. The whole discussion enters another plane when we leave the intellectualist and perceptual notion of revelation behind us, and escape from the doctrinaire forms of religion to a religion of spiritual, ethical, and personal relations; when we transcend classic forms of belief, and give scope to the romantic claims of direct feeling and original experience ; when the fixity of an initial system gives way to the results of historical inquiry both as to the absoluteness of the original revelation in Christ's person and as to the relativity of its subsequent course in the Church's thought. A conception of authority is reached which not only allows criticism but demands it—which is indeed the true nature of the Reformation as the action of the self-corrective and self-preservative spirit of the Gospel. The absoluteness of Christianity is to be sought only in its Gospel of grace : treated as the historic act of God for man's moral destiny and not for his scheme of truth. The antithesis of supernaturalism and rationalism goes out of date in its old form. The Gospel is no less critical of the past than creative of the future. The revelation in the Cross of God's holiness is equally a revelation of critical judgment and of creative grace.

There is then no authority for mere theological knowledge or statement. There are doctrines of salvation, but no saving doctrines. In a strict use of words, there is no such thing as saving truth. No machine ever sat or sits minting and issuing it as the one lawful currency for the Christian mind or the means of purchase for spiritual food. And no formal gift of it was ever made to man, and put in the Church's charge to keep undefiled. For the Protestant authority exists not in the theological form of dogma or statement, but in the evangelical form of historical grace, which is the soul and power of revelation. It is an authority truly religious. Our supreme good is not knowledge, not correct doctrine (which is a pagan perversion of Christianity caused by Greece, and loaded with intellectual pride). It is a moral thing, and essentially holy. It means more than a mystic union with the divine. It is the practical obedience and penitent response of faith in the historic grace

EPILOGUE 453

of Christ to the conscience. The Christian Gospel is an authority for the will, in the will's sphere of history; it is not for the intellect—except in so far as the intellect depends on the will. It is an authority which is felt primarily as living moral majesty, not as truth—as Christ was felt, not as the Scribes. That is, it is morally realised, not mentally; personally, not officially; ethically, and not æsthetically, not contemplatively. It is for conscience, not for thought, in the first place, nor for imagination. It so settles the whole moral man that in the region of truth there is entire flexibility and freedom. We have the liberty in that region which rests on final confidence and security in the moral region. Certainty of living faith in grace gives us liberty of thought in truth. To be sure, doctrine is implicit and integral to Christianity, but it is not supreme. Christ comes full of grace and truth, but with the grace uppermost and always central. Grace represents the fixed, fontal, authoritative, evangelical element; truth, the element free, adjustable, and catholic. The one appeals to our personal life-conviction, the other to our scientific judgment. We own the authority of grace by impression and not perception, by conviction and not observation, by regeneration and not recantation, by life and not by thought. It is in personal relation with us. It is the authority in it that breeds the knowledge, the science, the theology. It is not the knowledge that is the ground of the authority; it is the authority that is the ground of the knowledge (though, of course, in the empirical order of time, the knowledge may come first). There is assent as well as trust; but the *fiducia* precedes the *assensus*, and produces it freely. The freedom that is worth most to Christian theology is not free thought but a free soul. It is not cosmic and rational, but ethical, vital, evangelical. It is not the freedom of the world's organised harmony, but the freedom of Christ's reconciliation, of free and freeing grace.

It is one of the fundamental mistakes we make about our own Protestantism to say that the authority is the conscience, and the Christian conscience in particular. Not so. The authority is nothing in us, but something in history. It is something given us. What is in us only recognises it. And the conscience which now recognises it has long been created by it. The conscience recognises the tone of injunction, but what is enjoined is given by history, and has passed into the historic consciousness. We have the inner intuition of what is really a great historic teleology. But it is not gathered up from all history by an induction, which, as history is far from finished, could never give us anything final or authoritative. It is defined in it at a fixed point by faith in the experienced revelation of final purpose within God's act of Gospel there. The authority is not the conscience, but it is offered to it. The conscience of God is not latent in our conscience, but revealed to it in history. It is history centred in Christ, it is not conscience, that is the real court of morals. And it is there accordingly that we find the authority for Christian faith and Christian theology, for faith and theology both. It is the glory of Protestantism that we have the same source and standard for both in the grace of God. That is the historic spring of both, and the constant life and measure of both. We have an external authority which is not foreign to the soul, yet not native to it. It is not so much mystic at the heart of man's depths; it is historic in the midst of man's career. Our theology rests on no other foundation than our religion. Our religion rests on a theological fact and its nature.

There is but one thing that corresponds to all the

EPILOGUE

conditions of an authority : that is ethical, revealed, historic, personal, synthetic, and for ever miraculous to natural thought. There is one thing powerful over us for ever, because, though morally intelligible, it is for ever marvellous and inexplicable, beyond discovery, the very soul and essence of revelation. It is the creative grace of God toward human sin in Jesus Christ and His holy Atonement. This is intelligible to no reason. It is for ever amazing. It is only taken home by living faith to moral need. It is the moral core and reality of the Gospel—the thing that saves Christianity from the sentimentalism and rationalism and unreality that so easily beset it through the stimulus it brings to heart and mind. Grace is not irrational in the sense of being foreign to reason, but it is not in the reason of it that its authority resides. There is nothing which is such a surprise, such a permanent surprise, and such a growing surprise to reason as grace ; yet it is in the act and agent of grace that our moral experience finds authority at its final source, however seldom that source is visited by the soul or the society grace controls.

It has been said, " All that is absolute in the natural conscience is the sense of obligation. ' You *must* do what is right.' Yes, but it does not tell us what is right. That is the judgment of the reason according to circumstances. The real conscience of the conscience is the Gospel. This not only brings absolute obligation but absolute right and truth. It not only satisfies the natural conscience, its forerunner, but it opens to it a new world, it provides a new ideal and standard which it guarantees as the final reality. It reveals in the conscience new needs, and raises it to appreciate the moral value and right of a doctrine like Atonement, which to its natural light seemed strange and incredible " (note in Bertrand's *Redemption*, p. 494). Yes, apart from His revelation of His own moral nature there is absolutely no reason why God should forgive and redeem men. All the reason we know, apart from His own revelation of Himself and His purpose, is against it. There is nothing we have less natural reason to expect, except in so far as reasonable expectation has been coloured by the foregone revelation itself in the course of history. There is nothing, moreover, that so far passes human power as to forgive, in the deep, real, ultimate, divine sense of the word. As a revelation, grace is absolutely synthetic. It unites what it was beyond man's power to unite—sin, love, holiness, and judgment; and it unites them for ever in endless beauty and power, in the one object of faith and source of human morals—the Cross of Jesus Christ as the spring of the New Humanity.

The grace of God in the historic Cross of Christ must be the one source of morals and seal of authority for a race that is redeemed or nothing, redeemed or lost. The greatest fact in social ethics is also the most formidable and intractable; it is the fact of sin and the sense of guilt. All morals are academic which fail to recognise this—the real royalty of the moral, its actual wreck, and its imperative redemption. Whoever masters that fact of sin masters the conscience, and so, through the primacy of the moral, the whole of human life. The Redeemer from moral death is the seat of final authority for a moral humanity. Anything we believe about Incarnation, anything we glorify in it, springs from our faith in Redemption. Our final moral standard is the Gospel of the Cross with its ethical restitution of things, its restoration of all things from our moral centre. It was the eternal and immutable morality of holiness that was effectually established there for history and for ever.

There are ultimately no ethics, therefore, but

EPILOGUE 457

theological. The natural conscience, were it accessible, would certainly be an object of scientific interest. But, strictly speaking (as has already been hinted), in civilised communities to-day it does not exist. It is a mere abstraction of thought. What does exist is a historic product, deeply, permanently, and universally moulded by the Christian ethic of sin and redemption which for two thousand years has been shaping European morals. The authority that lifts its head in the individual conscience rises in an area which is never found detached, but always closing a long historical development, whose influence we may feel in weight more than we can measure in extent. Every conscience we interrogate has this long social history for its *prius*, and, indeed, its progenitor. And the solemnity of the moral world within each of us is the accumulated and condensed sanctity of centuries of belief, ages of conscience, and millions of wills bowed before the holy order and urgency which wakes human faith, or, if we break with it, makes human tragedy. What the historic student of the actual situation has to count with is either the Christian conscience in more or less definite form, or some reaction from it more or less indebted to it.

For practical purposes, upon the scale of all human life and of the whole, passionate, actual soul, we must deal with the evangelical conscience shaped by faith in the grace of God redeeming in Jesus Christ. That is the true and typical human conscience as things are. Sin is not an influence which affects but a sectional conscience, or troubles but a few members of the race. In so far as it is real at all, it affects and vitiates the whole conscience, the whole man, that is, and the whole race in its moral aspect and reliability. That follows from the unity of personality and of the race, from our solidarity. There is no such thing as a natural conscience giving the normal material for ethics, with a redemptive provision of a supplementary, religious, and corrective kind for those abnormal cases that have erred and strayed. In so far as ethical science proceeds on such a basis it is meagre and scholastic, and draws too little on the tragic, volitional, and religious experience in history for an adequate or sympathetic account of human nature. For the actual moral life of the race as we find it to our hand forgiveness has the place of a constitutive principle, and not of an accident or supplement.

Redemption, taken in earnest, is critically constructive for the whole man and for all men. It is the divine judgment acting as re-creation. It is not a mere contribution to the future, but its one condition, not to say creation. It makes a new conscience for the race, with an authority seated in the source of the new creation—in the grace and Gospel of God in Christ's Cross. The principles of the new and normal conscience are drawn from the nature of that Cross, from its moral theology, from its revelation of holiness, and not from any intuitions of natural goodness, or even of Christian piety. If (by such an admission as Huxley's) it is only by something in the nature of a miracle that humane ethics arise out of cosmic order and reverse the machinery, it is but lifting the statement to a higher plane by historic sense when we say that the conscience of the new race rests on the moral miracle in the Cross. And it is but a corollary of the same when we say that it is in the Forgiver and Redeemer of the Cross that the seat of moral, and so of all, authority for the renovated race must be found. The holy is the real. The ethics of the realist future must be the explication of the holiness revealed and effected with absolute cruciality for the race in the Cross; and the obedience of the future must be to the Christ of the Cross. The holy is the final moral authority. And the supreme

EPILOGUE

revelation of the holy is in the harmonised judgment and grace of the Cross, at once critical and creative for the whole of society. The faith which answers that and is made by it is the moral marrow of the race. The seat of authority coincides with the seat of the Gospel. It has always been where mankind found the power of God; and it must increasingly be where sinful man finds the power of a holy God for eternal salvation. And experience finds this but in Christ and in His Cross, in the victories achieved thereby in our own life, and the conquests gathered from the evangelisation thereby of the world.

For all ethics drawn from real life the great human soul is lamed and doomed by the malady of sin. We struggle not only with misfortune nor with fate, but with some curse. And the total and ultimate moral situation of the race is thus not moral only, but religious. The malady and the remedy are religious both. The Lord of the race is not simply the genius of excellence, nor " a self-transcending goodness," even when that goodness is viewed as a personal ideal. He is a Redeemer, who not only *embodies* goodness for our gaze, but *enacts* it for our salvation ; who not only startles us with the wonder and love of our ideal selves, but *intervenes* with His goodness in redemptive action as the only condition of our power to fulfil ourselves, appreciate His revelation, or share His life ; who not only reveals His kingdom, but *establishes* it in moral reality for ever with a spiritual finality historically perfectible.

But He is especially King and Lord when we realise *how* He became Redeemer, and what is the nature of His saving act. His authority does not rest simply on our grateful sense of the fact. That experience is too subjective and unstable for a seat of authority spiritual, absolute, and eternal. It is not simply that He produces on us the æsthetic impression of one in whom all human goodness foreruns itself, and all the soul's moral future is set forth by anticipation as an ideal to man and a pledge to God. It is not alone that we are melted and mastered by the spectacle of His grace. The seat of His eternal authority is neither in our wonder, fascination, nor gratitude. He rules neither as ideal nor as helper. His throne has a deeper and more objective base. By his personal act of holiness in a universal crisis He honoured for us that holy law which our worst sin could never unseat, against which the most titanic human defiance breaks in vain. He even becomes for us that self-satisfying law. He has taken over in His person all the lien held upon our conscience by all the moral order of the world, all the holy righteousness of God. By His perfect obedience, His acceptance of holy judgment, His perfect fulfilment and satisfaction of God's holiness. He is identified with it. He becomes the reversionary, therefore, of all its claims upon the race. By His perfect satisfaction [1] of God's holiness, He becomes the trustee of it for God among men. Because He took man's judgment He became man's judge. There is a close inner unity between sacrifice and judgment. "The saints shall judge the earth"; and the saints are such by their relation to divine sacrifice. The supreme sacrifice is in principle the final judgment, and the supreme victim the last judge. He who absorbed the curse and dissipated it acquires the monopoly of human blessing. And He who met the whole demand of holiness with His person becomes the law's Lord, in as much as holiness is above mere righteousness. So by the objective nature, and not by the mere impress, of His work for us He becomes

---

[1] By satisfaction is meant no equivalency of penalty, but adequacy of practical recognition. The idea is qualitative and not quantitative.

EPILOGUE

our King—the conscience of the conscience, Himself the living and holy law which is our moral ultimate. He is thus the fountain of moral honour, and the centre of moral authority, for ever and for all. He would indeed be supreme if our orderly moral nature were only constituted in Him; He is more profoundly and vitally supreme because our disordered nature is in Him redeemed. And this line of thought will be the more confirmed as the Christian psychology of the future explores the subjective experience and sets forth in fresh light the nature of the new creation.

It is easy to anticipate an objection which arises to the line of thought here pursued. It is an objection too congenial to the spirit of the age to be easily overlooked; indeed, no one is quite equipped for dealing with this whole subject if it has not arisen in his own thoughts, and been not only laid as a spectre of the mind but fought as a recalcitrancy of the will. There is a tendency to dwell in a region where it seems narrow to personalise, immodest to define, and overbold to be as positive or ethical about spiritual process as a word like redemption implies. There are few who have not felt at least the germs of that common reluctance to submit thought to the personal category, and will to a personal control. And there are many, not unspiritual, who never overcome their repugnance to accepting redemption as the fundamental note of the religious and moral life. Redemption in their case, like personality in the case of others, seems to imply a limitation of thought and an archaism of belief. It claims in the Redeemer an exclusiveness of authority, and a uniqueness of nature, foreign to modern views of religious science, of human progress, and of personal independence. Like the Pessimists, like a thinker so fine as von Hartmann, they will more readily admit a redemptive process than reduce it to the act of a Redeemer. And while they believe in a divine Humanity, it seems an indignity to condense it and submit it to the absolute authority of any one that arose in its midst.

But for the purposes of religion it is power that we need more than breadth ; it is control as the condition of freedom ; it is height, depth, and quality of soul more than range ; it is security more than progress, and divinity more than fraternity. The passion of inclusion has overreached the soul's own comprehensive power ; and we are losing real width of vision because our levelling instincts have dragged us from the commanding heights. There is a sacred narrowness, like that of the mountain peak, which raises us much more than it limits us, and increases our range while it straitens our steps. To be just to mankind is not to be diffuse in our loyalties, grudging towards an elect, or cold in our worship of a Unique. " To be just," says Baudelaire, " criticism must be partial and passionate, with a point of view which is exclusive indeed, but which opens new horizons." And another says, " L'amour, c'est choisir." It is so with regard to our moral Critic, Judge, and Saviour. The Eternal Equity is partial to us. The moral universe is not a windless vacuum. Its justice is not absolute poise. It is too full of holy passion to leave room for absolutely impartial (and impossible) judgments, whether in man or God. The Judge after all is just—because He is on our side, a just God and a Saviour. And we cannot be just unless we are on His.

Personality and partiality mean here but the concentration so essential for conviction and power. The lack of certainty to-day is not only due to the many things and the many points of view, but still more to the weakness of will which refuses to select and concentrate. Much more doubt is voluntary and culpable than it is the fashion to admit. It is more due to poverty than to veracity of soul. The mental confusion is due to some moral indecision and discursiveness. It is not wholly mental error, but to some extent moral flatness (to say the least), which causes so many to pass over the historic Christ as lightly as they do in their survey of the field of fact. There is some moral anesthesia in their incapacity to be arrested and detained. There is a lack of moral insight and of moral perspective, due to an absence of moral culture. But we have come to a time when it is the element of command rather than comprehension, of power rather than breadth, that we need in our faith. And for this end a Person has more value than a process, and a Redeemer than an ideal. We may or may not be "broad," but positive and objective we must be. We may or may not be "liberal," but we must have liberty. And the first condition of positiveness in our creed or freedom in our Soul, or liberty in the State, is a sure, clear, personal and historic authority whose writ runs to the very centre of the will and the recesses of the soul. The present decay in the matter of public liberty and its vigilance is more than concurrent with the decay of sure faith in a divine authority.

II

The word evangelical has, even within the Church, fallen into discredit, for various reasons, some better and some worse. And its place has been taken by such a word as mystical. Shrewd publishers welcome the one word in a title and frown at the other. This may be a straw, but there is a current beneath it. It means at bottom the same thing as the aversion from the name Protestant, with its victory of power and faith, and the culture of the word Catholic, with its comfort of taste and love. It is parallel with the abeyance of the moral note in religion and the culture of the spiritual, the retreat of the prophetic note in preaching and the cult of the saintly, the loss of the apostolic note, the forcing of " the wooing note," and the consequent anemia of the pulpit. It means the decay of the ethical and the growth of the sympathetic, the sacrifice of Pauline to Franciscan piety, the retirement, for some, of interest in God's revealed will behind the psychology of the Soul and its adventures in religion or among the religions, and the departure, for others, and especially for some young and cultured piety, of the humility which inever thinks of humility, and their pre-occupation with an adolescent spiritual self-consciousness, rising on occasion to spiritual " side." The subjectivity represented by Christian Science is only the extreme expression of that spiritual egoism which marks much of the temper of the time. What has been called " lay religion " becomes more and more identified with what has also been named " practical mysticism " —a vague religiosity or a warm spirituality, associated with sympathetic and beneficent action for social welfare, but without positive belief, or sure footing in a revelation—with atmosphere but no truth. This is a very valuable thing in its way, but it is not Christianity. It dissipates Christ in a Christian nimbus. He is lost in the temperature He created. He perishes of spontaneous combustion. His centre of gravity is removed from the conscience to the consciousness, from the soul to the heart, and he subsides in a gorgeous cloud of sunset dust. The note of mystic love submerges the word of moral grace; and the wonders love can work in neglected hearts obscure the miracle of mercy to the evil soul.

Now truly there is much need for the culture of the deep things in our religion. We are dying of so many worlds, so much to do. We gulp our spiritual food in quick meals. Our activity obsesses us.

EPILOGUE

While we are busy here and there the Spirit is gone. We need time and facility to collect our soul from the energies of enterprise or the manufacture of impression, and to retire to the energy of insight. We need more mystic souls and mystic hours. But the true mysticism is not raptly dwelling in the mystery of God, it is really living on His miracle. It is not prolonged elation but sure salvation. And the only mysticism with a lease of life is that which surrounds the moral miracle which makes Christianity in the end evangelical or nothing. It is the mysticism of the cross.

I have said more than once that the contact of God with the soul is in its nature a miracle. This might very well seem like taking refuge in an asylum of ignorance, and saving ourselves the trouble of really wrestling with the matter by escaping into a dark and warm mist. But miracle is something more than mystery, if we keep our moral wits about us. Since it belongs to revelation it has uppermost the element not of dark but of light, and the movement not of mere emergence but creation. If religion is not mystic, indeed, it is not religion; and it is truly intelligible only to its initiates and regenerates, and not to the world. But in Christianity the mysticism is not psychological but historic, not temperamental but moral. It is not a frame of subjective mood but a relation to an objective grace of God. What is uppermost is not what we feel but what makes us feel. The site of our contact with God is not our rising and falling moods but our conscience. And its perfection is not the prayer of quiet, the deep, withdrawn, and silent rapture of the spiritual adept, but the justified faith which is a life-confidence with God through Jesus Christ. It is the miracle of the new moral creation, the peace which is less calm than trust, the mysticism of the conscience released and remade by a diviner act of power than creates and rounds the worlds. It is moral regeneration and not mystic absorption, nor even habitual charity. It is love which is an act of grace in us and not simply a process of suffusion. It is the conscious miracle of the New Creation and the constant obedience of faith to the New Creator.

As the ultimate idea of authority is religious, and not only so but Christian, and as it is bound up with the central Christian idea of the New Creation, it will be well to protect ourselves against misconceptions of what that means.

What it means positively is much more a matter of faith's experience than of psychological description. It is the new life of faith taken in infinite moral earnest. It is salvation as God's holy and crucial action and not simply His tender mercy. It is intelligible only to its adepts, the new creatures. But its scientific description is beyond us. We have no deep psychology of what takes place in regeneration, nor can we set forth the exact relation of the old man to the new. The origin of faith is to science a mystery, like the origin of all life.

As to what it does not mean, we may say this.

1. It means nothing metaphysical. It is not a nature process in any sense, not in a subliminal, far less in a magical, sense. It is a moral and spiritual thing. It belongs to the region of the personal life and to its ethical methods. There is no change of any subliminal substance, no conversion of finite essence to infinite, of earthly corporeality into heavenly, to make a physical foundation for the development of salvation. All such ideas belong to an outgrown stage of thought, whose metaphysic of static being is superseded by the metaphysic of energetic idealism, and existence is held

to be due to the standing act of a divine personality instead of the immobile presence of an infinite substance.

2. It follows that the New Creation cannot be construed by the categories of physical Omnipotence or Causation; but " of His own *Will* begat He us." It is to be treated as a moral creation and not a physical; the new departure is personal and not material; it is of righteousness and not of being; and the creative act giving spiritual freedom is exercised upon a will which has already risen to psychological freedom over the necessities of natural force. As with the gift of our first freedom a creature of the wild rises to be a child of nature, so with the gift of our second the child of nature rises to be a son of God.

3. It is not meant that in everyone's Christian experience we should demand the vivid and crucial lines that mark the conversion of a Paul, an Augustine, or a Luther. When we speak of the New Creation we mean to express something decisive and peculiar for the Christian religion, the Christian idea, and not for the experience in every case. We mean what makes the Church the Church and not the individual a confessor. We express, as it was expressed by the classic exponents of it and its representative souls, the nature of the change from a childhood of Nature to a childhood of God, its breach with law and its home in grace, the passage from death to life. What Paul meant by this deepest and most comprehensive description of the Christian salvation was that the new life was disparate with all else in existence, which he counted but dross if he might be found in Christ. The new-born man has arrived by crisis at what really makes man man. It is the rise to power in man of the really spiritual, the coming of the Holy Ghost. The spirit that worked *on* the soul now rules *in* it. The new Humanity is the only true Humanity. It alone

reaches the life destined by God for Humanity, and reaches it out of wreck. We have here the end of one creative range and the beginning of another. We now live in Christ, Who is not of the created world, and Who alone is in miraculous command of its forces. It is a creative act that sets man in Christ, one inexplicable, if not unintelligible, to the first creation (though with a real nexus). Eye hath not seen, nor ear heard what God reveals by His Spirit. Faith taken in final earnest is not sentiment, not creed, not morality, not conduct or even character; it is regeneration. It is not simply a new degree but a new departure, not a higher phase but a holy work. Revelation is Redemption and Redemption is Creation. The supernatural is not merely transcendent but also creative. It gives a new state of the *whole man*, not a new angle to which the old man is turned, not a sectional repair, not a fresh annexe. There is a "totality" in it, an eternal crisis, a passage from death to life, a unique lawlessness, a change to which nothing in the world is comparable, and to express which Paul had to seek an inadequate metaphor in the most tremendous and solemn and pregnant thing ever done in the world up to Christ.

This change the individual Christian realises more and more. It is gradually appropriated in perhaps most cases. But a new Creation is the nature of what is appropriated. That is the thing objectively done. From God's side it is creation, the miracle of a new moral personality, though not a new constitution for human nature. Of course, what is creation from God's side may be felt by us, reared in the Christian Church and kingdom so created, as evolution, as mere sanctification and not regeneration. What for Him is an act is for us a process, till we evolve to the power of seeing it as God does and knowing as we are known.

EPILOGUE

All mystic religion which is not the mysticism of the new conscience and the new imperative, but is only the mysticism of the new sympathy, is not Protestant but Catholic. Its spread among the religiously minded means, as certainly as history can mean anything, our reconquest by Catholicism, and in the end by Curialism. We are Catholic whenever love casts down faith to a second place. That is a more welcome and insidious danger than priests and masses. Pietism has no real weapon against Rome. They are too much akin—pre-eminently subjective both. They both mean the canonisation of mutual love at the cost of sole grace, the nurture of the heart at the cost of the conscience, the pursuit of communion without justification, the foundation of religion upon something else than forgiveness, or upon absolution at the cost of a forgiveness truly ethical and holy, of a grace more moral than magical. But such a holy love, founding us on forgiveness, is the only power that can save love, and therefore religion, from natural degeneration. It is the ethical element of the holy, of love in the superlative terms of the conscience, of love as a holy gift and grace, that alone keeps love from sinking in the history and experience of man, through a natural religion to a depraved. This ethic of the holy, as it is the humbling element in God's love, is *the* sanative element in the Christian forgiveness. It is its eternity. It provides the final and perpetual authority, with a right which a moral Creator alone can claim over the whole of life. Love is bound to become debased in human history, but for the moral holy action of God's grace in Christ, whose sphere, heritage, and reversion all history is. The kingdom of Christ is but the expansion on the scale of all Humanity of the moral sovereignty He acquired by His forgiveness and redemption.

Christian mysticism therefore reposes, not on the depths of subliminal being, which give no footing for any authority that royalises life, but upon the miracle of the forgiven conscience of the world and its holy redemption. At the central point of life, at its moral focus, at its productive core there takes place the creative miracle which gives all miracles their meaning and their worth. They are there only as outcrops of Christ's work of creative grace. That is the native region and family home of Christian mysticism, the mystery of the forgiven and re-created conscience. We dwell reverently on the mystery of generation; the miracle of regeneration is more solemn still. And it is more intelligible to our experience however inexplicable.

Religion is not a mystic union with the divine independent of historic mediation. Nor is Christ but the superlative of this choice faculty of the soul. But He is the Creator of the possibility of that mysticism which keeps at its heart the moral crisis of the race, the mystery of sin, the miracle of its conquest; and which therefore carries the race's moral future. It is the mystery and miracle of the Cross, where all of Christ was gathered up in one eternal, effective, inexplicable act that meant and means more for the world than its creation. It is quite true that the essence of Christianity is mystery. It is not merely sane and rational. But it is such a mystery as this. It is the moral miracle of the historic yet eternal action of the holy on souls guilty of historic sin.

The history which culminated in Christianity, the history of Israel, and especially its prophecy, was not an evolutionary refinement of ethic; it was a demand of the conscience of God on the prophet, and by the prophet on the recalcitrant people. The ethical growth of the nation was not a case of evolution

EPILOGUE

but of a new creating Word, whose divine power should transcend the forces even of the moral world and its social culture. It was not simply the moral side of civilisation; but civilisation was confronted and invaded at its centre by the will and purpose and Word of God. God's love to His people was not mere nurture, it was redemption from contempt and despite of His love. The nation arose out of Egypt in a redemption whose miraculous form was but a way of putting its miraculous nature.

And this was the note perfected in Christ. God's love became in Him and His Cross the moral miracle of forgiveness, of salvation. It was moralised, from God's heart to man's, by holy judgment and holy grace. *The* fact of the Christian's spiritual world is a moral fact. It is a moral miracle. He lives in a world of it—not in the poetic and imaginary sense, when everything is said to be miracle, but in the moral, the historic, sense that everything radiates now from the miracle of the new creation of the conscience in Christ, and shines in that mystic light. He lives in God's saving will and not His immanent presence; for immanence is not yet intimacy, nor is omnipresence communion. His object is not the cultivation of his soul in love but the obedience of faith in grace. If he trusts God's grace God will see to his love and his spiritual culture generally. Few things are so dangerous as the deliberate culture of the soul, and the pursuit of sanctity as a vocation in life. Seek first the kingdom, the authority, of God and you will find your soul and all else. It is better to cultivate Christ than our soul. To develop insight into the Cross is more than to court perfection or nurse our spiritual beauty. Covet earnestly the better gift.

There is a kind of mysticism which becomes but visionary, and it is the kind detached from its creative spring in the work of Christ for the guilty soul and upon it. All true and healthy communion with God is the communion of that work, with its power to give us the whole moral mystery and mastery of the world. Our whole communion with God is the amplification of our communion of His forgiveness in Christ's Cross. It is the vast spiritual dialectic of that new creation. It is not sporadic " visions and revelations of the Lord." It is the perfecting of the revelation final in redemption. We do not say enough when we say it is in Christ. Christ does not become absolutely regal and universal except in His Cross, and in the new moral creation of the race there. That alone commits and pledges us to a faith which is more absolute and eternal than any mere loyalty or susceptibility. The inner life of Christ is but impressionist for us without the absolute mastery of this new creation of our moral self in the Cross. We get the true mysticism in the conscience and the mysticism of the conscience, in the moral miracle of its historical regeneration. And we get that only in the Cross of the whole Christ, whose one end, both as He lived, died, and revived, was that He might be *Lord* both of the dead and living.

If ever such a moralising of revelation and of religion seem a reduction of its note of love, a blanching of its tender mercy, and a flattening of its mystic strain, that is because of a defective grasp of the moral situation, in which divine love has lost in pity its commanding note of holiness, or else holiness has lost the solemn note of conscience either in the pietisms of a too subjective sanctity or in the aridities of a too forensic system. The whole wealth of the soul's world issues at last from the creative Cross of Christ, His conquest of all things there, and His gift of all things richly to enjoy in a God Whom

EPILOGUE

we live only to glorify for the fulness of that cosmic Redemption.

And this is the last and fontal authority for the whole of life. Subjectivism ends in nihilism. A religion merely mystic contains no moral ground of authority. But authority there must be, else there is no religion, and no society; and a moral ground it must have else it has no right. There is no authority in a religion of mere love (which makes it popular with a crowd); but only in the holiness which makes love truly, if slowly, divine, which makes it to judge, to save, and to re-create, from the guilty, humbled, and regenerate conscience outward.

I will end on my keynote.

There is another counterpart of authority than certainty, and one more spiritual than obedience. It is humility, which is freedom's elder twin and guide. That we should have all but lost this sovereign feature from so much of our religion of the Kingdom is not surprising in the decay of authority or its debasement, and especially in the abeyance of that superlative form of authority which the mystic of the conscience calls holiness, and which enjoins us, if we would be perfect as our Father, to be holy as He is holy, and humbled to the very Cross. The holiness of God is beyond our definition, for it is God the holy; and we cannot define a person, far less the absolute Person. It is not simply His perfection either in thought or act. Its appeal is to something beyond both mind and will. It carries us deeper into God and man. We cannot define it, we can but realise it. And, as it is the last reality, we can but realise it in the last and highest energy of the soul. It is that in God which emerges upon us and comes home to us only in our worship. It changes that worship from dull abasement before God's power, or dumb amazement at the wealth of His nature, to the deepest adoration of what He personally is, and is for us. Its counterpart in us and our religion is the humility that worship at once rears and perfects. And it is as much beyond righteousness in Him as humility is beyond mere obedience or justice in us. Humility is not a chain of submissive acts, but the habitual and total and active obedience of the whole soul to the Holy in His act, to that which alone both abashes and exalts the whole soul, and severs it from the world by every step of its assumption into God. Religion never confers such distinction upon the soul as in its humility, since nothing so exalts the common to the choice as the dignity placed upon us by the communion of the Holy; Whose very anger turned on the world is a patent of nobility for it,[1] Whose judgment is its glory, and His saints its peers. The true authority cannot return to order, secure, and distinguish society without a religious revolution. It cannot till humility pull down self-satisfaction on the one hand or lift up self-prostration on the other, and take the place both of self-worship or self's dishonour. Yet it is never the mere breaking of self that makes humility, as it does not make true repentance or confession; it is the sight, sense, and confession of that ineffable sanctity which comes home to us but in adoration, and makes such hours the ruling and creative hours of life. For in that holiness we are neither passive, soft, nor weak; we are touched by the one authority and reality of life; and in the amazement, the miracle, that He should come to us Who is sublimely separate from all the sinful world, we have the exalted humility which teaches us to love

---

[1] "Was Thine anger against the rivers or Thy wrath against the sea."—HAB. iii. 8.

the world in godly sort, and is the secret of the obedience that at once controls life and inspires it. To know such a God is to be crushed, to be known of Him is to sit in heavenly places. This holiness is that in love which humiliates us, not in gratitude merely, but in adoration ; and in the act it takes us into the fellowship of what is the one power and reality of life and eternity. The last authority of the soul for ever is the grace of a holy God, the holiness of His gracious love in Jesus Christ. And this is the last reality of things, the last rest of all hearts, and the last royalty of all wills.

www.ingramcontent.com/pod-product-compliance
Lightning Source LLC
Chambersburg PA
CBHW071136300426
44113CB00009B/988